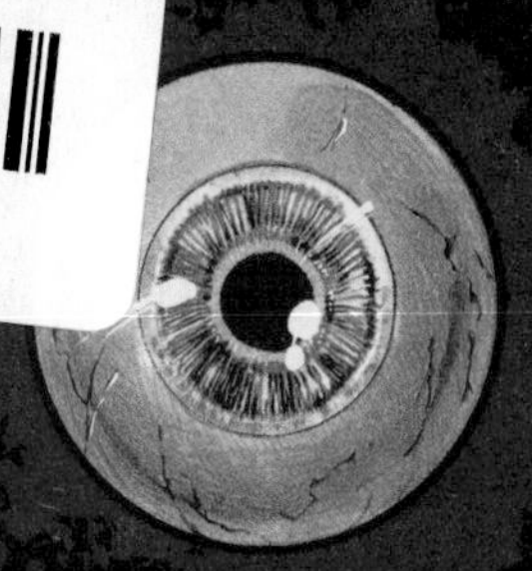

MEGUMI OSUGA

FILTHY.
MY DESK IS ABSOLUTELY COVERED IN STUFF. YOU KNOW IT'S JUST
SAD WHEN YOU START NAMING THE SPIDERS THAT SHOW UP. I HAVE
A FEELING THAT TODAY JUST MIGHT BE THE DAY TO HOLD A BIG
WORKPLACE CLEANING.

MEGUMI OSUGA

BORN DECEMBER 21 IN CHIBA PREFECTURE, MEGUMI OSUGA MADE HER
DEBUT WITH *TONPACHI*, WHICH RAN IN *SHONEN SUNDAY R*, AND HAD A
SHORT SERIES IN *SHONEN SUNDAY SUPER* CALLED *HONOU NO ANA NO YOMI*.
IN 2007, HER SERIALIZATION OF *MAOH: JUVENILE REMIX* STARTED IN
SHONEN SUNDAY.

KOTARO ISAKA

BORN IN 1971 IN CHIBA PREFECTURE, KOTARO ISAKA IS ONE OF THE MOST
POPULAR JAPANESE NOVELISTS AND HAS RECEIVED NUMEROUS AWARDS.
HE HAS MANY TITLES UNDER HIS BELT, MOST OF WHICH HAVE BEEN
TURNED INTO LIVE-ACTION MOVIES.

MAOH JUVENILE REMIX

MAOH: JUVENILE REMIX
Volume 03

Shonen Sunday Edition

Original Story by **KOTARO ISAKA**
Story and Art by **MEGUMI OSUGA**

© 2007 Kotaro ISAKA, Megumi OSUGA/Shogakukan
All rights reserved.
Original Japanese edition "MAOH JUVENILE REMIX" published by SHOGAKUKAN Inc.

Logo and cover design created by Isao YOSHIMURA & Bay Bridge Studio.

Translation/Stephen Paul
Touch-up Art & Lettering/James Dashiell
Design/Sam Elzway
Editor/Alexis Kirsch

VP, Production/Alvin Lu
VP, Sales & Product Marketing/Gonzalo Ferreyra
VP, Creative/Linda Espinosa
Publisher/Hyoe Narita

Printed in the U.S.A.

Published by VIZ Media, LLC
P.O. Box 77010
San Francisco, CA 94107

10 9 8 7 6 5 4 3 2 1
First printing, November 2010

www.viz.com

MANGA STARTS ON SUNDAY
SHONEN SUNDAY

www.shonensunday.com

MAOH
JUVENILE REMIX

ORIGINAL STORY BY
KOTARO ISAKA

STORY AND ART BY
MEGUMI OSUGA

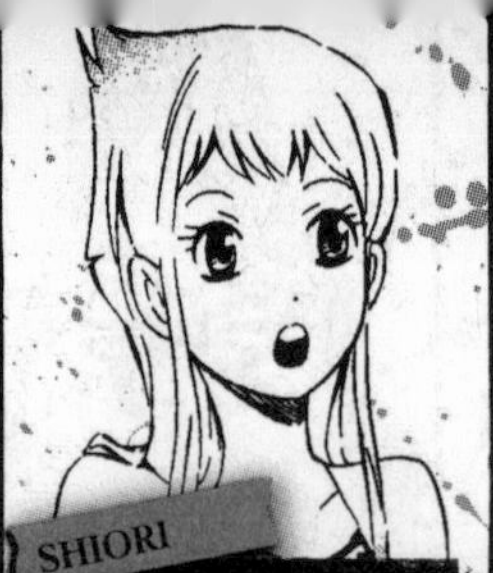

SHIORI

Junya's girlfriend. Placid and clumsy, she makes a good foil to Junya.

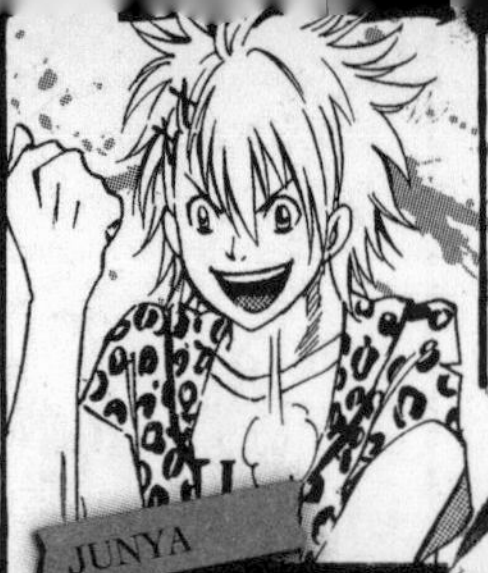

JUNYA

Ando's younger brother. Unlike his fretful sibling, Junya is optimistic and freewheeling.

THE STORY UNTIL NOW

Ando uses every bit of cunning at his disposal to avoid the assassination attempts of his mysterious would-be killer, Semi, but they will only give him so much time. Ultimately, it is only a sudden call from Semi's client that spares Ando's life. Put off by the suspicious nature of his contract, Semi drags Ando along to find the man who put out the hit. However, they learn little, other than that important figures within the New Urban Center Project are dying left and right, and the Project's recent push has come from the Anderson Group...

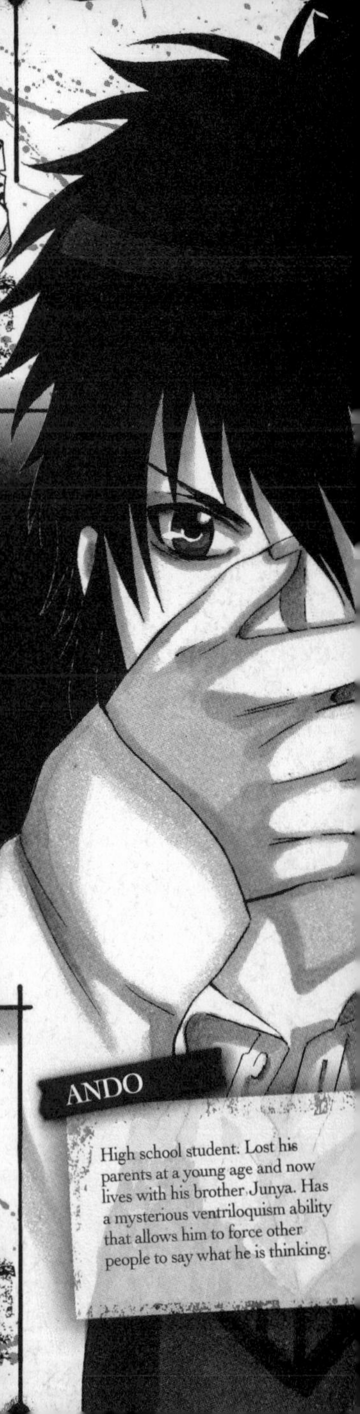

ANDO

High school student. Lost his parents at a young age and now lives with his brother Junya. Has a mysterious ventriloquism ability that allows him to force other people to say what he is thinking.

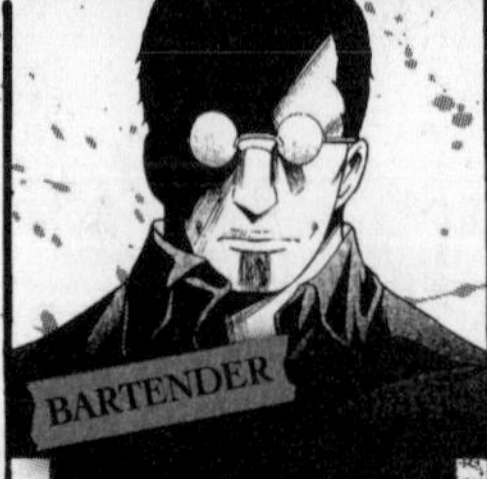

BARTENDER

Runs Cafe Duce. Is connected to Inukai somehow...

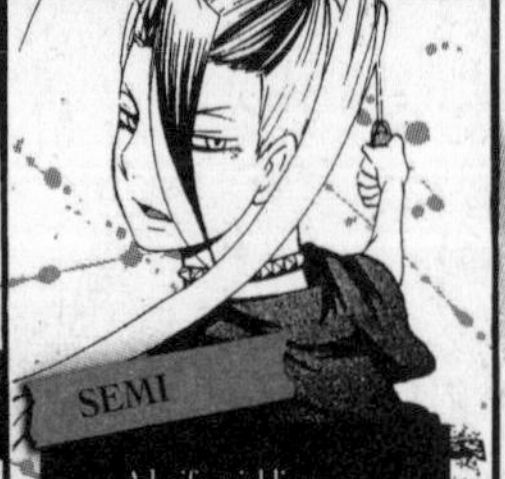

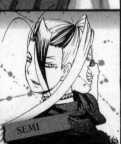

SEMI

A knife-wielding professional killer. Works for a man named Iwanishi.

KANAME

Ando's classmate.
A victim of bullies until he
met Inukai and joined
Grasshopper.

MACHIKO

Vice president of the
journalism club, of which the
Ando brothers are members.
Beautiful and aggressive.

Meanwhile, Inukai's arrest has given the
gangs free reign over the city. When Inukai is
released, he immediately quells the unrest,
except for a small group that takes a hostage.

The gangsters fire upon Inukai when he
approaches, but the bullet stops dead, inches
before Inukai's head. Nearby, Ando notices a
certain figure standing in the shadows. It was
the bartender from Duce, whom he also saw
after the incident at the theme park...

INUKAI

A young man who leads the vigilante group Grasshopper. He envelops
the town with his massive charisma,
but in his shadow lurks the specter
of violence and coercion.

DETECTIVE

Suspects that the fishy
incidents popping up

ANDERSON

President of the
Anderson Group, recent
heavy backers of the

CONTENTS

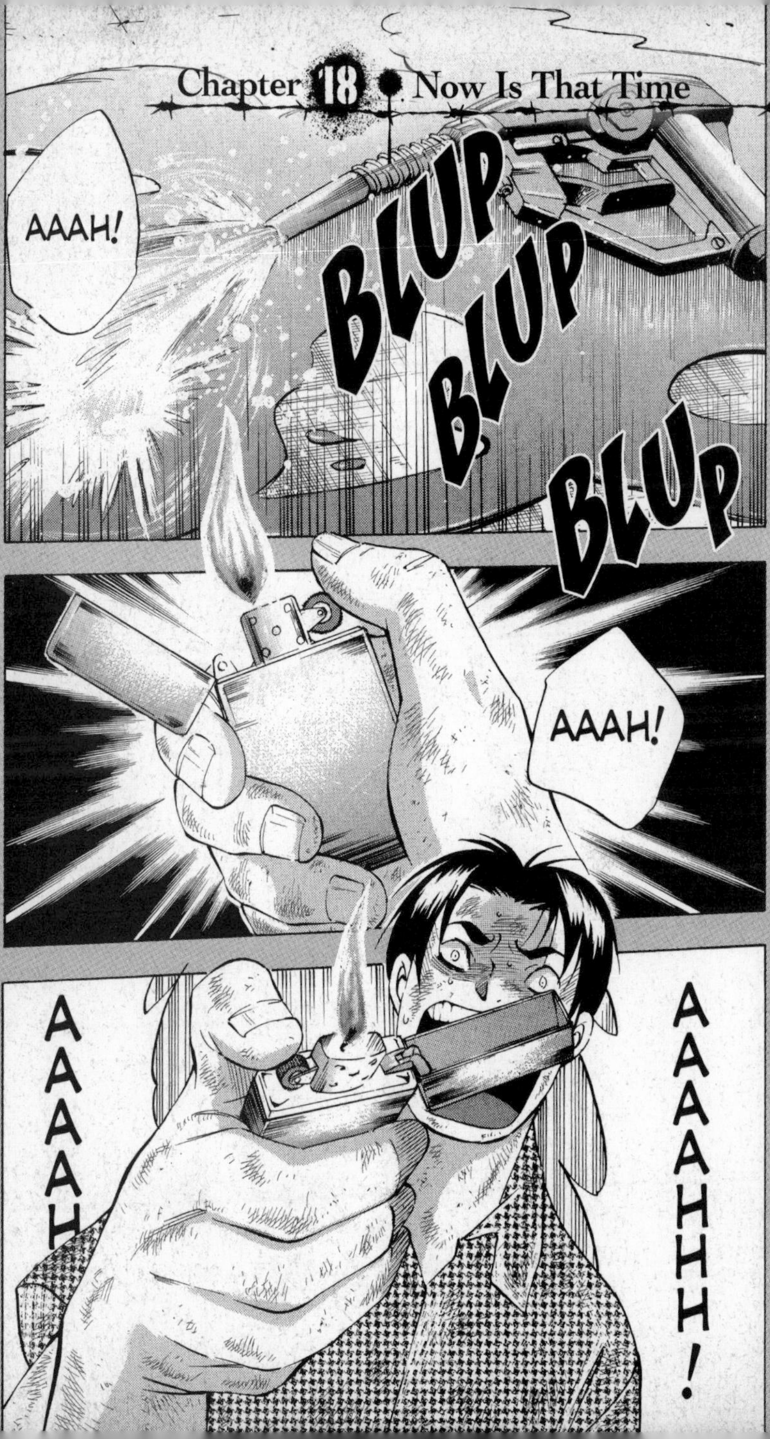
Chapter 18 Now Is That Time
AAAH!
BLUP
BLUP
BLUP
AAAH!
AAAAH
AAAAAHHH!

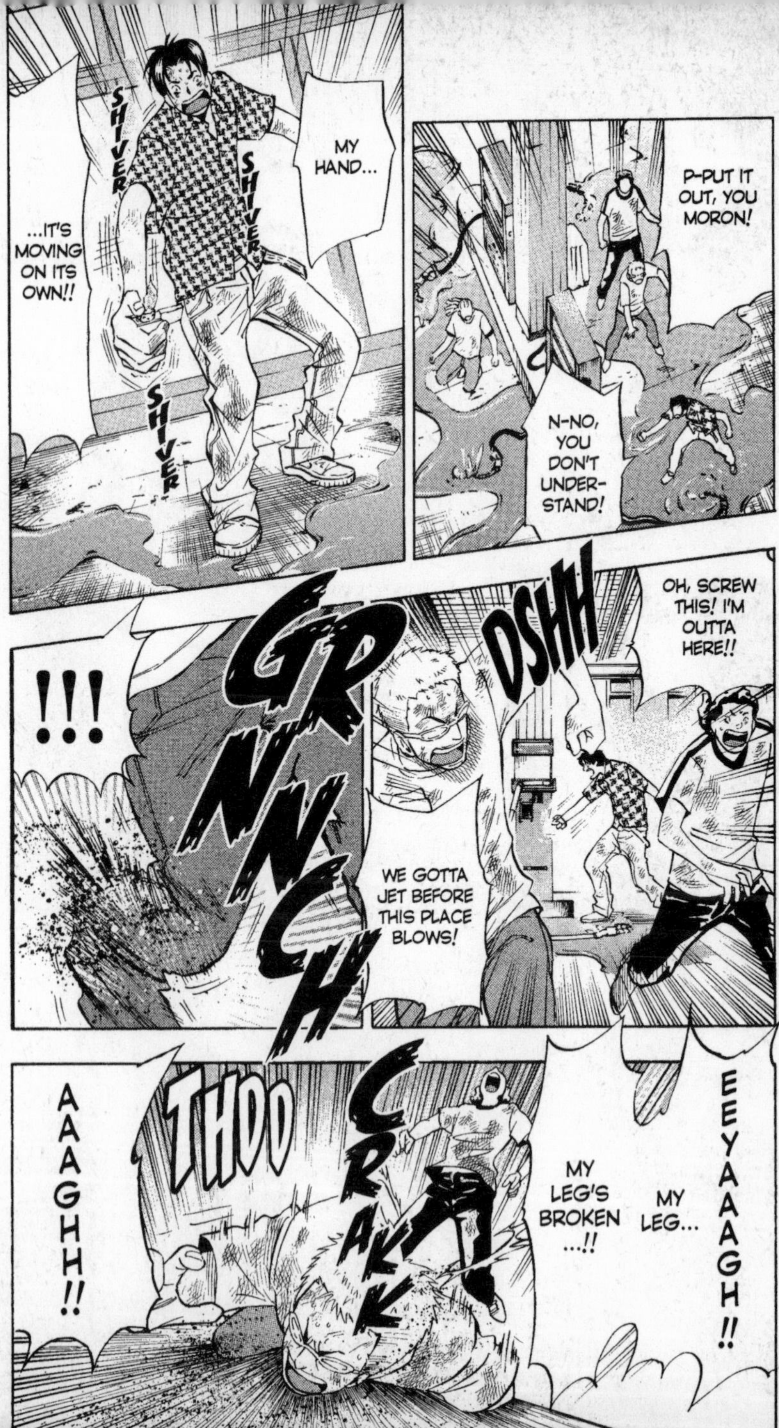
P-PUT IT OUT, YOU MORON!
N-NO, YOU DON'T UNDERSTAND!
MY HAND...
SHIVER
SHIVER
...IT'S MOVING ON ITS OWN!!
SHIVER
OH, SCREW THIS! I'M OUTTA HERE!!
DSHH
WE GOTTA JET BEFORE THIS PLACE BLOWS!
!!!
GRNNCH
EEYAAAGH!!
MY LEG...
MY LEG'S BROKEN ...!!
CRAKK
THOO
AAAAGHH!!

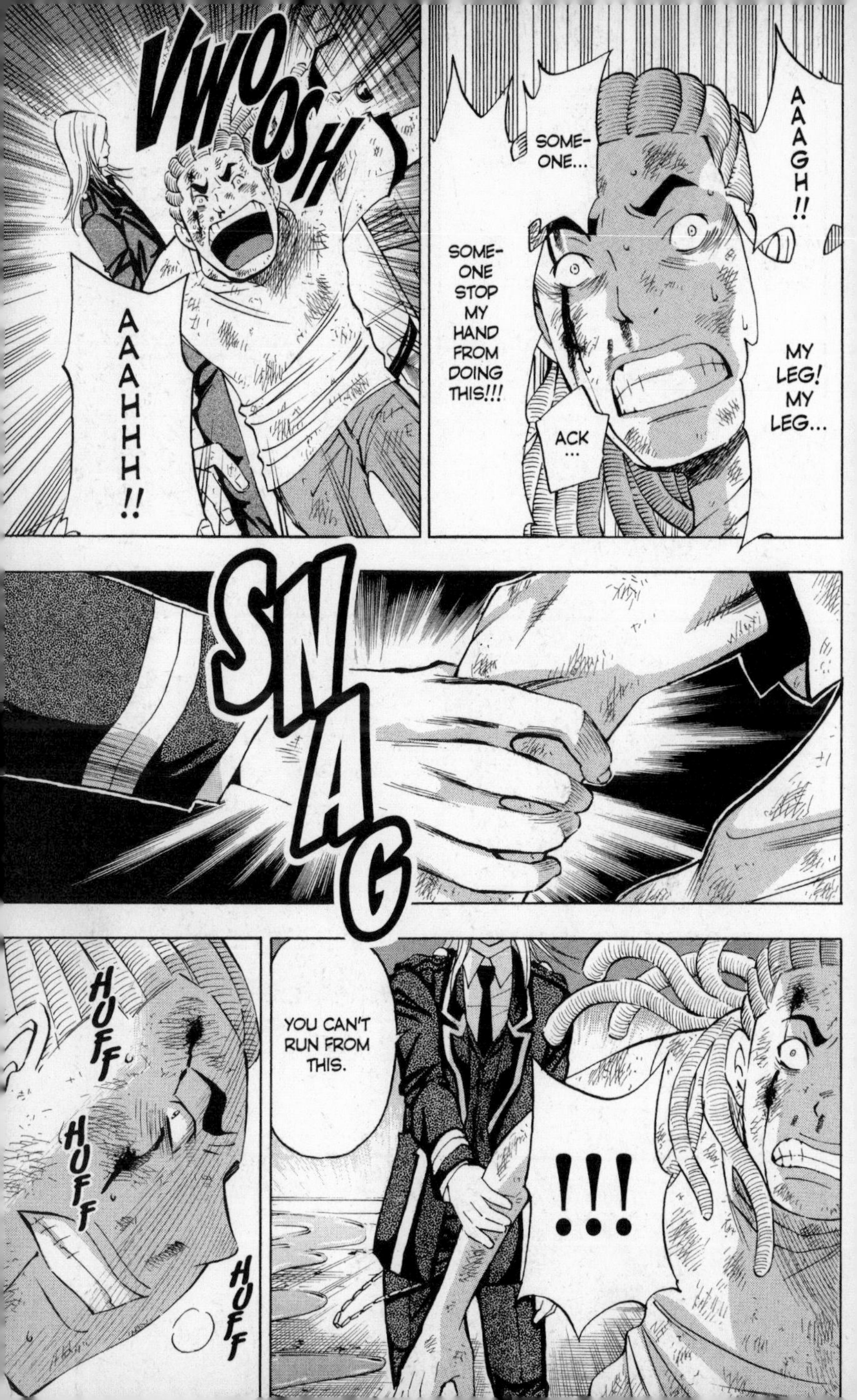
AAAGH!!
SOME-ONE...
MY LEG! MY LEG...
SOME-ONE STOP MY HAND FROM DOING THIS!!!
ACK...
VWOOSH
AAAHHH!!
SNAG
YOU CAN'T RUN FROM THIS.
!!!
HUFF
HUFF
HUFF

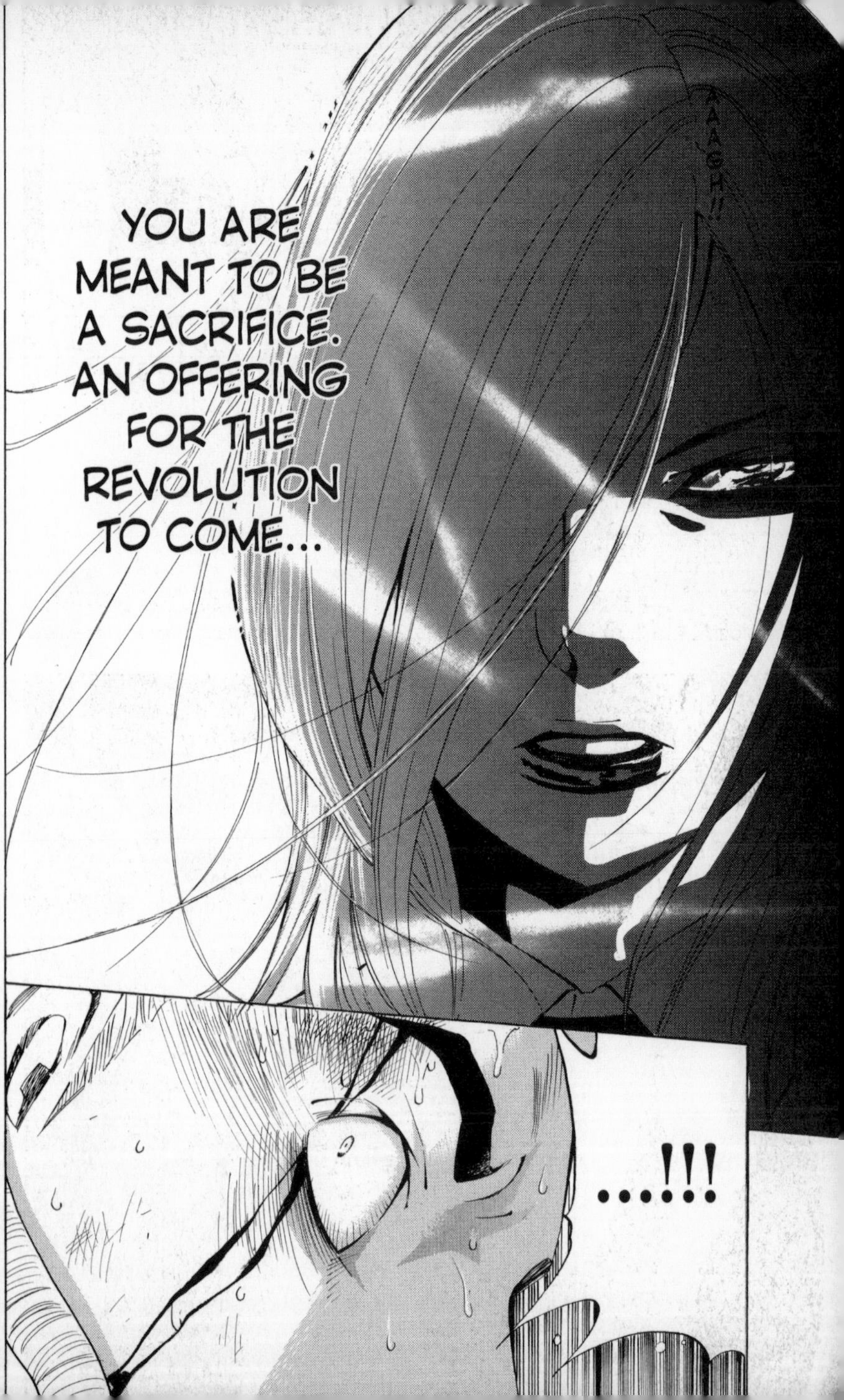
AAAGH!!
YOU ARE MEANT TO BE A SACRIFICE. AN OFFERING FOR THE REVOLUTION TO COME...
...!!!

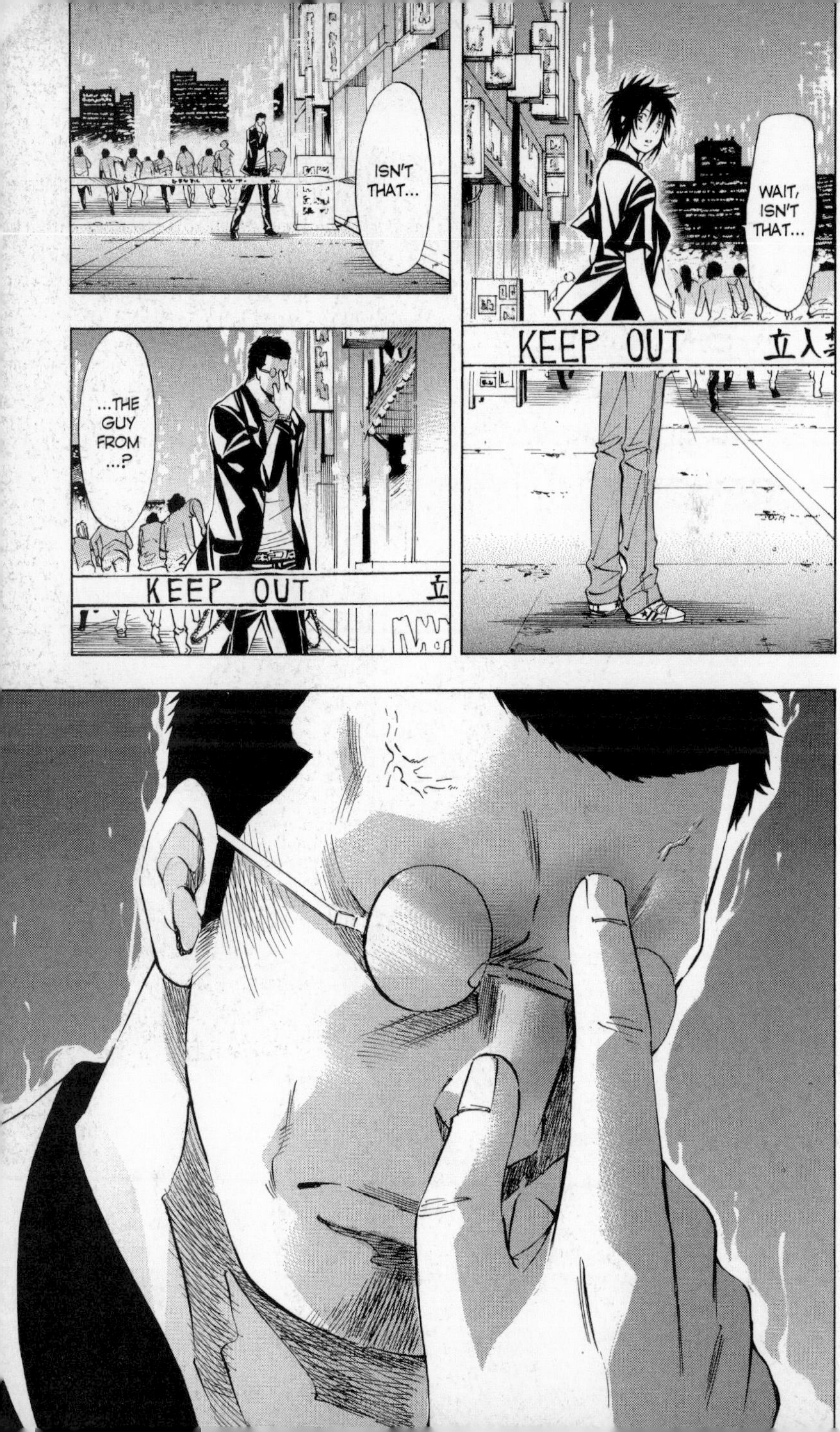
WAIT, ISN'T THAT...
KEEP OUT 立入
ISN'T THAT...
...THE GUY FROM ...?
KEEP OUT 立

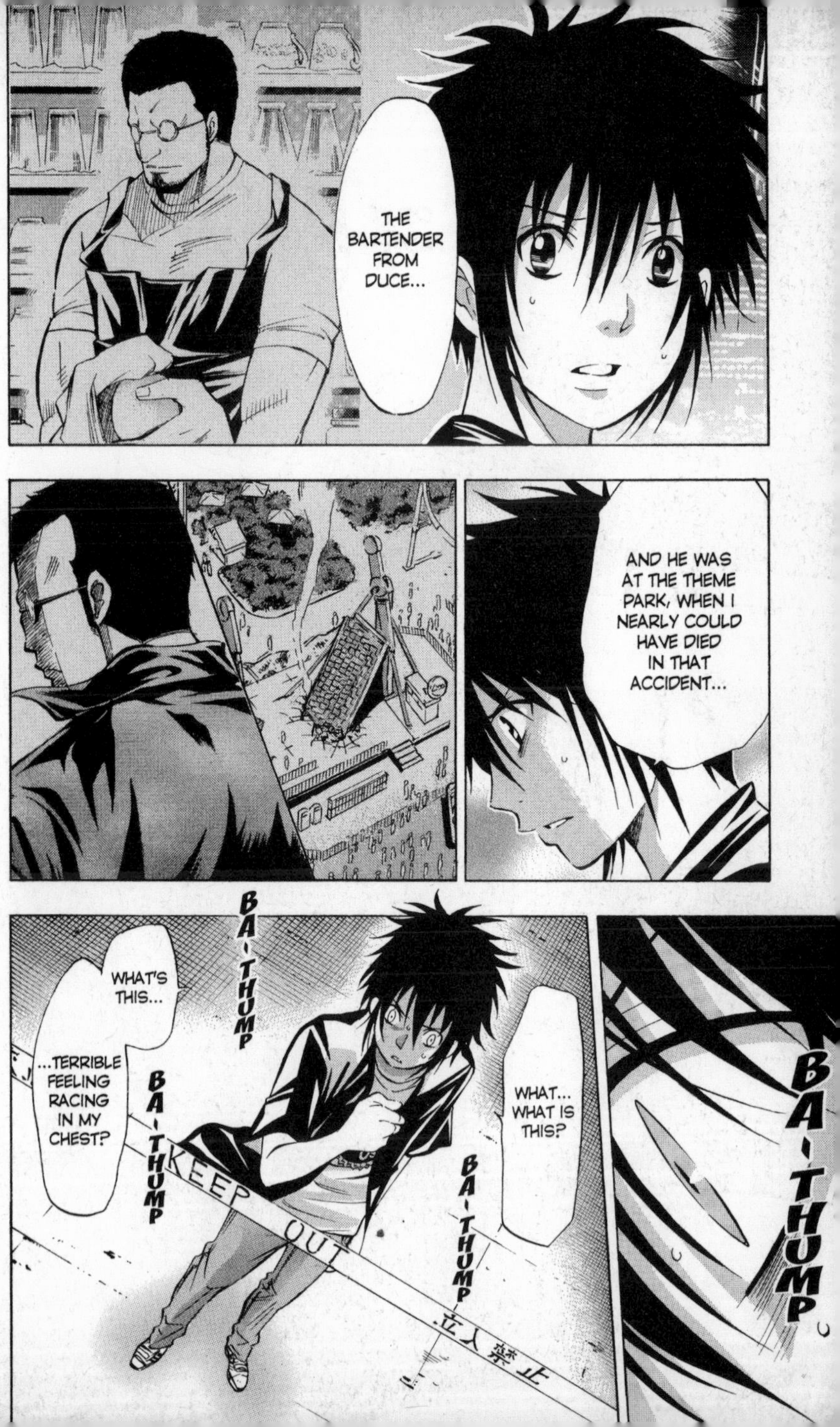
THE BARTENDER FROM DUCE...
AND HE WAS AT THE THEME PARK, WHEN I NEARLY COULD HAVE DIED IN THAT ACCIDENT...
BA-THUMP
WHAT... WHAT IS THIS?
BA-THUMP
BA-THUMP
WHAT'S THIS...
...TERRIBLE FEELING RACING IN MY CHEST?
BA-THUMP
KEEP OUT
立入禁止

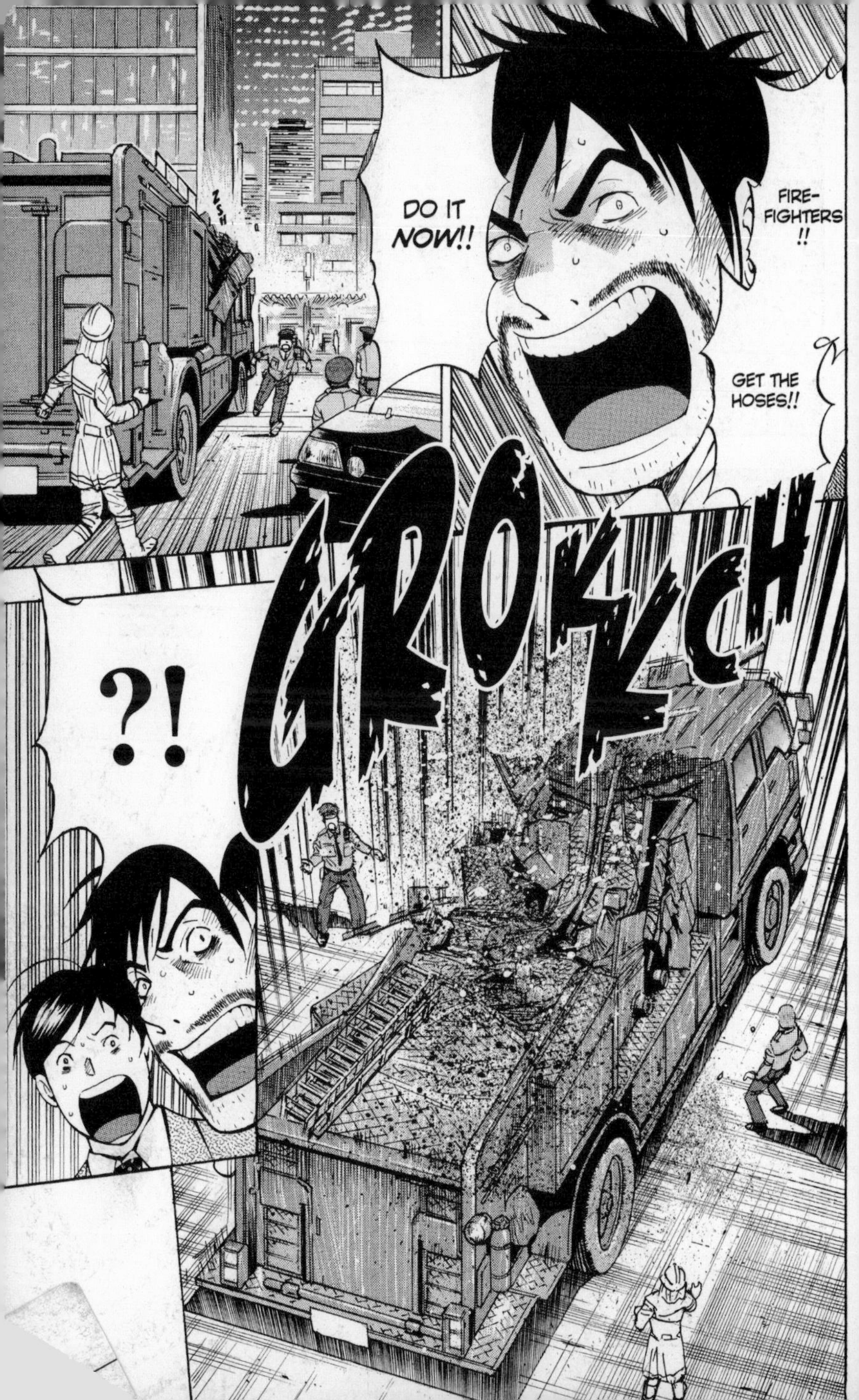
FIRE-FIGHTERS!!
GET THE HOSES!!
DO IT NOW!!
ZSH
GROKCH
?!

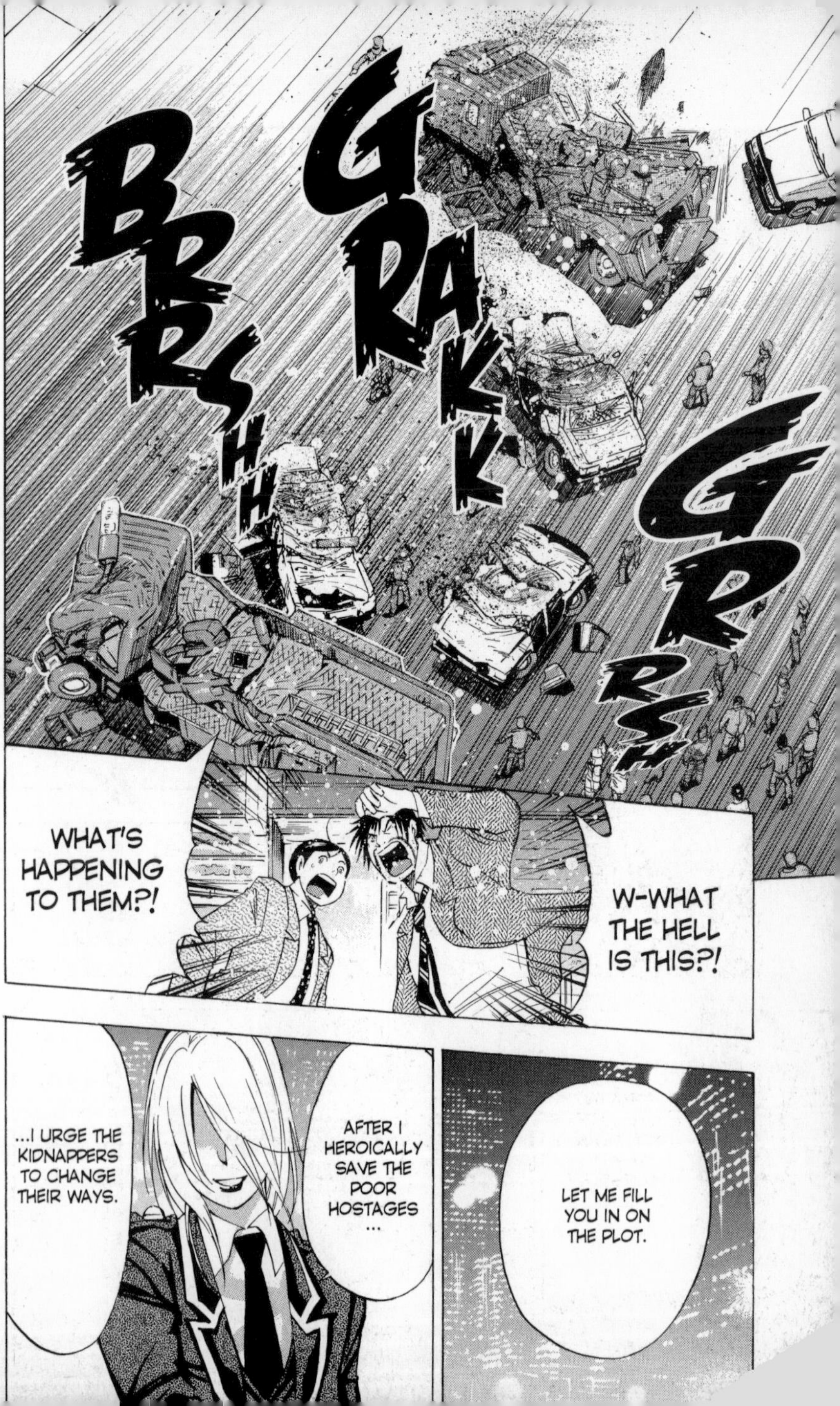
GRRSH
GRAKK
BRRSHH
W-WHAT THE HELL IS THIS?!
WHAT'S HAPPENING TO THEM?!
LET ME FILL YOU IN ON THE PLOT.
AFTER I HEROICALLY SAVE THE POOR HOSTAGES ...
...I URGE THE KIDNAPPERS TO CHANGE THEIR WAYS.

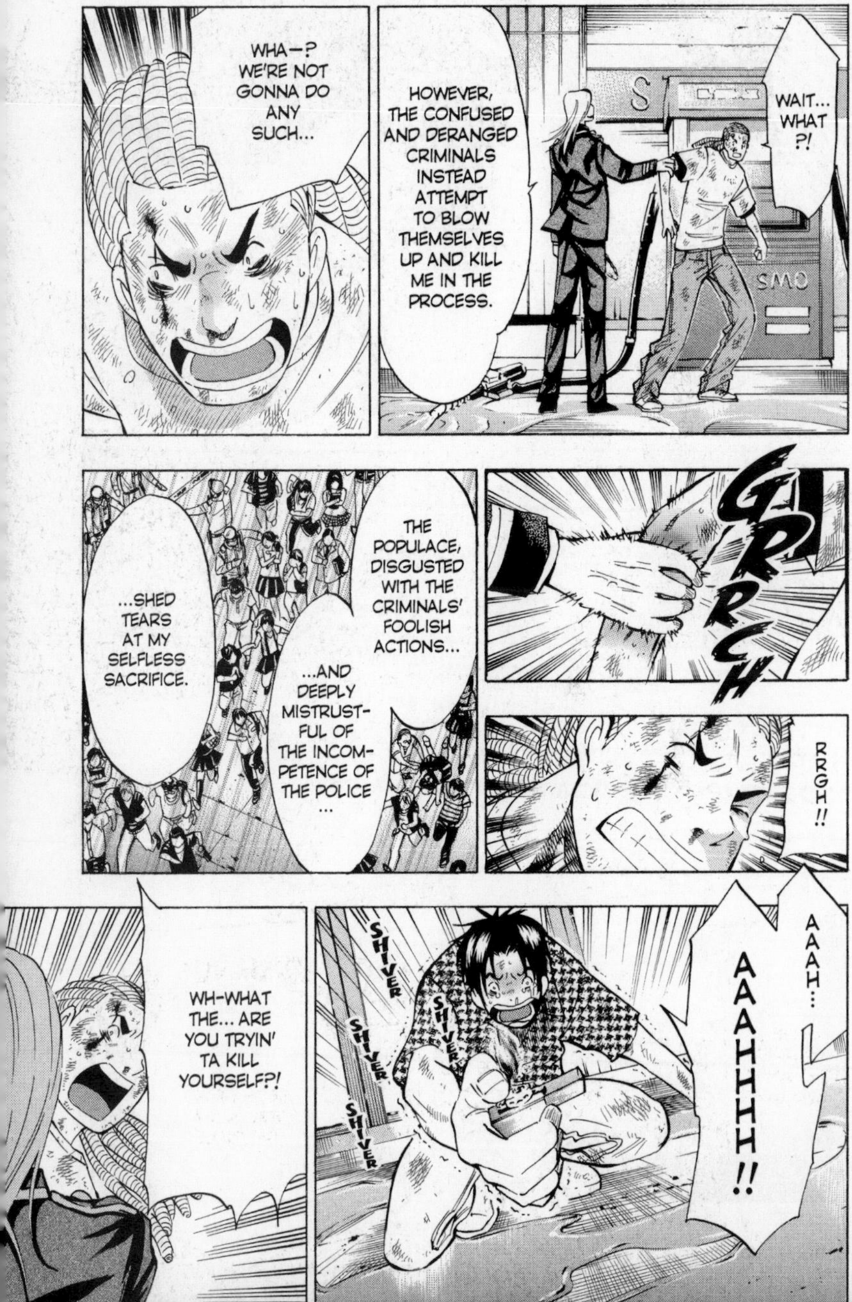
WAIT... WHAT?!
HOWEVER, THE CONFUSED AND DERANGED CRIMINALS INSTEAD ATTEMPT TO BLOW THEMSELVES UP AND KILL ME IN THE PROCESS.
S
SMO
WHA—? WE'RE NOT GONNA DO ANY SUCH...
GRRRCH
RRGH!!
THE POPULACE, DISGUSTED WITH THE CRIMINALS' FOOLISH ACTIONS...
...AND DEEPLY MISTRUST-FUL OF THE INCOM-PETENCE OF THE POLICE ...
...SHED TEARS AT MY SELFLESS SACRIFICE.
AAAH... AAAHHHH!!
SHIVER
SHIVER
SHIVER
SHIVER
WH-WHAT THE... ARE YOU TRYIN' TA KILL YOURSELF?!

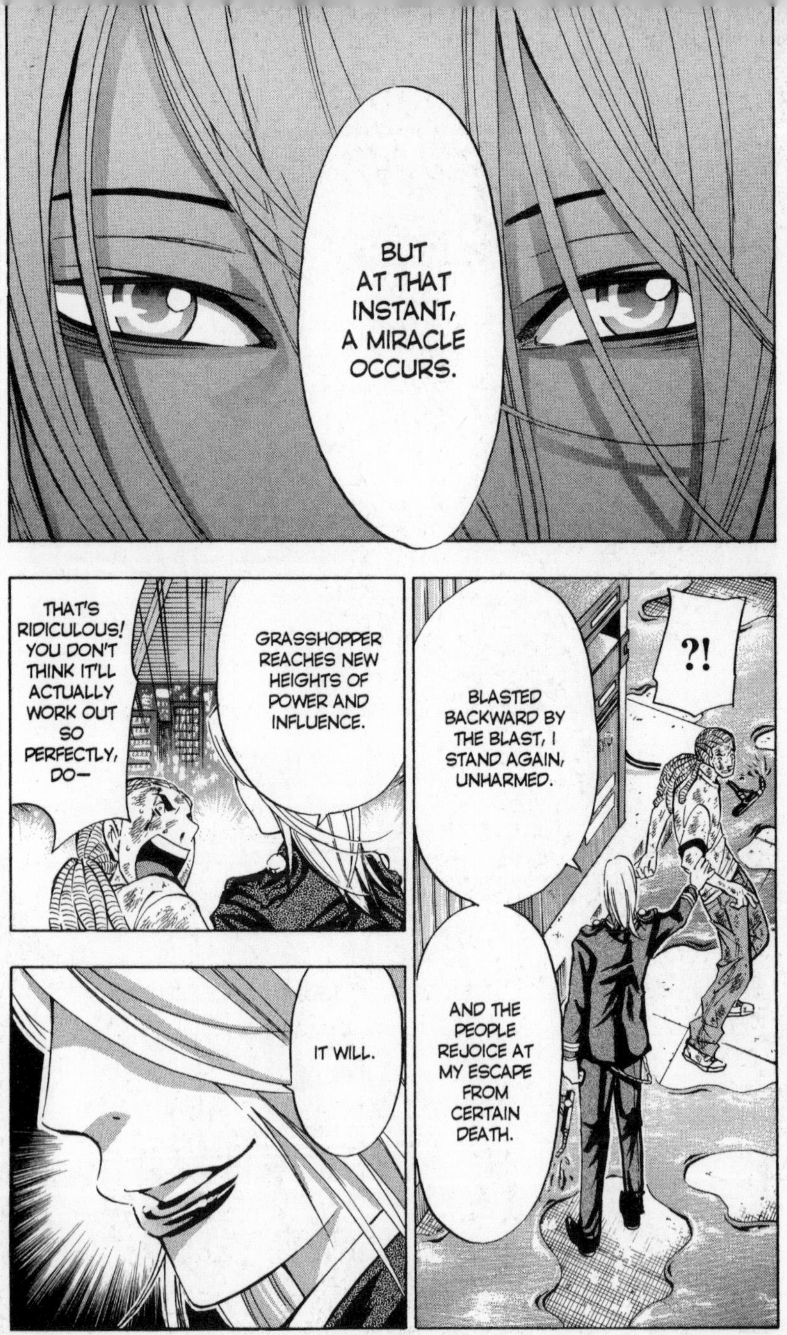
BUT AT THAT INSTANT, A MIRACLE OCCURS.
?!
BLASTED BACKWARD BY THE BLAST, I STAND AGAIN, UNHARMED.
AND THE PEOPLE REJOICE AT MY ESCAPE FROM CERTAIN DEATH.
GRASSHOPPER REACHES NEW HEIGHTS OF POWER AND INFLUENCE.
THAT'S RIDICULOUS! YOU DON'T THINK IT'LL ACTUALLY WORK OUT SO PERFECTLY, DO—
IT WILL.

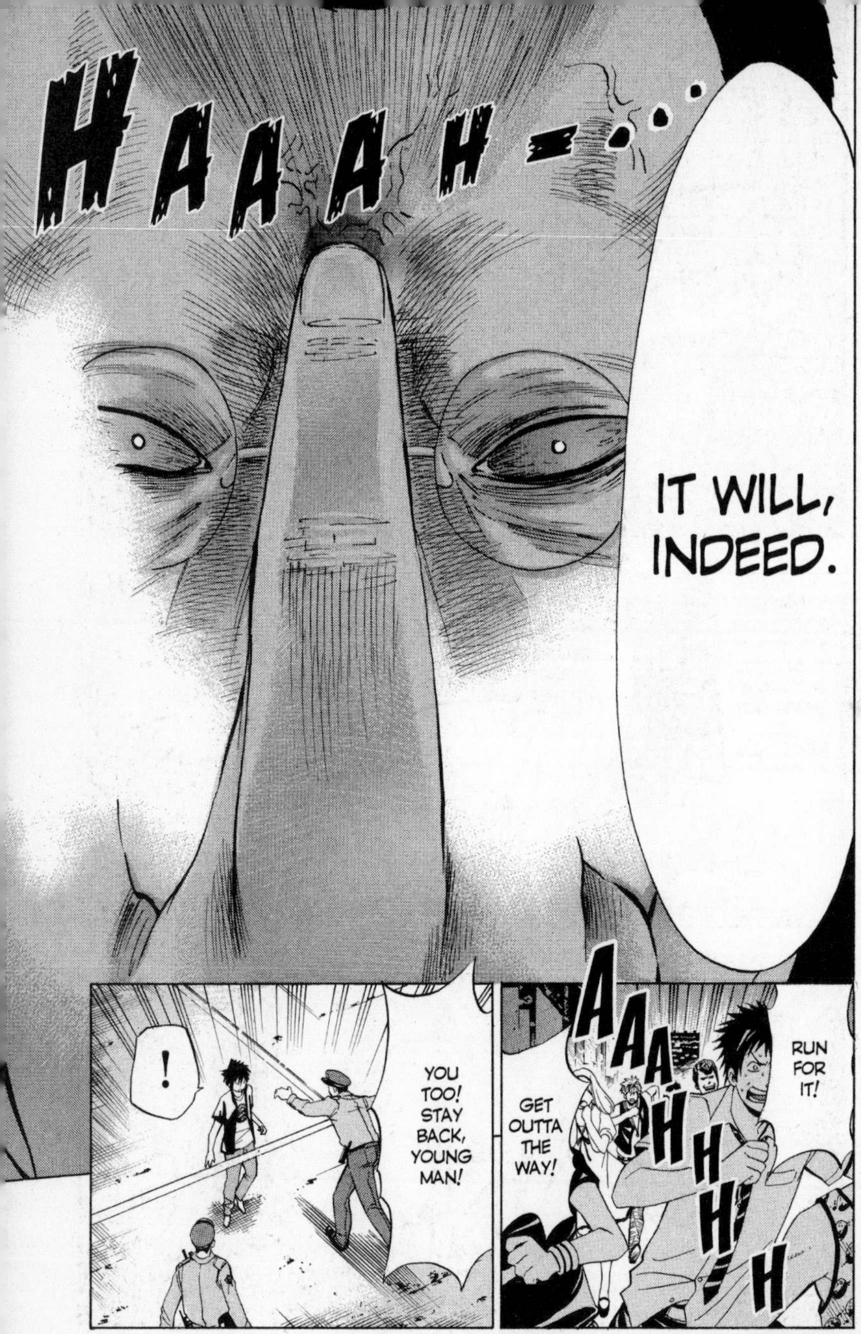
IT WILL, INDEED.
HAAAAH—...
RUN FOR IT!
AAAHHHHHH
GET OUTTA THE WAY!
YOU TOO! STAY BACK, YOUNG MAN!
!

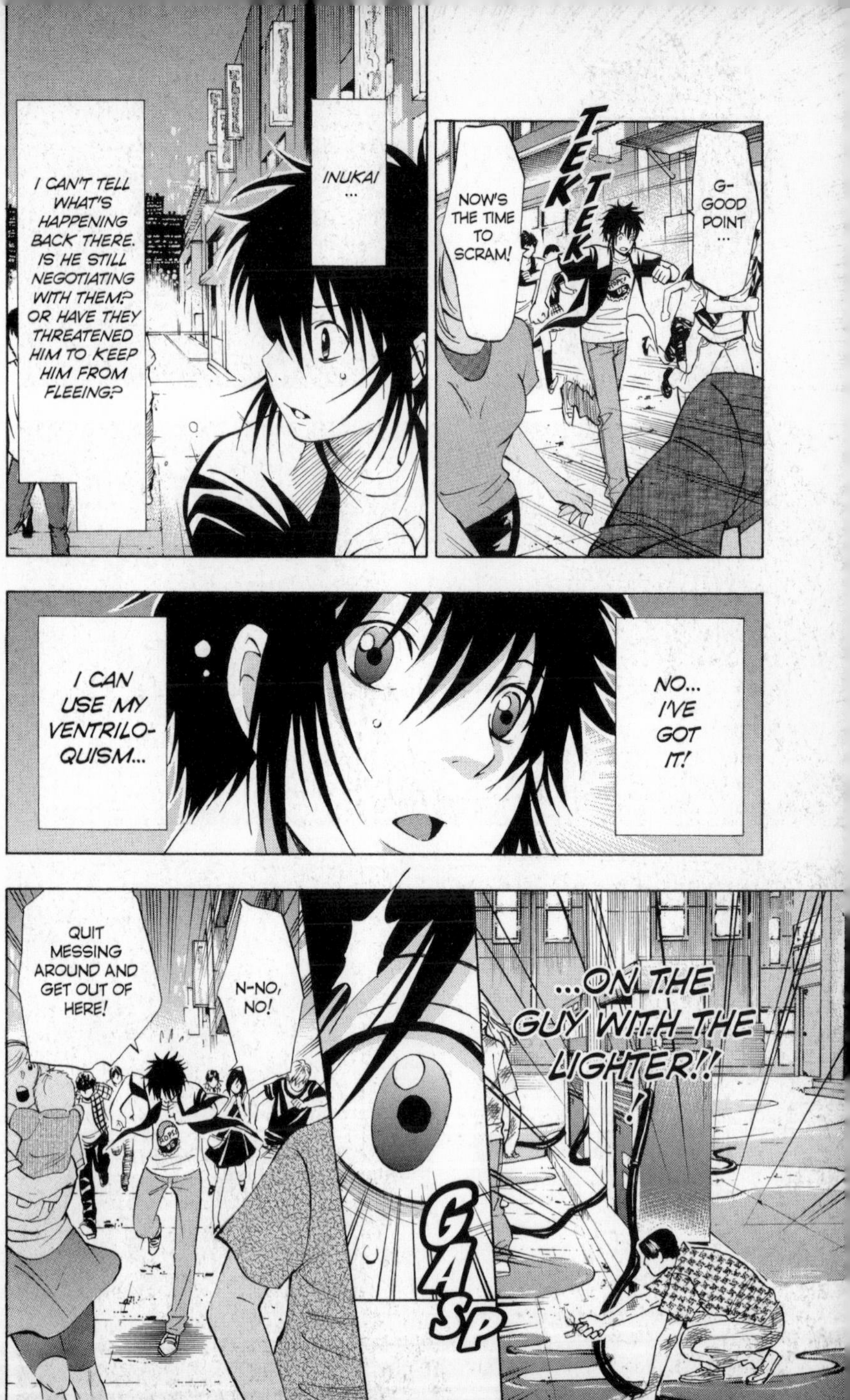
NOW'S THE TIME TO SCRAM!
TEK TEK
G-GOOD POINT...
INUKAI...
I CAN'T TELL WHAT'S HAPPENING BACK THERE. IS HE STILL NEGOTIATING WITH THEM? OR HAVE THEY THREATENED HIM TO KEEP HIM FROM FLEEING?
NO... I'VE GOT IT!
I CAN USE MY VENTRILO-QUISM...
...ON THE GUY WITH THE LIGHTER!!!
GASP
QUIT MESSING AROUND AND GET OUT OF HERE!
N-NO, NO!

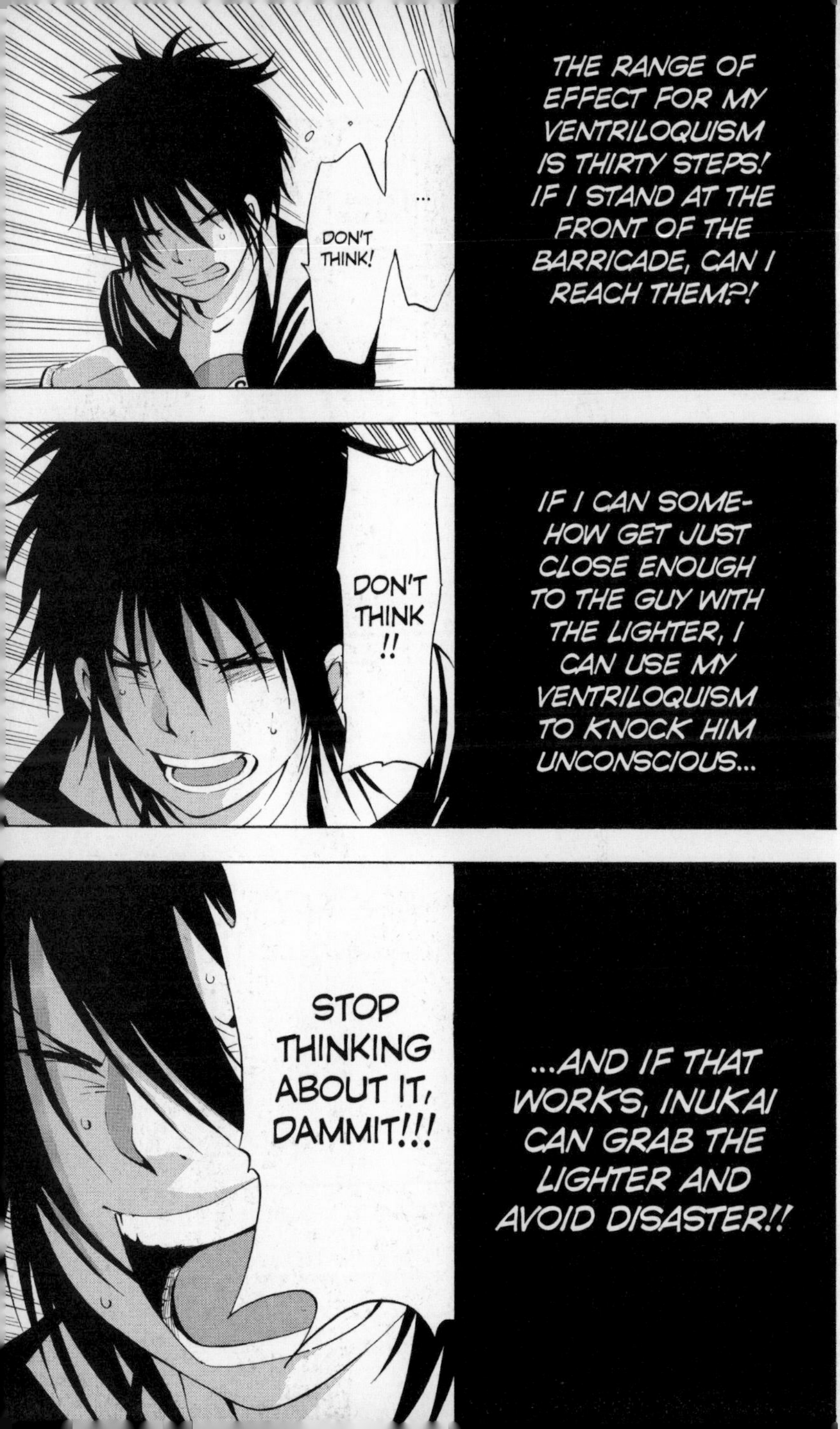
THE RANGE OF EFFECT FOR MY VENTRILOQUISM IS THIRTY STEPS! IF I STAND AT THE FRONT OF THE BARRICADE, CAN I REACH THEM?!
...
DON'T THINK!
IF I CAN SOME-HOW GET JUST CLOSE ENOUGH TO THE GUY WITH THE LIGHTER, I CAN USE MY VENTRILOQUISM TO KNOCK HIM UNCONSCIOUS...
DON'T THINK!!
...AND IF THAT WORKS, INUKAI CAN GRAB THE LIGHTER AND AVOID DISASTER!!
STOP THINKING ABOUT IT, DAMMIT!!!

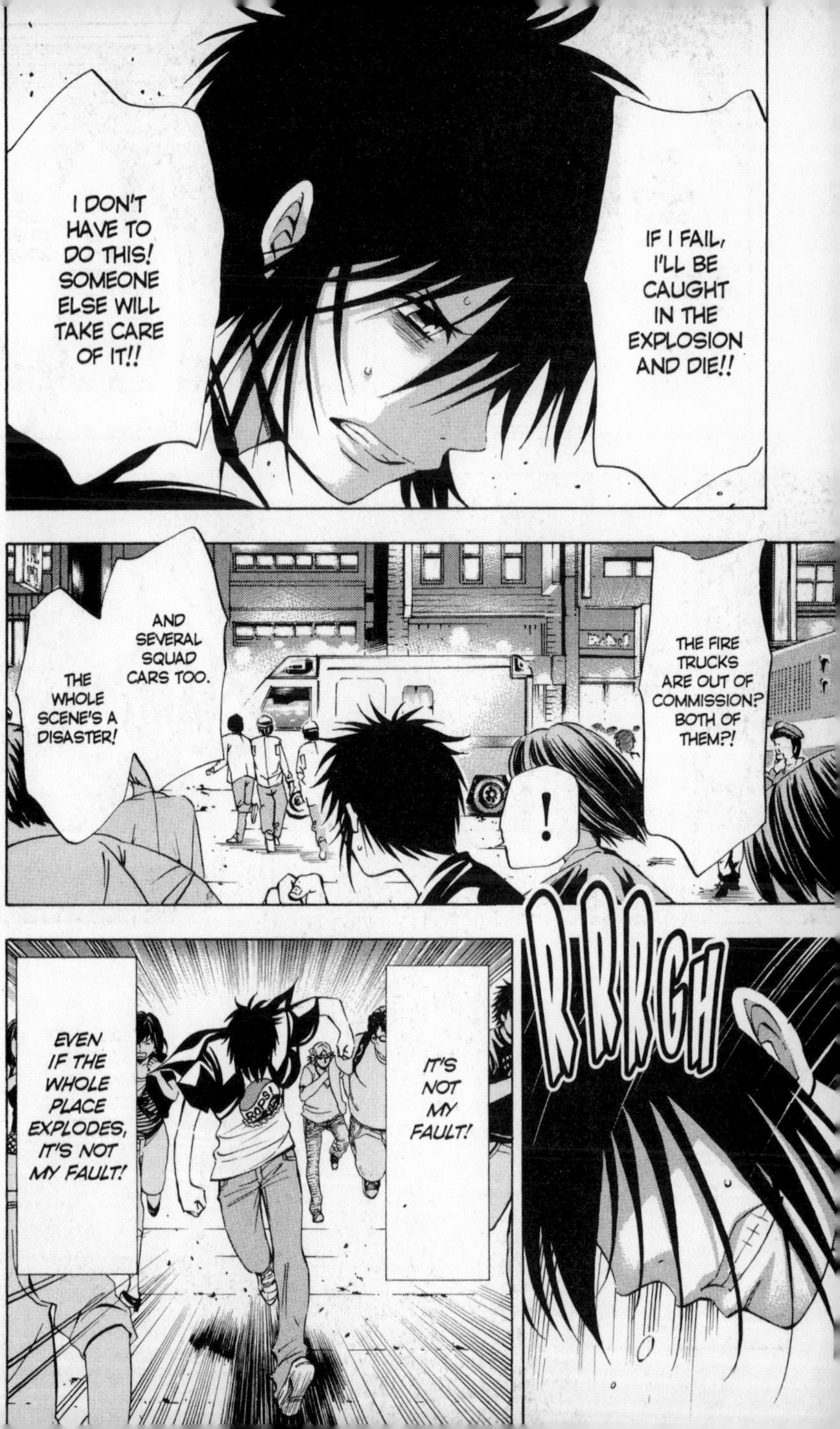
IF I FAIL, I'LL BE CAUGHT IN THE EXPLOSION AND DIE!!
I DON'T HAVE TO DO THIS! SOMEONE ELSE WILL TAKE CARE OF IT!!
THE FIRE TRUCKS ARE OUT OF COMMISSION? BOTH OF THEM?!
!
AND SEVERAL SQUAD CARS TOO.
THE WHOLE SCENE'S A DISASTER!
RRRGH
IT'S NOT MY FAULT!
EVEN IF THE WHOLE PLACE EXPLODES, IT'S NOT MY FAULT!

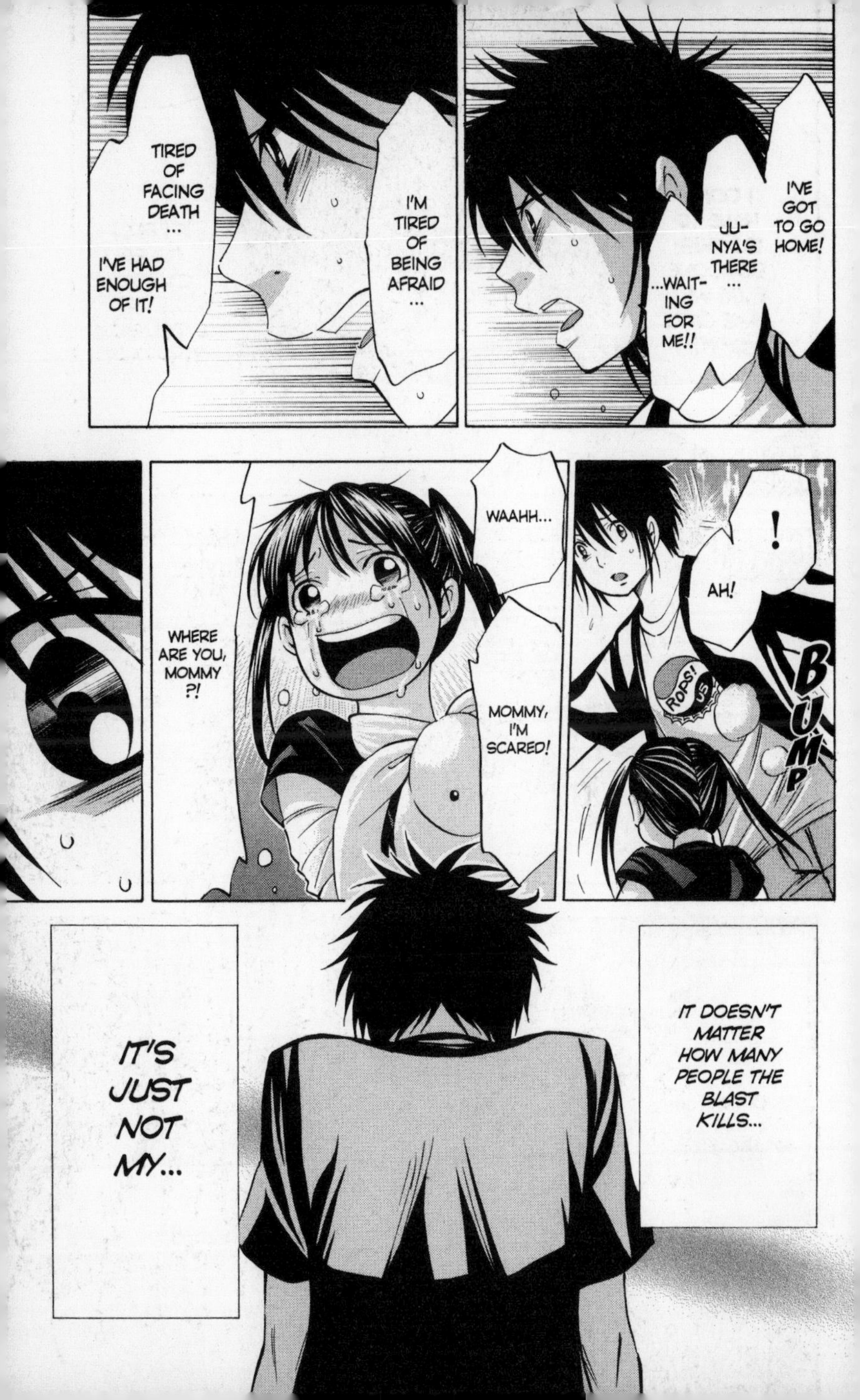
I'VE GOT TO GO HOME!
JU-NYA'S THERE...
...WAIT-ING FOR ME!!
I'M TIRED OF BEING AFRAID...
TIRED OF FACING DEATH...
I'VE HAD ENOUGH OF IT!
!
AH!
BUMP
WAAHH...
MOMMY, I'M SCARED!
WHERE ARE YOU, MOMMY?!
IT DOESN'T MATTER HOW MANY PEOPLE THE BLAST KILLS...
IT'S JUST NOT MY...

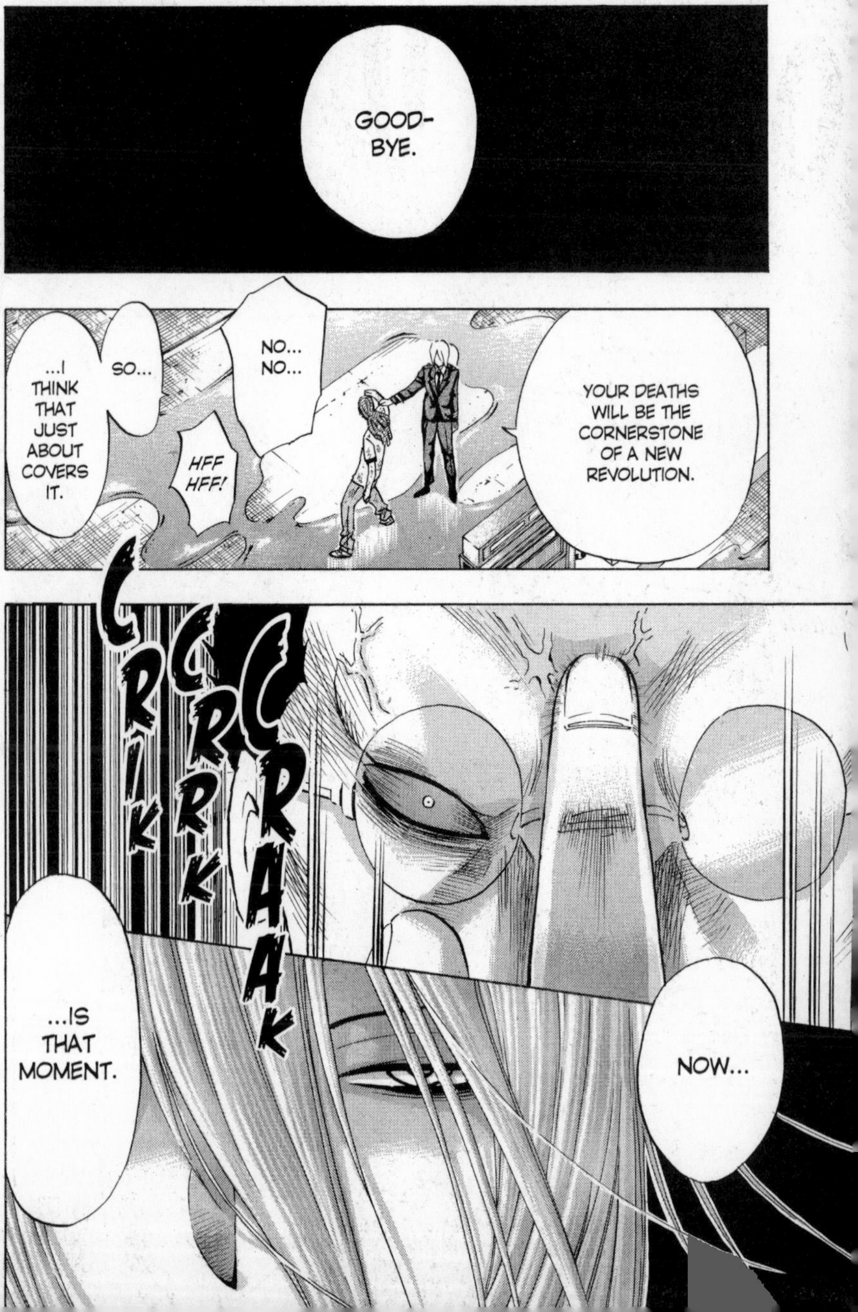
GOOD-BYE.
YOUR DEATHS WILL BE THE CORNERSTONE OF A NEW REVOLUTION.
NO... NO...
HFF HFF!
SO...
...I THINK THAT JUST ABOUT COVERS IT.
CRAAK
CRRK
CRIK
NOW...
...IS THAT MOMENT.

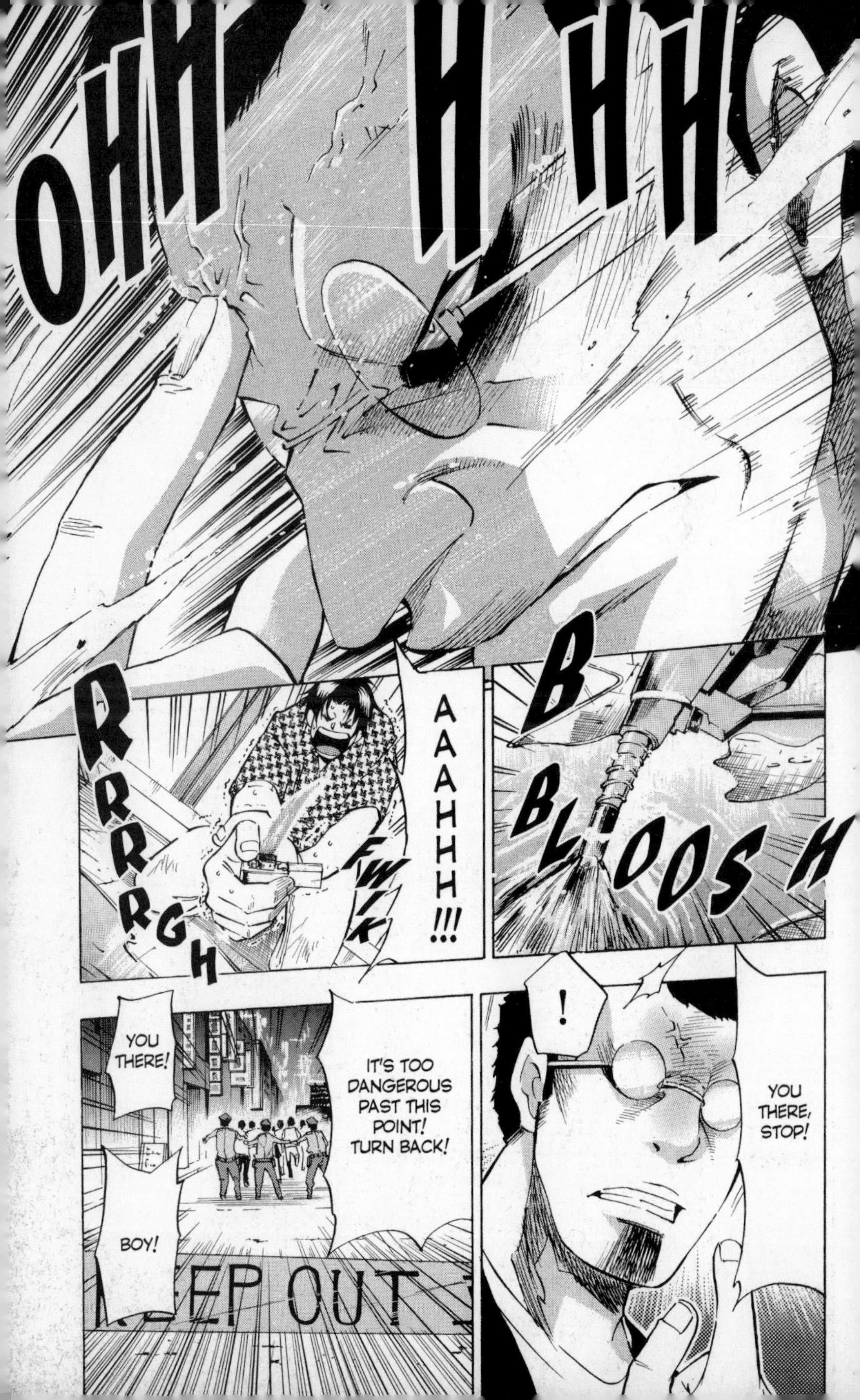
BBLOOSH
AAAHHHH!!!
FWIK
RRRRRGH
!
YOU THERE, STOP!
YOU THERE!
IT'S TOO DANGEROUS PAST THIS POINT! TURN BACK!
BOY!

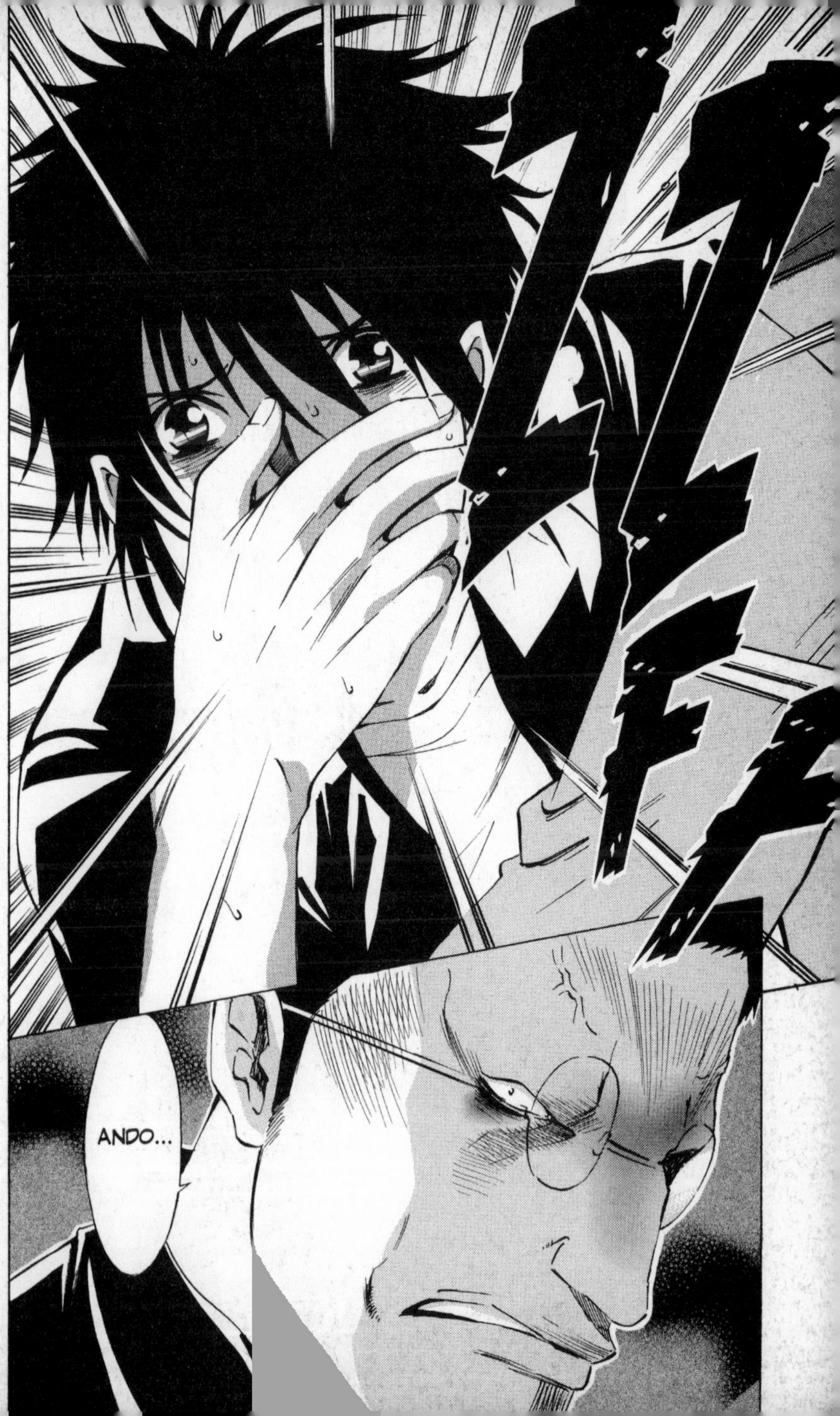
ANDO...

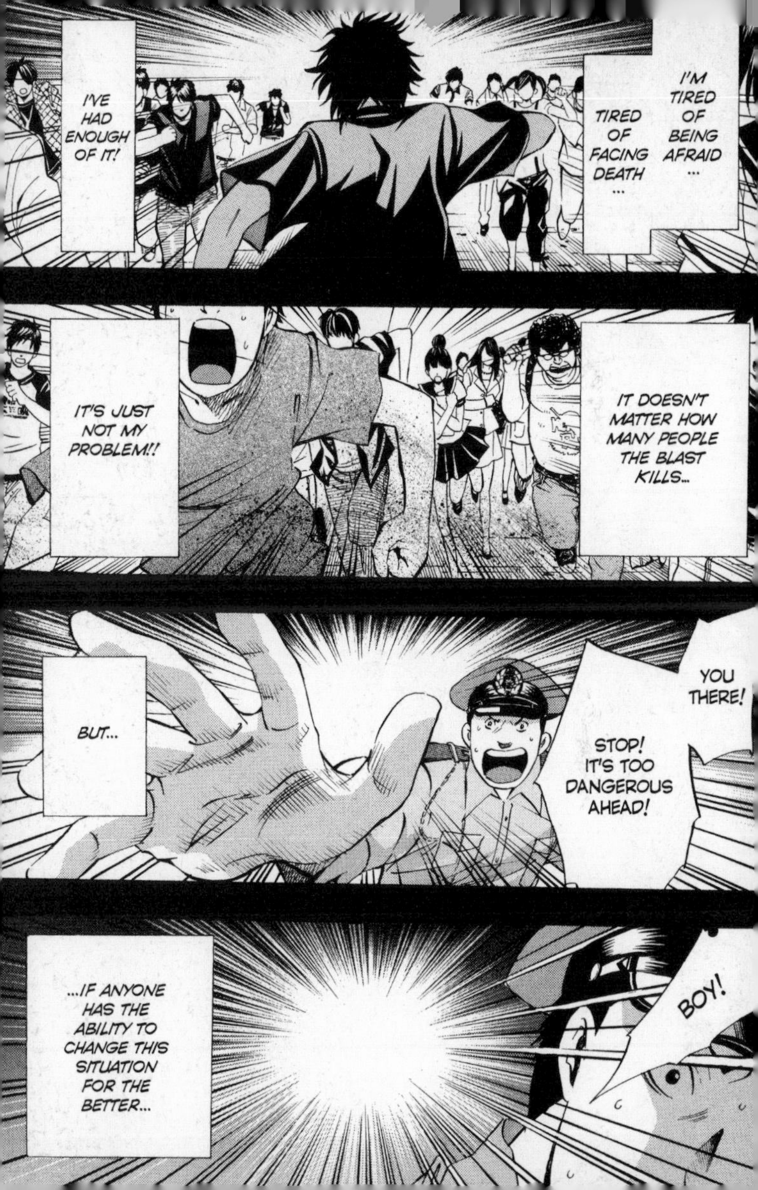
I'M TIRED OF BEING AFRAID...
TIRED OF FACING DEATH...
I'VE HAD ENOUGH OF IT!
IT DOESN'T MATTER HOW MANY PEOPLE THE BLAST KILLS...
IT'S JUST NOT MY PROBLEM!!
YOU THERE!
STOP! IT'S TOO DANGEROUS AHEAD!
BUT...
BOY!
...IF ANYONE HAS THE ABILITY TO CHANGE THIS SITUATION FOR THE BETTER...

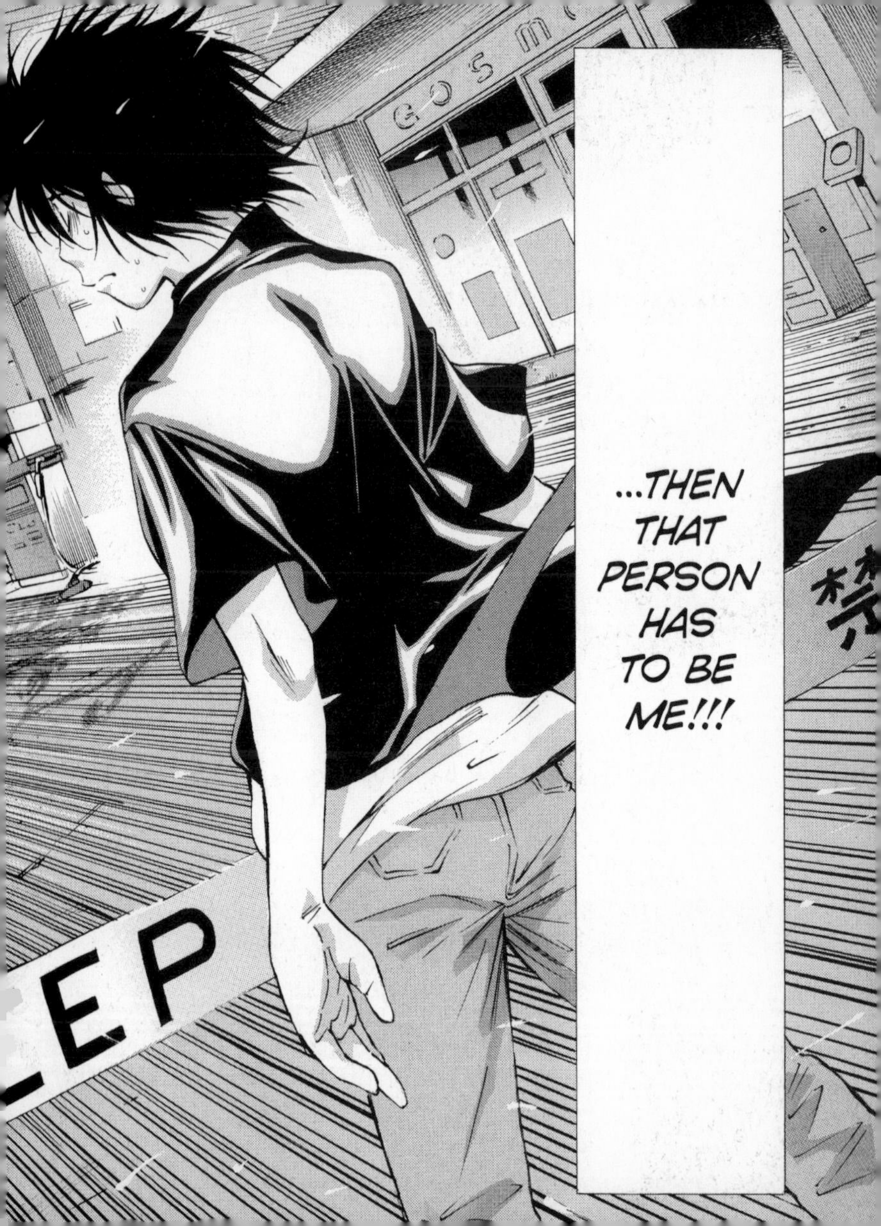
...THEN THAT PERSON HAS TO BE ME!!!

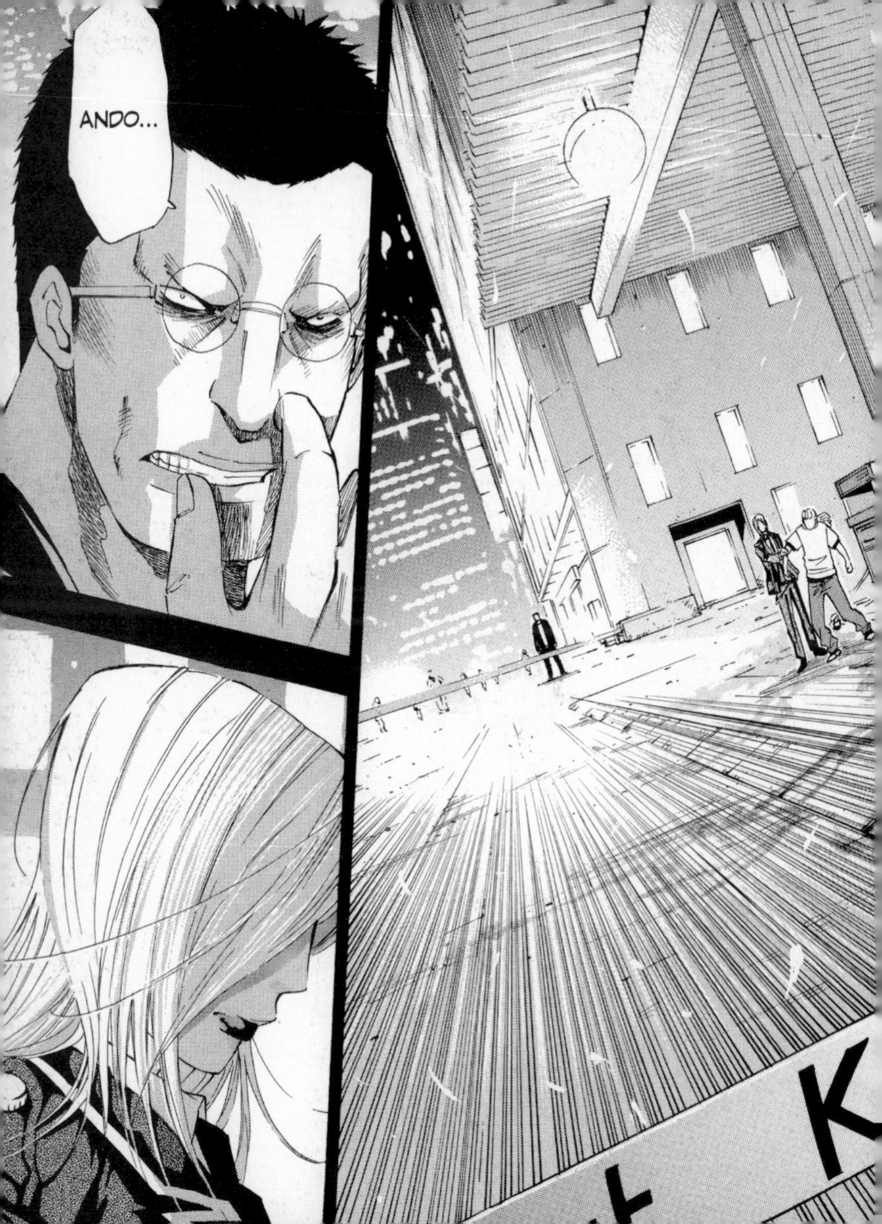
K
ANDO...

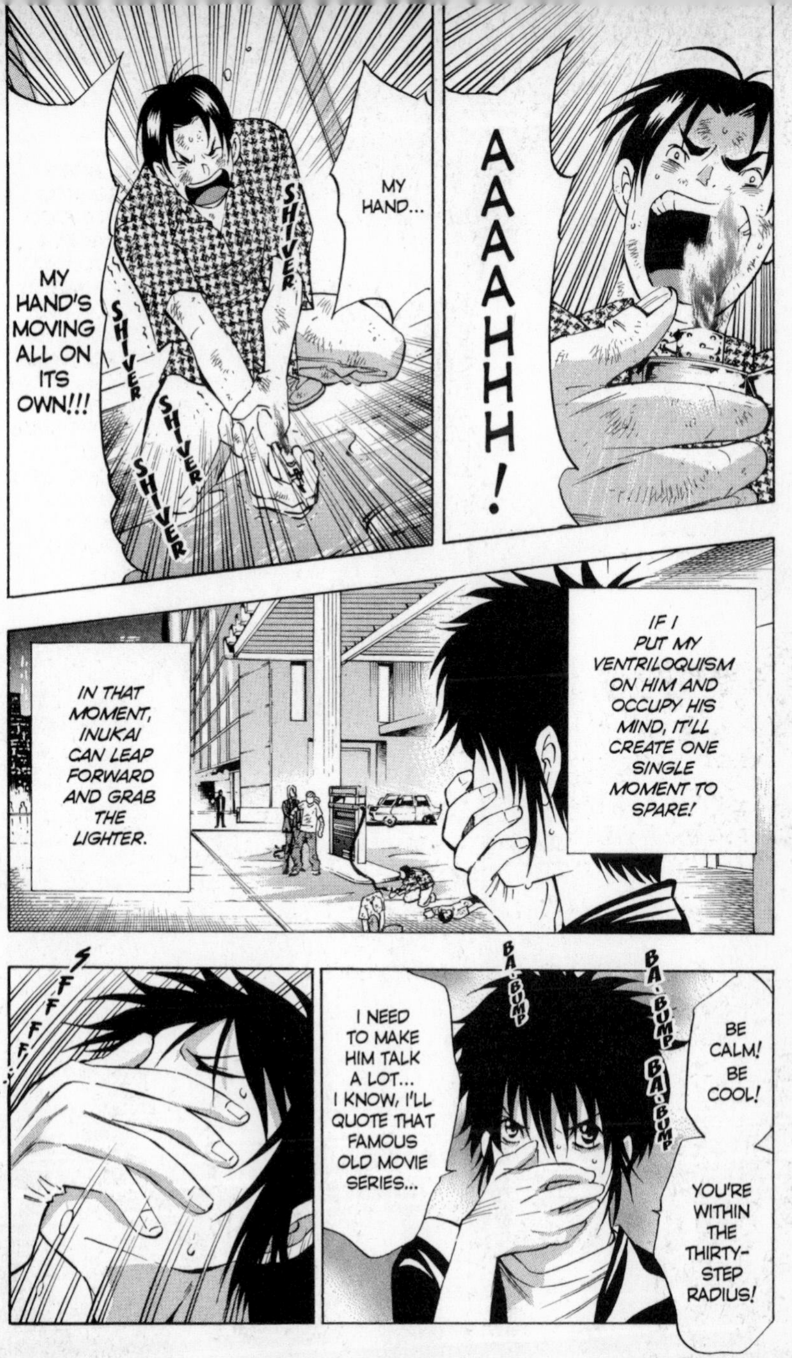
AAAAHHH!
MY HAND...
SHIVER
SHIVER
SHIVER
SHIVER
SHIVER
MY HAND'S MOVING ALL ON ITS OWN!!!
IF I PUT MY VENTRILOQUISM ON HIM AND OCCUPY HIS MIND, IT'LL CREATE ONE SINGLE MOMENT TO SPARE!
IN THAT MOMENT, INUKAI CAN LEAP FORWARD AND GRAB THE LIGHTER.
BA-BUMP
BA-BUMP
BA-BUMP
BE CALM! BE COOL!
YOU'RE WITHIN THE THIRTY-STEP RADIUS!
I NEED TO MAKE HIM TALK A LOT... I KNOW, I'LL QUOTE THAT FAMOUS OLD MOVIE SERIES...
SFFFF

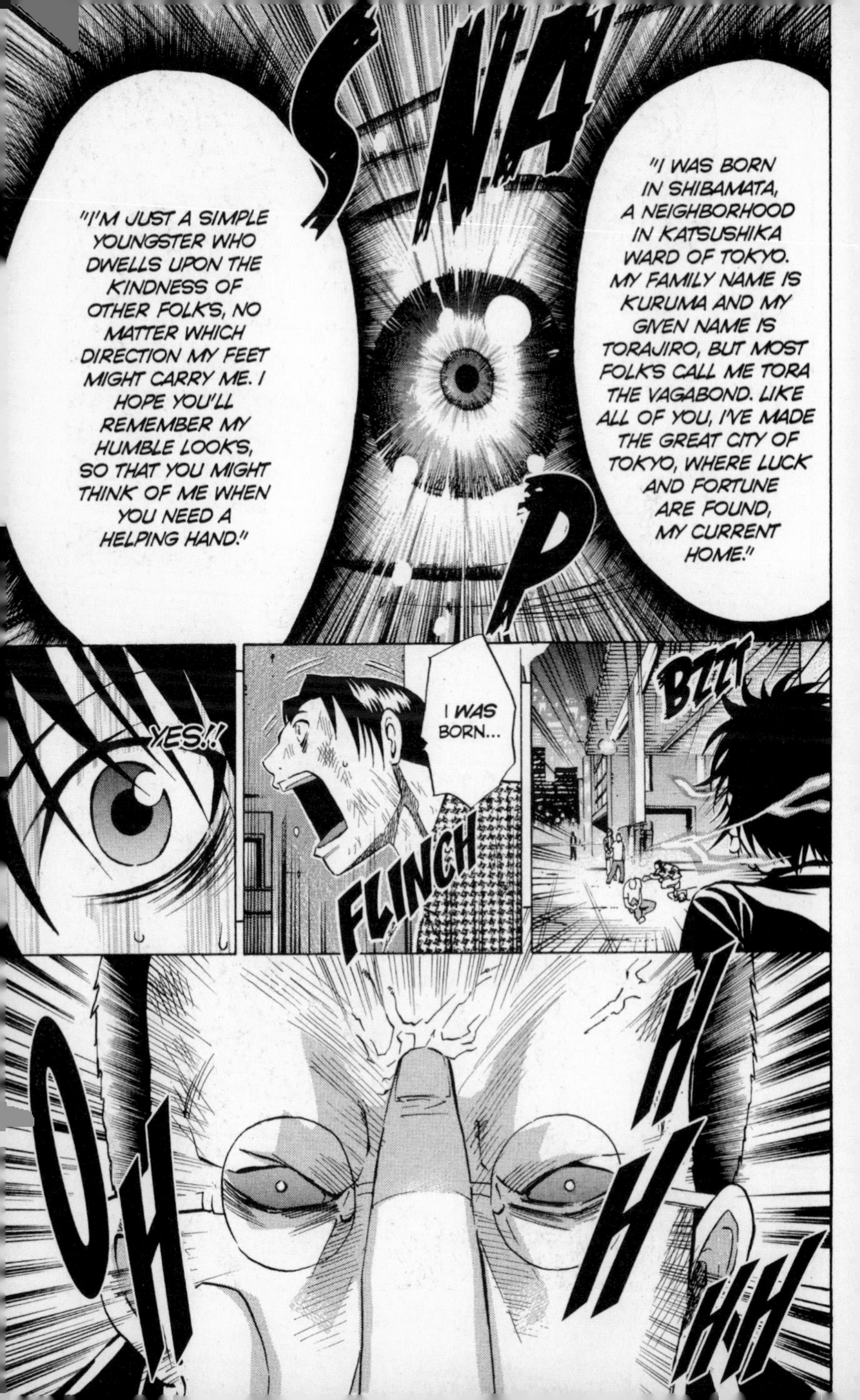
SNAP
"I WAS BORN IN SHIBAMATA, A NEIGHBORHOOD IN KATSUSHIKA WARD OF TOKYO. MY FAMILY NAME IS KURUMA AND MY GIVEN NAME IS TORAJIRO, BUT MOST FOLKS CALL ME TORA THE VAGABOND. LIKE ALL OF YOU, I'VE MADE THE GREAT CITY OF TOKYO, WHERE LUCK AND FORTUNE ARE FOUND, MY CURRENT HOME."
"I'M JUST A SIMPLE YOUNGSTER WHO DWELLS UPON THE KINDNESS OF OTHER FOLKS, NO MATTER WHICH DIRECTION MY FEET MIGHT CARRY ME. I HOPE YOU'LL REMEMBER MY HUMBLE LOOKS, SO THAT YOU MIGHT THINK OF ME WHEN YOU NEED A HELPING HAND."
BZZT
I WAS BORN...
FLINCH
YES!!

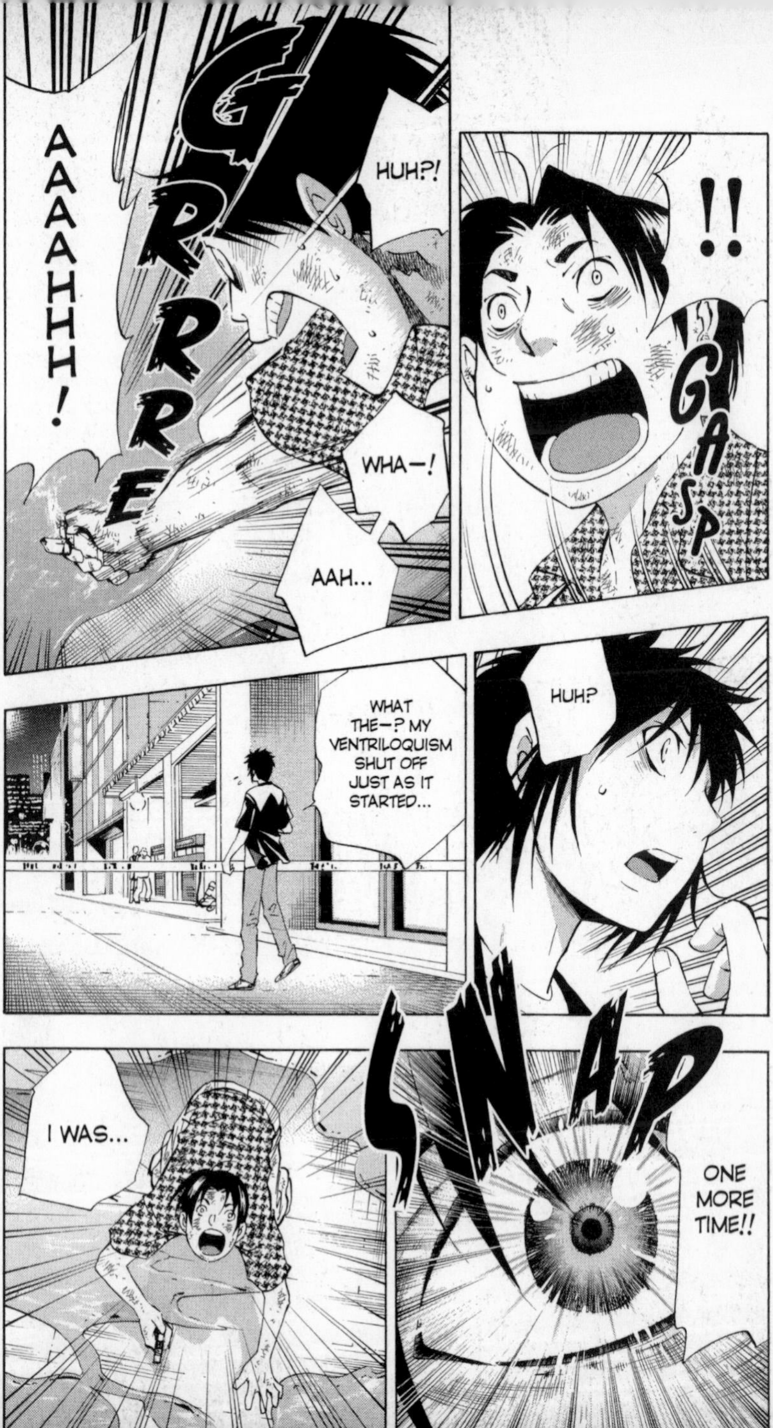
!!
GASP
HUH?!
WHA—!
AAH...
GRRRE
AAAAHHH!
HUH?
WHAT THE—? MY VENTRILOQUISM SHUT OFF JUST AS IT STARTED...
ONE MORE TIME!!
SNAP
I WAS...

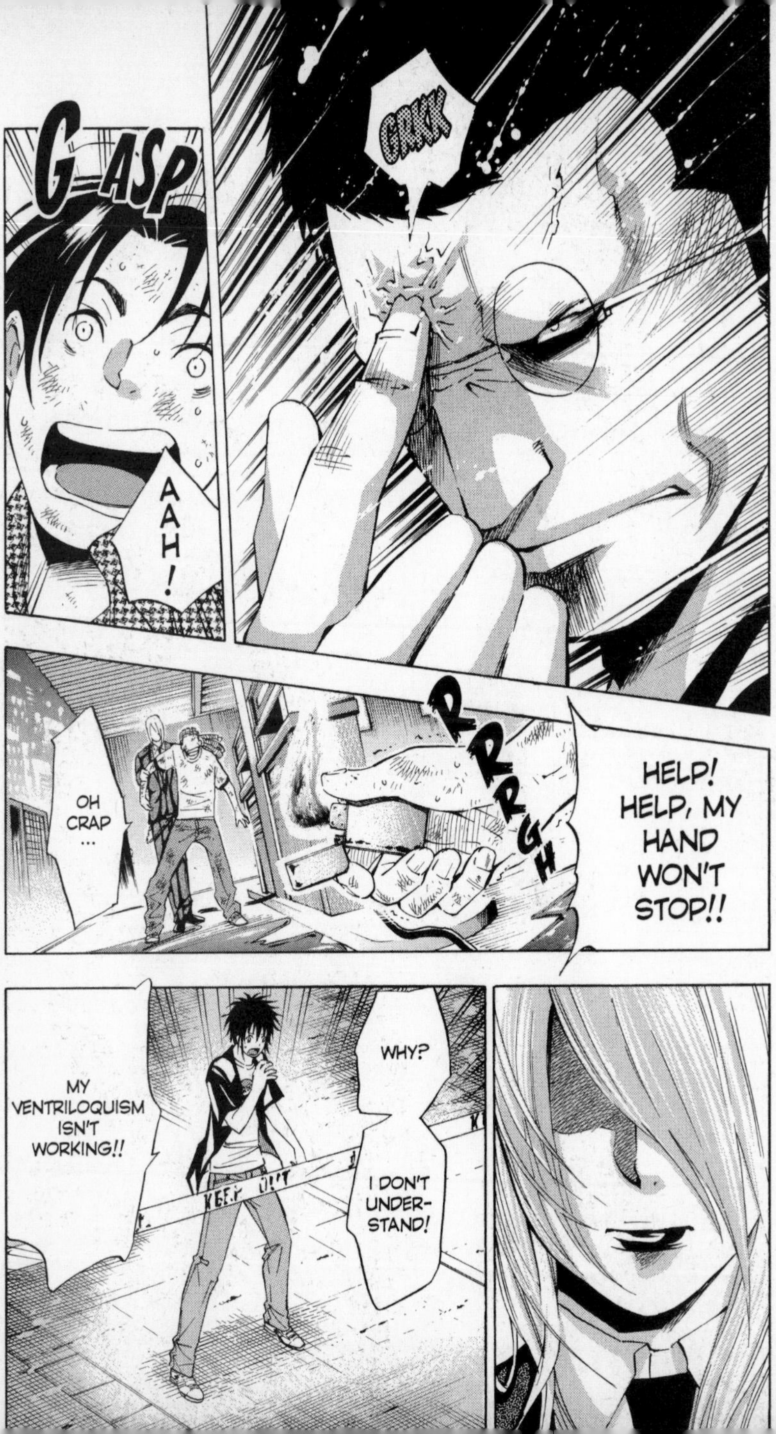
GRKK
GASP
AAH!
HELP! HELP, MY HAND WON'T STOP!!
RRRGH
OH CRAP ...
WHY?
I DON'T UNDERSTAND!
MY VENTRILOQUISM ISN'T WORKING!!

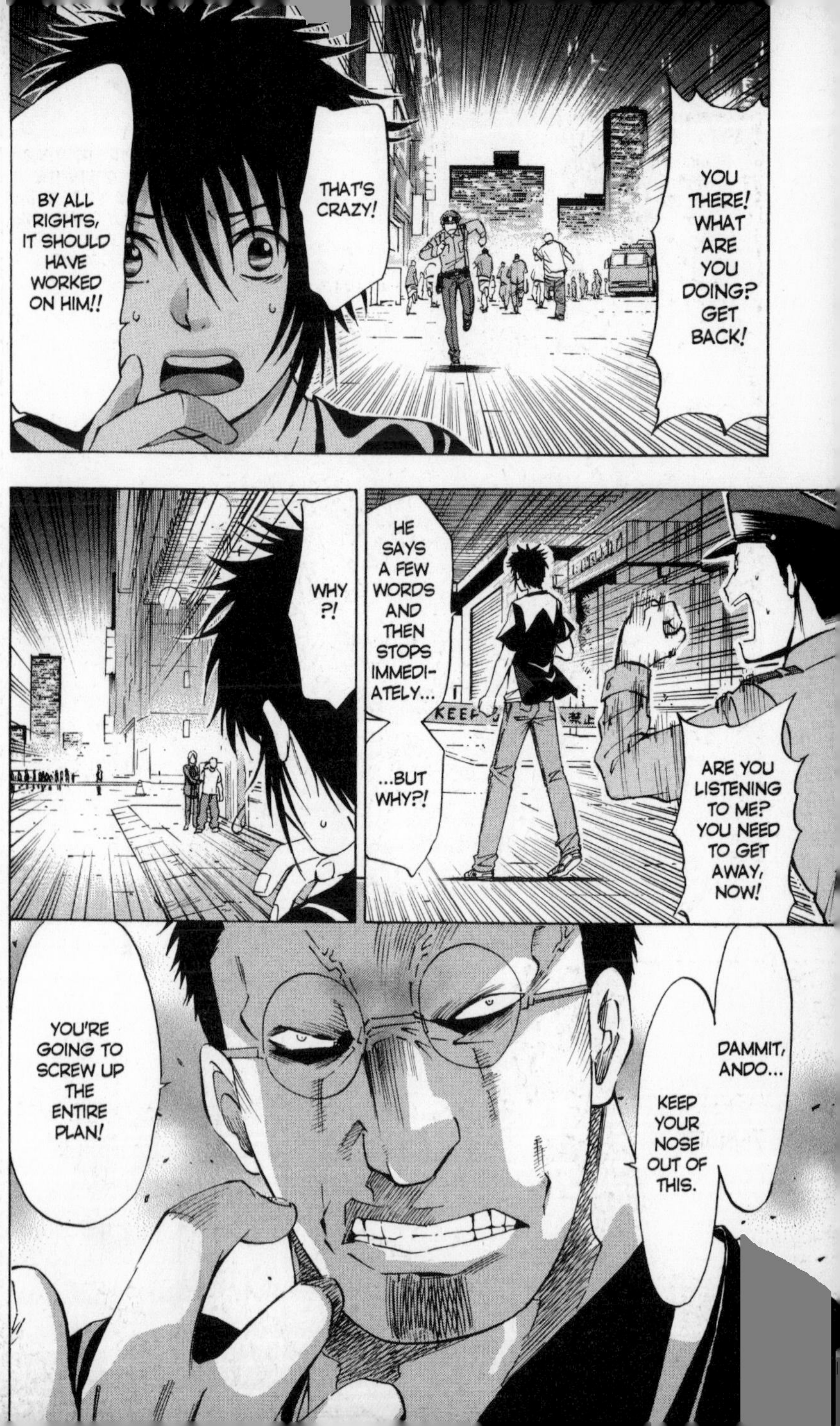
YOU THERE! WHAT ARE YOU DOING? GET BACK!
THAT'S CRAZY!
BY ALL RIGHTS, IT SHOULD HAVE WORKED ON HIM!!
ARE YOU LISTENING TO ME? YOU NEED TO GET AWAY, NOW!
HE SAYS A FEW WORDS AND THEN STOPS IMMEDIATELY...
...BUT WHY?!
WHY?!
DAMMIT, ANDO...
KEEP YOUR NOSE OUT OF THIS.
YOU'RE GOING TO SCREW UP THE ENTIRE PLAN!

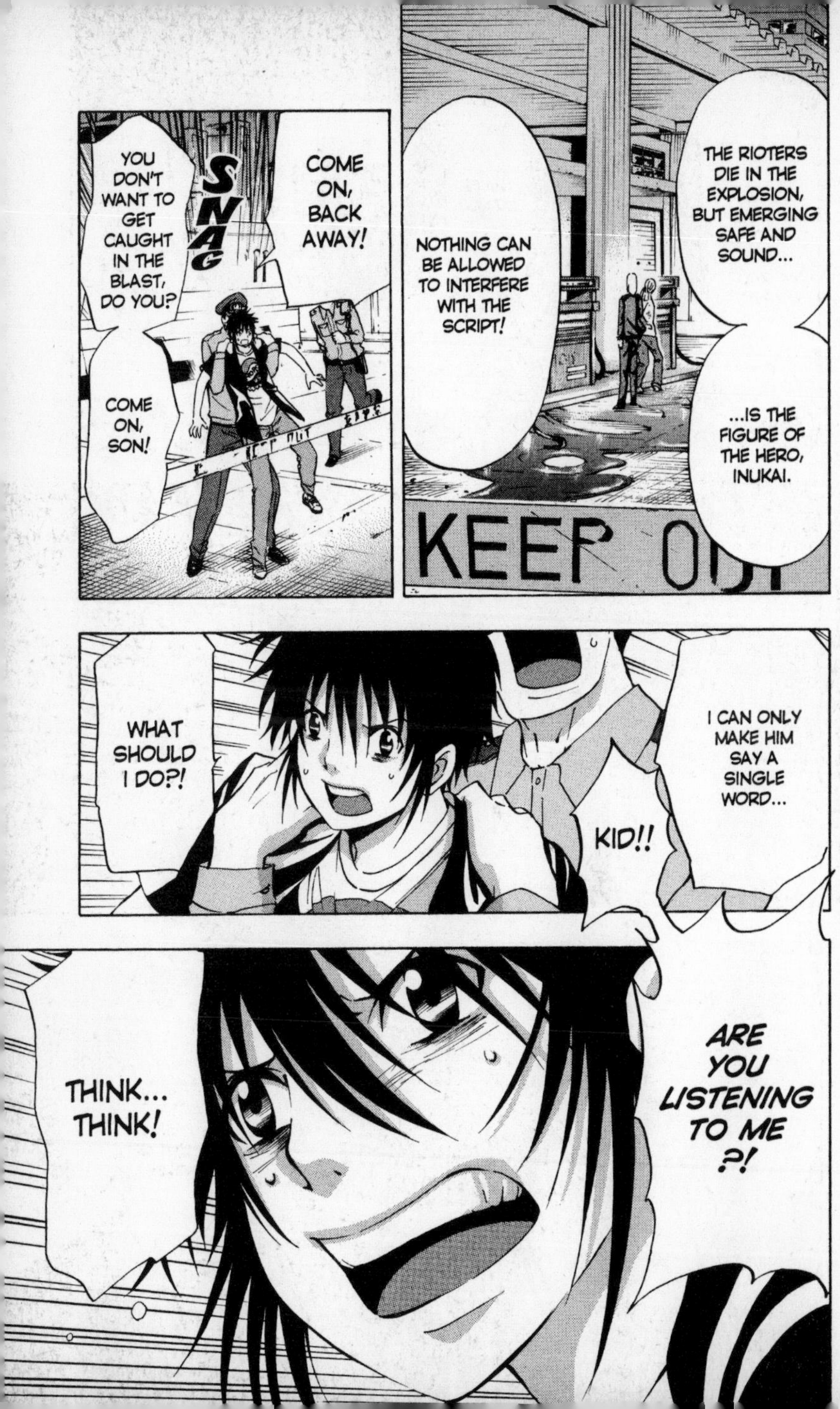
THE RIOTERS DIE IN THE EXPLOSION, BUT EMERGING SAFE AND SOUND...
...IS THE FIGURE OF THE HERO, INUKAI.
NOTHING CAN BE ALLOWED TO INTERFERE WITH THE SCRIPT!
KEEP
COME ON, BACK AWAY!
SNAG
YOU DON'T WANT TO GET CAUGHT IN THE BLAST, DO YOU?
COME ON, SON!
I CAN ONLY MAKE HIM SAY A SINGLE WORD...
KID!!
WHAT SHOULD I DO?!
ARE YOU LISTENING TO ME ?!
THINK... THINK!

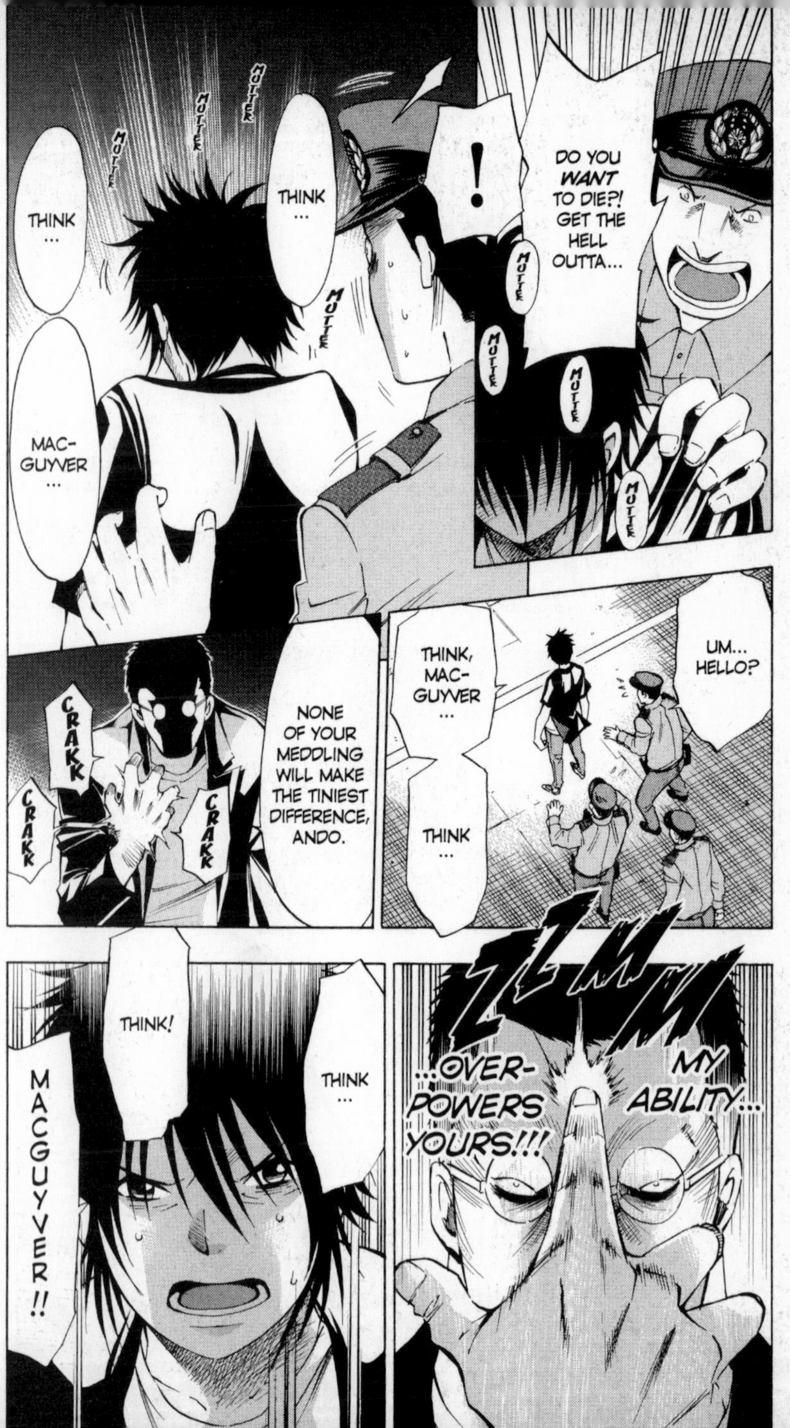
DO YOU *WANT* TO DIE?! GET THE HELL OUTTA...
!
MUTTER
MUTTER
MUTTER
MUTTER
THINK ...
MUTTER
MUTTER
MUTTER
THINK ...
MUTTER
MAC-GUYVER ...
UM... HELLO?
THINK, MAC-GUYVER ...
THINK ...
NONE OF YOUR MEDDLING WILL MAKE THE TINIEST DIFFERENCE, ANDO.
CRAKK
CRAKK
CRAKK
MY ABILITY...
...OVER-POWERS YOURS!!!
THINK ...
THINK!
MACGUYVER!!

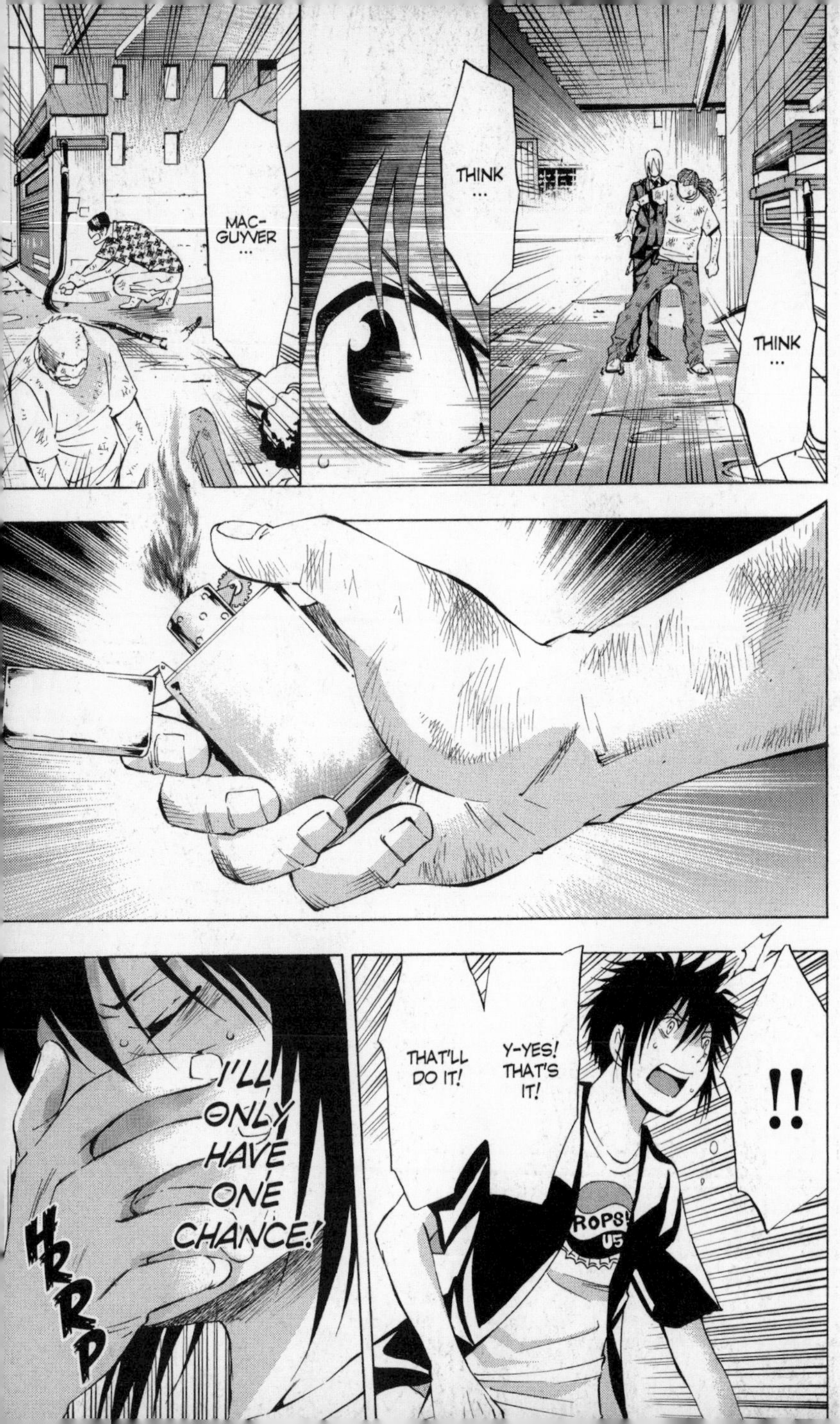
THINK ...
THINK ...
MAC-GUYVER ...
!!
Y-YES! THAT'S IT!
THAT'LL DO IT!
I'LL ONLY HAVE ONE CHANCE!
HRRP

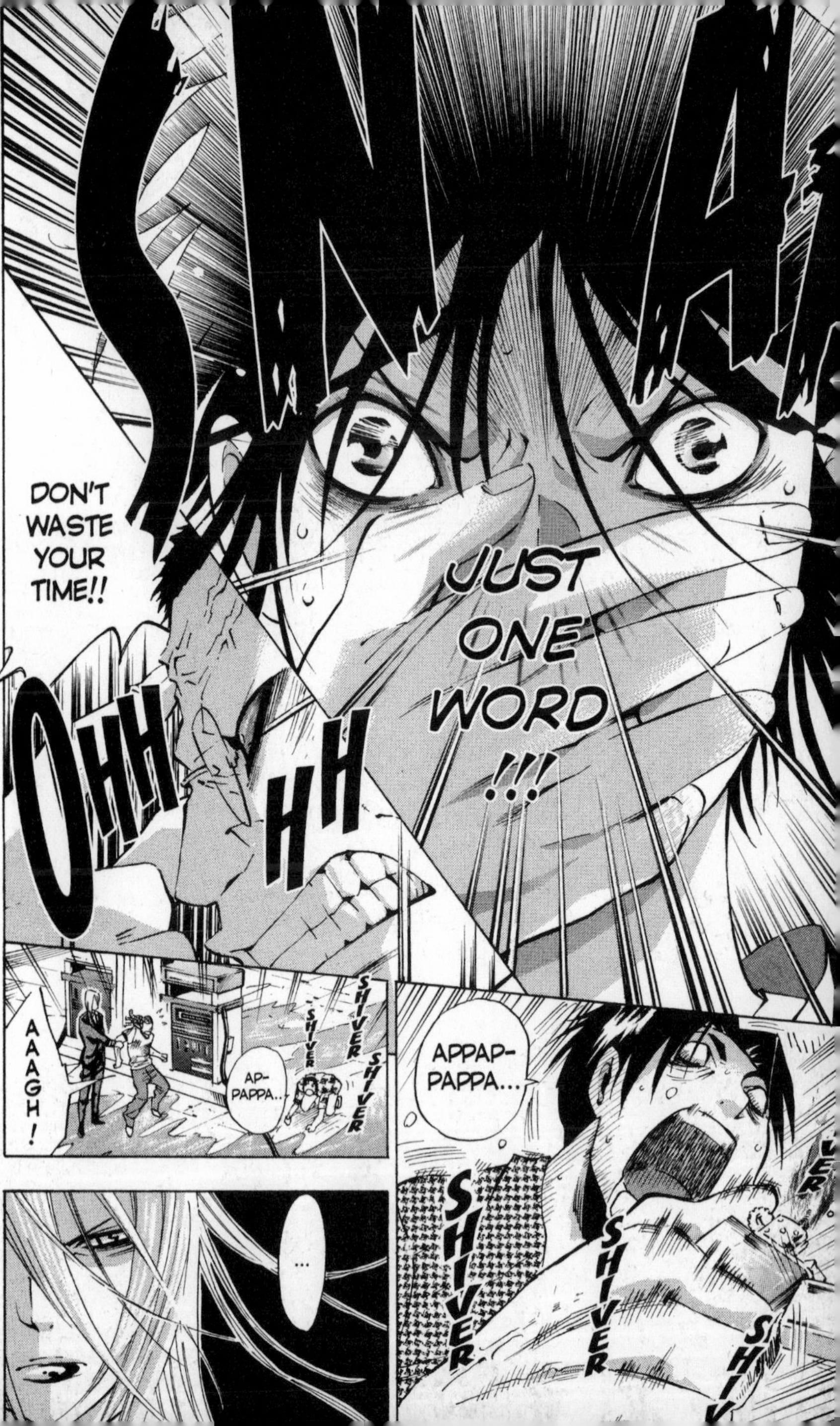
JUST ONE WORD!!!
DON'T WASTE YOUR TIME!!
OHHHH
APPAP-PAPPA...
SHIVER
SHIVER
SHIV
VER
SHIVER SHIVER
SHIVER
AP-PAPPA...
AAAGH!
...

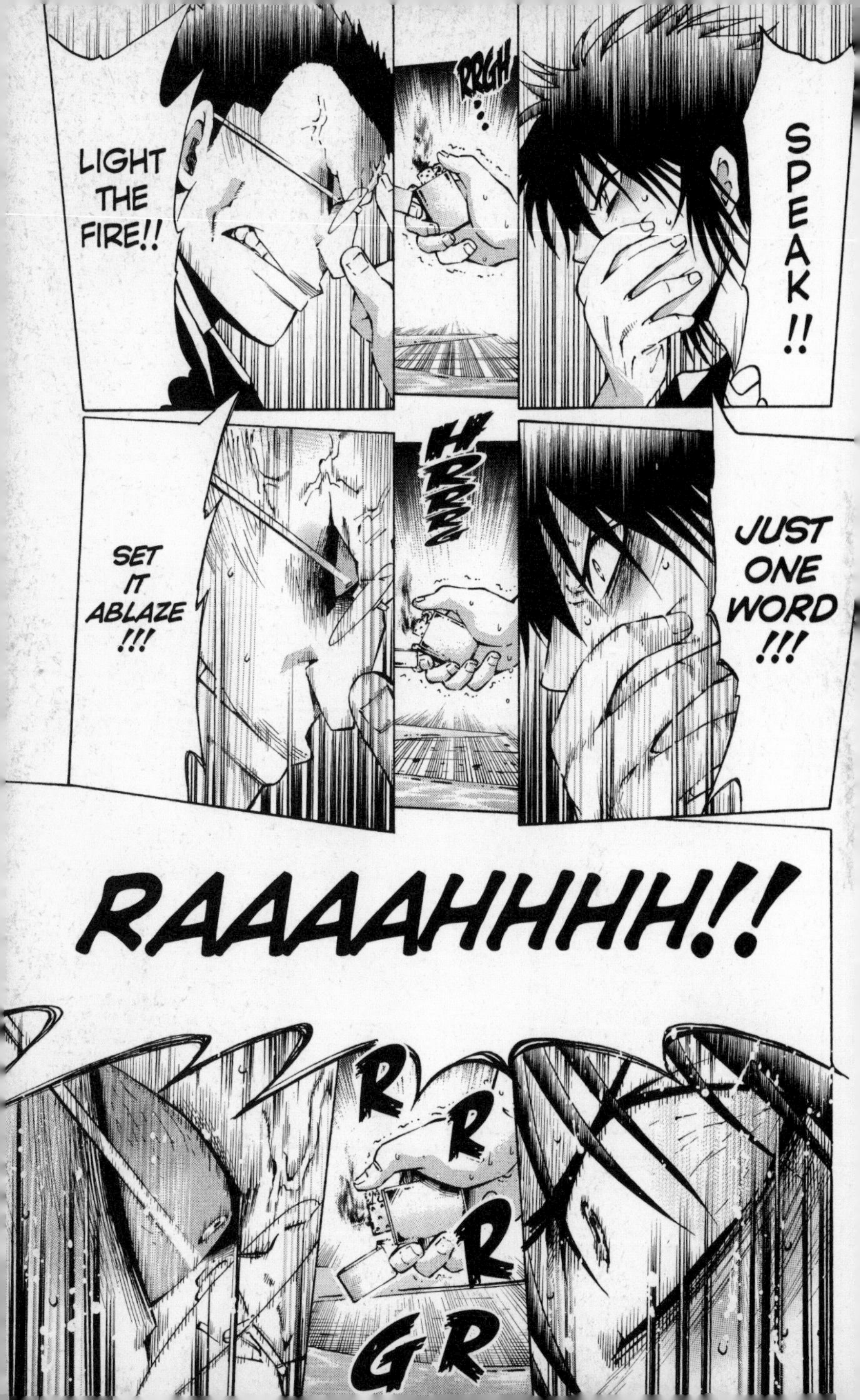
SPEAK!!
RRGH...
LIGHT THE FIRE!!
JUST ONE WORD!!!
HRRRG
SET IT ABLAZE!!!
RAAAAHHHH!!
RRRR
GR

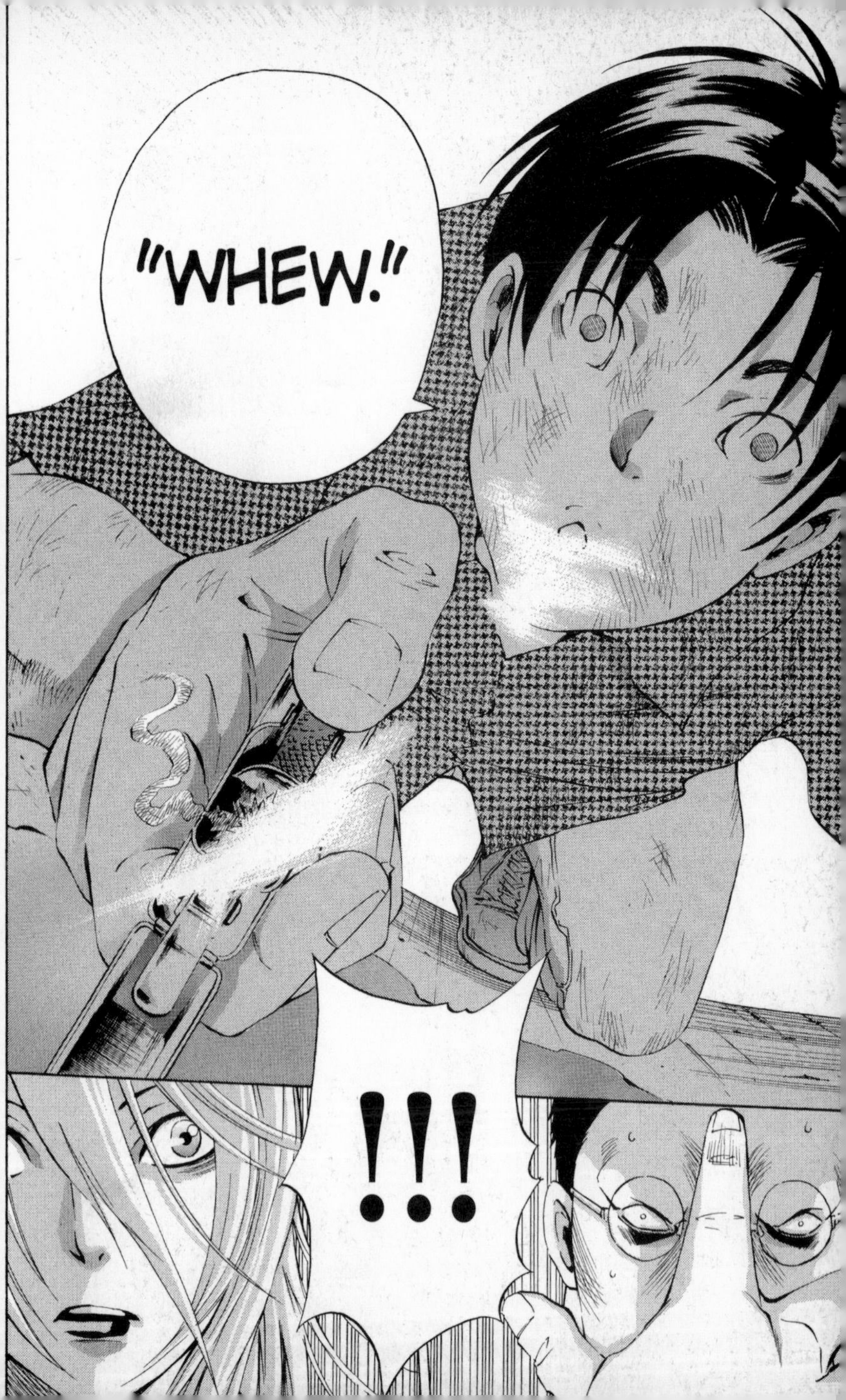
"WHEW."
!!!

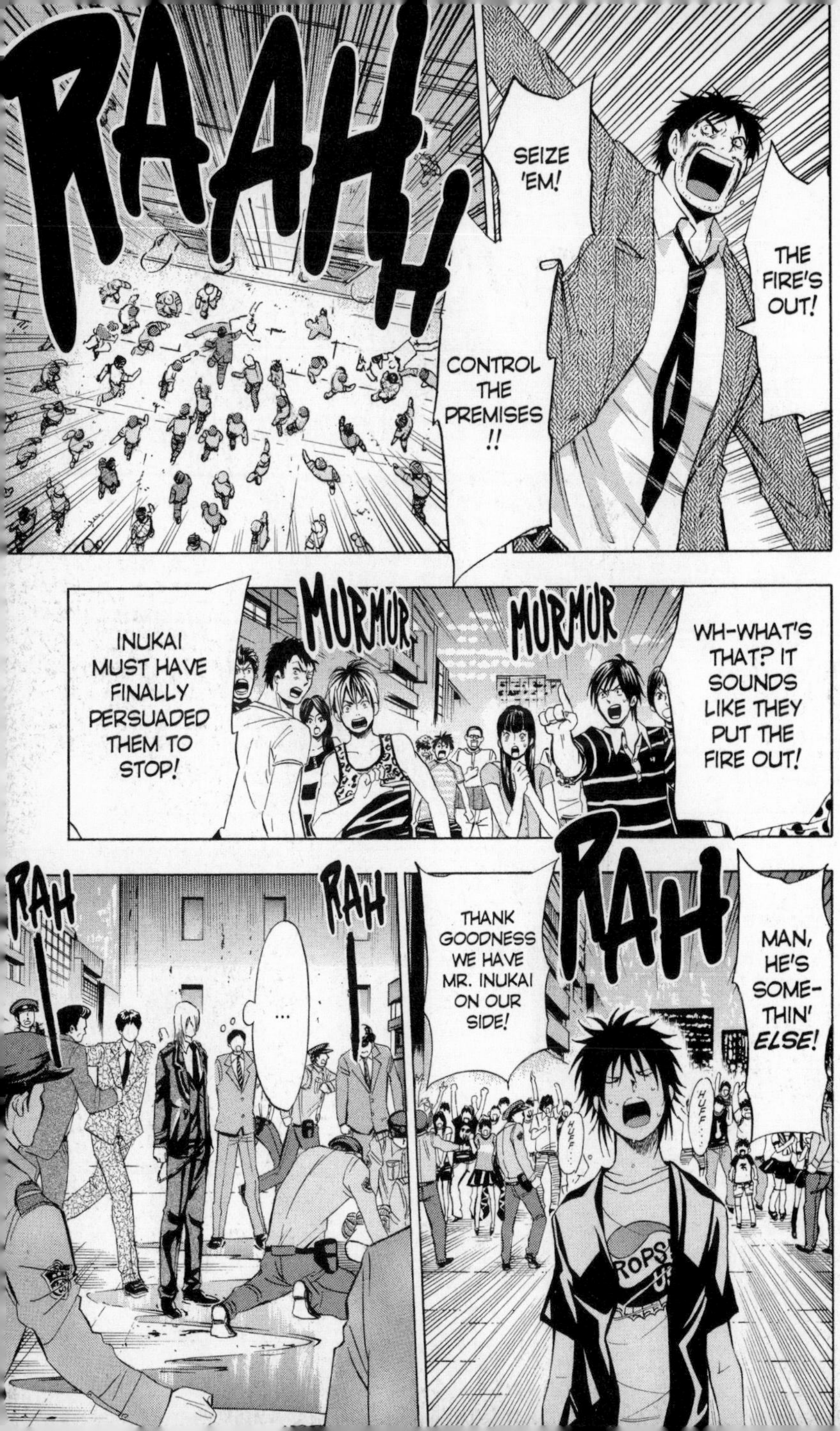
THE FIRE'S OUT!
SEIZE 'EM!
CONTROL THE PREMISES!!
RAAHH
WH-WHAT'S THAT? IT SOUNDS LIKE THEY PUT THE FIRE OUT!
MURMUR
MURMUR
INUKAI MUST HAVE FINALLY PERSUADED THEM TO STOP!
MAN, HE'S SOME-THIN' *ELSE*!
RAH
THANK GOODNESS WE HAVE MR. INUKAI ON OUR SIDE!
HUFF...
HUFF...
RAH
...
RAH

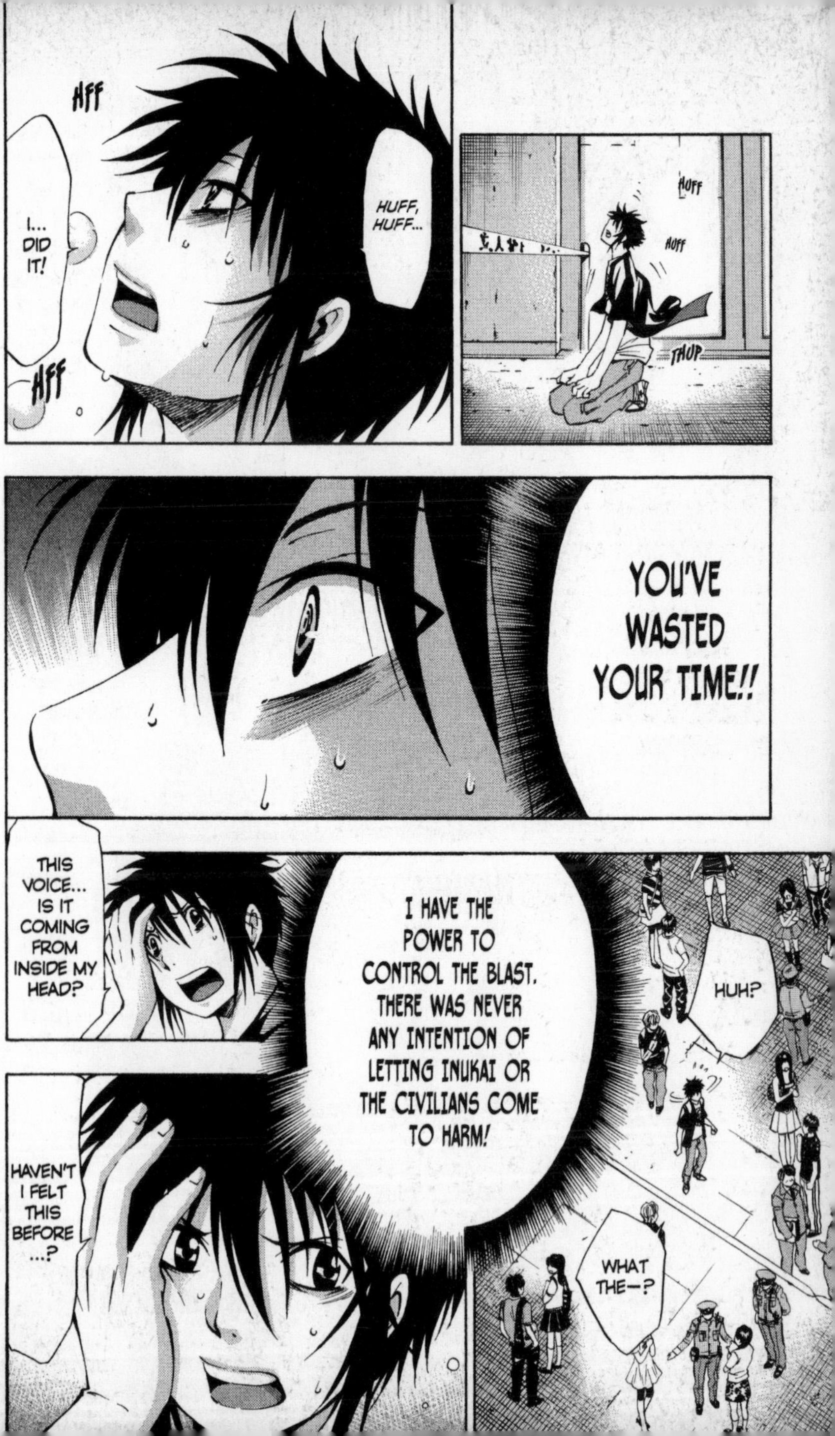
HUFF
HUFF
THUP
HUFF, HUFF...
HFF
I... DID IT!
HFF
YOU'VE WASTED YOUR TIME!!
HUH?
WHAT THE—?
THIS VOICE... IS IT COMING FROM INSIDE MY HEAD?
I HAVE THE POWER TO CONTROL THE BLAST. THERE WAS NEVER ANY INTENTION OF LETTING INUKAI OR THE CIVILIANS COME TO HARM!
HAVEN'T I FELT THIS BEFORE ...?

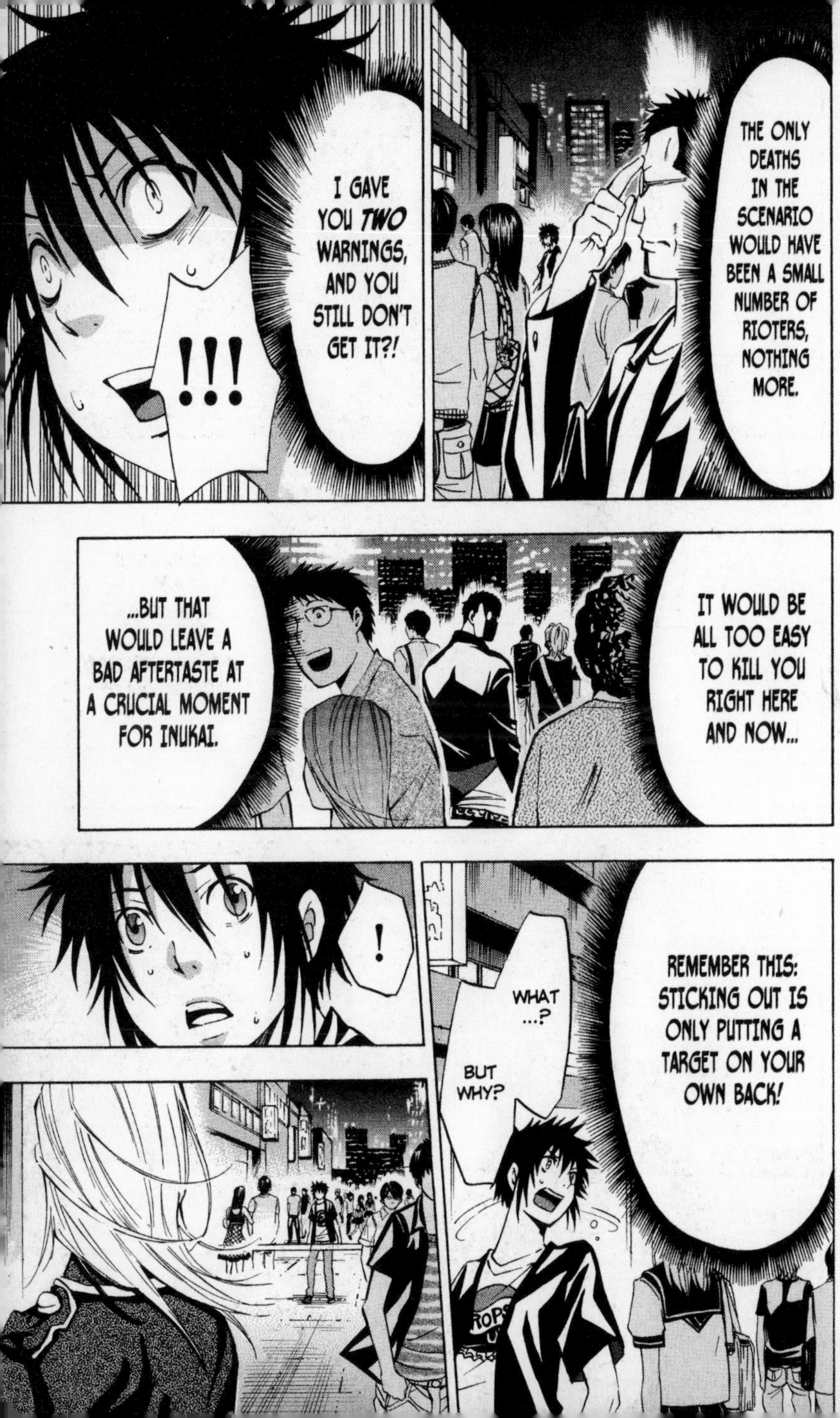
THE ONLY DEATHS IN THE SCENARIO WOULD HAVE BEEN A SMALL NUMBER OF RIOTERS, NOTHING MORE.
I GAVE YOU *TWO* WARNINGS, AND YOU STILL DON'T GET IT?!
!!!
IT WOULD BE ALL TOO EASY TO KILL YOU RIGHT HERE AND NOW...
...BUT THAT WOULD LEAVE A BAD AFTERTASTE AT A CRUCIAL MOMENT FOR INUKAI.
REMEMBER THIS: STICKING OUT IS ONLY PUTTING A TARGET ON YOUR OWN BACK!
WHAT ...?
BUT WHY?
!

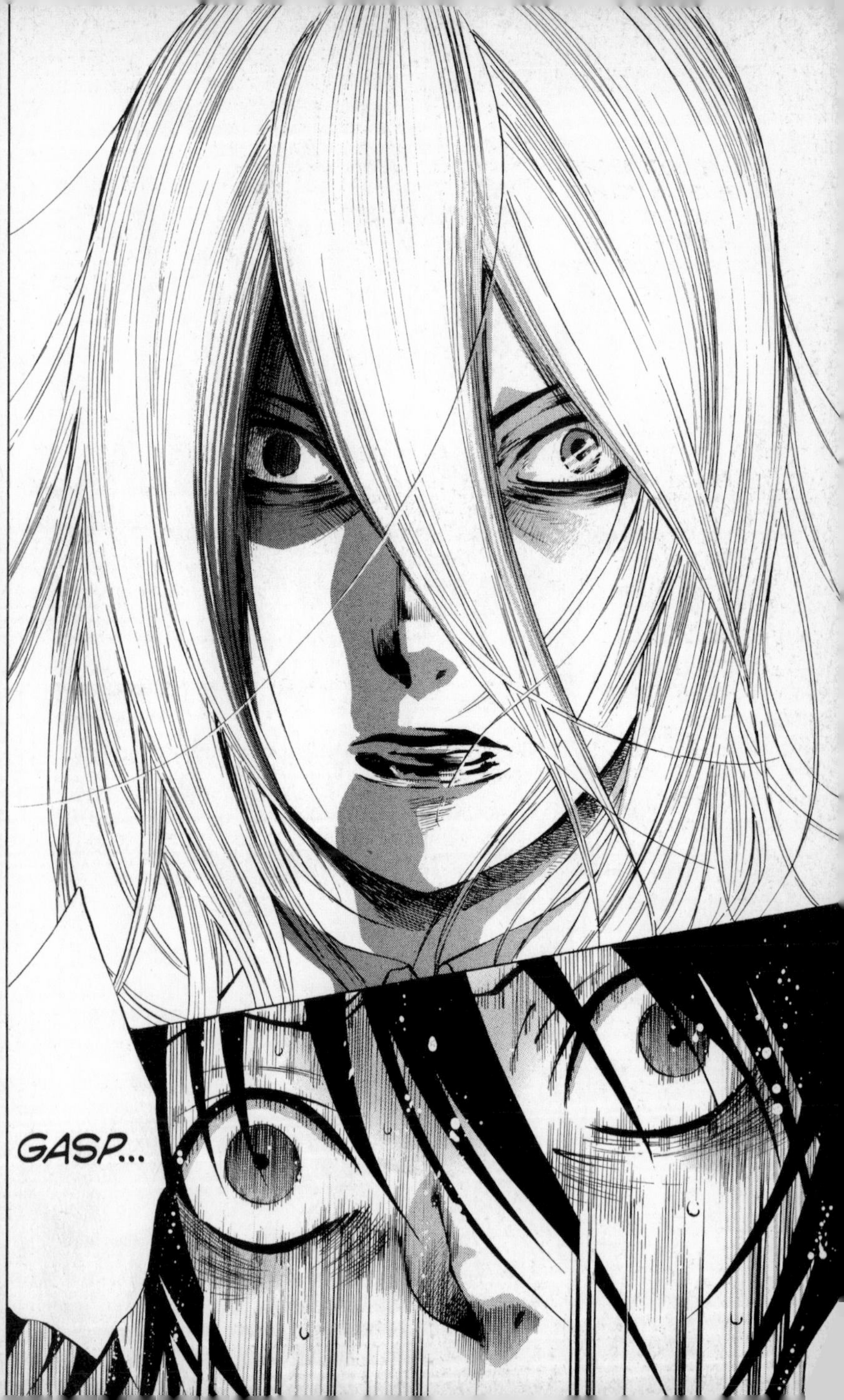
GASP...

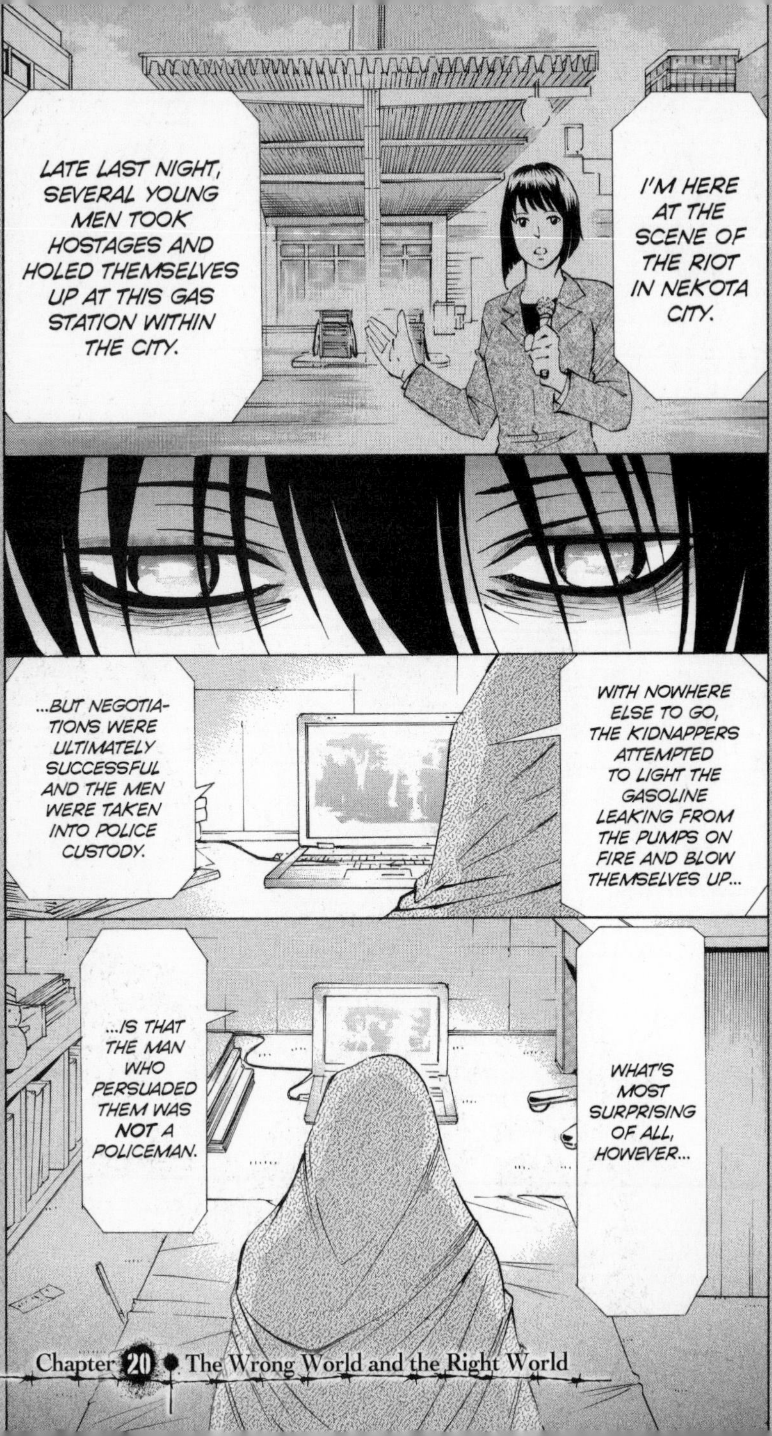
I'M HERE AT THE SCENE OF THE RIOT IN NEKOTA CITY.
LATE LAST NIGHT, SEVERAL YOUNG MEN TOOK HOSTAGES AND HOLED THEMSELVES UP AT THIS GAS STATION WITHIN THE CITY.
WITH NOWHERE ELSE TO GO, THE KIDNAPPERS ATTEMPTED TO LIGHT THE GASOLINE LEAKING FROM THE PUMPS ON FIRE AND BLOW THEMSELVES UP...
...BUT NEGOTIA-TIONS WERE ULTIMATELY SUCCESSFUL AND THE MEN WERE TAKEN INTO POLICE CUSTODY.
WHAT'S MOST SURPRISING OF ALL, HOWEVER...
...IS THAT THE MAN WHO PERSUADED THEM WAS **NOT** A POLICEMAN.

Chapter 20 • The Wrong World and the Right World

Chapter 20 The Wrong World and the Right World

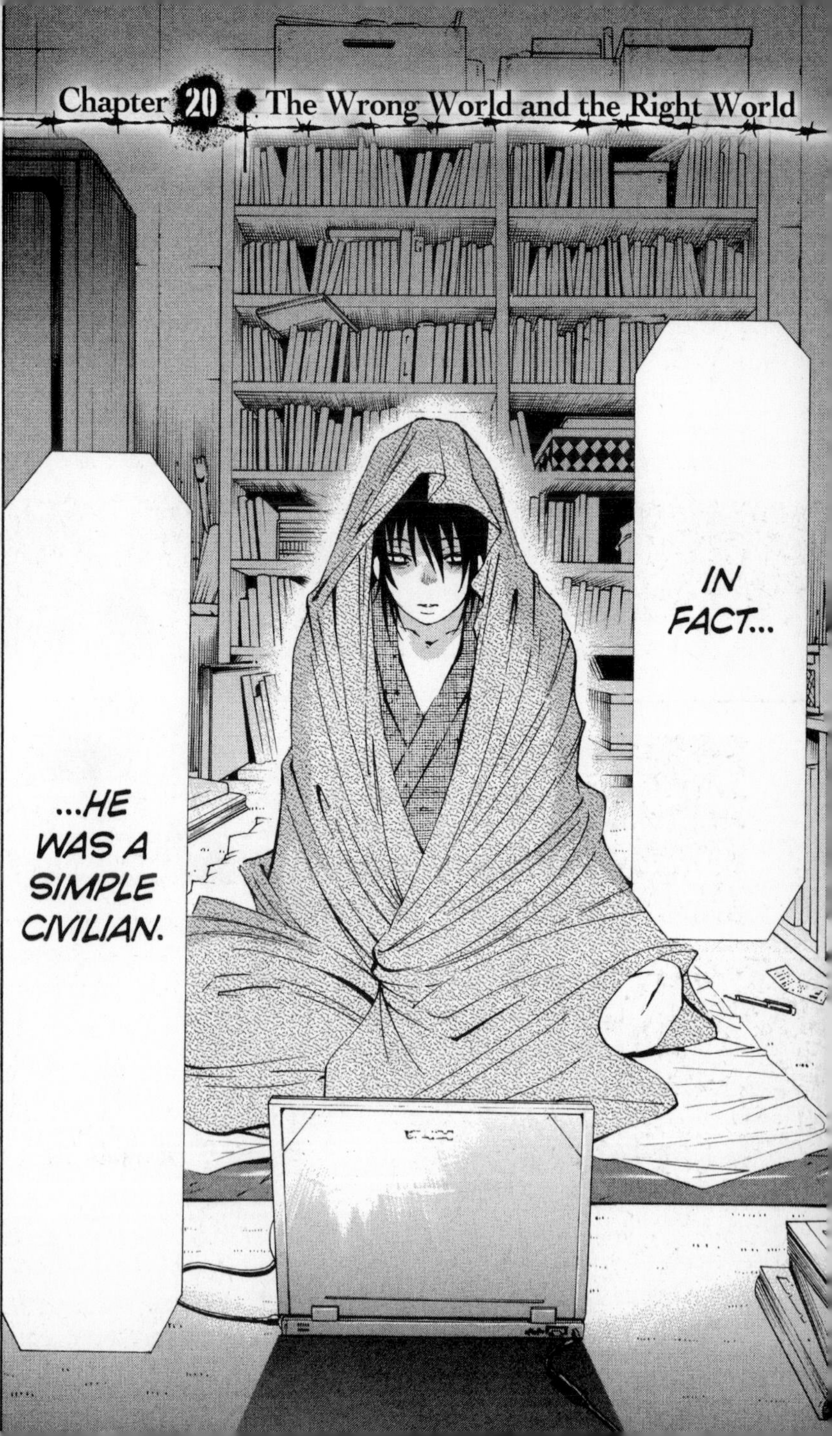
IN FACT...
...HE WAS A SIMPLE CIVILIAN.

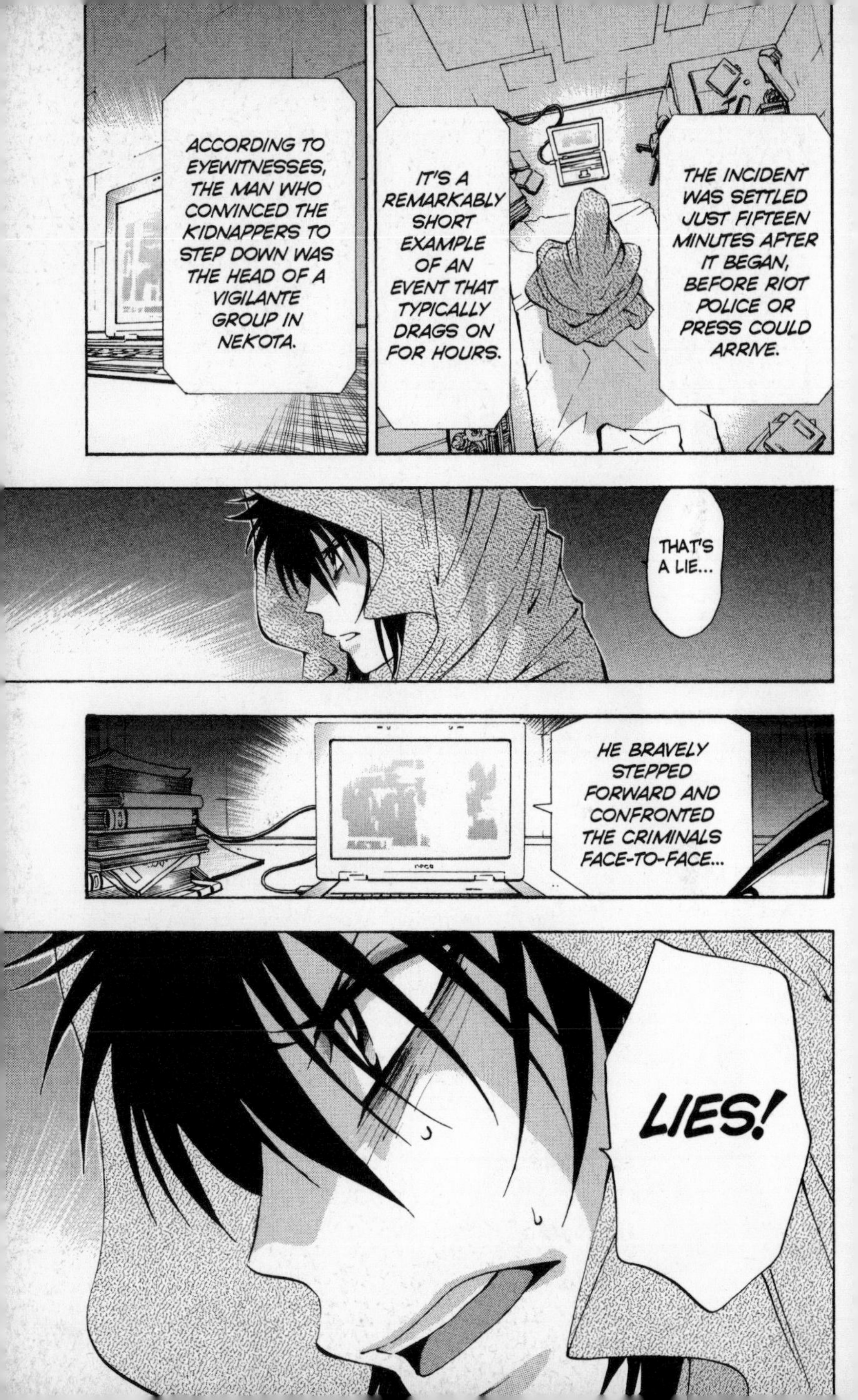
THE INCIDENT WAS SETTLED JUST FIFTEEN MINUTES AFTER IT BEGAN, BEFORE RIOT POLICE OR PRESS COULD ARRIVE.
IT'S A REMARKABLY SHORT EXAMPLE OF AN EVENT THAT TYPICALLY DRAGS ON FOR HOURS.
ACCORDING TO EYEWITNESSES, THE MAN WHO CONVINCED THE KIDNAPPERS TO STEP DOWN WAS THE HEAD OF A VIGILANTE GROUP IN NEKOTA.
THAT'S A LIE...
HE BRAVELY STEPPED FORWARD AND CONFRONTED THE CRIMINALS FACE-TO-FACE...
LIES!

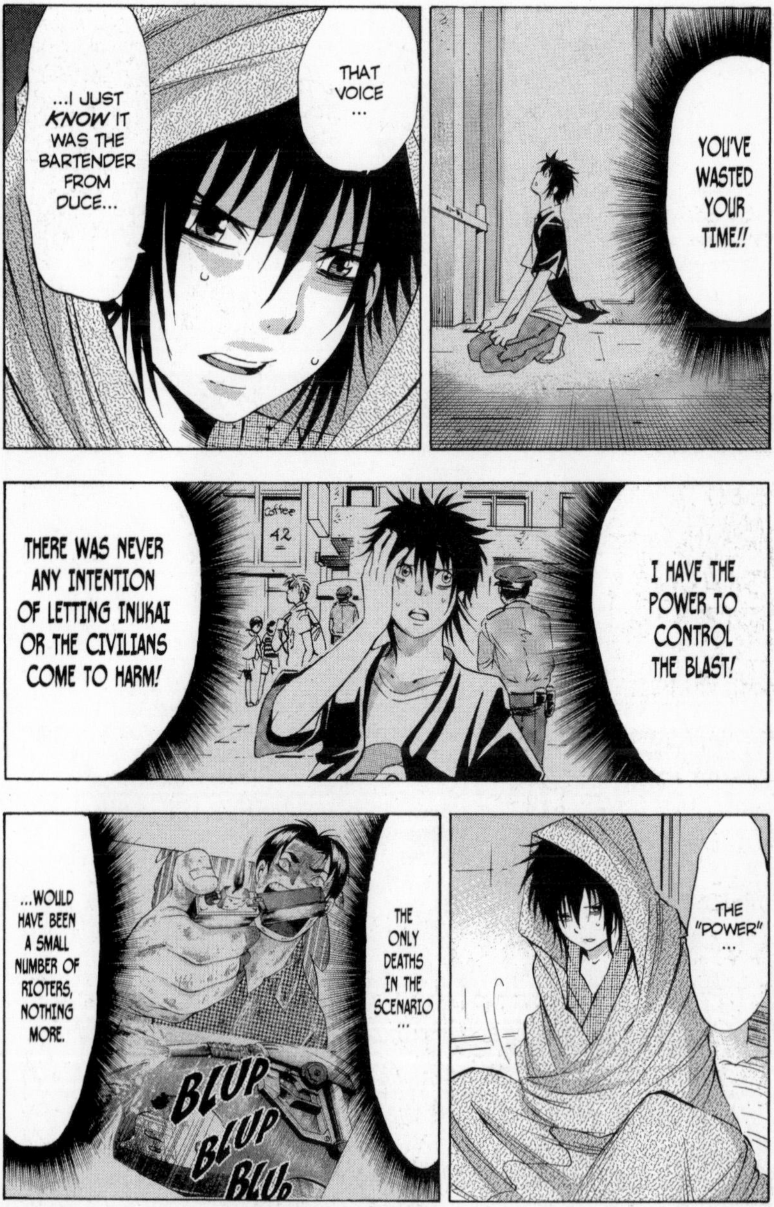
YOU'VE WASTED YOUR TIME!!
THAT VOICE ...
...I JUST *KNOW* IT WAS THE BARTENDER FROM DUCE...
I HAVE THE POWER TO CONTROL THE BLAST!
THERE WAS NEVER ANY INTENTION OF LETTING INUKAI OR THE CIVILIANS COME TO HARM!
Coffee 42
THE "POWER" ...
THE ONLY DEATHS IN THE SCENARIO ...
...WOULD HAVE BEEN A SMALL NUMBER OF RIOTERS, NOTHING MORE.
BLUP
BLUP

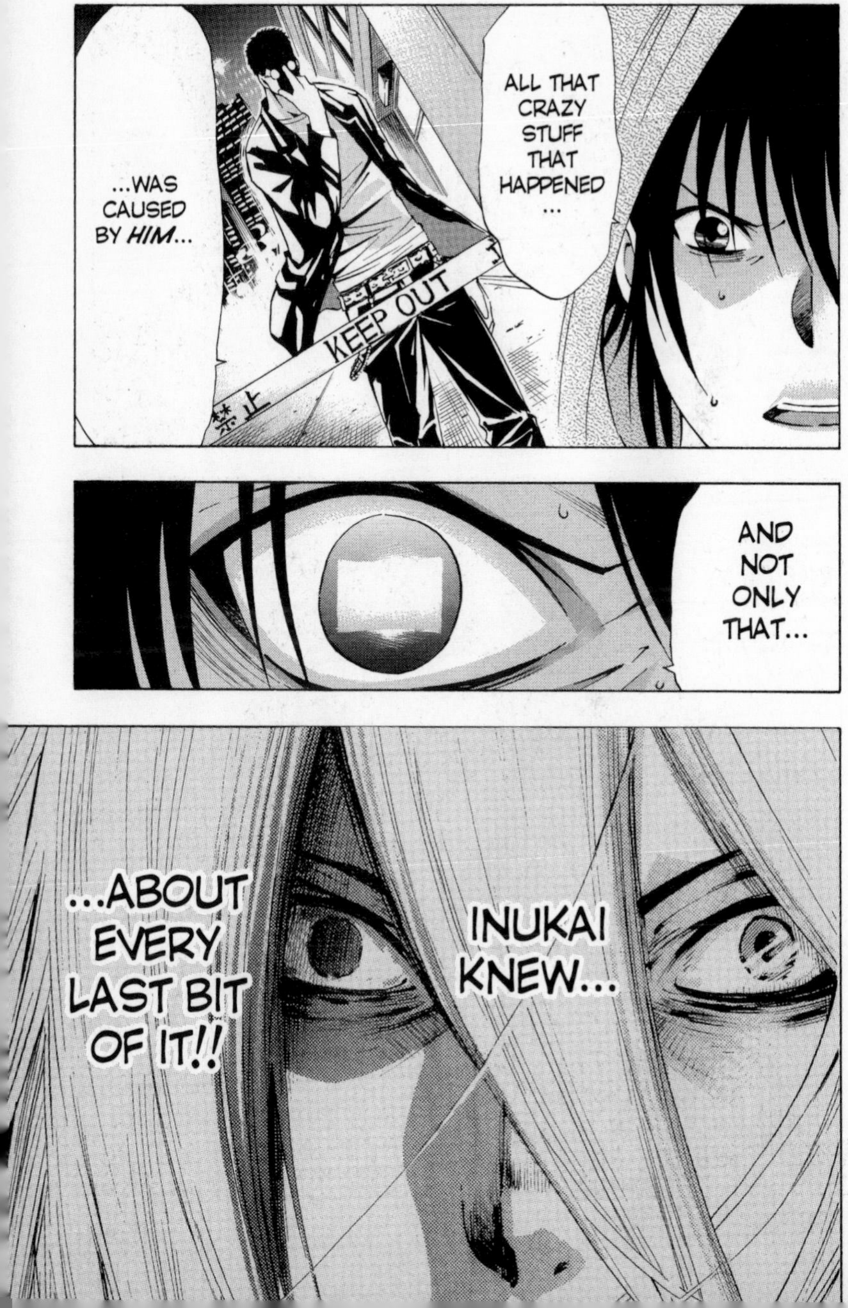
ALL THAT CRAZY STUFF THAT HAPPENED ...
...WAS CAUSED BY *HIM*...
KEEP OUT
禁止
AND NOT ONLY THAT...
INUKAI KNEW...
...ABOUT EVERY LAST BIT OF IT!!

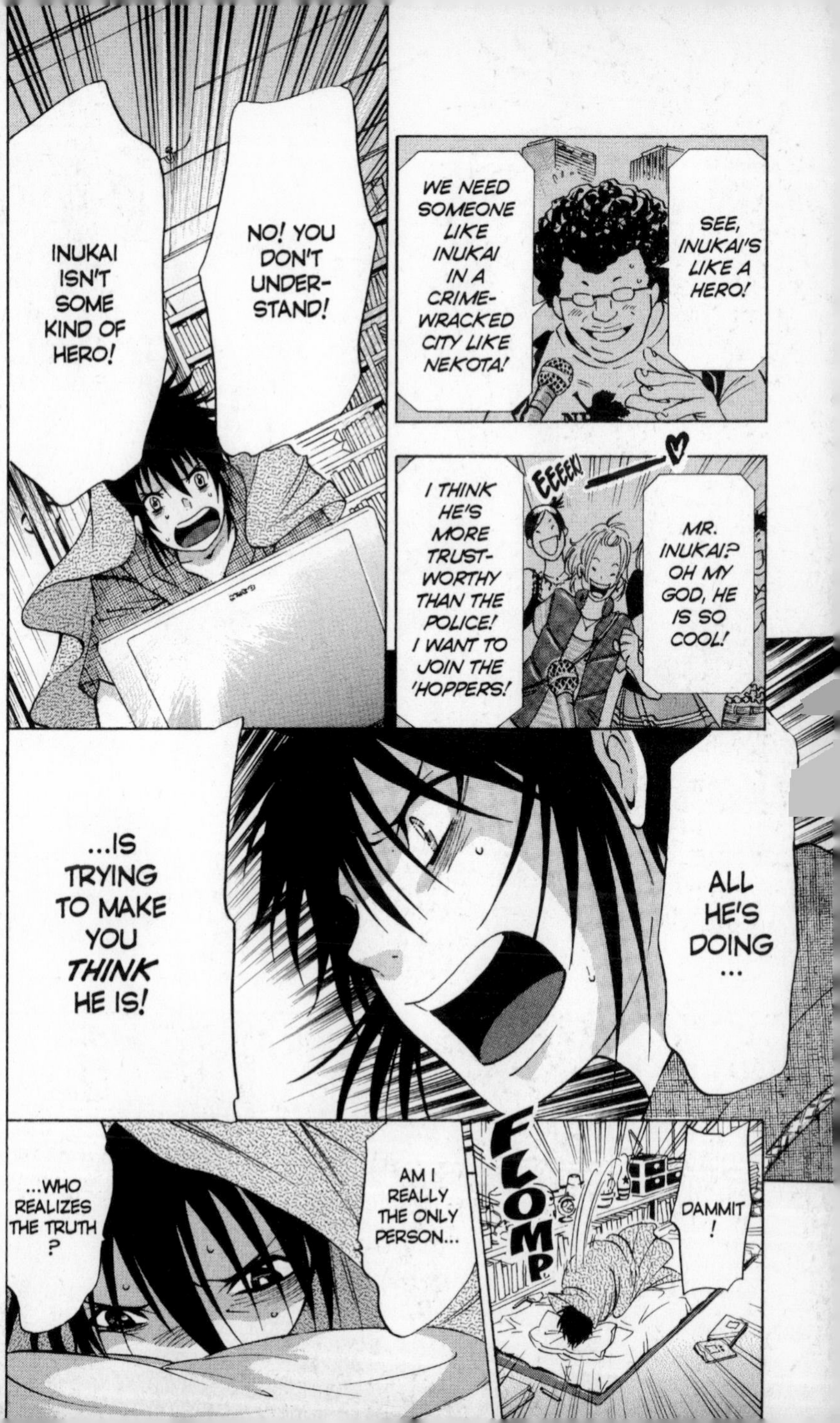
SEE, INUKAI'S LIKE A HERO!
WE NEED SOMEONE LIKE INUKAI IN A CRIME-WRACKED CITY LIKE NEKOTA!
MR. INUKAI? OH MY GOD, HE IS SO COOL!
EEEEK!
I THINK HE'S MORE TRUST-WORTHY THAN THE POLICE! I WANT TO JOIN THE 'HOPPERS!
NO! YOU DON'T UNDER-STAND!
INUKAI ISN'T SOME KIND OF HERO!
ALL HE'S DOING ...
...IS TRYING TO MAKE YOU *THINK* HE IS!
DAMMIT!
FLOMP
AM I REALLY THE ONLY PERSON...
...WHO REALIZES THE TRUTH?

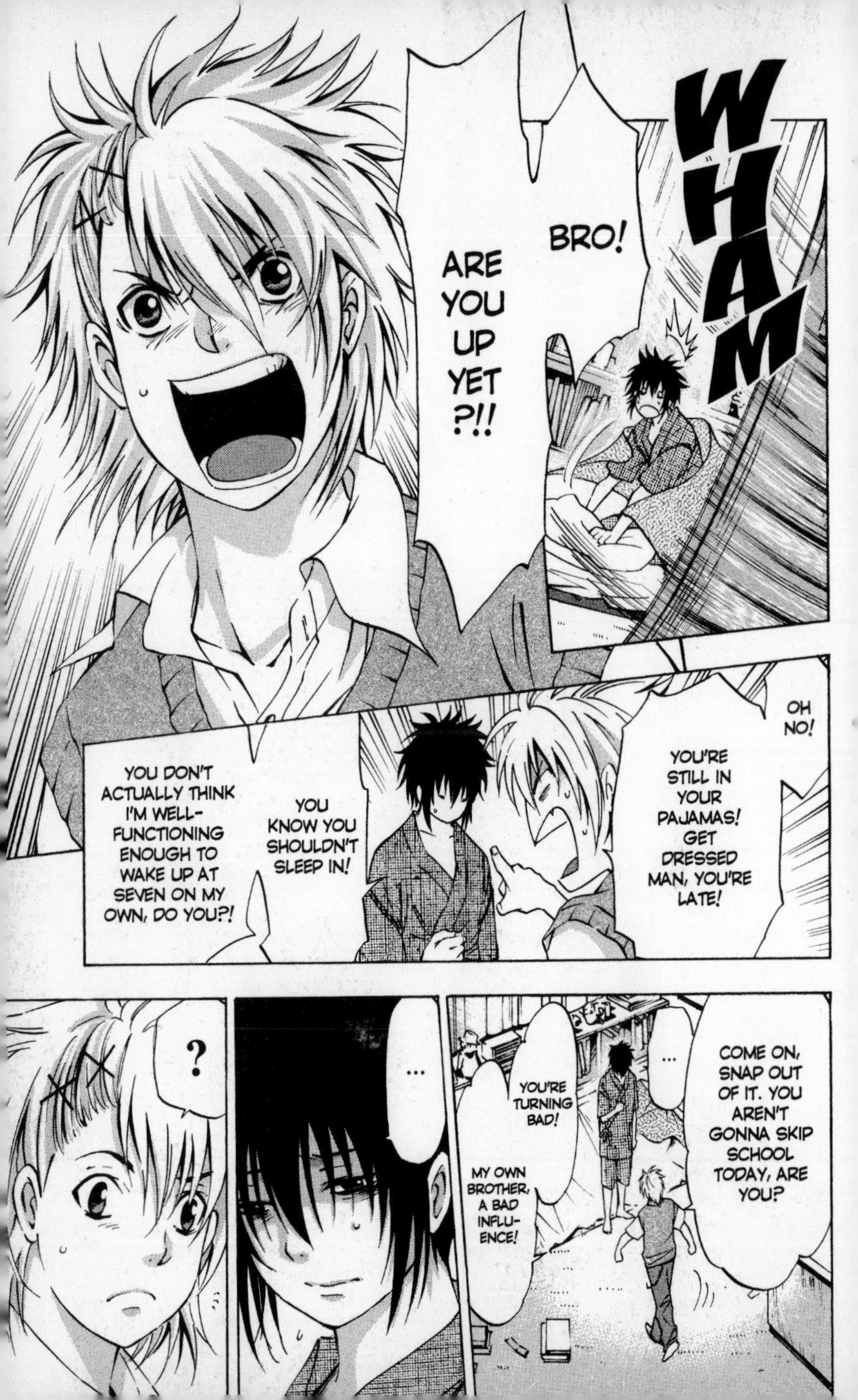
WHAM
BRO!
ARE YOU UP YET?!!
OH NO!
YOU'RE STILL IN YOUR PAJAMAS! GET DRESSED MAN, YOU'RE LATE!
YOU KNOW YOU SHOULDN'T SLEEP IN!
YOU DON'T ACTUALLY THINK I'M WELL-FUNCTIONING ENOUGH TO WAKE UP AT SEVEN ON MY OWN, DO YOU?!
COME ON, SNAP OUT OF IT. YOU AREN'T GONNA SKIP SCHOOL TODAY, ARE YOU?
...
YOU'RE TURNING BAD!
MY OWN BROTHER, A BAD INFLU-ENCE!
...
?

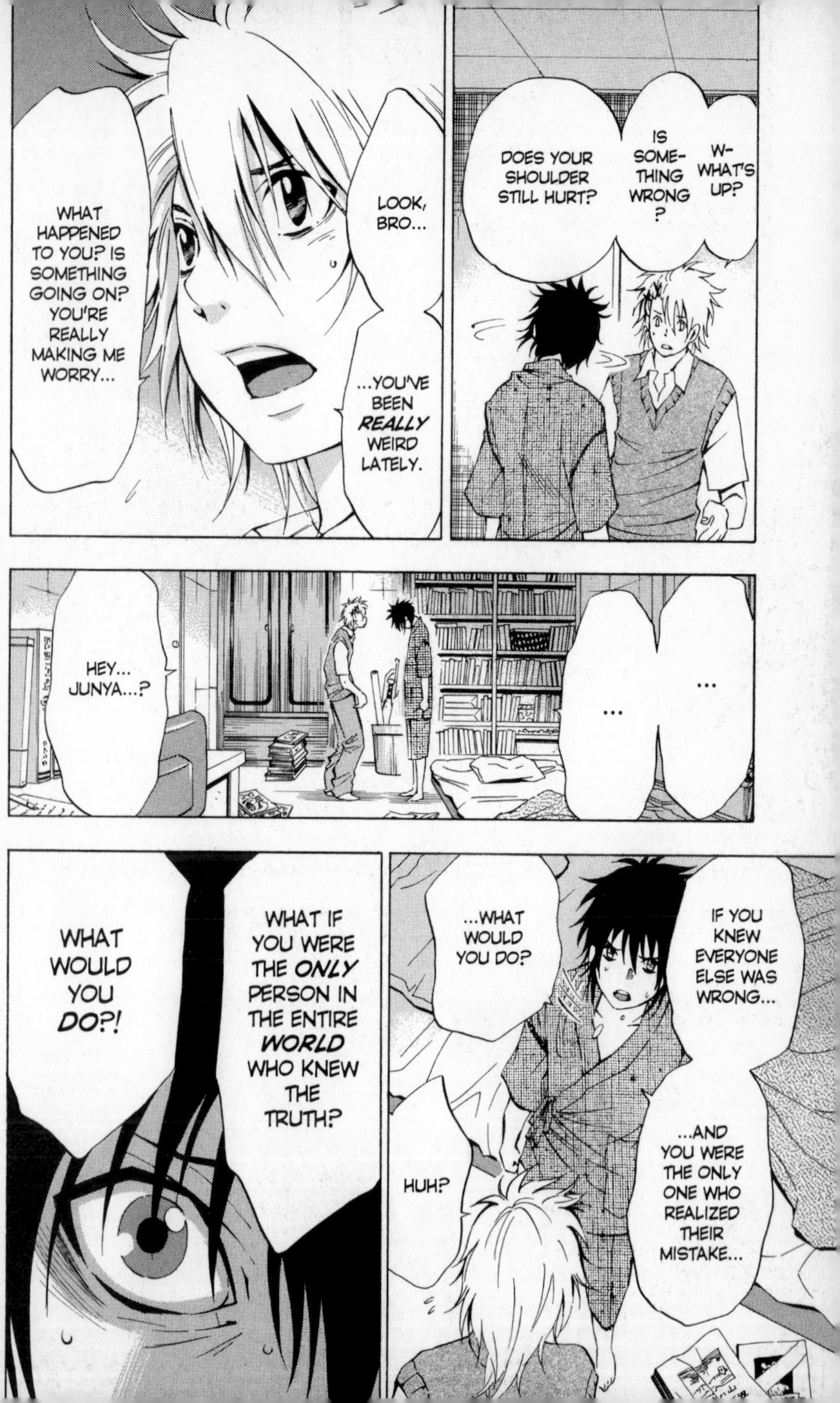
W- WHAT'S UP?
IS SOME-THING WRONG?
DOES YOUR SHOULDER STILL HURT?
LOOK, BRO...
...YOU'VE BEEN *REALLY* WEIRD LATELY.
WHAT HAPPENED TO YOU? IS SOMETHING GOING ON? YOU'RE REALLY MAKING ME WORRY...
...
...
HEY... JUNYA...?
IF YOU KNEW EVERYONE ELSE WAS WRONG...
...AND YOU WERE THE ONLY ONE WHO REALIZED THEIR MISTAKE...
...WHAT WOULD YOU DO?
HUH?
WHAT IF YOU WERE THE *ONLY* PERSON IN THE ENTIRE *WORLD* WHO KNEW THE TRUTH?
WHAT WOULD YOU *DO*?!

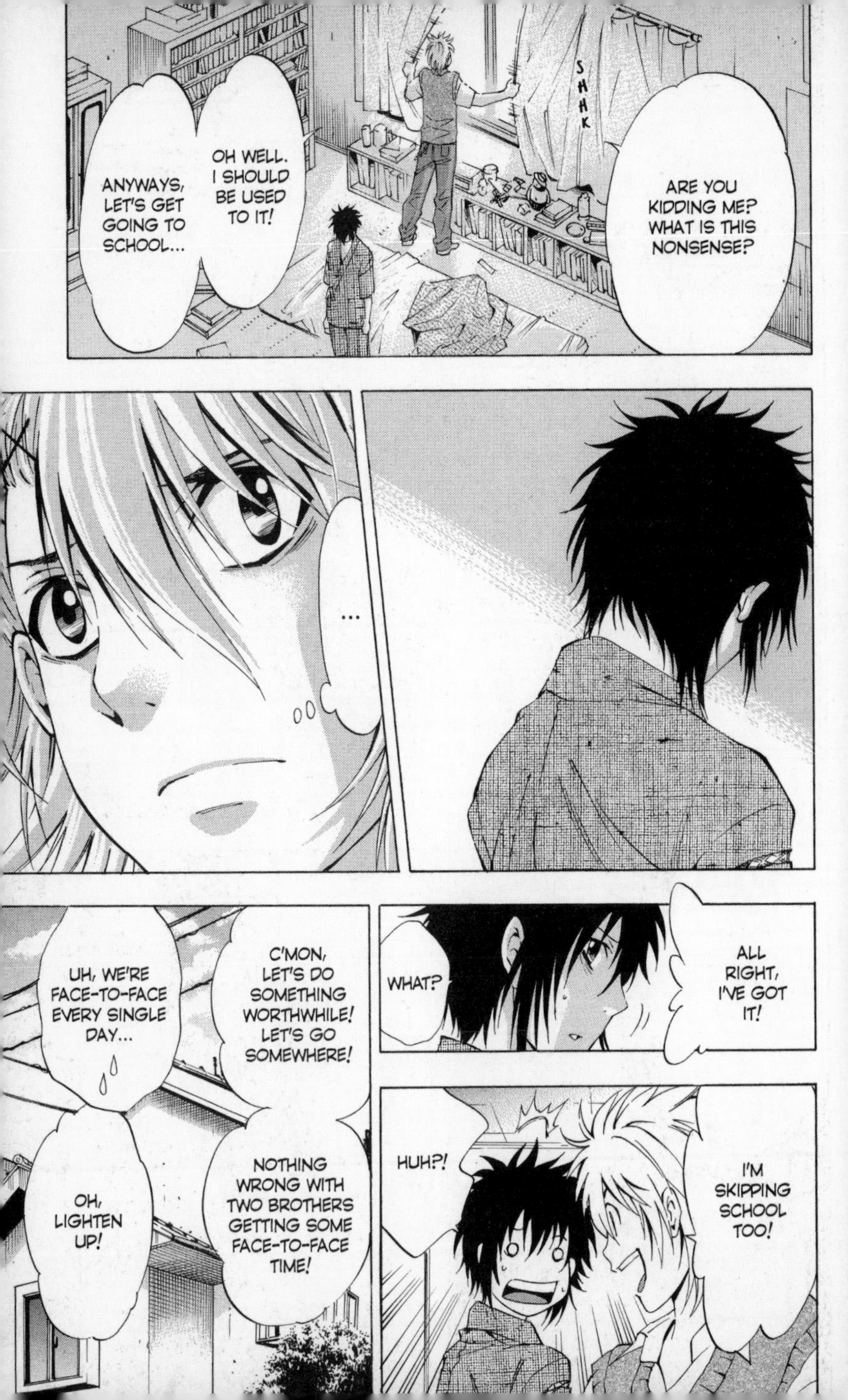
ARE YOU KIDDING ME? WHAT IS THIS NONSENSE?
SHHK
OH WELL. I SHOULD BE USED TO IT!
ANYWAYS, LET'S GET GOING TO SCHOOL...
...
ALL RIGHT, I'VE GOT IT!
WHAT?
I'M SKIPPING SCHOOL TOO!
HUH?!
C'MON, LET'S DO SOMETHING WORTHWHILE! LET'S GO SOMEWHERE!
UH, WE'RE FACE-TO-FACE EVERY SINGLE DAY...
NOTHING WRONG WITH TWO BROTHERS GETTING SOME FACE-TO-FACE TIME!
OH, LIGHTEN UP!

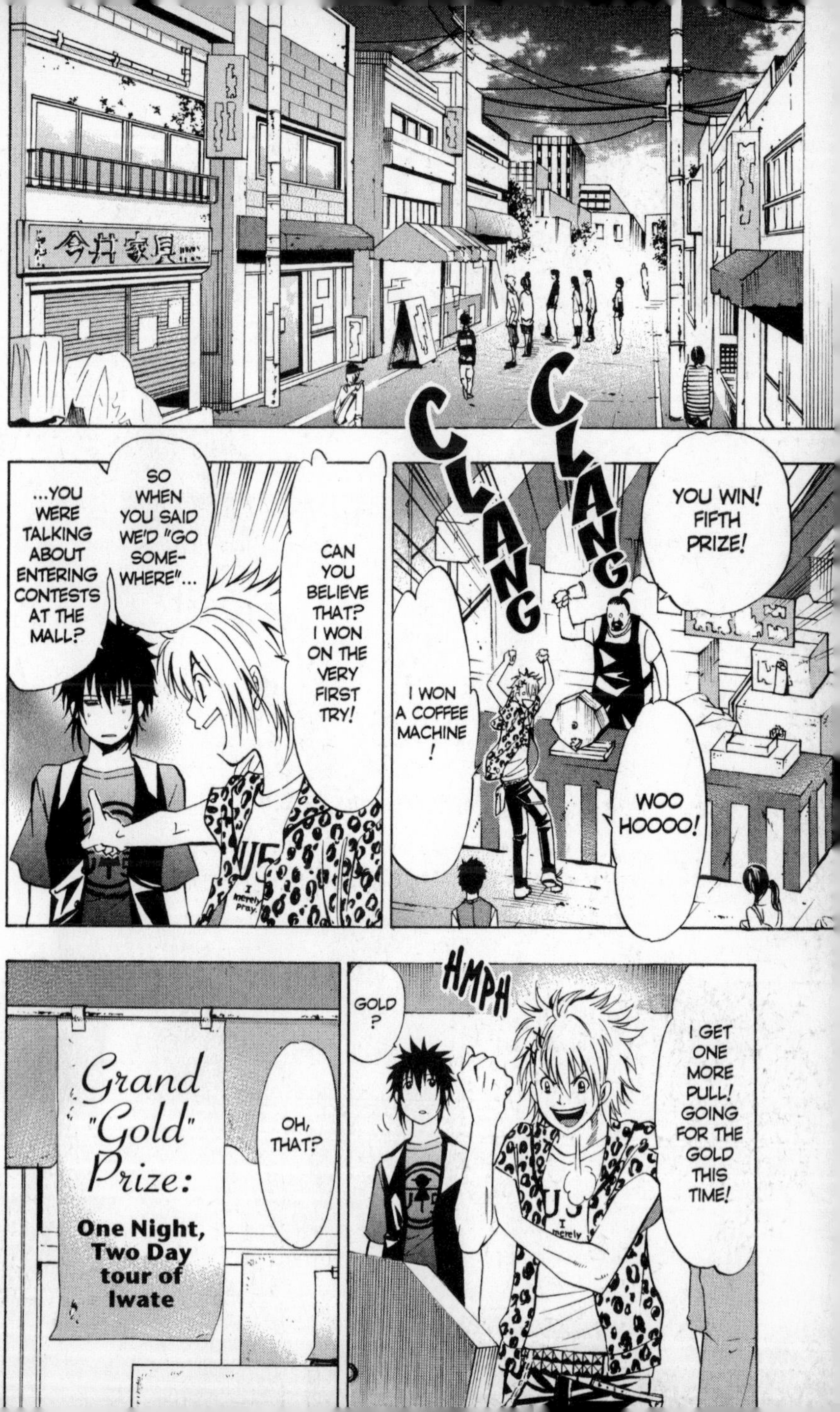
今井家具
YOU WIN! FIFTH PRIZE!
CLANG CLANG
WOO HOOOO!
I WON A COFFEE MACHINE!
CAN YOU BELIEVE THAT? I WON ON THE VERY FIRST TRY!
SO WHEN YOU SAID WE'D "GO SOME-WHERE"...
...YOU WERE TALKING ABOUT ENTERING CONTESTS AT THE MALL?
I merely pray.
HMPH
I GET ONE MORE PULL! GOING FOR THE GOLD THIS TIME!
GOLD?
OH, THAT?
Grand "Gold" Prize:
One Night, Two Day tour of Iwate

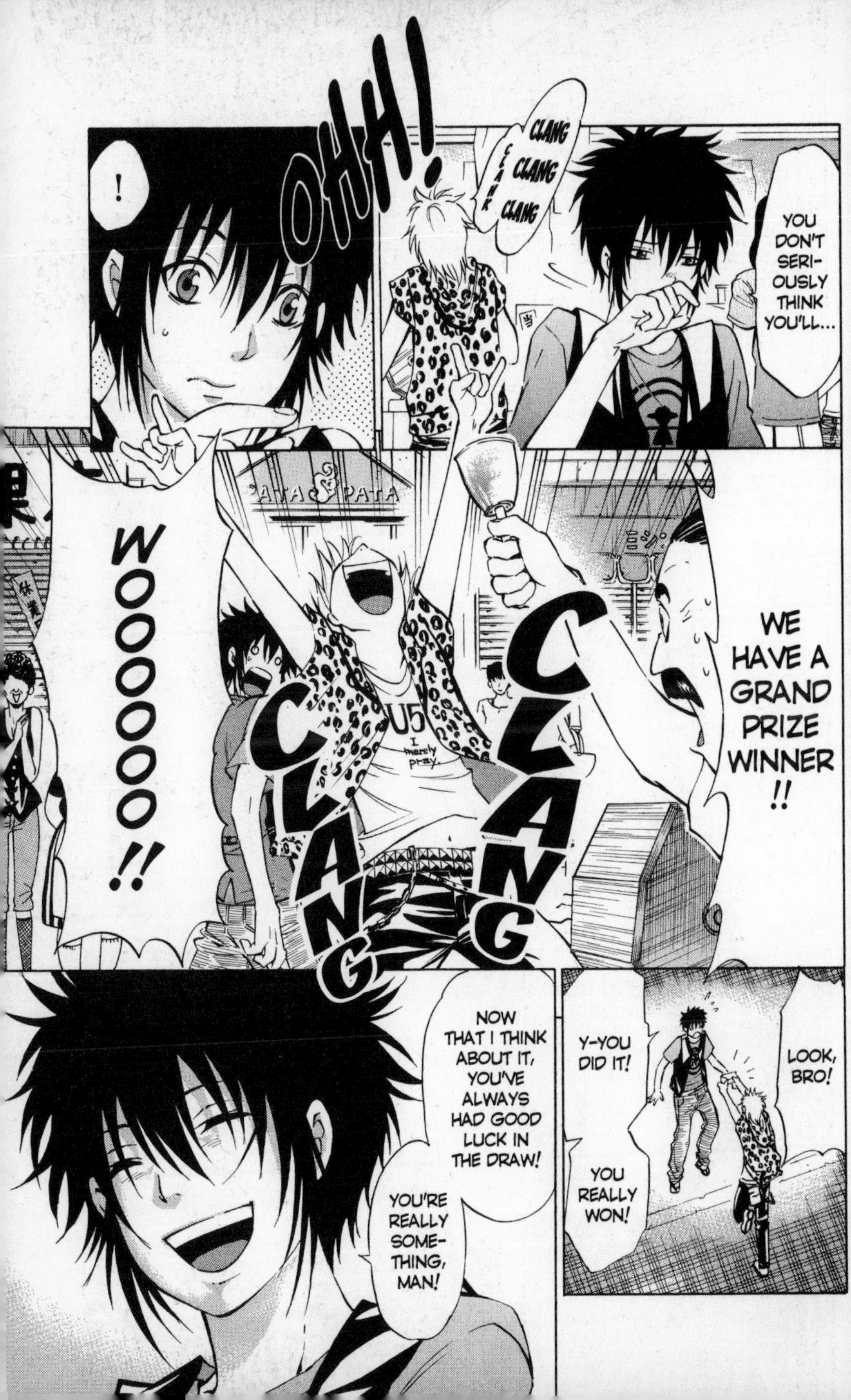
YOU DON'T SERIOUSLY THINK YOU'LL...
CLANG CLANG CLANG
CLANK
OHH!
!
WE HAVE A GRAND PRIZE WINNER!!
CLANG
CLANG
PATA PATA
U5 I merely pray.
WOOOOOOO!!
LOOK, BRO!
Y-YOU DID IT!
YOU REALLY WON!
NOW THAT I THINK ABOUT IT, YOU'VE ALWAYS HAD GOOD LUCK IN THE DRAW!
YOU'RE REALLY SOMETHING, MAN!

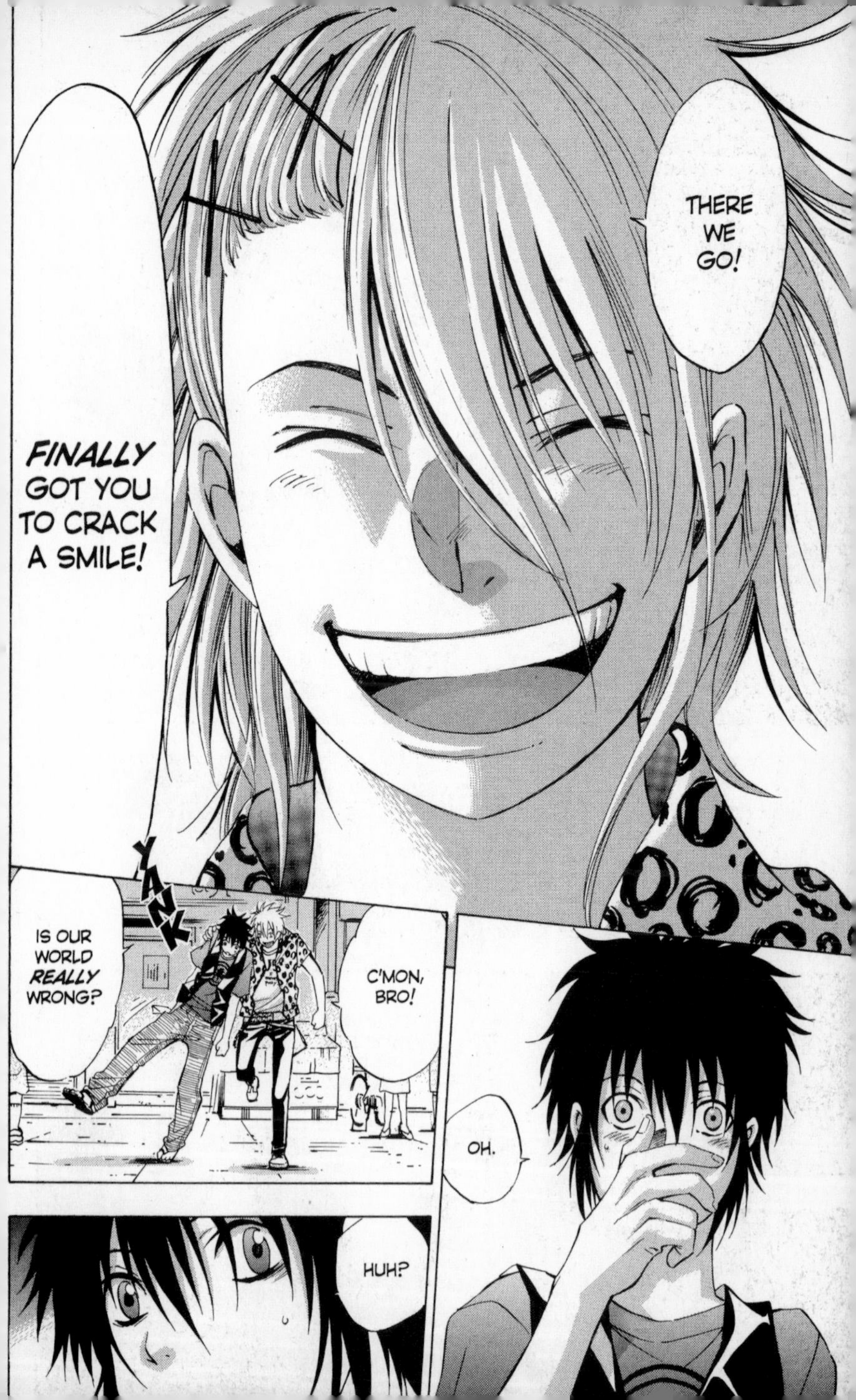
THERE WE GO!
FINALLY GOT YOU TO CRACK A SMILE!
OH.
YANK
C'MON, BRO!
IS OUR WORLD REALLY WRONG?
HUH?

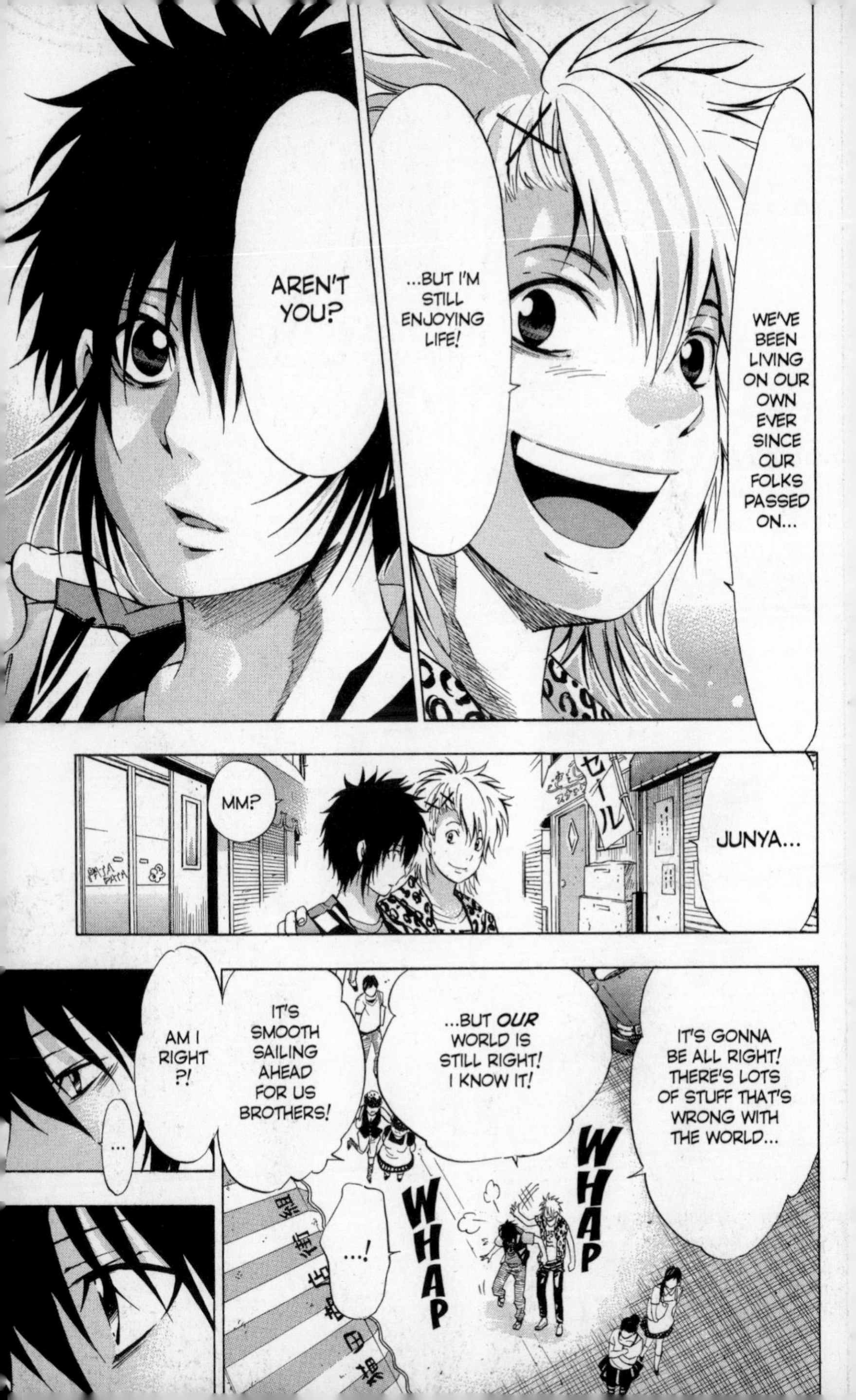
WE'VE BEEN LIVING ON OUR OWN EVER SINCE OUR FOLKS PASSED ON...
...BUT I'M STILL ENJOYING LIFE!
AREN'T YOU?
JUNYA...
MM?
IT'S GONNA BE ALL RIGHT! THERE'S LOTS OF STUFF THAT'S WRONG WITH THE WORLD...
...BUT *OUR* WORLD IS STILL RIGHT! I KNOW IT!
WHAP
WHAP
IT'S SMOOTH SAILING AHEAD FOR US BROTHERS!
AM I RIGHT ?!
...!
...

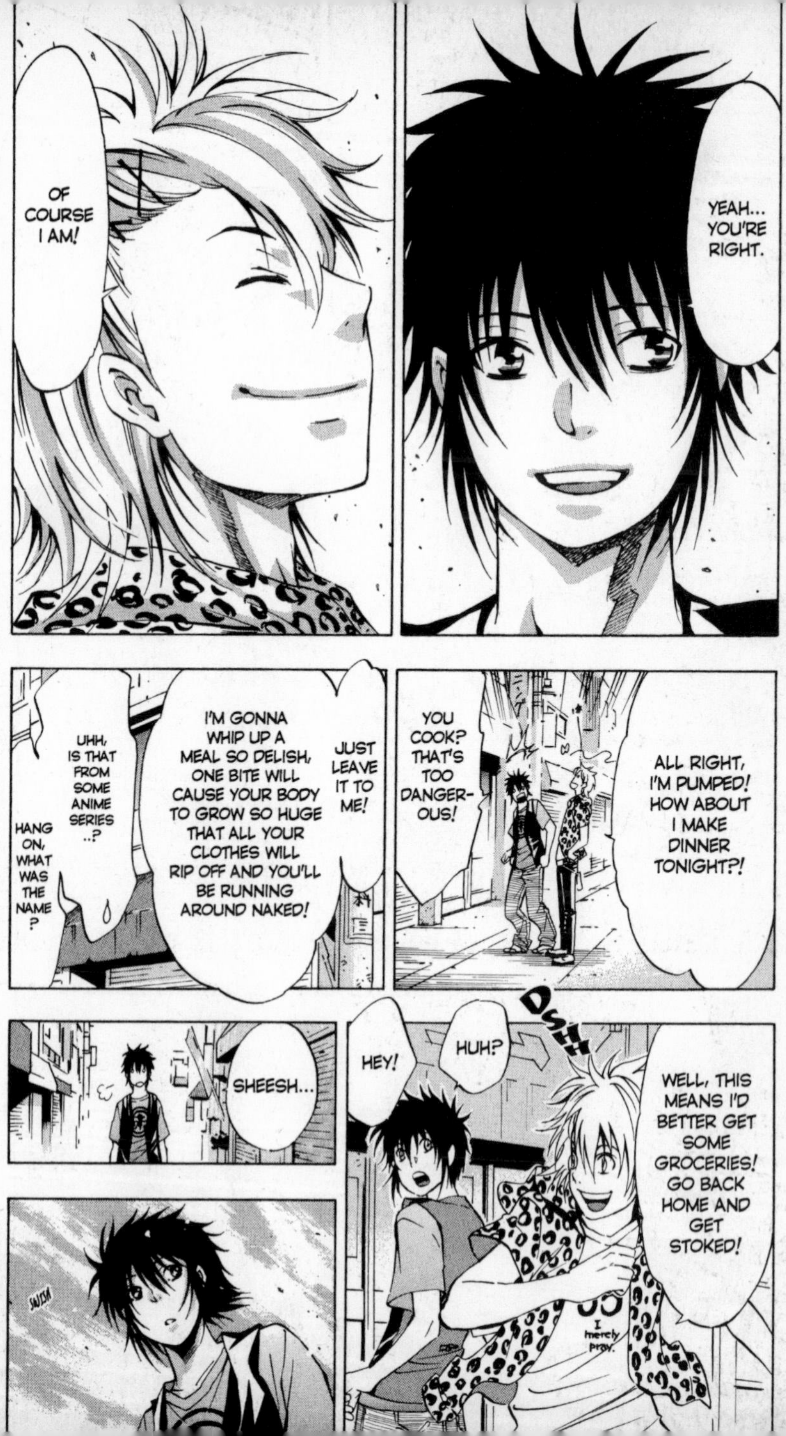
YEAH... YOU'RE RIGHT.
OF COURSE I AM!
ALL RIGHT, I'M PUMPED! HOW ABOUT I MAKE DINNER TONIGHT?!
YOU COOK? THAT'S TOO DANGER-OUS!
JUST LEAVE IT TO ME!
I'M GONNA WHIP UP A MEAL SO DELISH, ONE BITE WILL CAUSE YOUR BODY TO GROW SO HUGE THAT ALL YOUR CLOTHES WILL RIP OFF AND YOU'LL BE RUNNING AROUND NAKED!
UHH, IS THAT FROM SOME ANIME SERIES ..?
HANG ON, WHAT WAS THE NAME ?
WELL, THIS MEANS I'D BETTER GET SOME GROCERIES! GO BACK HOME AND GET STOKED!
DSHH
HUH?
HEY!
I merely pray.
SHEESH...

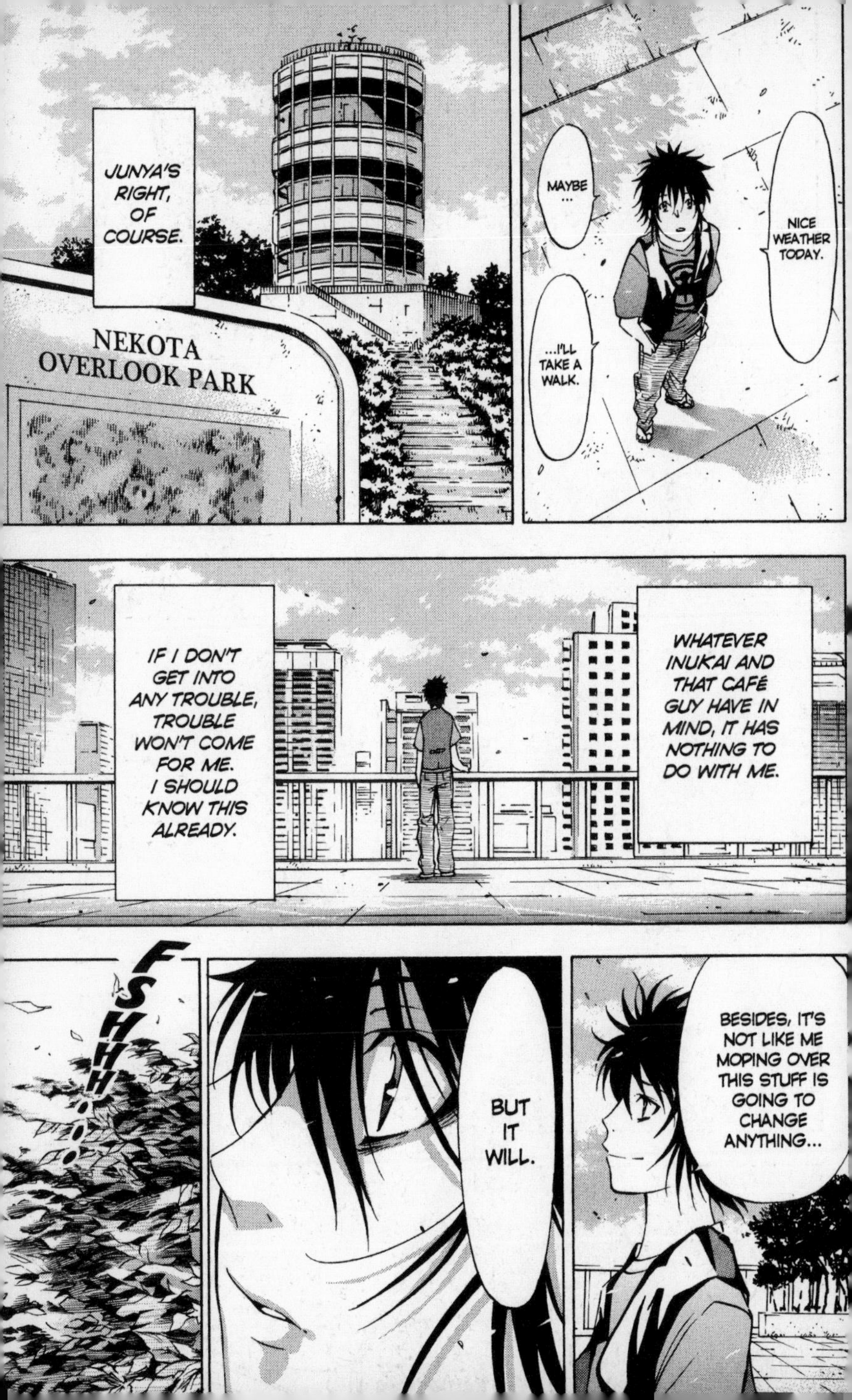
NICE WEATHER TODAY.
MAYBE...
...I'LL TAKE A WALK.
JUNYA'S RIGHT, OF COURSE.
NEKOTA OVERLOOK PARK
WHATEVER INUKAI AND THAT CAFÉ GUY HAVE IN MIND, IT HAS NOTHING TO DO WITH ME.
IF I DON'T GET INTO ANY TROUBLE, TROUBLE WON'T COME FOR ME. I SHOULD KNOW THIS ALREADY.
BESIDES, IT'S NOT LIKE ME MOPING OVER THIS STUFF IS GOING TO CHANGE ANYTHING...
BUT IT WILL.
FSHHH...

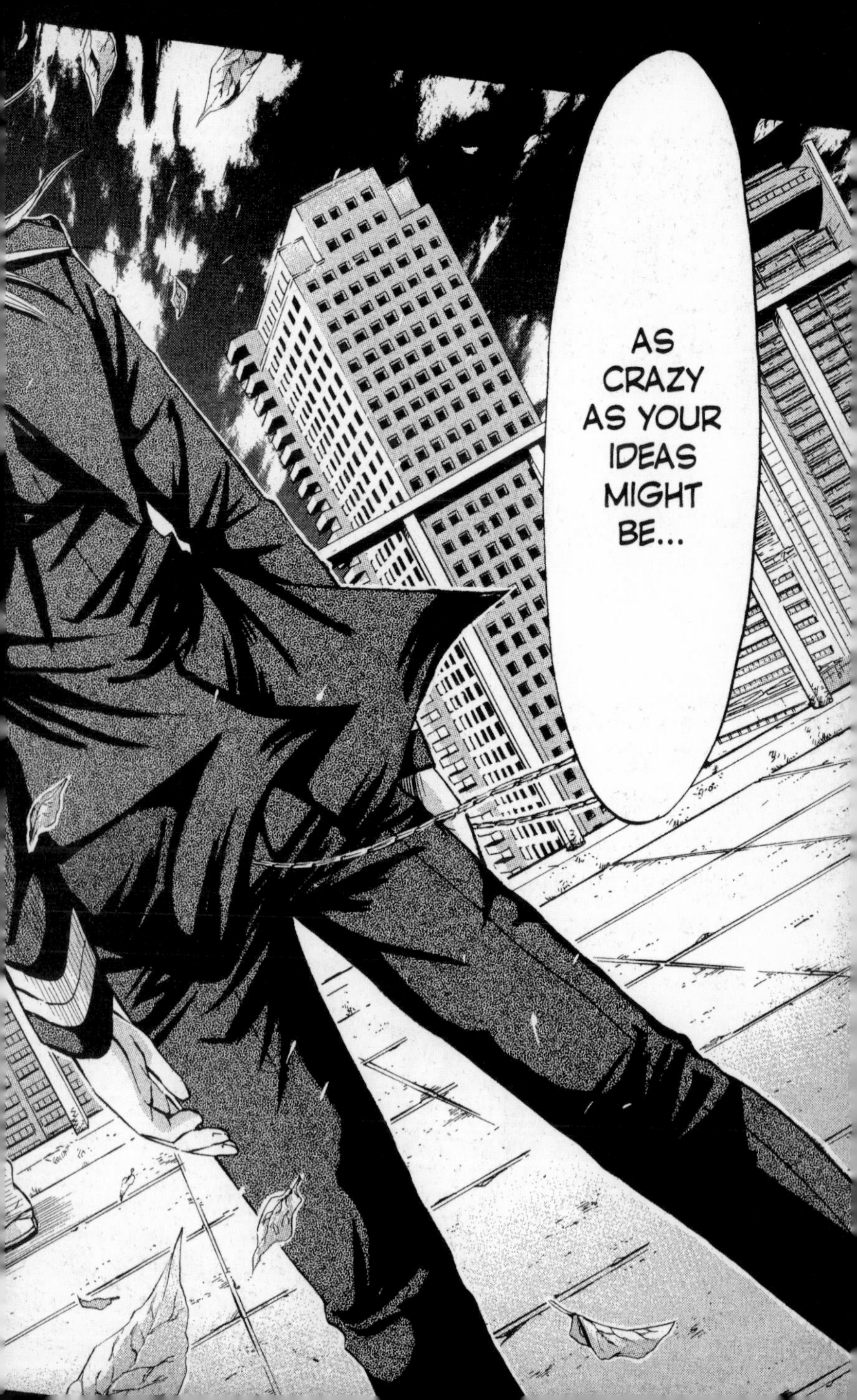
AS CRAZY AS YOUR IDEAS MIGHT BE...

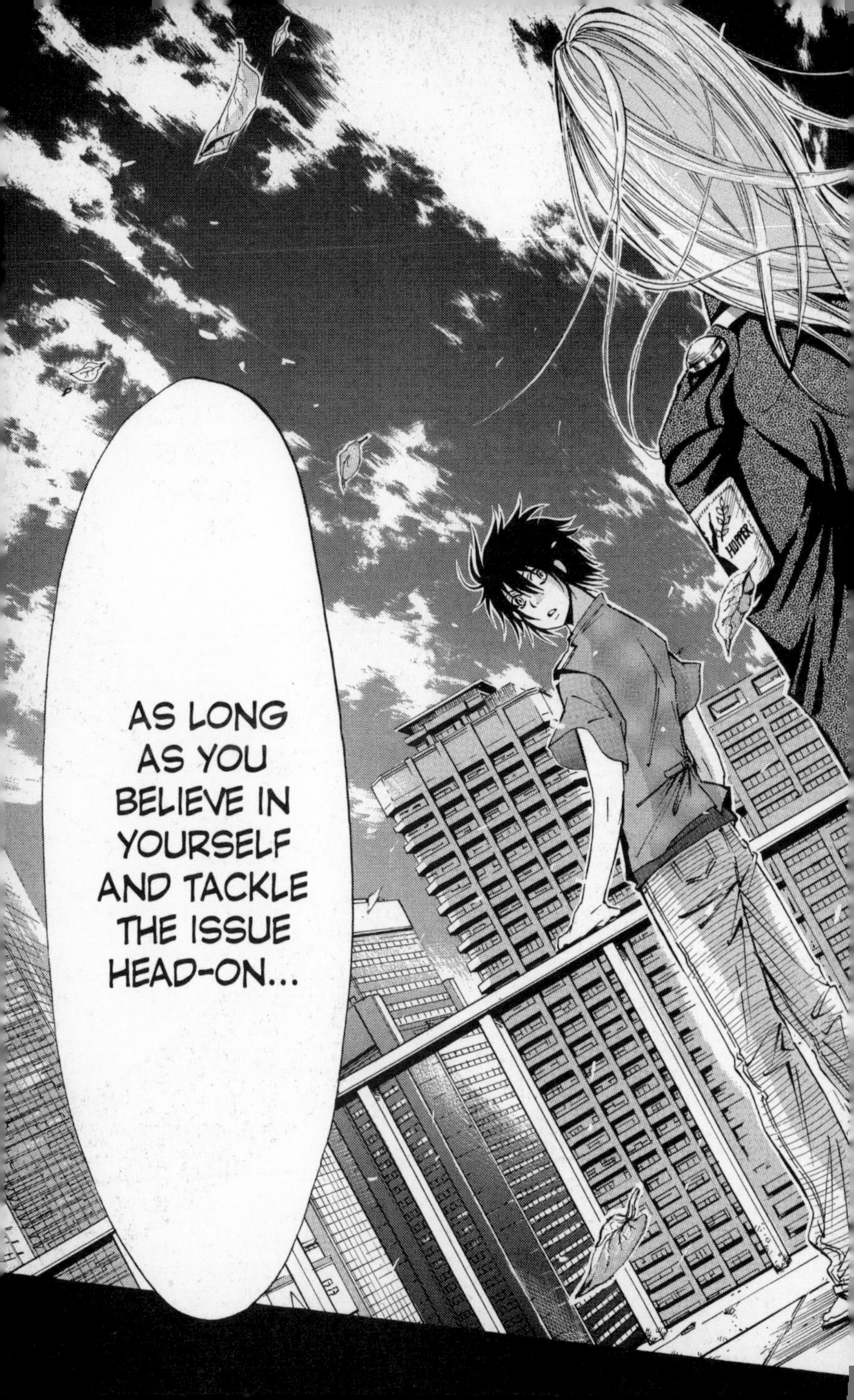
AS LONG AS YOU BELIEVE IN YOURSELF AND TACKLE THE ISSUE HEAD-ON...
HOPPER

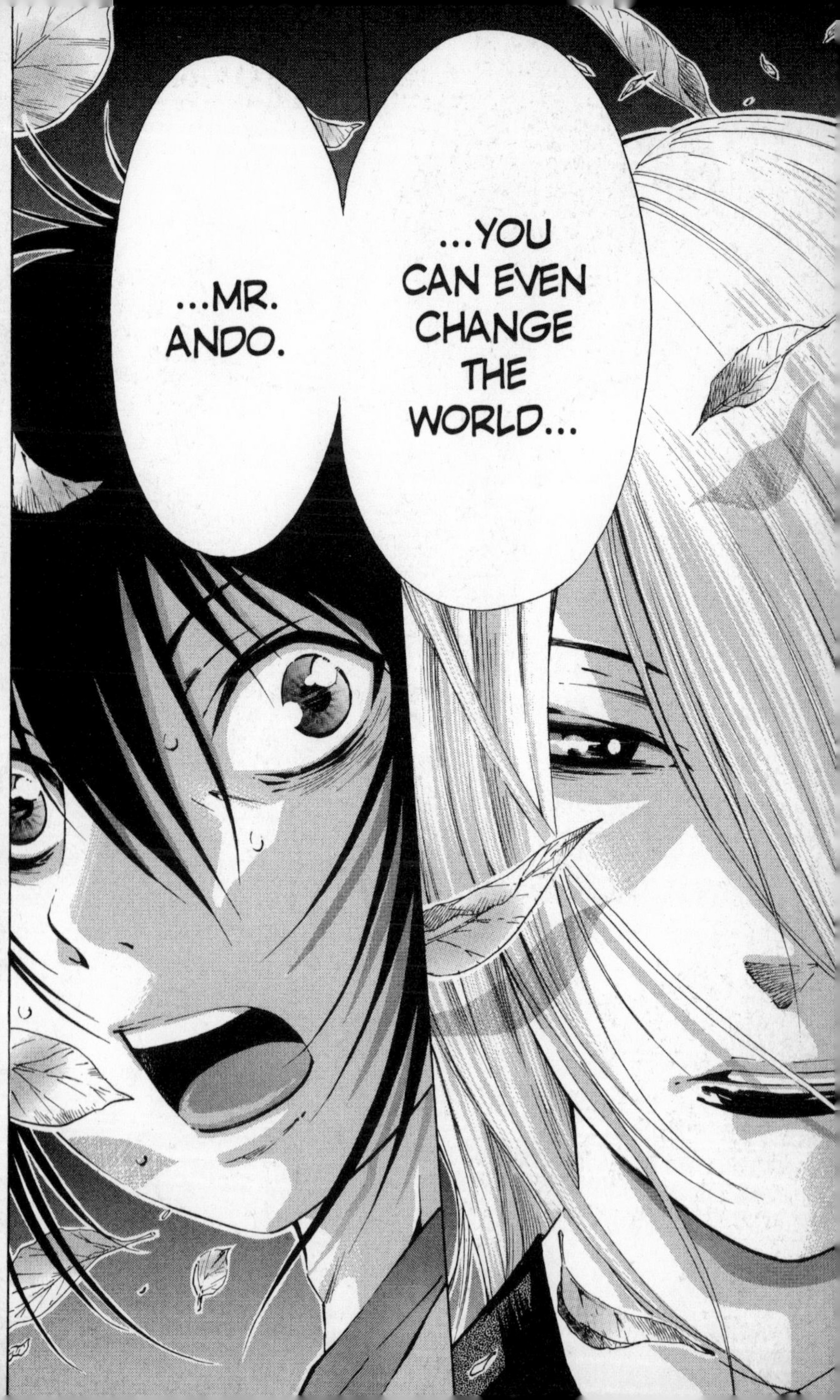
...YOU CAN EVEN CHANGE THE WORLD...
...MR. ANDO.

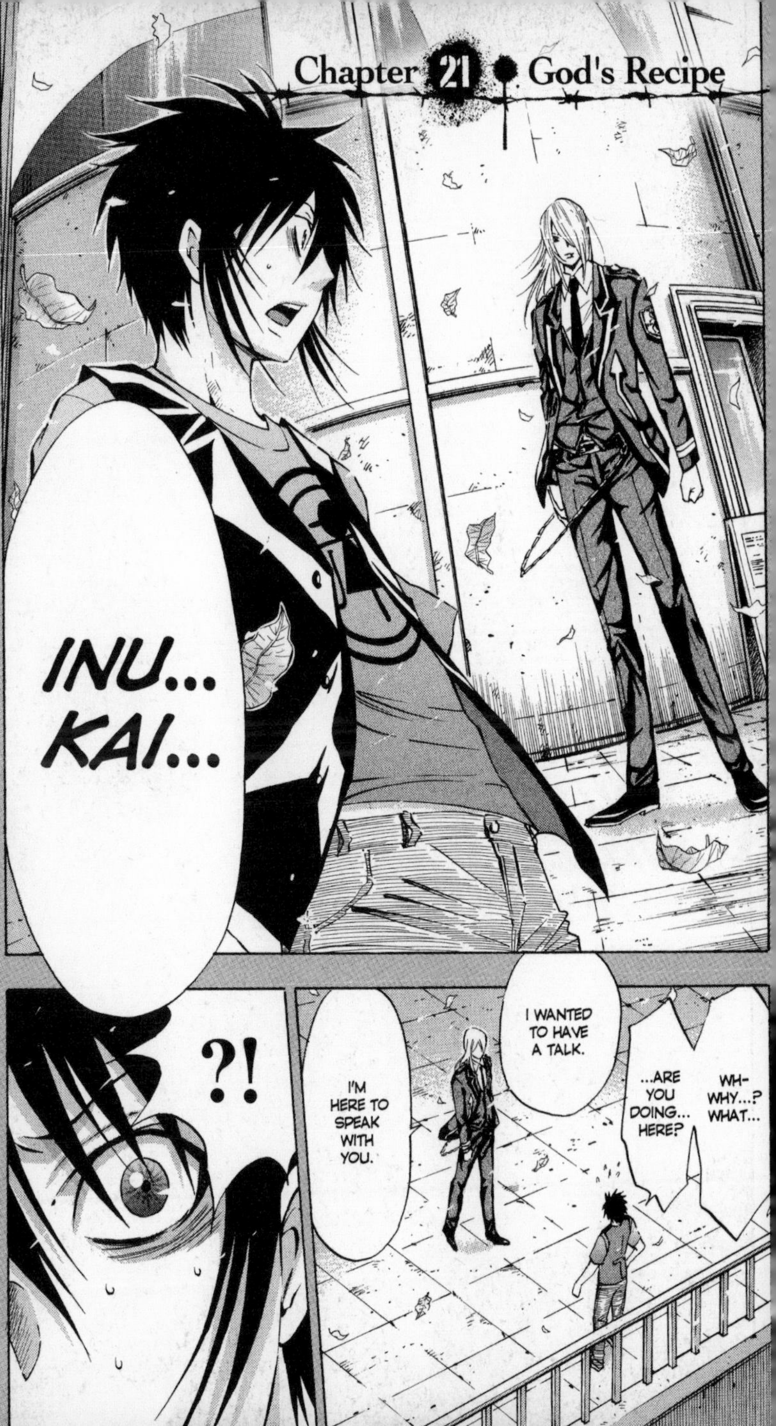
Chapter 21 God's Recipe
INU... KAI...
WH- WHY...? WHAT...
...ARE YOU DOING... HERE?
I WANTED TO HAVE A TALK.
I'M HERE TO SPEAK WITH YOU.
?!

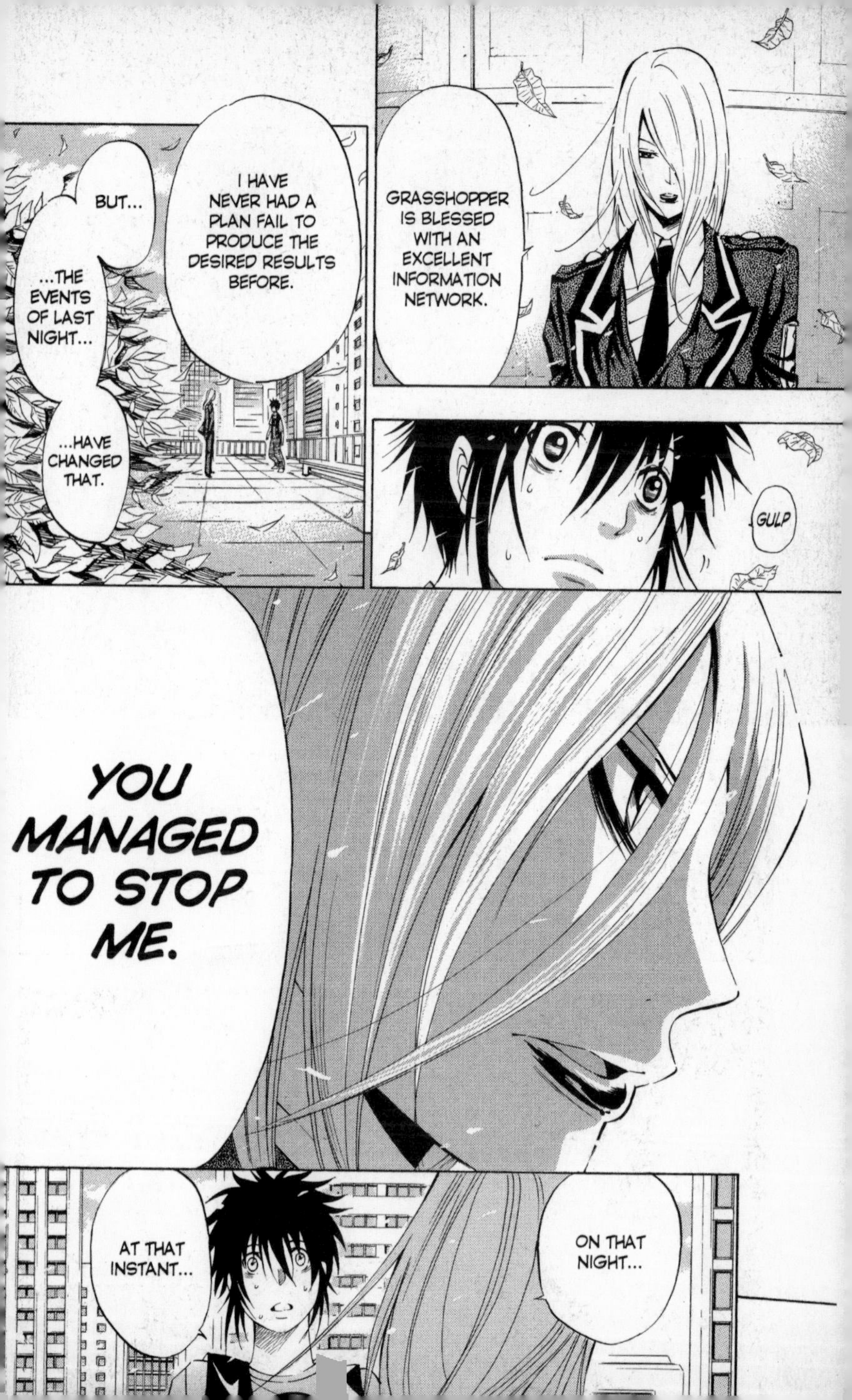
GRASSHOPPER IS BLESSED WITH AN EXCELLENT INFORMATION NETWORK.
GULP
I HAVE NEVER HAD A PLAN FAIL TO PRODUCE THE DESIRED RESULTS BEFORE.
BUT...
...THE EVENTS OF LAST NIGHT...
...HAVE CHANGED THAT.
YOU MANAGED TO STOP ME.
ON THAT NIGHT...
AT THAT INSTANT...

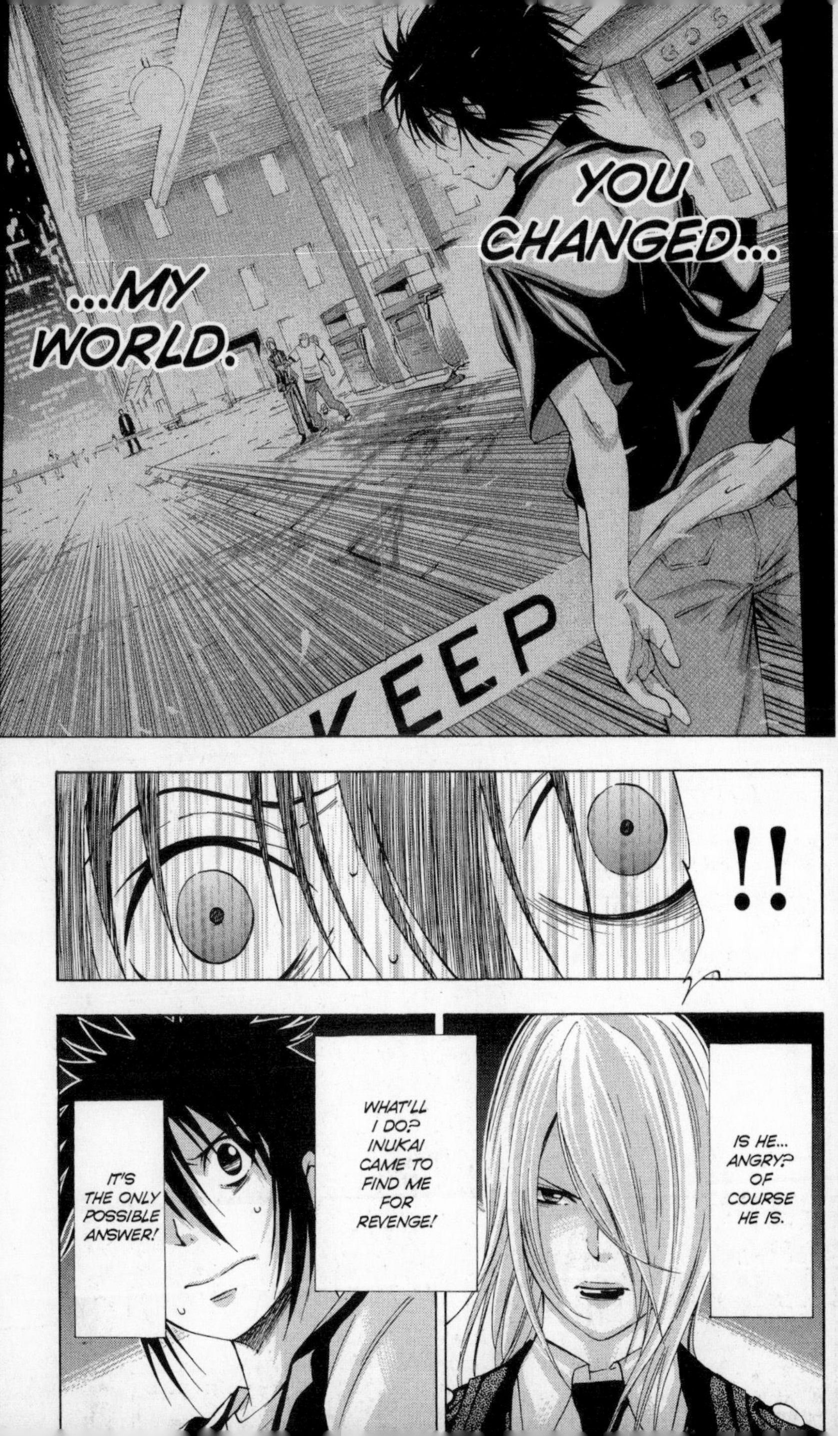

YOU CHANGED...
...MY WORLD.
KEEP
!!
IS HE... ANGRY? OF COURSE HE IS.
WHAT'LL I DO? INUKAI CAME TO FIND ME FOR REVENGE!
IT'S THE ONLY POSSIBLE ANSWER!

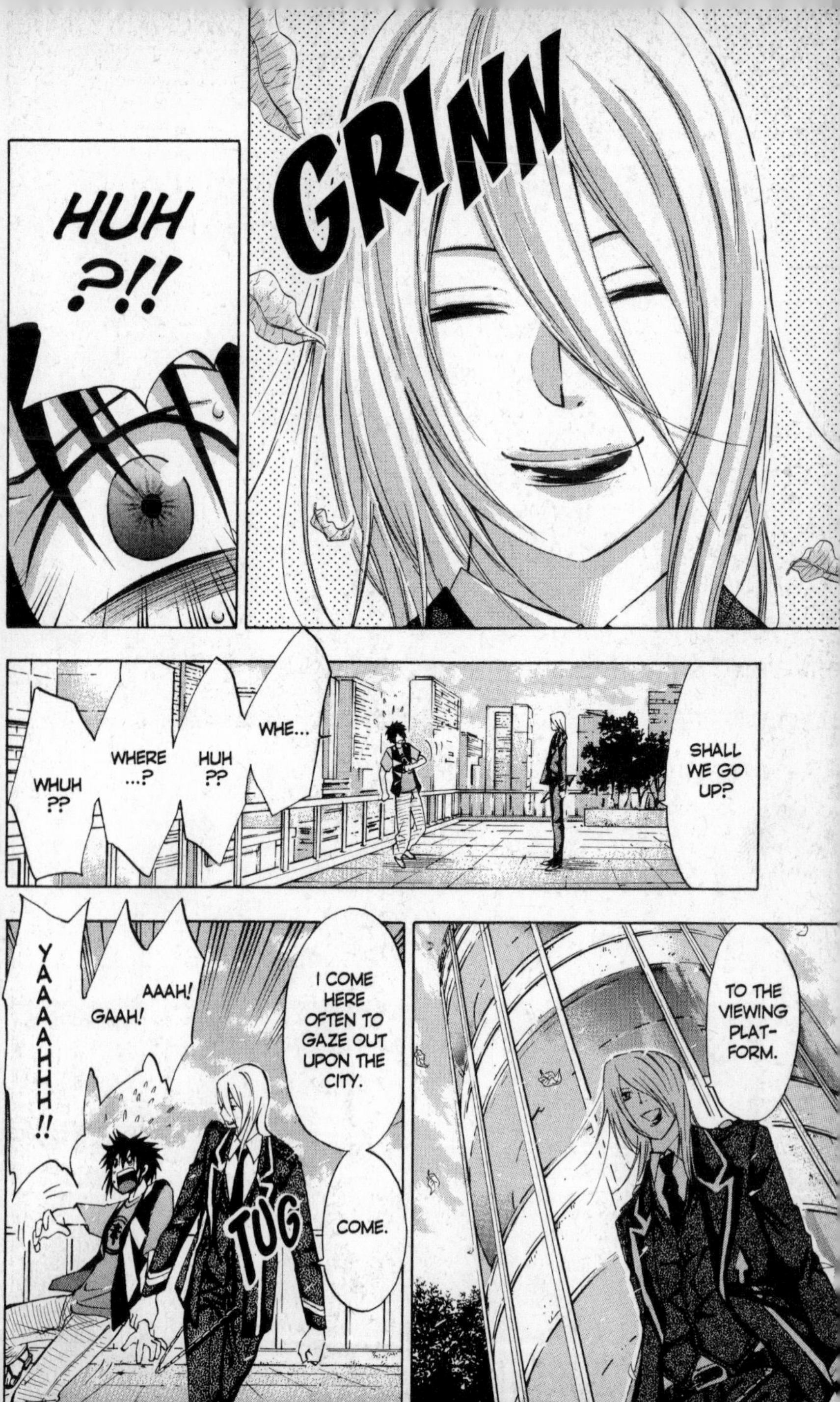
GRINN
HUH ?!!
SHALL WE GO UP?
WHE...
HUH ??
WHERE ...?
WHUH ??
TO THE VIEWING PLAT-FORM.
I COME HERE OFTEN TO GAZE OUT UPON THE CITY.
COME.
TUG
AAAH!
GAAH!
YAAAAAHHH!!

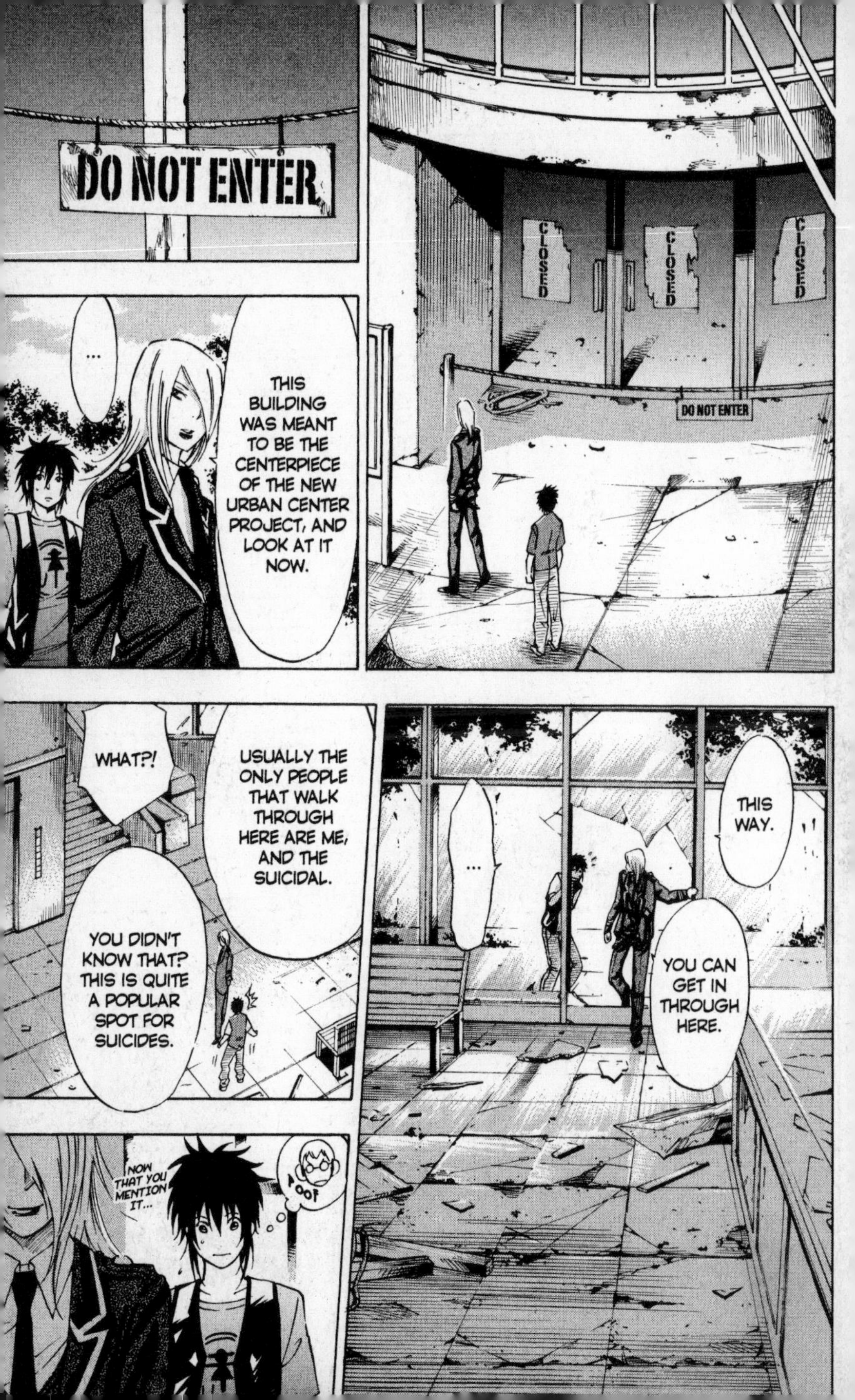
CLOSED
CLOSED
CLOSED
DO NOT ENTER
DO NOT ENTER
THIS BUILDING WAS MEANT TO BE THE CENTERPIECE OF THE NEW URBAN CENTER PROJECT, AND LOOK AT IT NOW.
...
THIS WAY.
YOU CAN GET IN THROUGH HERE.
...
USUALLY THE ONLY PEOPLE THAT WALK THROUGH HERE ARE ME, AND THE SUICIDAL.
WHAT?!
YOU DIDN'T KNOW THAT? THIS IS QUITE A POPULAR SPOT FOR SUICIDES.
POOF
NOW THAT YOU MENTION IT...

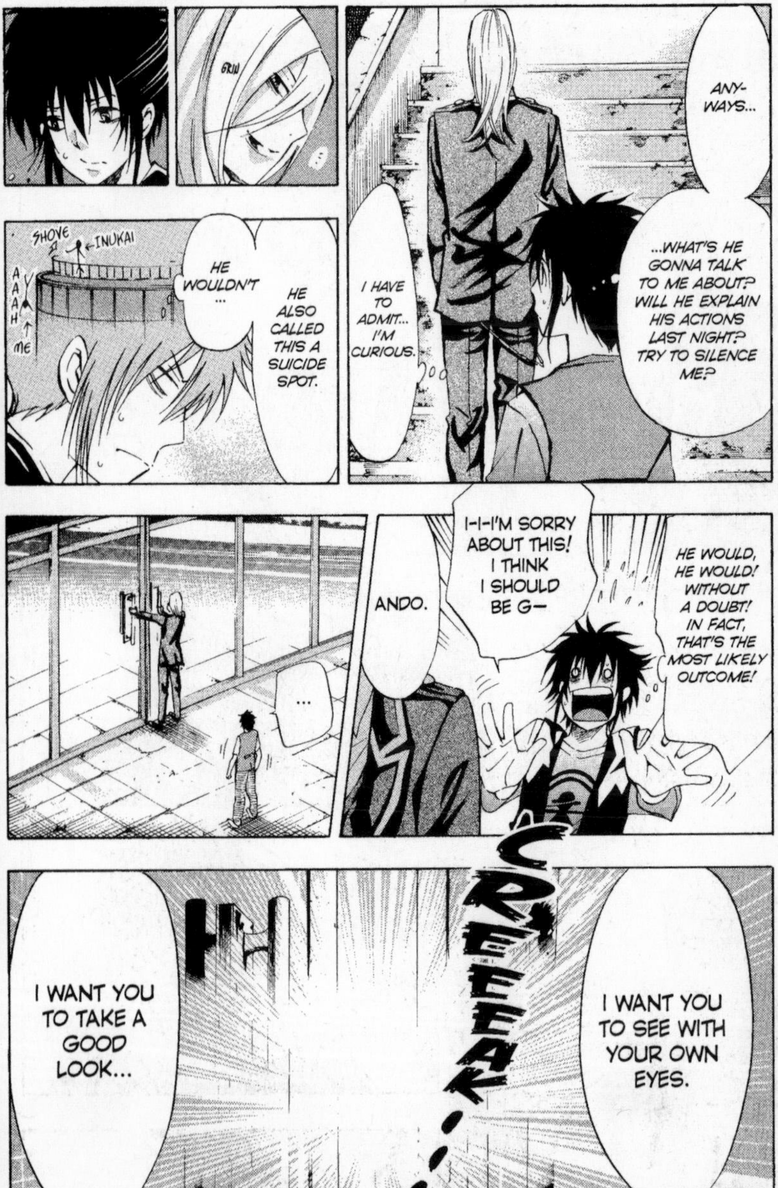
ANY-WAYS...
...WHAT'S HE GONNA TALK TO ME ABOUT? WILL HE EXPLAIN HIS ACTIONS LAST NIGHT? TRY TO SILENCE ME?
I HAVE TO ADMIT... I'M CURIOUS.
GRIN
...
HE ALSO CALLED THIS A SUICIDE SPOT.
HE WOULDN'T ...
SHOVE
INUKAI
AAAAH
ME
HE WOULD, HE WOULD! WITHOUT A DOUBT! IN FACT, THAT'S THE MOST LIKELY OUTCOME!
I-I-I'M SORRY ABOUT THIS! I THINK I SHOULD BE G—
ANDO.
...
I WANT YOU TO SEE WITH YOUR OWN EYES.
CREEEAK...
I WANT YOU TO TAKE A GOOD LOOK...

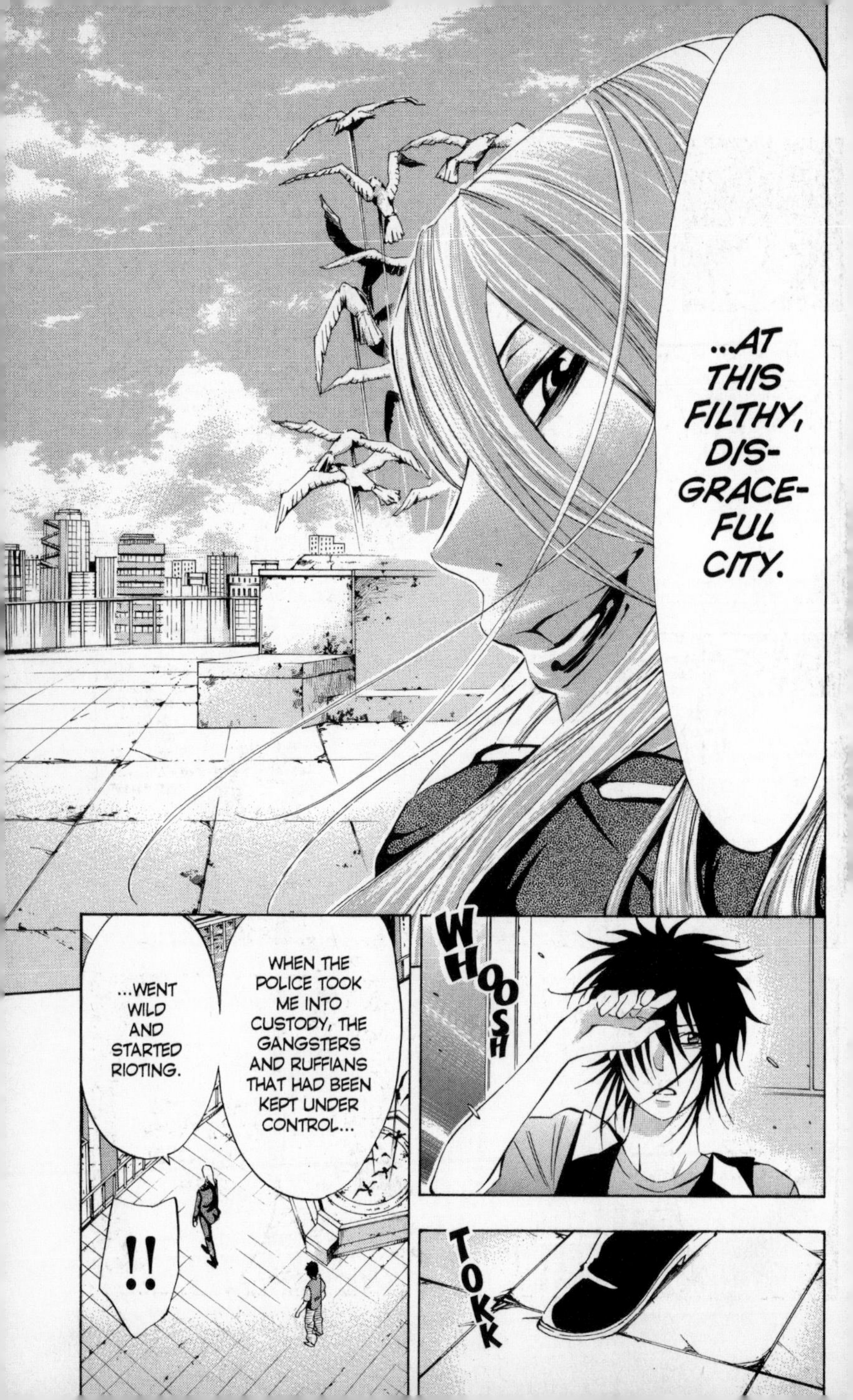
...AT THIS FILTHY, DIS-GRACE-FUL CITY.
WHOOSH
TOKK
WHEN THE POLICE TOOK ME INTO CUSTODY, THE GANGSTERS AND RUFFIANS THAT HAD BEEN KEPT UNDER CONTROL...
...WENT WILD AND STARTED RIOTING.
!!

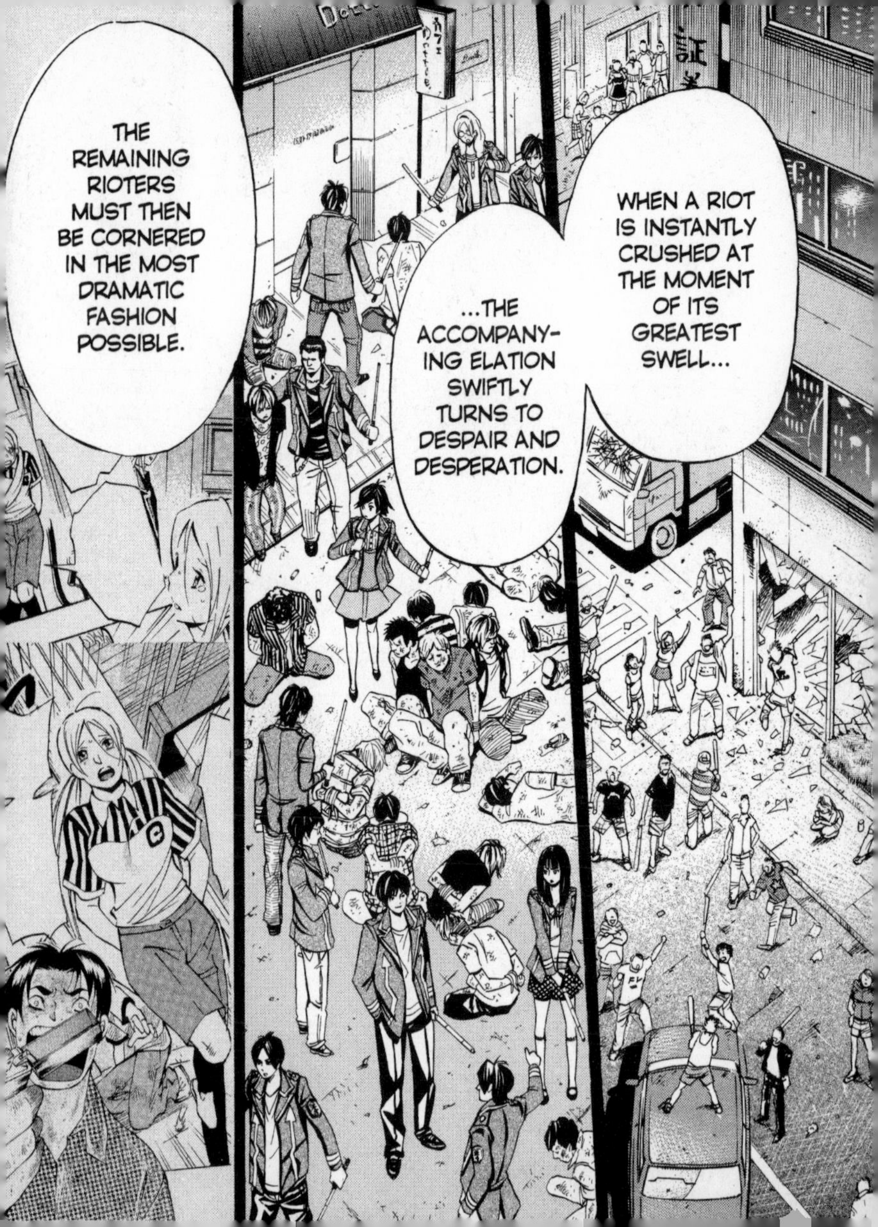
WHEN A RIOT IS INSTANTLY CRUSHED AT THE MOMENT OF ITS GREATEST SWELL...
...THE ACCOMPANYING ELATION SWIFTLY TURNS TO DESPAIR AND DESPERATION.
THE REMAINING RIOTERS MUST THEN BE CORNERED IN THE MOST DRAMATIC FASHION POSSIBLE.

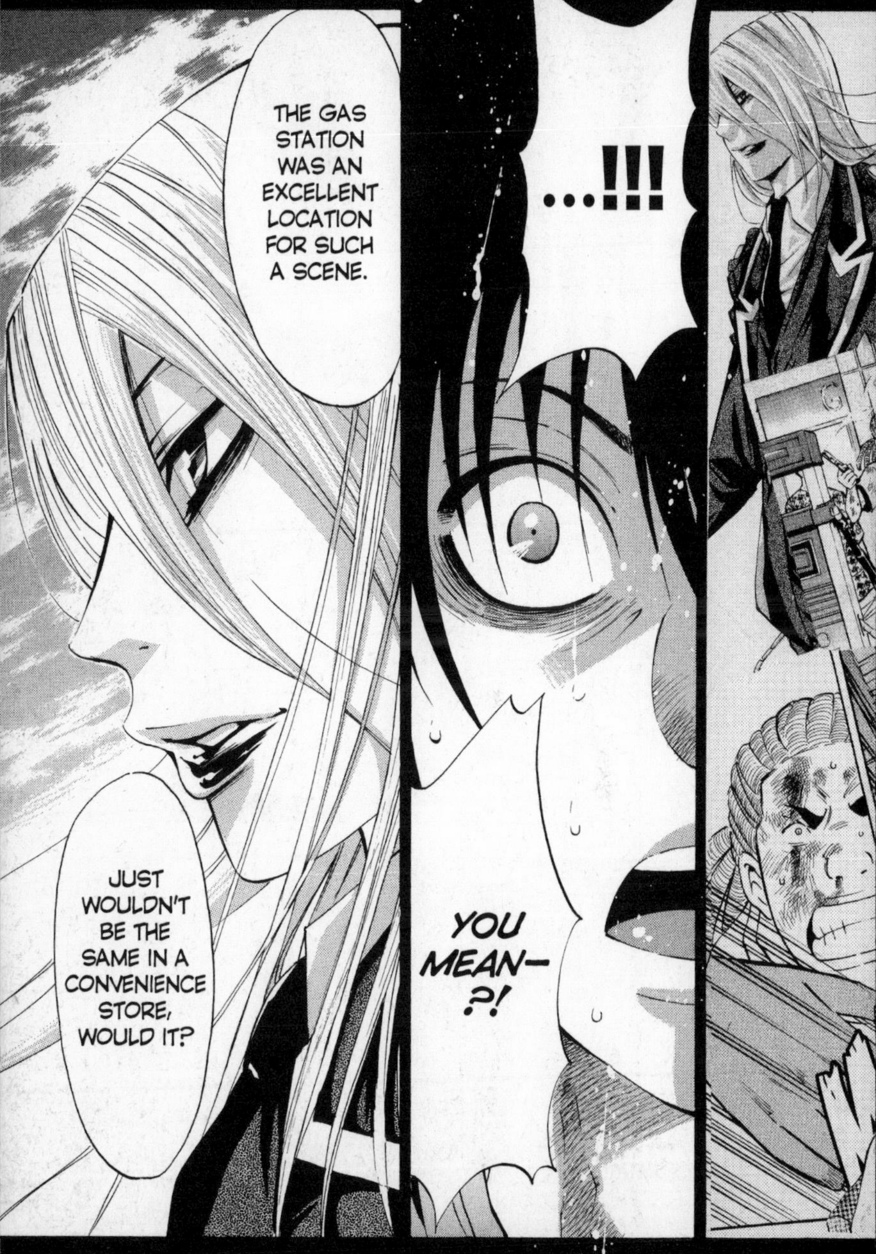
...!!!
YOU MEAN— ?!
THE GAS STATION WAS AN EXCELLENT LOCATION FOR SUCH A SCENE.
JUST WOULDN'T BE THE SAME IN A CONVENIENCE STORE, WOULD IT?

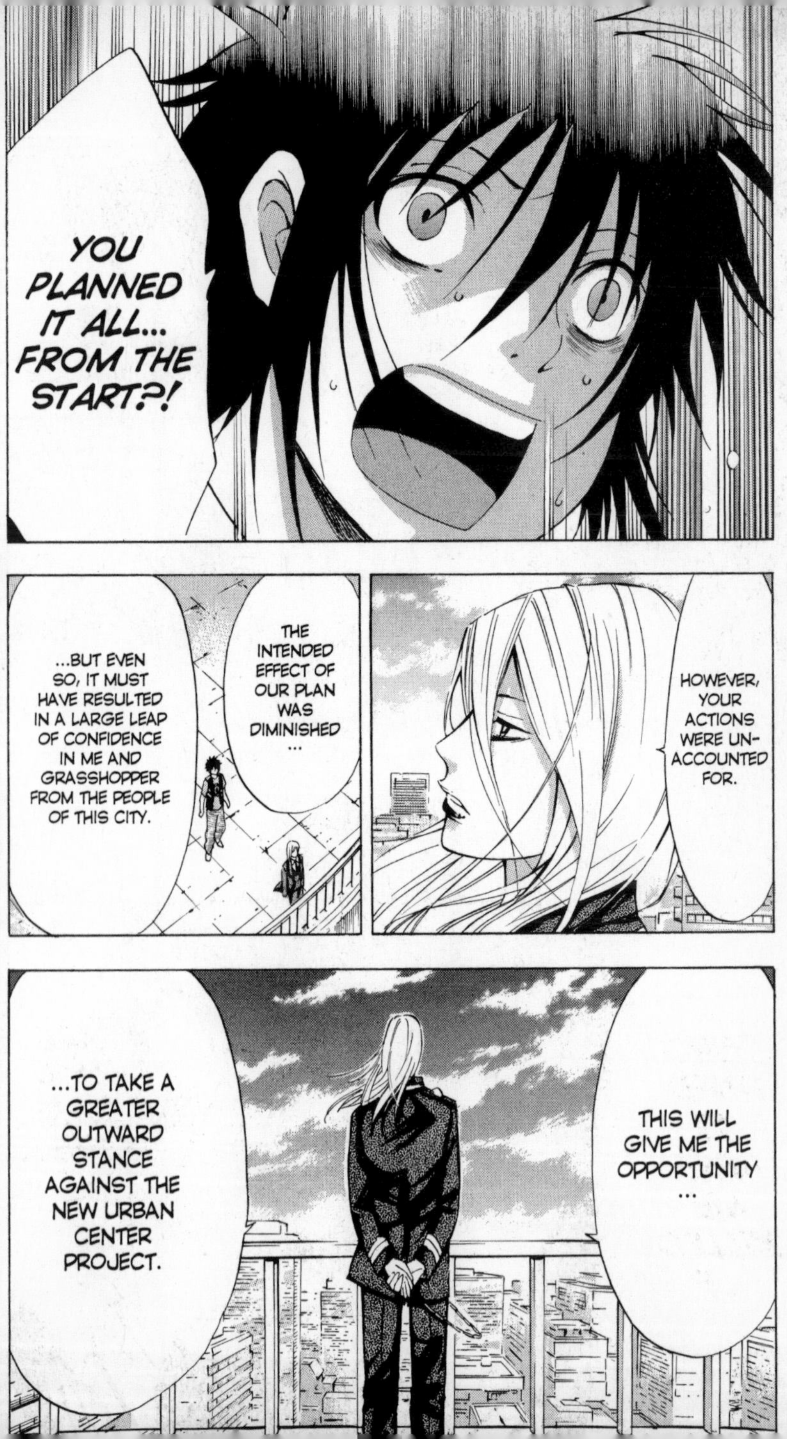
YOU PLANNED IT ALL... FROM THE START?!
HOWEVER, YOUR ACTIONS WERE UN-ACCOUNTED FOR.
THE INTENDED EFFECT OF OUR PLAN WAS DIMINISHED...
...BUT EVEN SO, IT MUST HAVE RESULTED IN A LARGE LEAP OF CONFIDENCE IN ME AND GRASSHOPPER FROM THE PEOPLE OF THIS CITY.
THIS WILL GIVE ME THE OPPORTUNITY...
...TO TAKE A GREATER OUTWARD STANCE AGAINST THE NEW URBAN CENTER PROJECT.

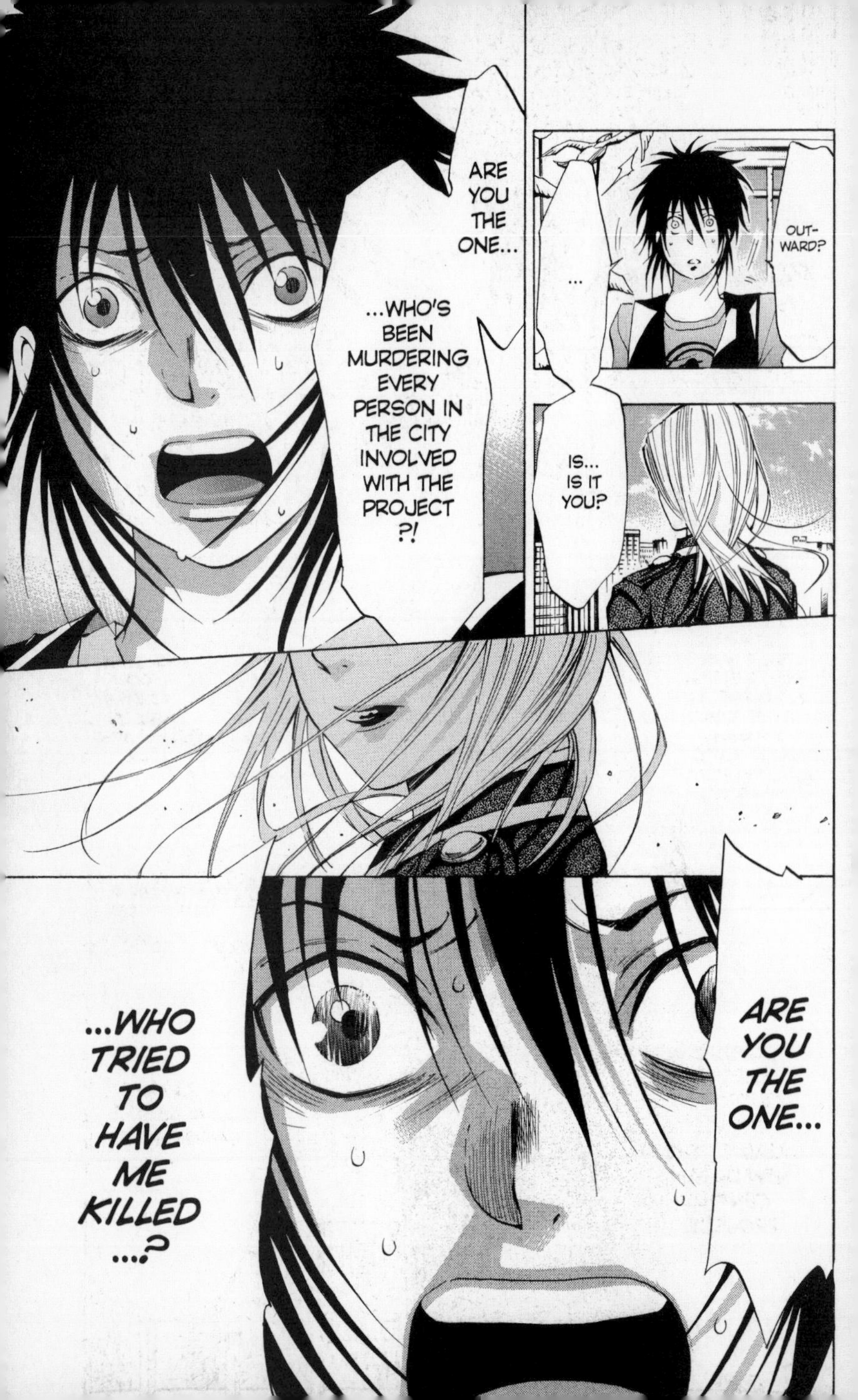
OUT-WARD?
...
IS... IS IT YOU?
ARE YOU THE ONE...
...WHO'S BEEN MURDERING EVERY PERSON IN THE CITY INVOLVED WITH THE PROJECT ?!
ARE YOU THE ONE...
...WHO TRIED TO HAVE ME KILLED ...?

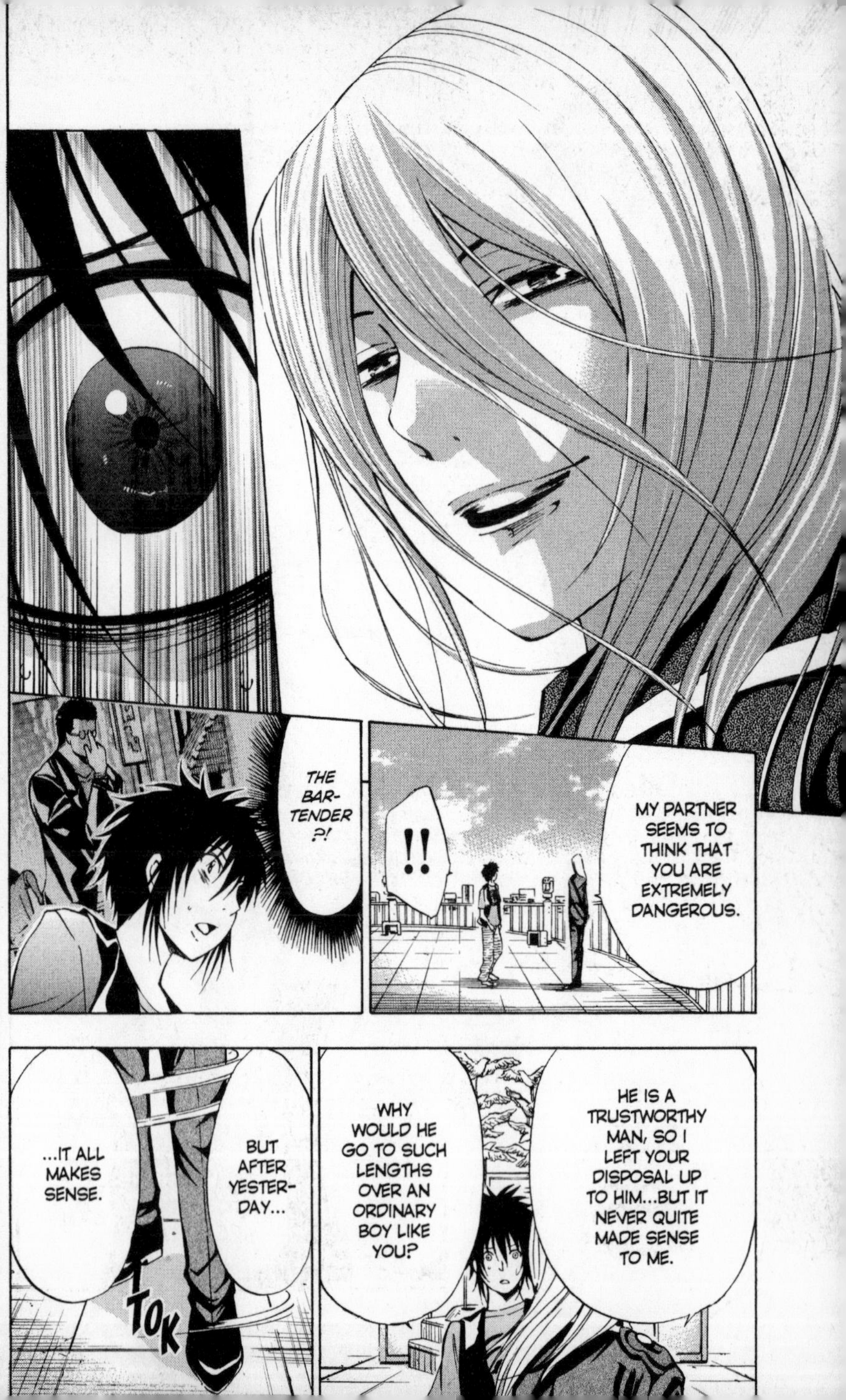
MY PARTNER SEEMS TO THINK THAT YOU ARE EXTREMELY DANGEROUS.
!!
THE BAR-TENDER?!
HE IS A TRUSTWORTHY MAN, SO I LEFT YOUR DISPOSAL UP TO HIM...BUT IT NEVER QUITE MADE SENSE TO ME.
WHY WOULD HE GO TO SUCH LENGTHS OVER AN ORDINARY BOY LIKE YOU?
BUT AFTER YESTER-DAY...
...IT ALL MAKES SENSE.
TOK

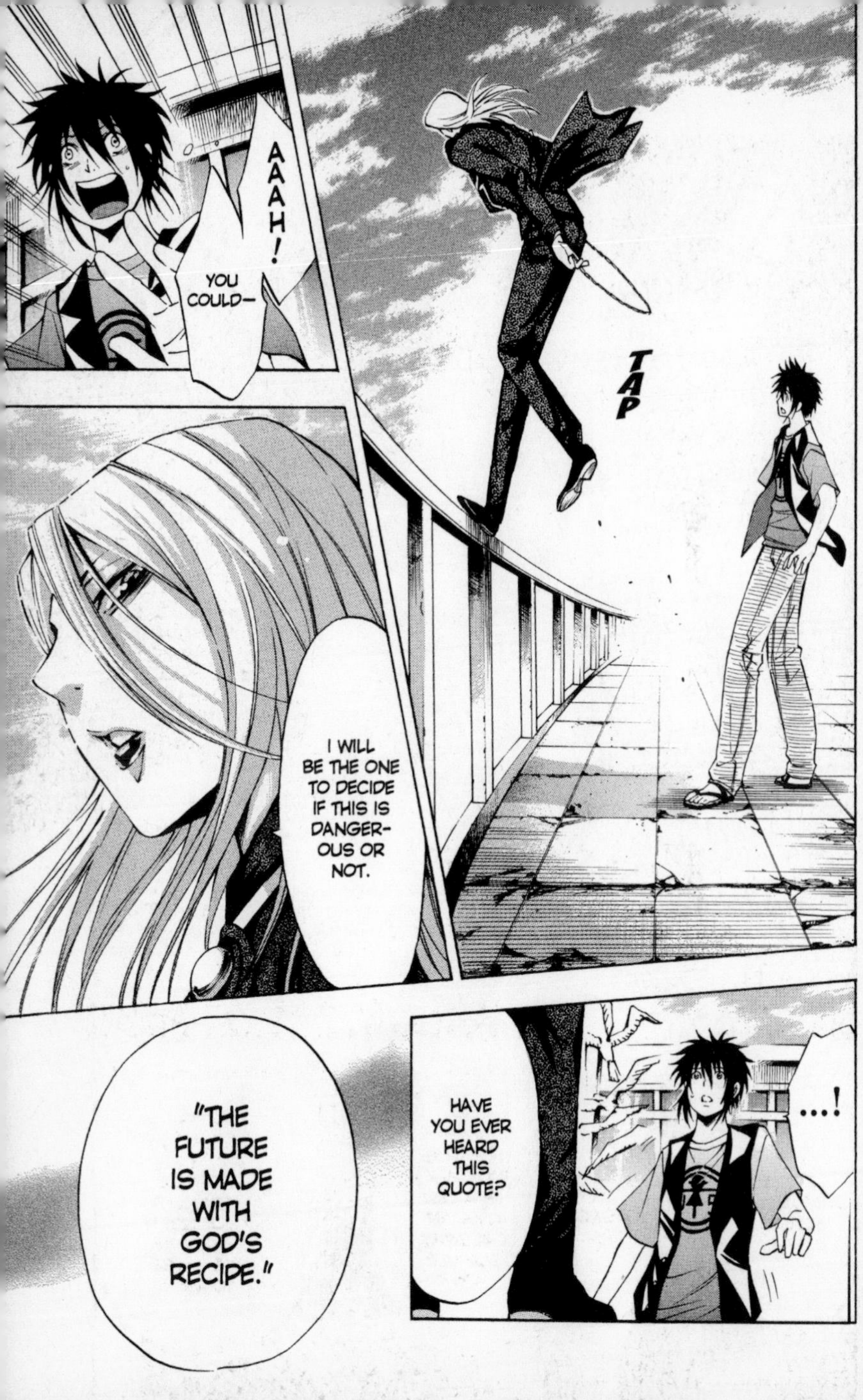
TAP
AAAH! YOU COULD—
I WILL BE THE ONE TO DECIDE IF THIS IS DANGEROUS OR NOT.
...!
HAVE YOU EVER HEARD THIS QUOTE?
"THE FUTURE IS MADE WITH GOD'S RECIPE."

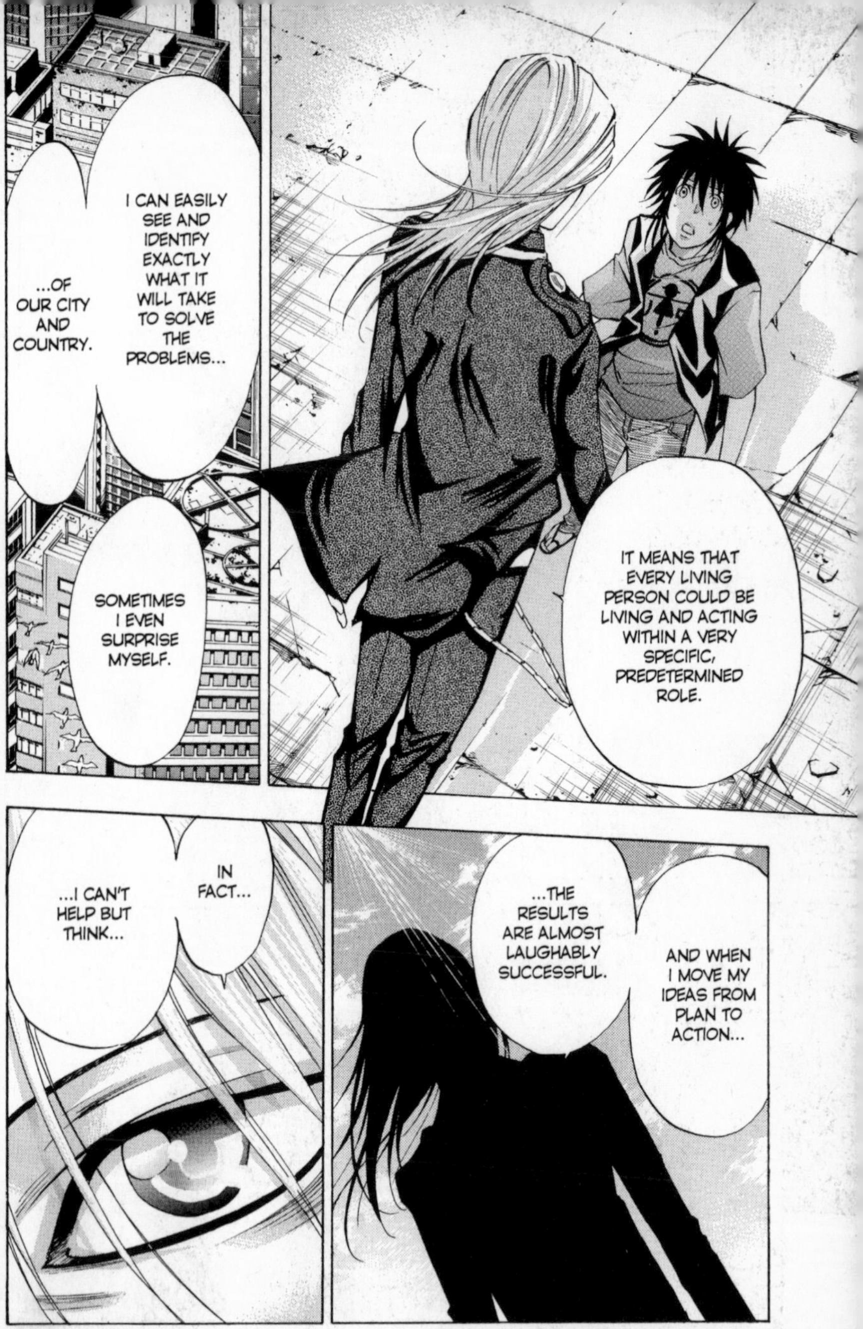
IT MEANS THAT EVERY LIVING PERSON COULD BE LIVING AND ACTING WITHIN A VERY SPECIFIC, PREDETERMINED ROLE.
I CAN EASILY SEE AND IDENTIFY EXACTLY WHAT IT WILL TAKE TO SOLVE THE PROBLEMS...
...OF OUR CITY AND COUNTRY.
SOMETIMES I EVEN SURPRISE MYSELF.
AND WHEN I MOVE MY IDEAS FROM PLAN TO ACTION...
...THE RESULTS ARE ALMOST LAUGHABLY SUCCESSFUL.
IN FACT...
...I CAN'T HELP BUT THINK...

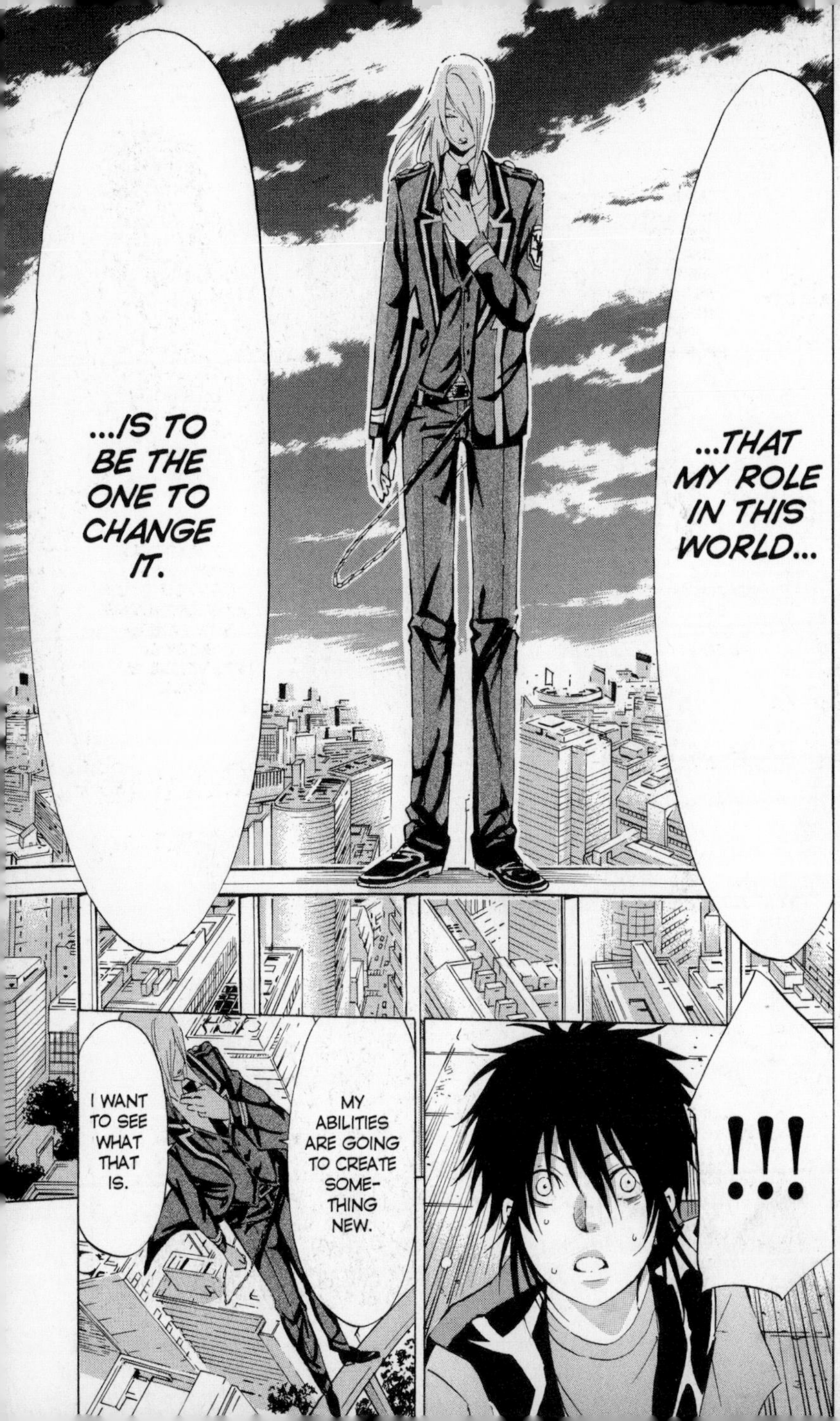
...THAT MY ROLE IN THIS WORLD...
...IS TO BE THE ONE TO CHANGE IT.
!!!
MY ABILITIES ARE GOING TO CREATE SOME-THING NEW.
I WANT TO SEE WHAT THAT IS.

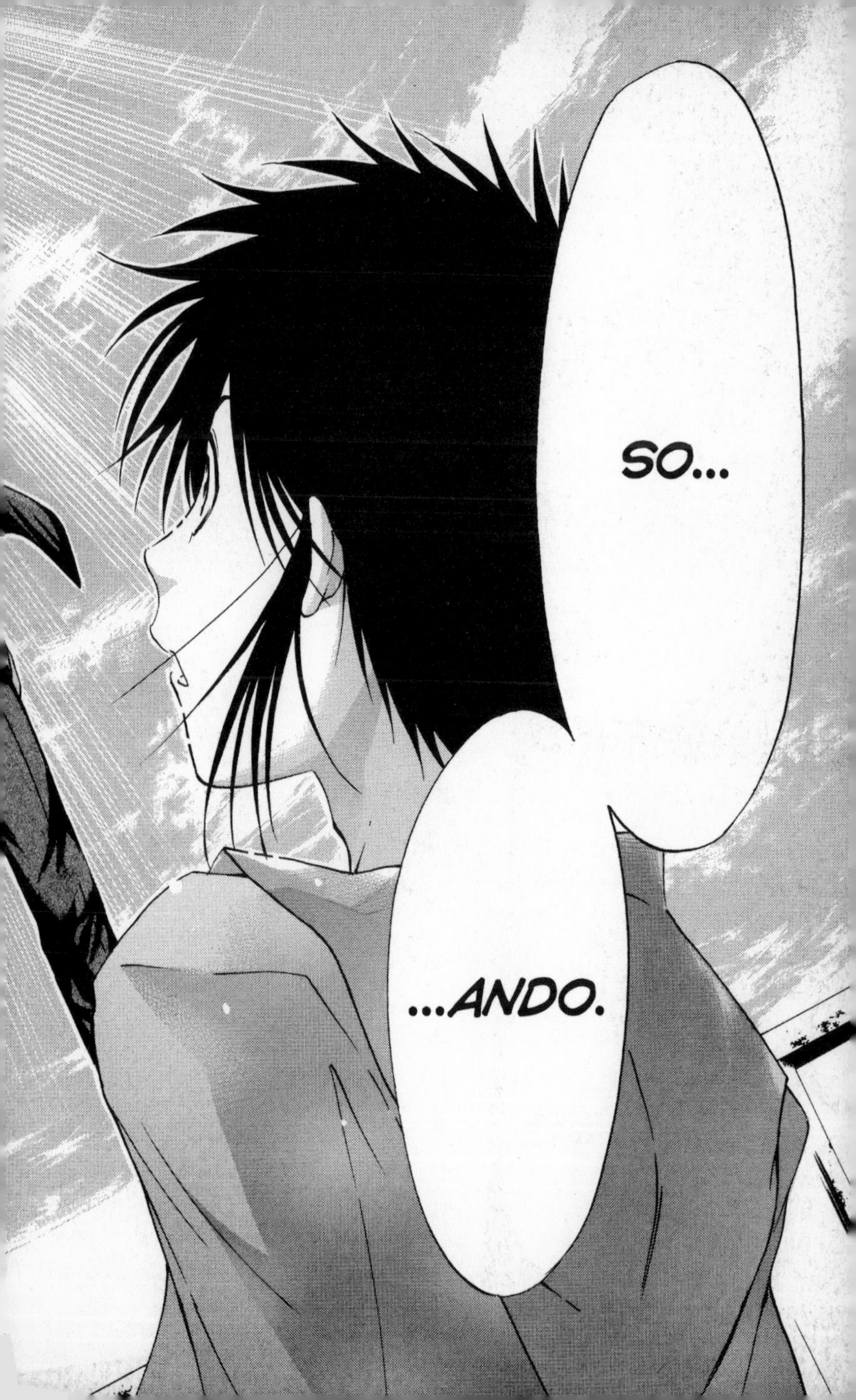
SO...
...ANDO.

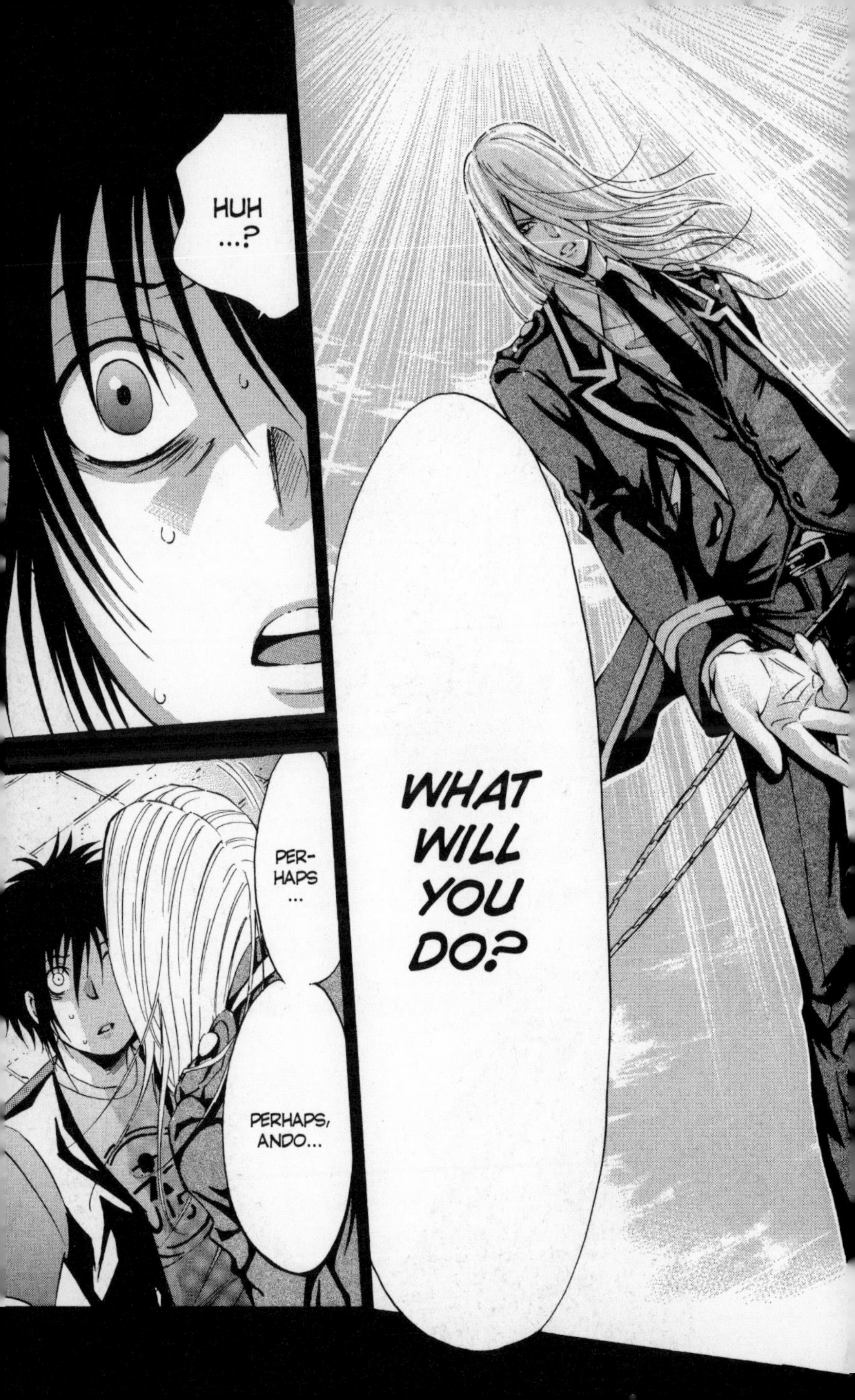
WHAT WILL YOU DO?
HUH ...?
PER-HAPS ...
PERHAPS, ANDO...

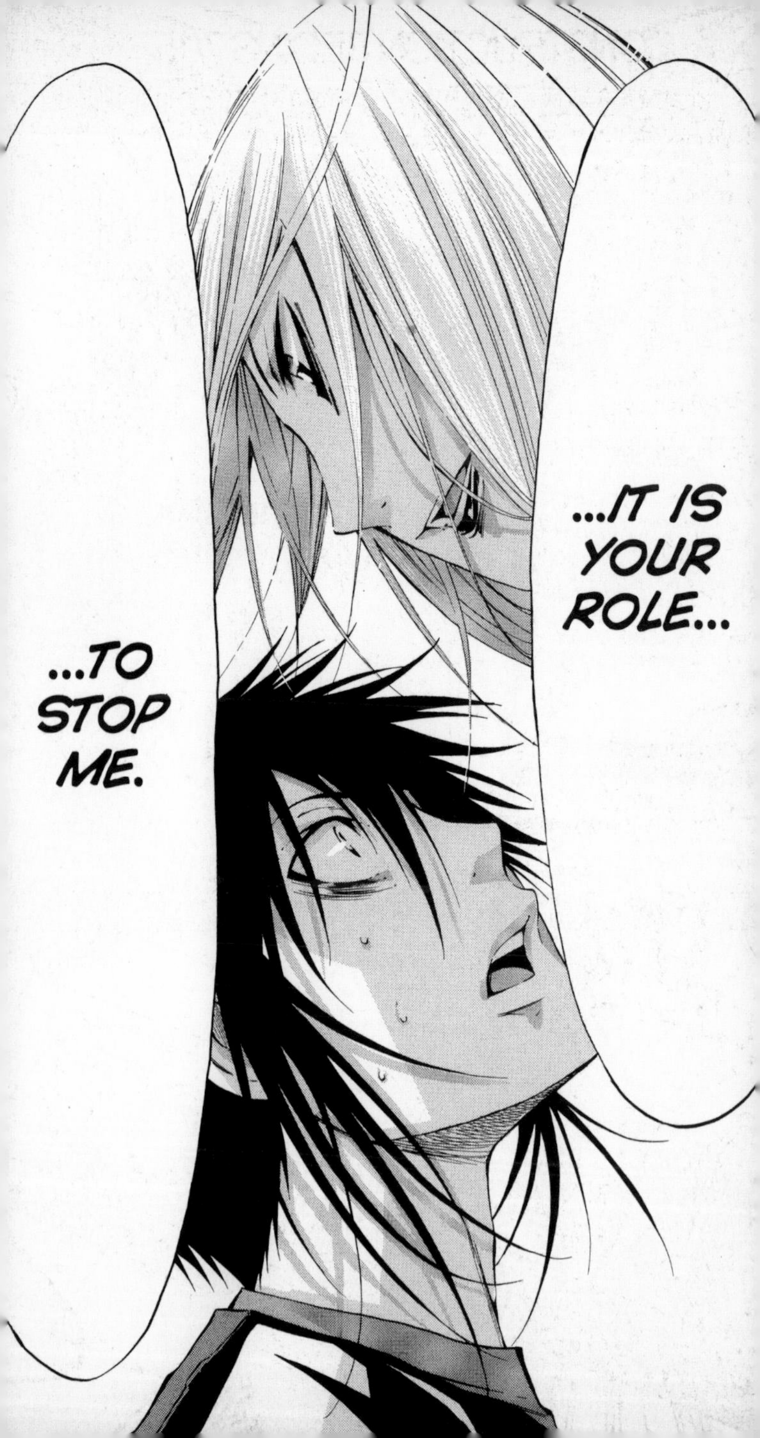
...IT IS YOUR ROLE...
...TO STOP ME.

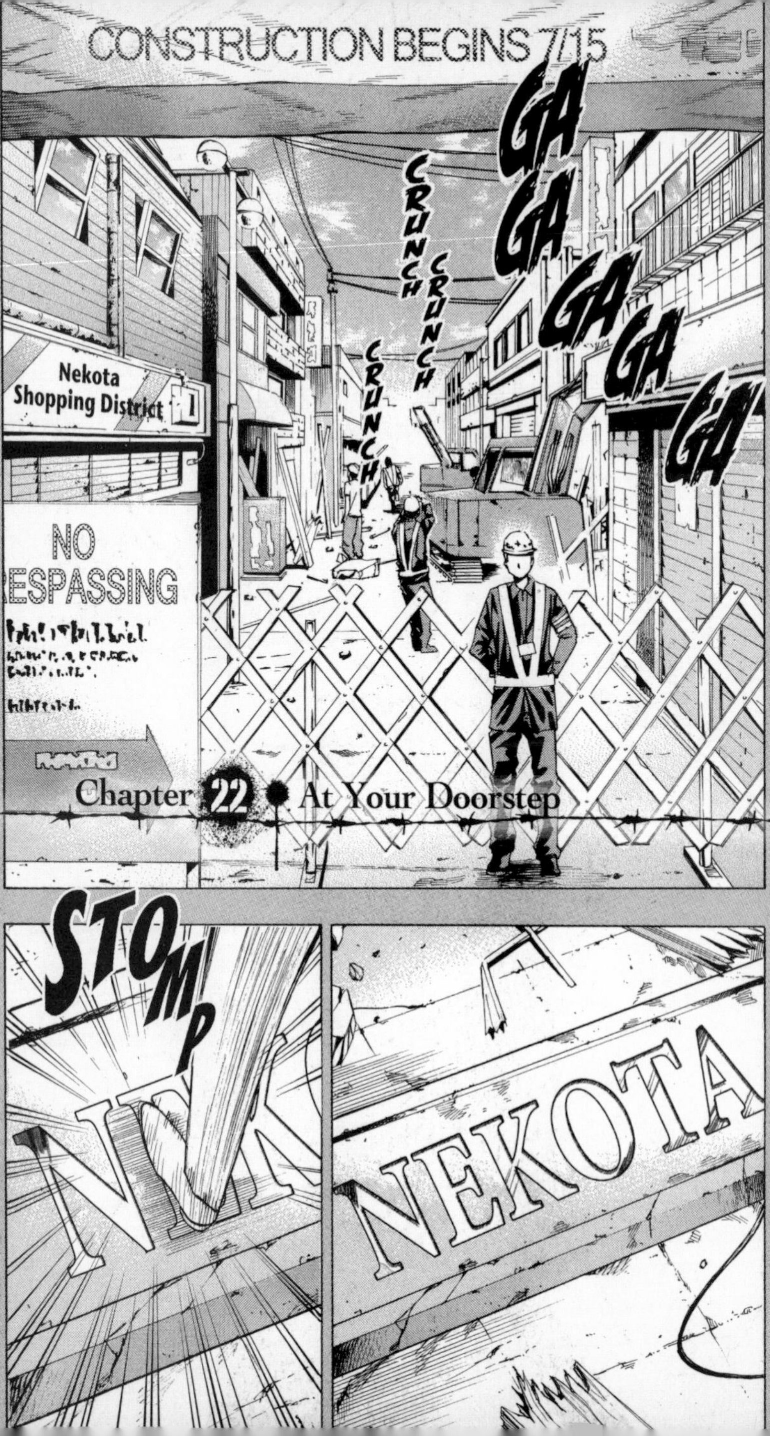
CONSTRUCTION BEGINS 7/15
GA GA GA GA GA GA
CRUNCH CRUNCH
CRUNCH
Nekota Shopping District 1
NO RESPASSING
Chapter 22 • At Your Doorstep
NEKOTA
STOMP

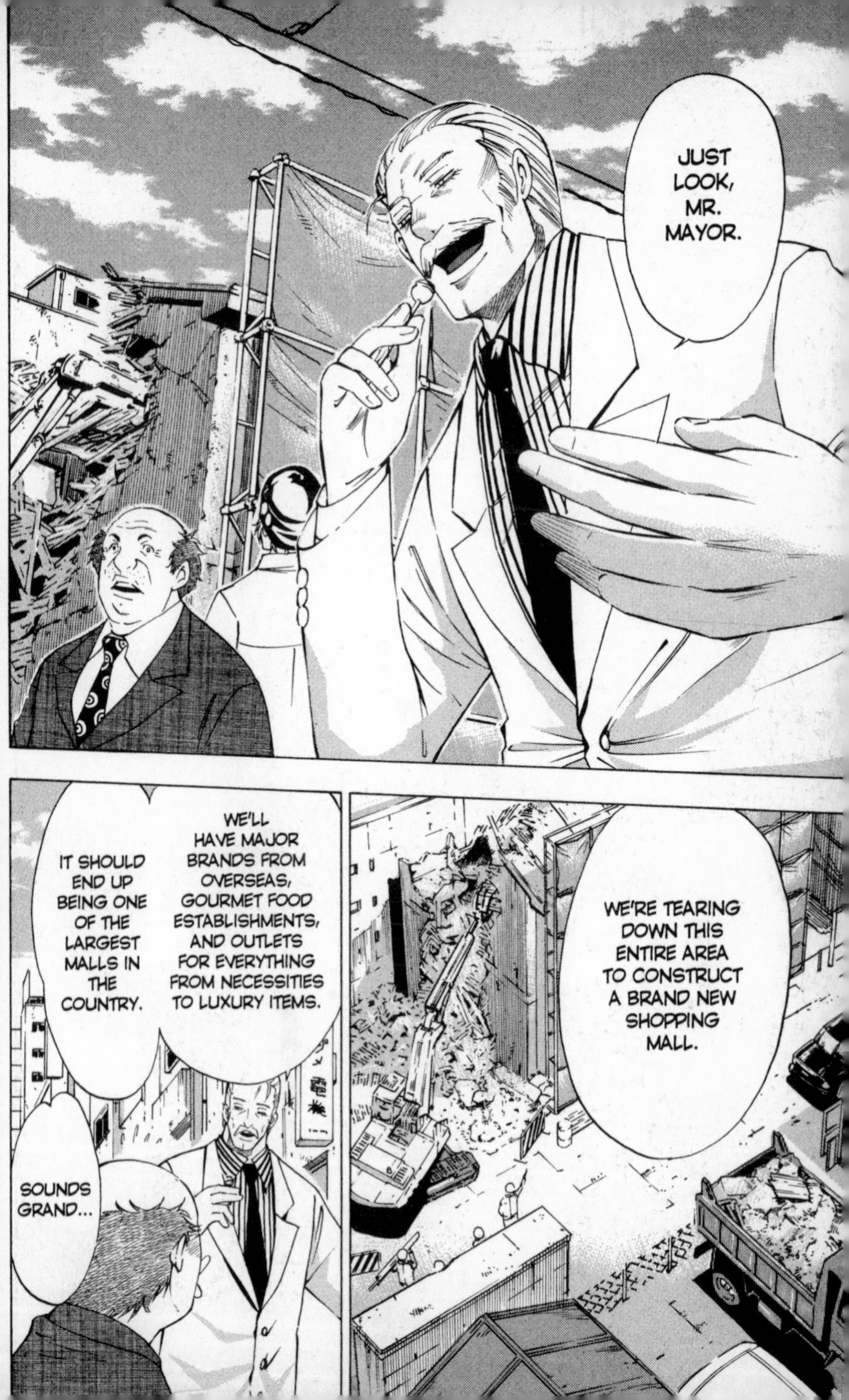
JUST LOOK, MR. MAYOR.
WE'RE TEARING DOWN THIS ENTIRE AREA TO CONSTRUCT A BRAND NEW SHOPPING MALL.
WE'LL HAVE MAJOR BRANDS FROM OVERSEAS, GOURMET FOOD ESTABLISHMENTS, AND OUTLETS FOR EVERYTHING FROM NECESSITIES TO LUXURY ITEMS.
IT SHOULD END UP BEING ONE OF THE LARGEST MALLS IN THE COUNTRY.
SOUNDS GRAND...

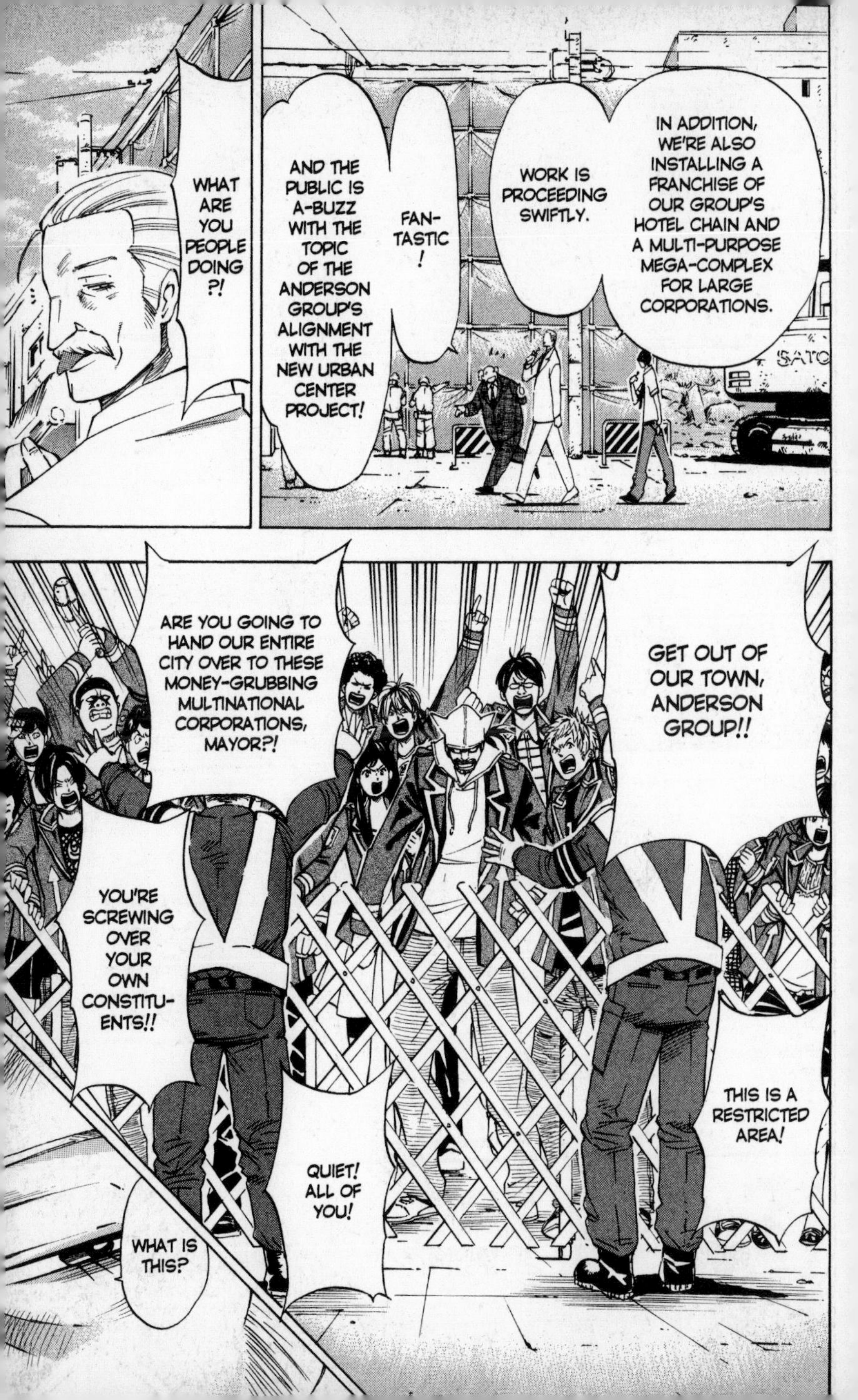
IN ADDITION, WE'RE ALSO INSTALLING A FRANCHISE OF OUR GROUP'S HOTEL CHAIN AND A MULTI-PURPOSE MEGA-COMPLEX FOR LARGE CORPORATIONS.
WORK IS PROCEEDING SWIFTLY.
FANTASTIC!
AND THE PUBLIC IS A-BUZZ WITH THE TOPIC OF THE ANDERSON GROUP'S ALIGNMENT WITH THE NEW URBAN CENTER PROJECT!
SATO
WHAT ARE YOU PEOPLE DOING?!
GET OUT OF OUR TOWN, ANDERSON GROUP!!
ARE YOU GOING TO HAND OUR ENTIRE CITY OVER TO THESE MONEY-GRUBBING MULTINATIONAL CORPORATIONS, MAYOR?!
YOU'RE SCREWING OVER YOUR OWN CONSTITUENTS!!
THIS IS A RESTRICTED AREA!
QUIET! ALL OF YOU!
WHAT IS THIS?

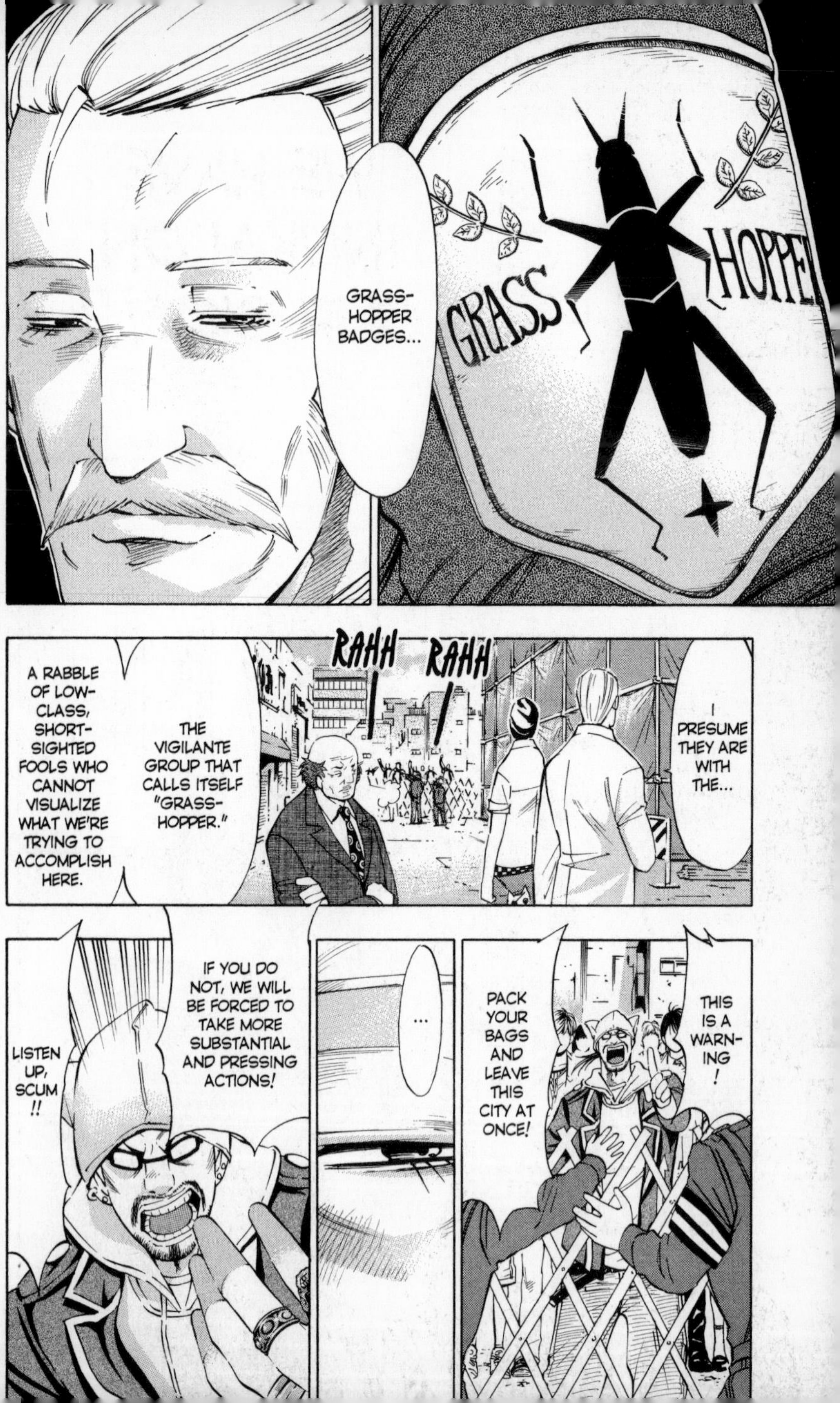
GRASS-HOPPER BADGES...
I PRESUME THEY ARE WITH THE...
RAHH RAHH
THE VIGILANTE GROUP THAT CALLS ITSELF "GRASS-HOPPER."
A RABBLE OF LOW-CLASS, SHORT-SIGHTED FOOLS WHO CANNOT VISUALIZE WHAT WE'RE TRYING TO ACCOMPLISH HERE.
THIS IS A WARN-ING!
PACK YOUR BAGS AND LEAVE THIS CITY AT ONCE!
...
IF YOU DO NOT, WE WILL BE FORCED TO TAKE MORE SUBSTANTIAL AND PRESSING ACTIONS!
LISTEN UP, SCUM!!

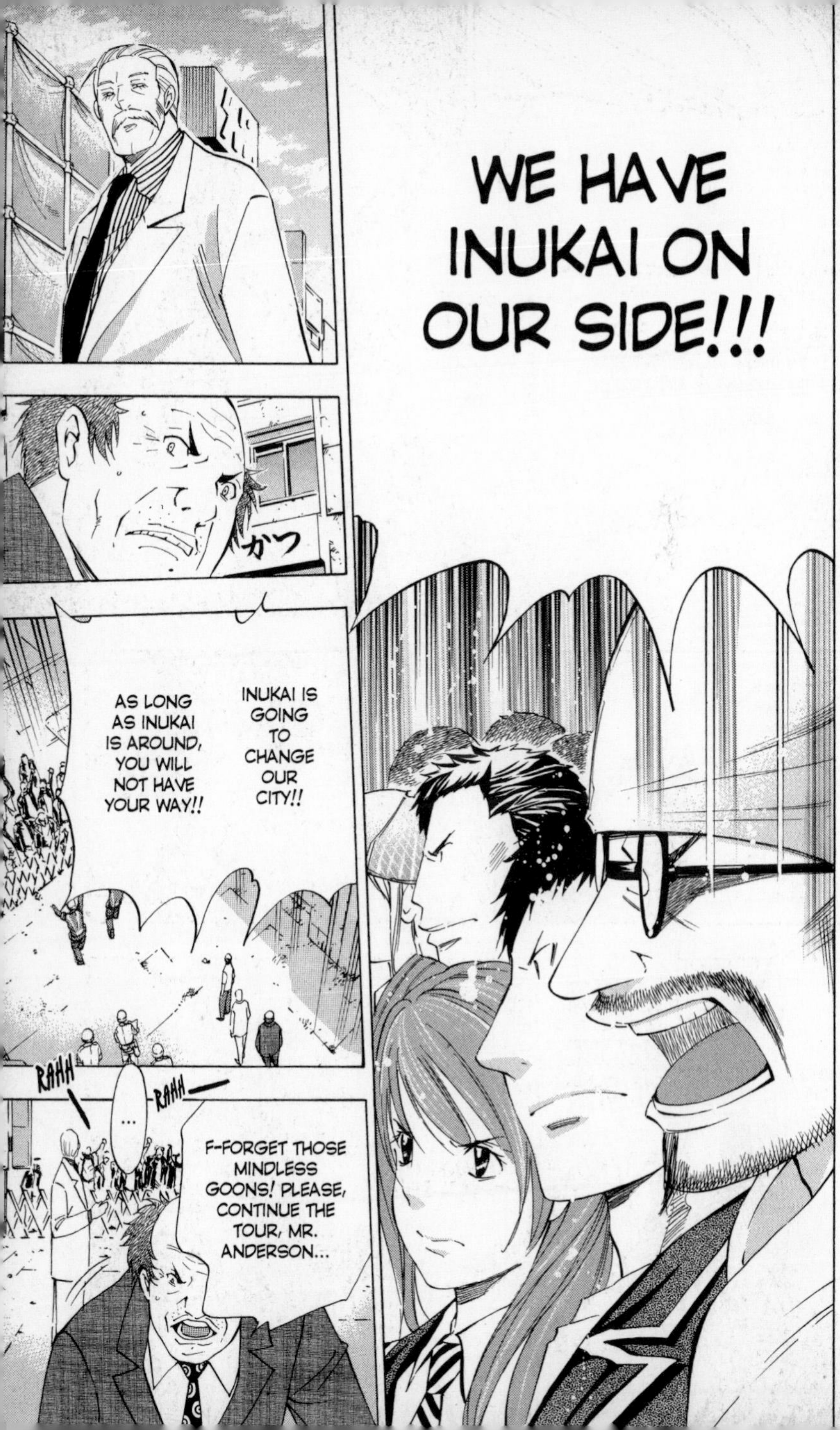
WE HAVE INUKAI ON OUR SIDE!!!
がつ
INUKAI IS GOING TO CHANGE OUR CITY!!
AS LONG AS INUKAI IS AROUND, YOU WILL NOT HAVE YOUR WAY!!
RAHH
...
RAHH
F-FORGET THOSE MINDLESS GOONS! PLEASE, CONTINUE THE TOUR, MR. ANDERSON...

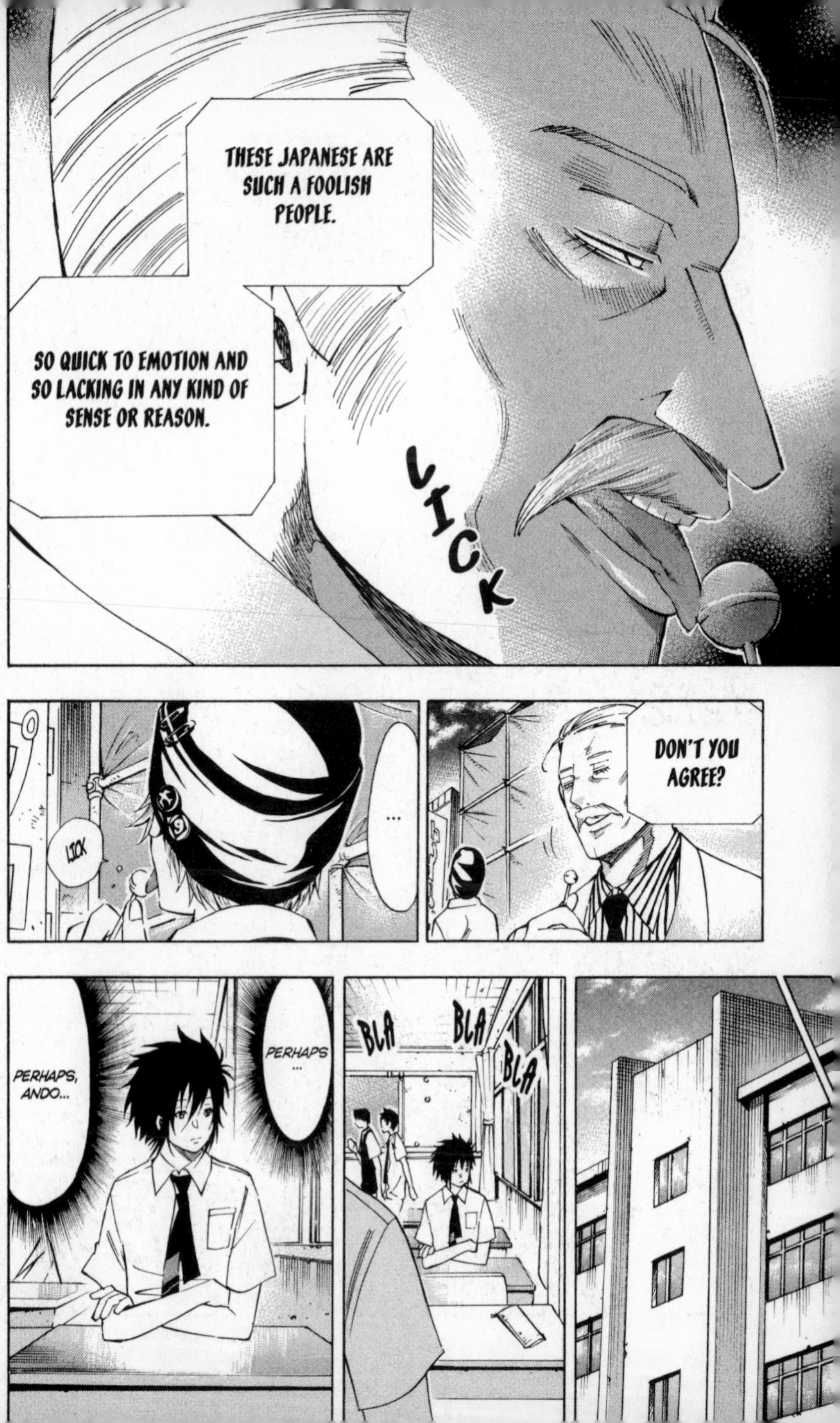
THESE JAPANESE ARE SUCH A FOOLISH PEOPLE.
SO QUICK TO EMOTION AND SO LACKING IN ANY KIND OF SENSE OR REASON.
LICK
DON'T YOU AGREE?
...
LICK
BLA
BLA
BLA
PERHAPS...
PERHAPS, ANDO...

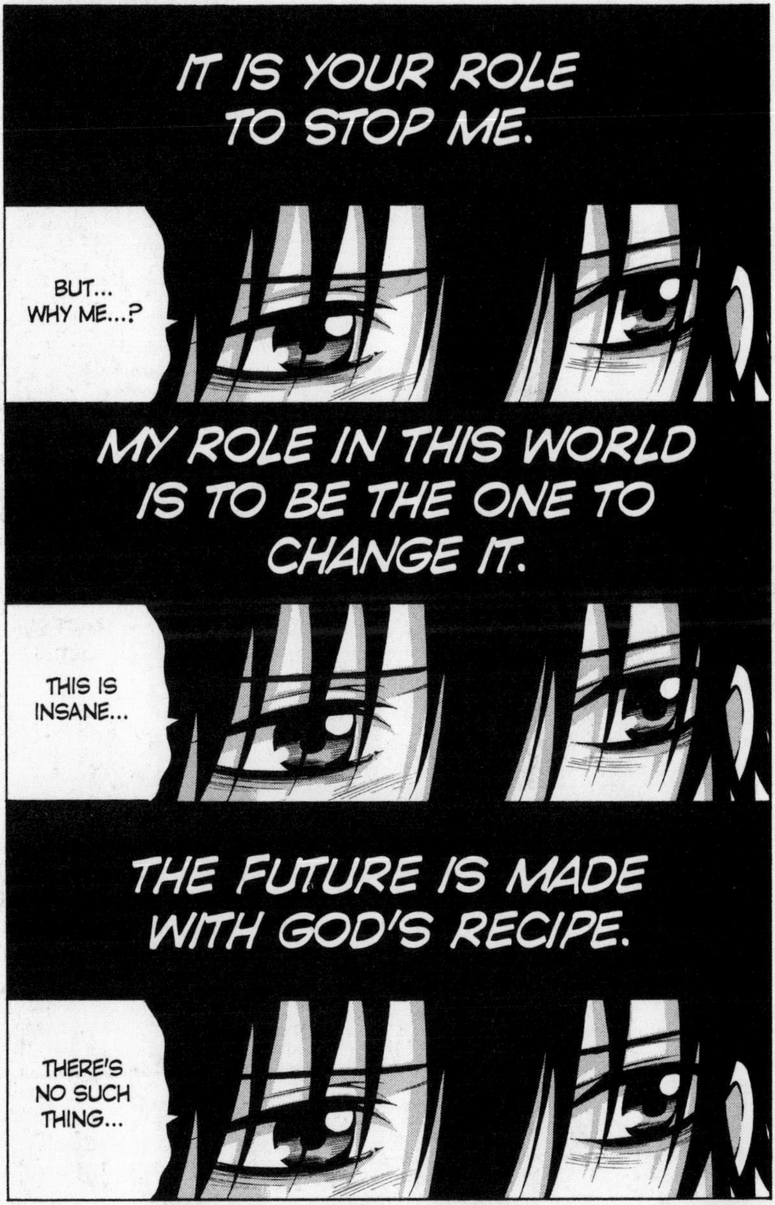
IT IS YOUR ROLE TO STOP ME.
BUT... WHY ME...?
MY ROLE IN THIS WORLD IS TO BE THE ONE TO CHANGE IT.
THIS IS INSANE...
THE FUTURE IS MADE WITH GOD'S RECIPE.
THERE'S NO SUCH THING...

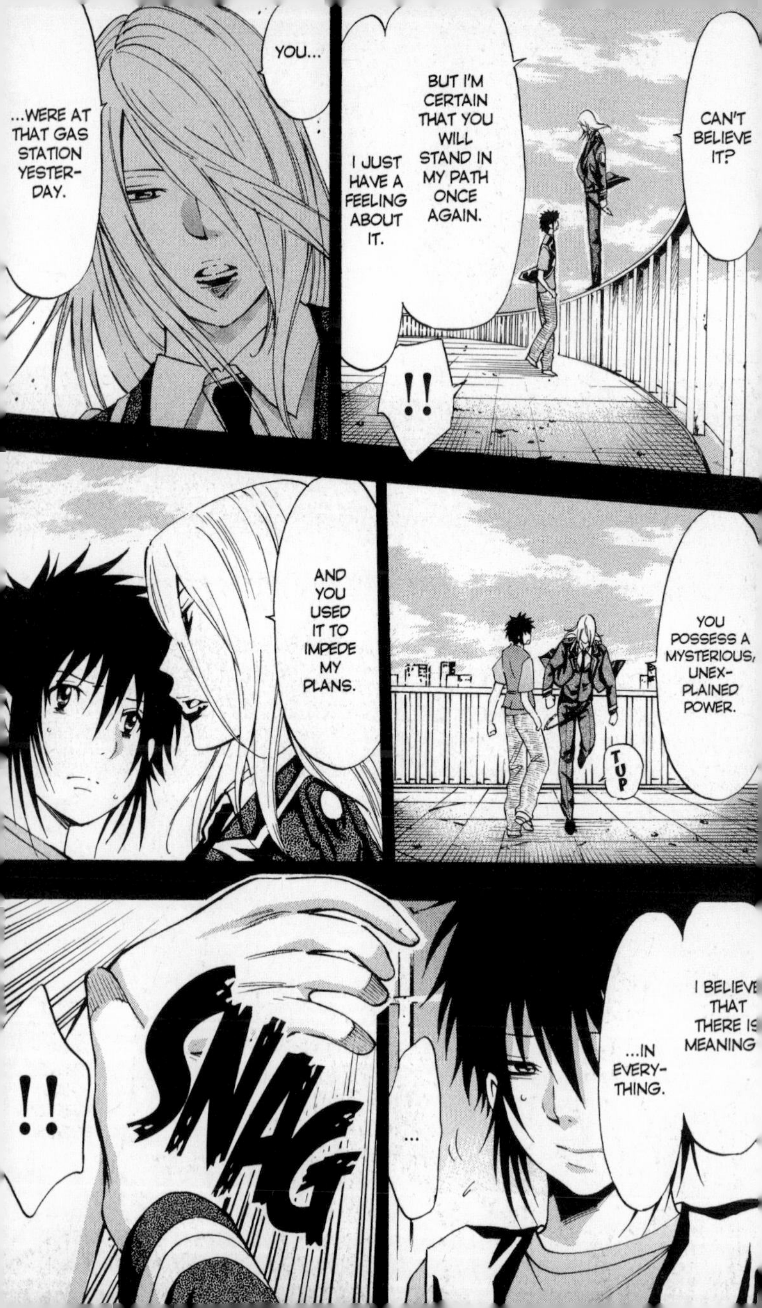
CAN'T BELIEVE IT?
BUT I'M CERTAIN THAT YOU WILL STAND IN MY PATH ONCE AGAIN.
I JUST HAVE A FEELING ABOUT IT.
!!
YOU...
...WERE AT THAT GAS STATION YESTER-DAY.
YOU POSSESS A MYSTERIOUS, UNEX-PLAINED POWER.
TUP
AND YOU USED IT TO IMPEDE MY PLANS.
I BELIEVE THAT THERE IS MEANING
...IN EVERY-THING.
...
SNAG
!!

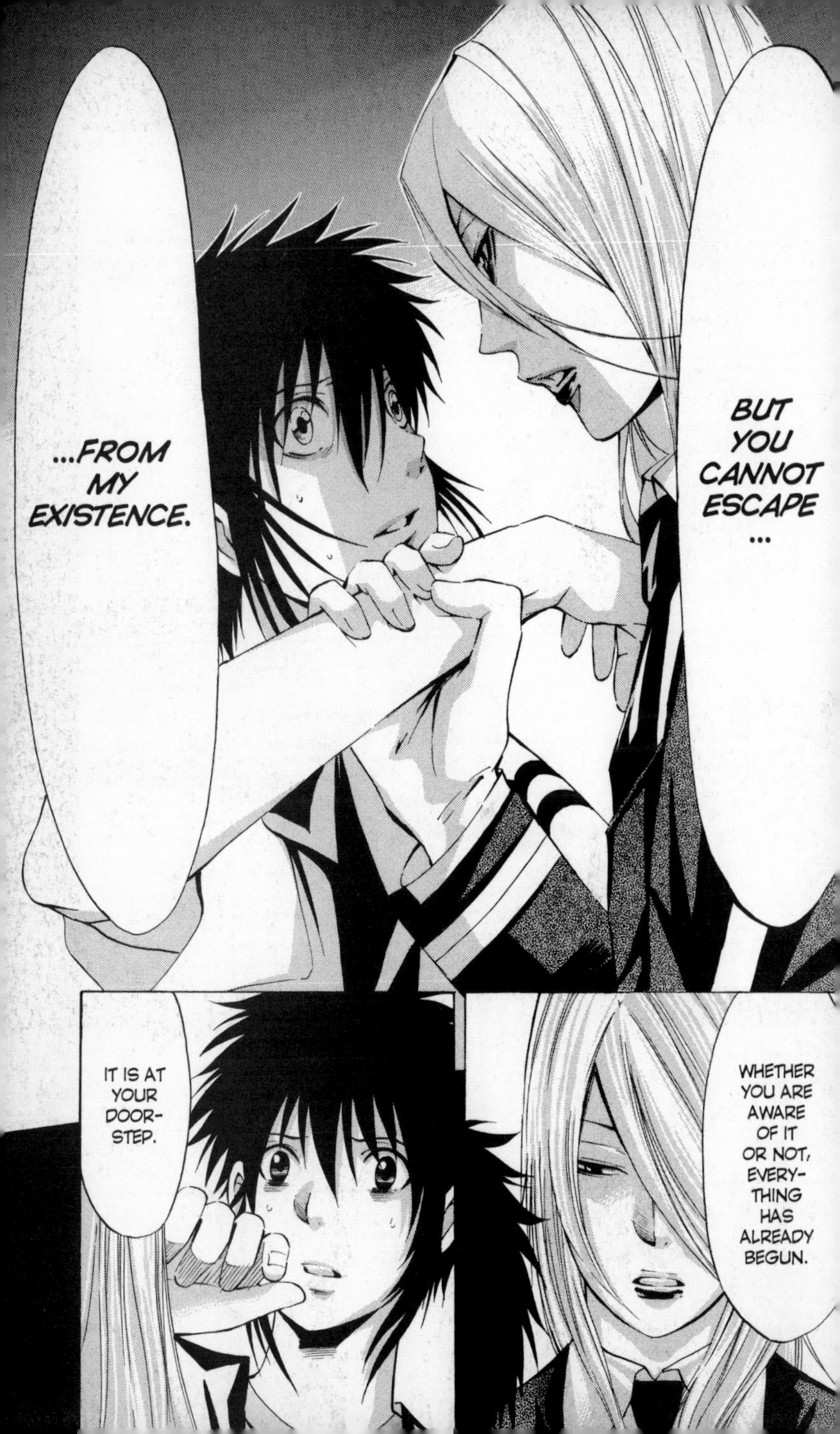
BUT YOU CANNOT ESCAPE...
...FROM MY EXISTENCE.
WHETHER YOU ARE AWARE OF IT OR NOT, EVERYTHING HAS ALREADY BEGUN.
IT IS AT YOUR DOORSTEP.

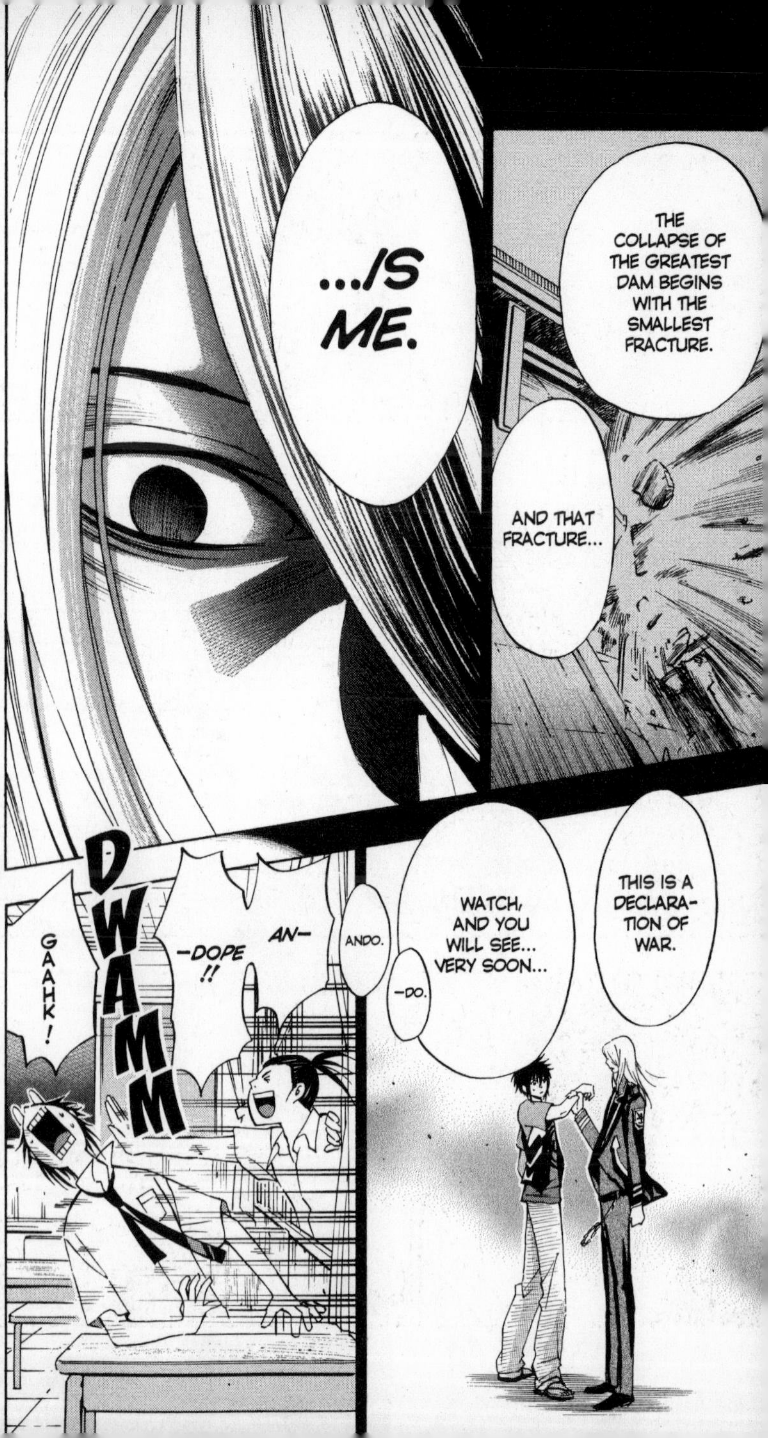
THE COLLAPSE OF THE GREATEST DAM BEGINS WITH THE SMALLEST FRACTURE.
AND THAT FRACTURE...
...IS ME.
THIS IS A DECLARATION OF WAR.
WATCH, AND YOU WILL SEE... VERY SOON...
ANDO.
-DO.
AN-
-DOPE!!
DWAMM
GAAHK!

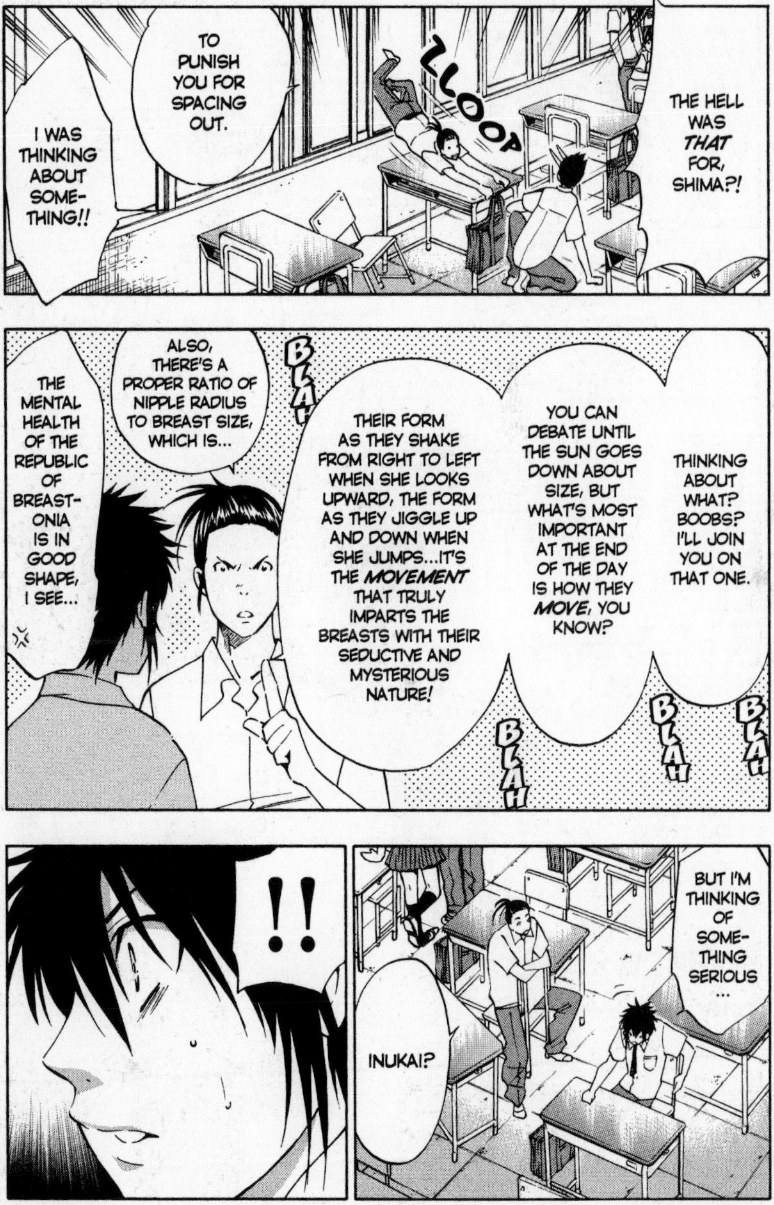
THE HELL WAS *THAT* FOR, SHIMA?!
ZLOOP
TO PUNISH YOU FOR SPACING OUT.
I WAS THINKING ABOUT SOME-THING!!
THINKING ABOUT WHAT? BOOBS? I'LL JOIN YOU ON THAT ONE.
BLAH
YOU CAN DEBATE UNTIL THE SUN GOES DOWN ABOUT SIZE, BUT WHAT'S MOST IMPORTANT AT THE END OF THE DAY IS HOW THEY *MOVE*, YOU KNOW?
BLAH
THEIR FORM AS THEY SHAKE FROM RIGHT TO LEFT WHEN SHE LOOKS UPWARD, THE FORM AS THEY JIGGLE UP AND DOWN WHEN SHE JUMPS...IT'S THE *MOVEMENT* THAT TRULY IMPARTS THE BREASTS WITH THEIR SEDUCTIVE AND MYSTERIOUS NATURE!
BLAH
BLAH
ALSO, THERE'S A PROPER RATIO OF NIPPLE RADIUS TO BREAST SIZE, WHICH IS...
THE MENTAL HEALTH OF THE REPUBLIC OF BREAST-ONIA IS IN GOOD SHAPE, I SEE...
BUT I'M THINKING OF SOME-THING SERIOUS...
INUKAI?
!!

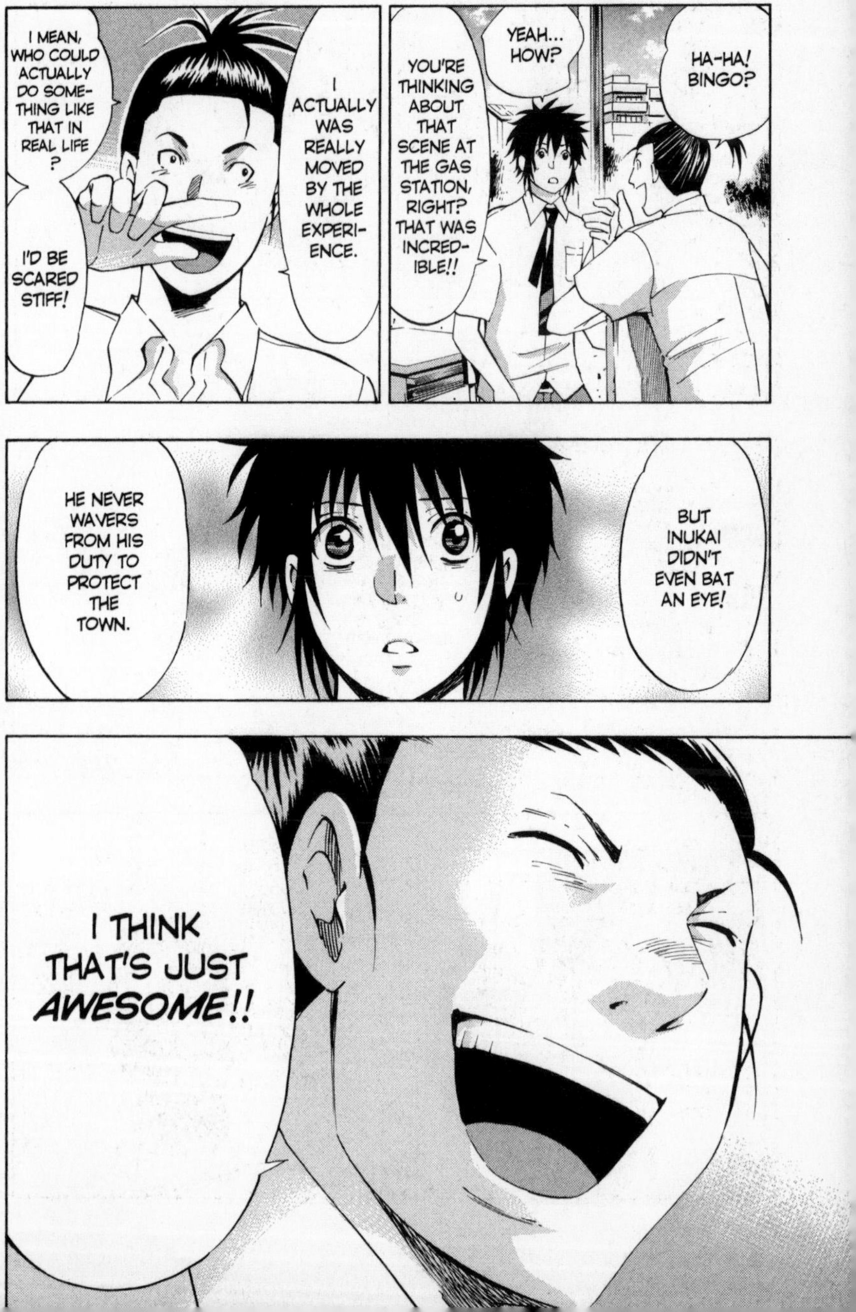
HA-HA! BINGO?
YEAH... HOW?
YOU'RE THINKING ABOUT THAT SCENE AT THE GAS STATION, RIGHT? THAT WAS INCREDIBLE!!
I ACTUALLY WAS REALLY MOVED BY THE WHOLE EXPERIENCE.
I MEAN, WHO COULD ACTUALLY DO SOMETHING LIKE THAT IN REAL LIFE?
I'D BE SCARED STIFF!
BUT INUKAI DIDN'T EVEN BAT AN EYE!
HE NEVER WAVERS FROM HIS DUTY TO PROTECT THE TOWN.
I THINK THAT'S JUST *AWESOME*!!

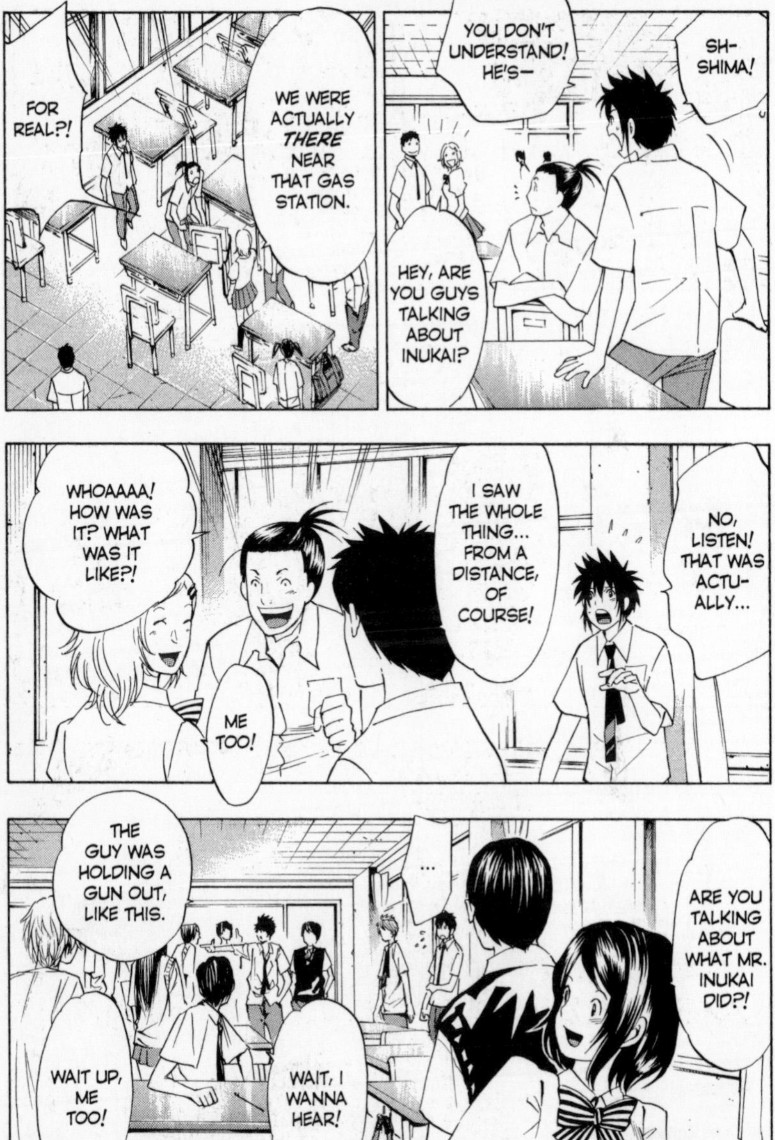
SH-SHIMA!
YOU DON'T UNDERSTAND! HE'S—
HEY, ARE YOU GUYS TALKING ABOUT INUKAI?
WE WERE ACTUALLY *THERE* NEAR THAT GAS STATION.
FOR REAL?!
NO, LISTEN! THAT WAS ACTU-ALLY...
I SAW THE WHOLE THING... FROM A DISTANCE, OF COURSE!
WHOAAAA! HOW WAS IT? WHAT WAS IT LIKE?!
ME TOO!
ARE YOU TALKING ABOUT WHAT MR. INUKAI DID?!
...
THE GUY WAS HOLDING A GUN OUT, LIKE THIS.
WAIT, I WANNA HEAR!
WAIT UP, ME TOO!

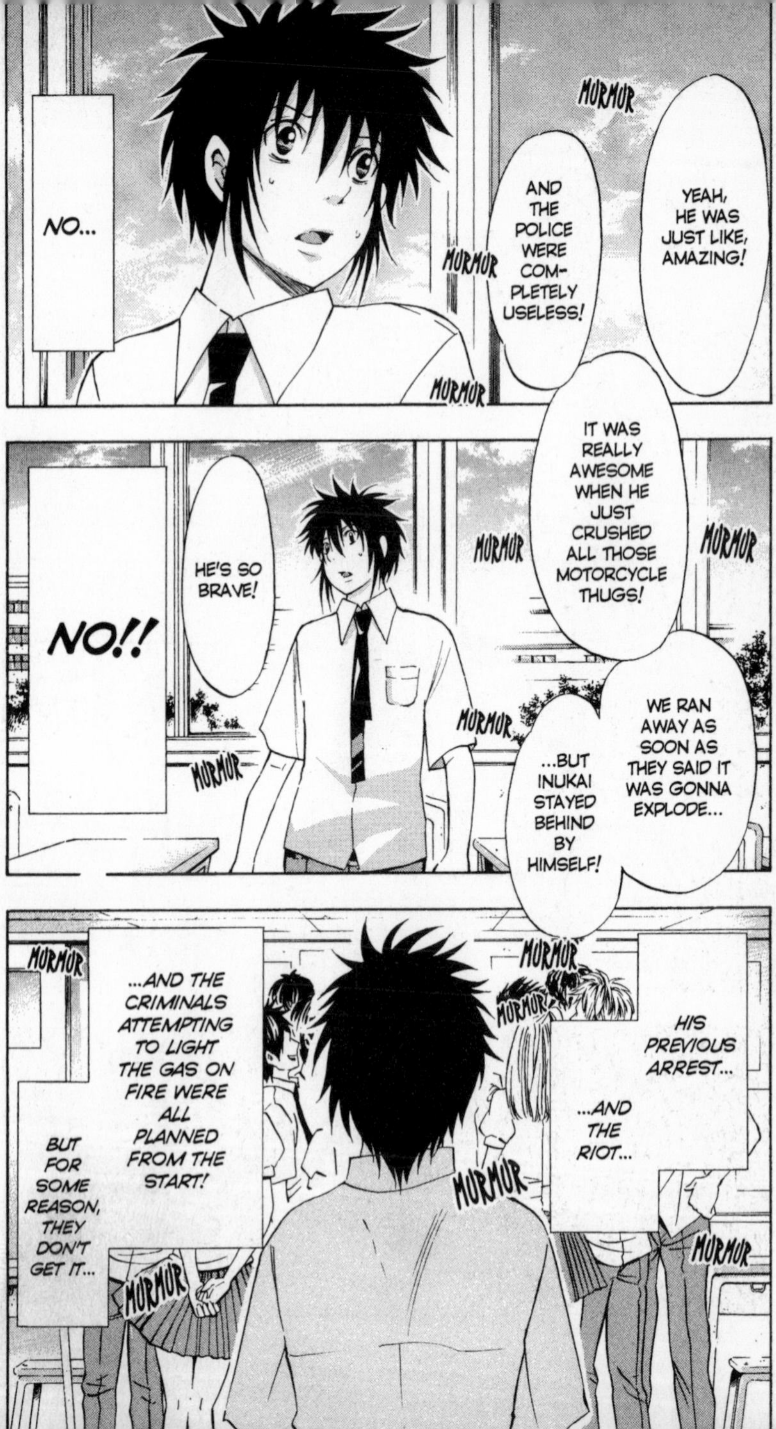
MURMUR
YEAH, HE WAS JUST LIKE, AMAZING!
AND THE POLICE WERE COM-PLETELY USELESS!
MURMUR
MURMUR
NO...
IT WAS REALLY AWESOME WHEN HE JUST CRUSHED ALL THOSE MOTORCYCLE THUGS!
MURMUR
MURMUR
HE'S SO BRAVE!
NO!!
WE RAN AWAY AS SOON AS THEY SAID IT WAS GONNA EXPLODE...
...BUT INUKAI STAYED BEHIND BY HIMSELF!
MURMUR
MURMUR
MURMUR
HIS PREVIOUS ARREST...
...AND THE RIOT...
MURMUR
MURMUR
...AND THE CRIMINALS ATTEMPTING TO LIGHT THE GAS ON FIRE WERE ALL PLANNED FROM THE START!
MURMUR
BUT FOR SOME REASON, THEY DON'T GET IT...
MURMUR

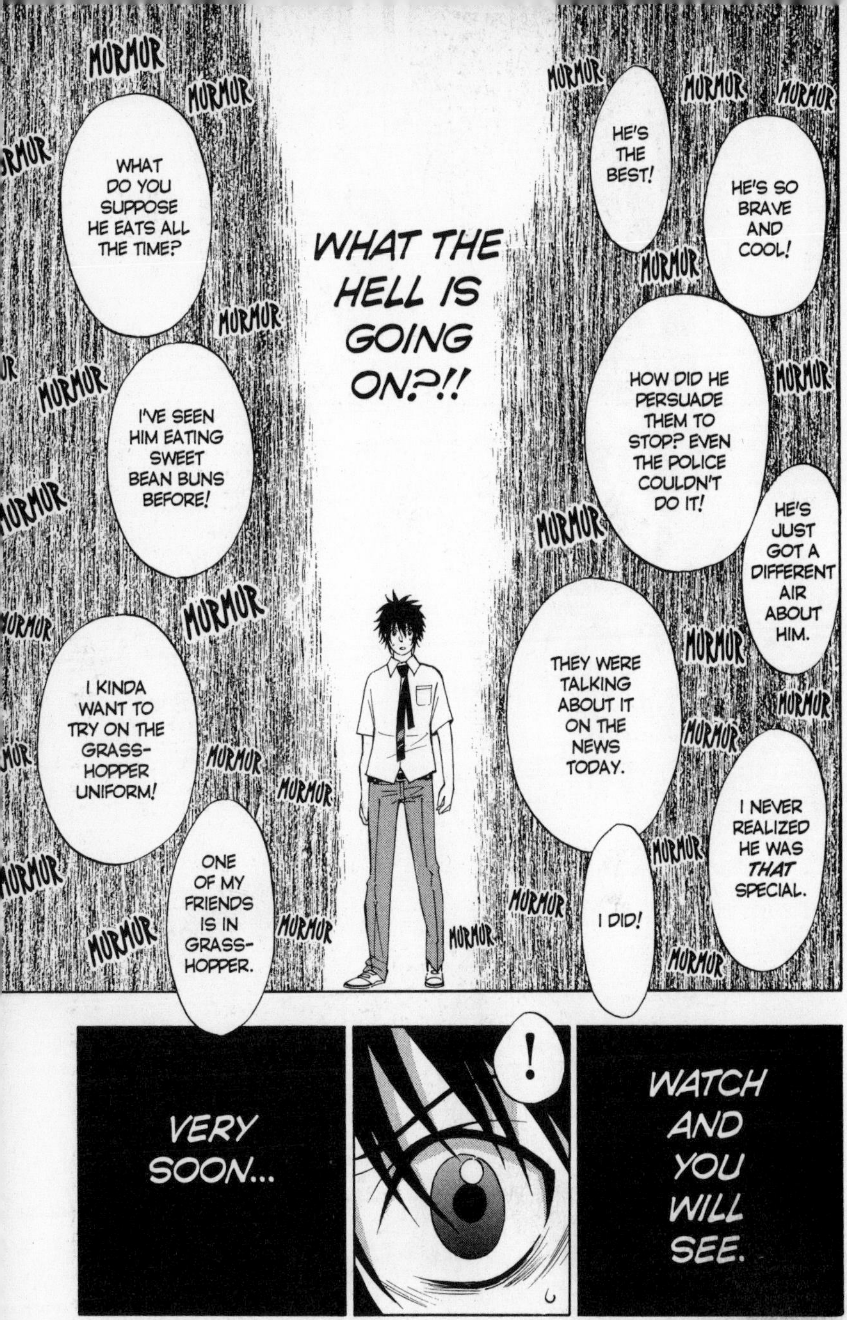
MURMUR
MURMUR
MURMUR
HE'S SO BRAVE AND COOL!
HE'S THE BEST!
MURMUR
HOW DID HE PERSUADE THEM TO STOP? EVEN THE POLICE COULDN'T DO IT!
MURMUR
HE'S JUST GOT A DIFFERENT AIR ABOUT HIM.
MURMUR
MURMUR
MURMUR
MURMUR
THEY WERE TALKING ABOUT IT ON THE NEWS TODAY.
I NEVER REALIZED HE WAS *THAT* SPECIAL.
MURMUR
I DID!
MURMUR
MURMUR
WHAT THE HELL IS GOING ON?!!
MURMUR
MURMUR
MURMUR
MURMUR
WHAT DO YOU SUPPOSE HE EATS ALL THE TIME?
MURMUR
MURMUR
I'VE SEEN HIM EATING SWEET BEAN BUNS BEFORE!
MURMUR
MURMUR
MURMUR
I KINDA WANT TO TRY ON THE GRASS-HOPPER UNIFORM!
MURMUR
MURMUR
MURMUR
ONE OF MY FRIENDS IS IN GRASS-HOPPER.
MURMUR
WATCH AND YOU WILL SEE.
!
VERY SOON...

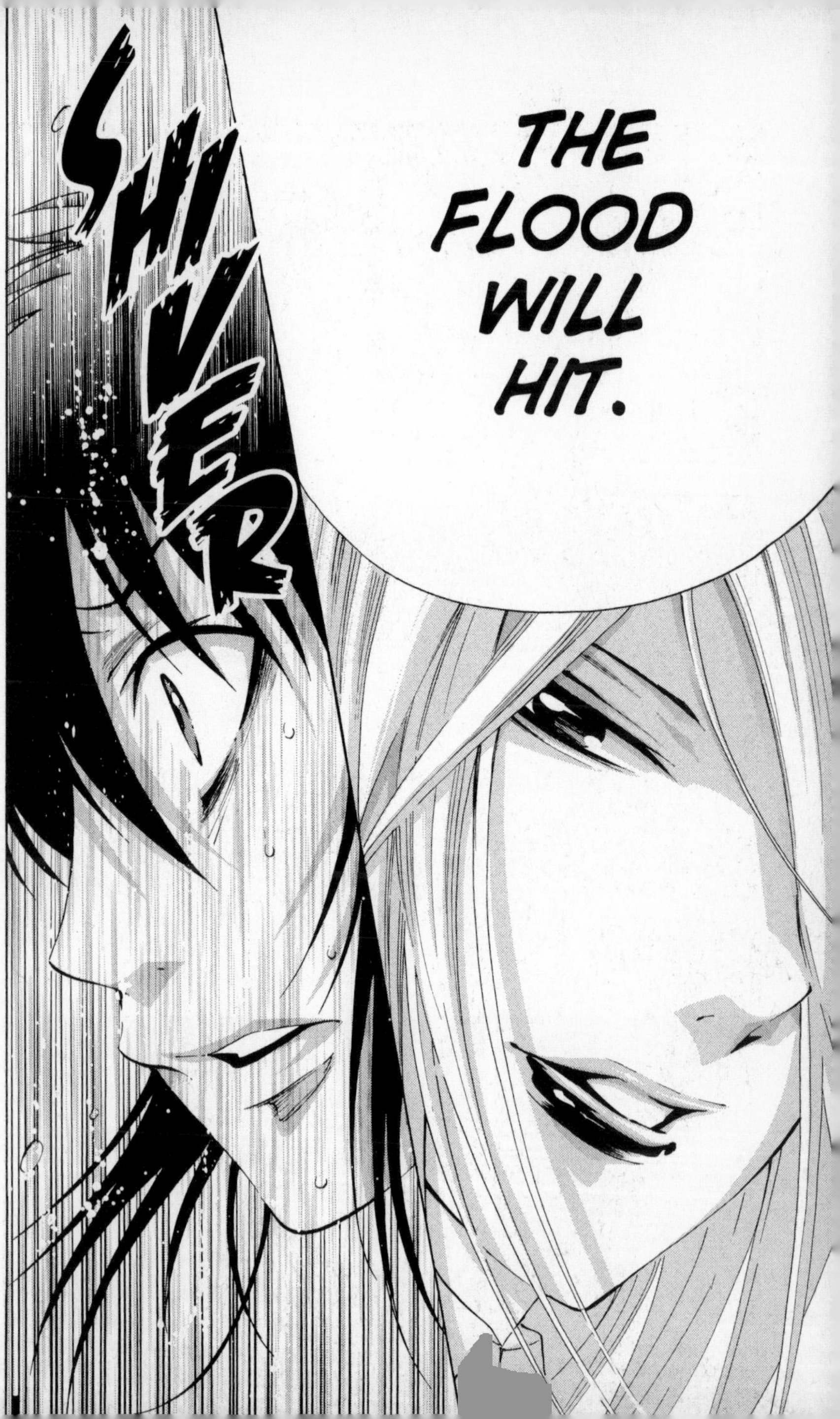
THE FLOOD WILL HIT.
SHIVER

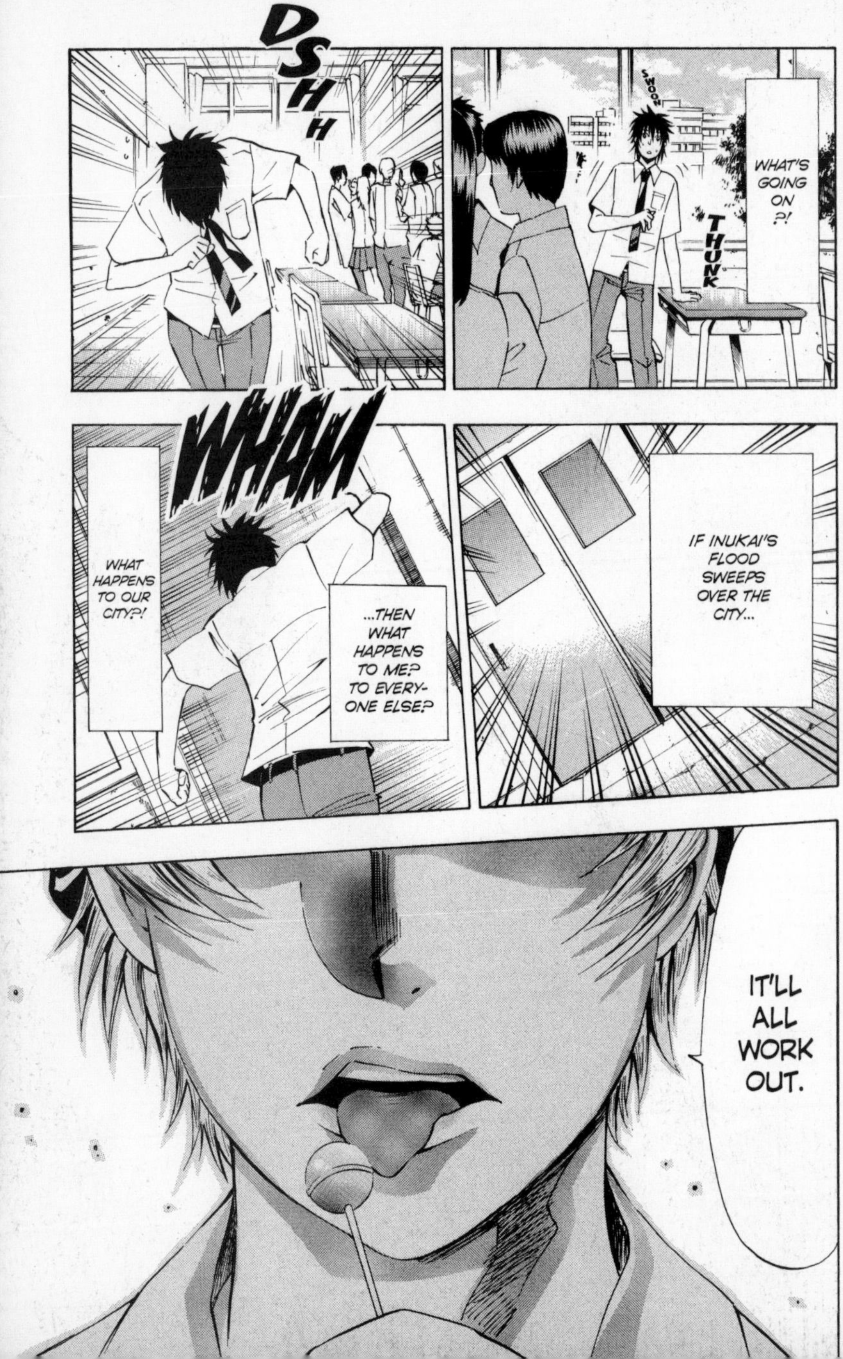
SWOON
THUNK
WHAT'S GOING ON ?!
DSHH
IF INUKAI'S FLOOD SWEEPS OVER THE CITY...
WHAM
...THEN WHAT HAPPENS TO ME? TO EVERY-ONE ELSE?
WHAT HAPPENS TO OUR CITY?!
IT'LL ALL WORK OUT.

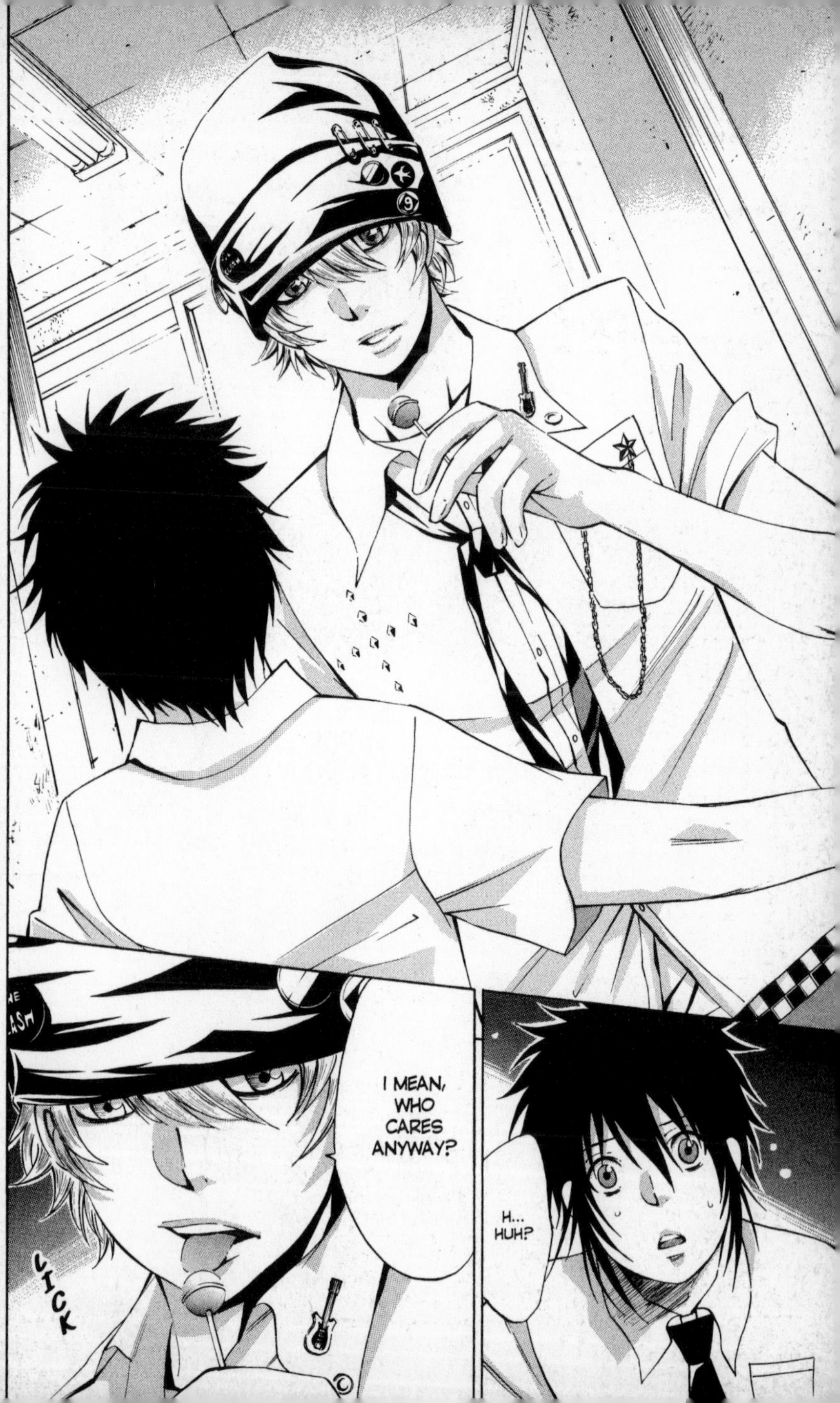
H... HUH?
I MEAN, WHO CARES ANYWAY?
LICK

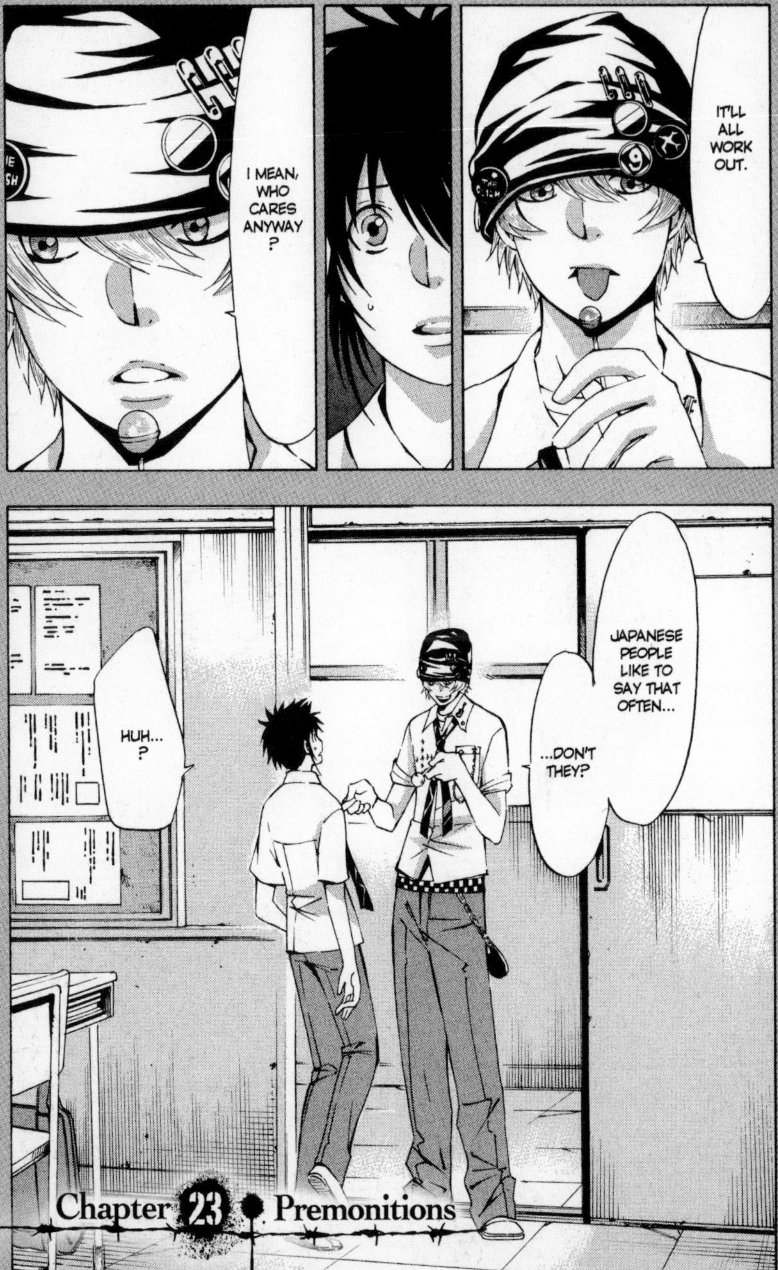
IT'LL ALL WORK OUT.
I MEAN, WHO CARES ANYWAY ?
JAPANESE PEOPLE LIKE TO SAY THAT OFTEN...
...DON'T THEY?
HUH... ?

Chapter 23 Premonitions

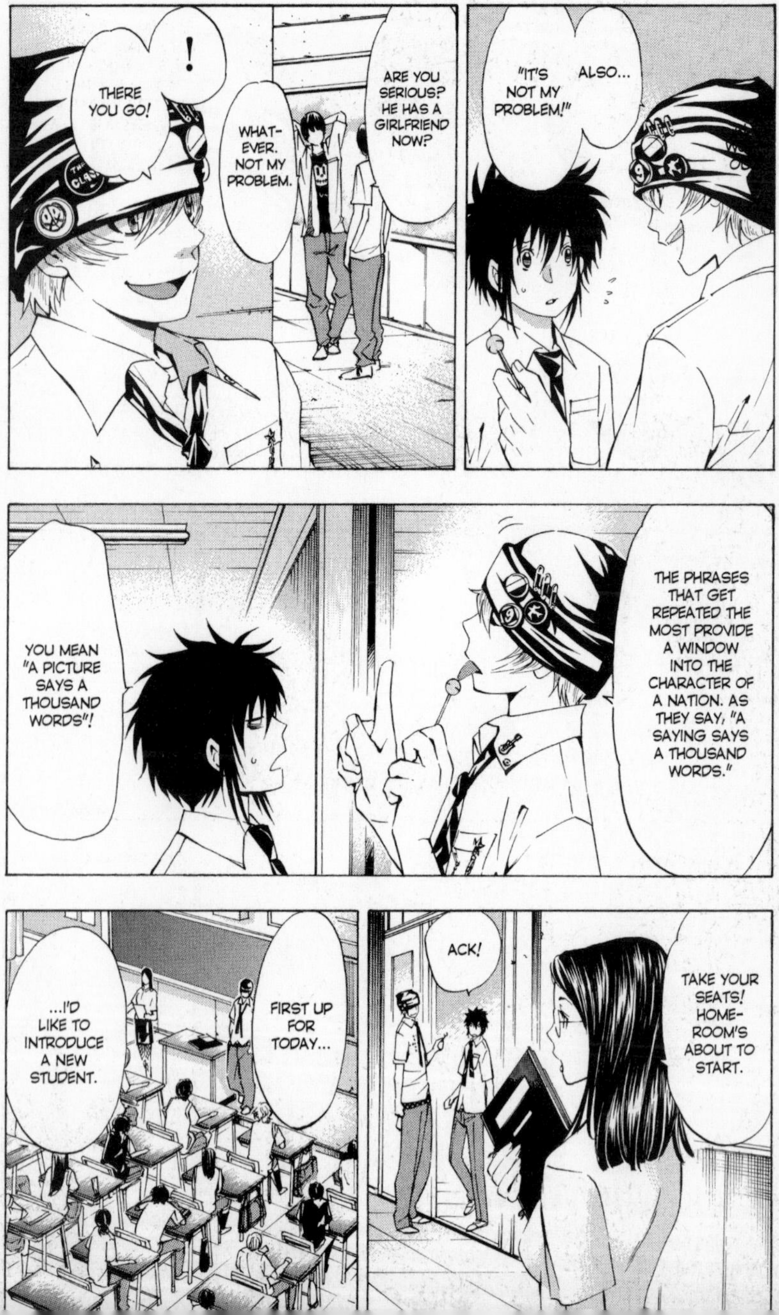
ALSO...
"IT'S NOT MY PROBLEM!"
ARE YOU SERIOUS? HE HAS A GIRLFRIEND NOW?
WHAT-EVER. NOT MY PROBLEM.
!
THERE YOU GO!
THE PHRASES THAT GET REPEATED THE MOST PROVIDE A WINDOW INTO THE CHARACTER OF A NATION. AS THEY SAY, "A SAYING SAYS A THOUSAND WORDS."
YOU MEAN "A PICTURE SAYS A THOUSAND WORDS"!
TAKE YOUR SEATS! HOME-ROOM'S ABOUT TO START.
ACK!
FIRST UP FOR TODAY...
...I'D LIKE TO INTRODUCE A NEW STUDENT.

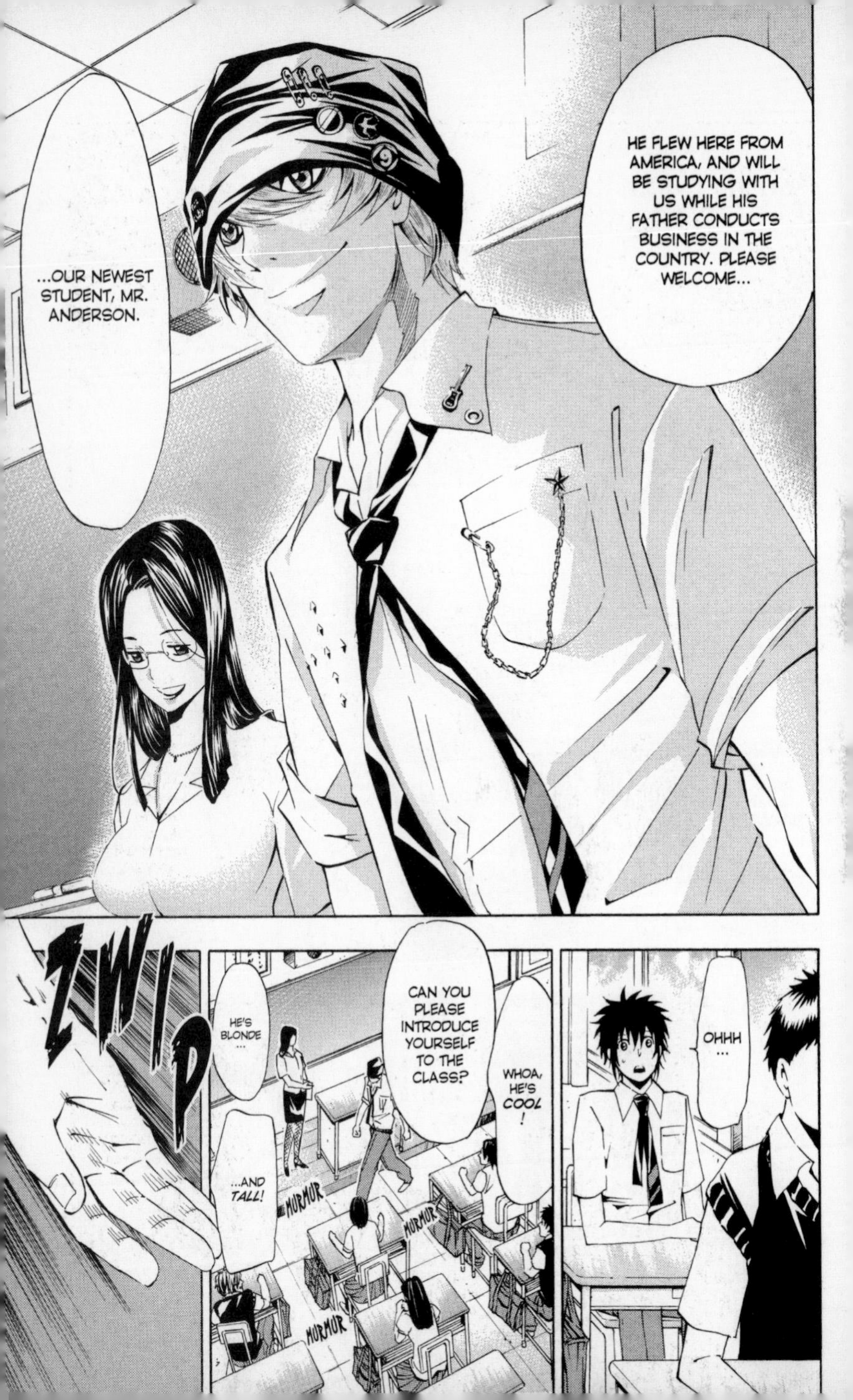
HE FLEW HERE FROM AMERICA, AND WILL BE STUDYING WITH US WHILE HIS FATHER CONDUCTS BUSINESS IN THE COUNTRY. PLEASE WELCOME...
...OUR NEWEST STUDENT, MR. ANDERSON.
OHHH ...
WHOA, HE'S *COOL*!
CAN YOU PLEASE INTRODUCE YOURSELF TO THE CLASS?
HE'S BLONDE ...
...AND *TALL*!
MURMUR
MURMUR
MURMUR
ZWIP

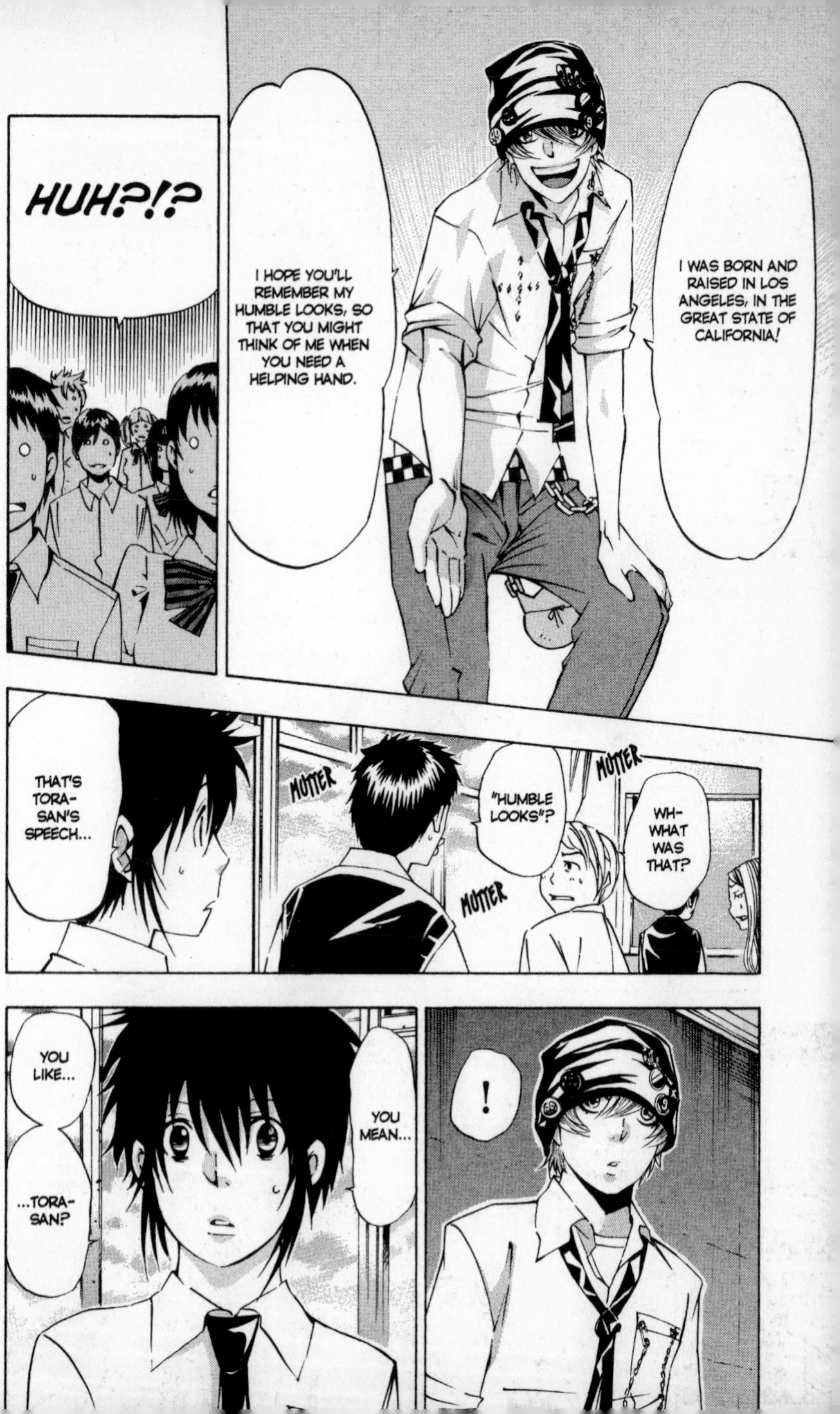
I WAS BORN AND RAISED IN LOS ANGELES, IN THE GREAT STATE OF CALIFORNIA!
I HOPE YOU'LL REMEMBER MY HUMBLE LOOKS, SO THAT YOU MIGHT THINK OF ME WHEN YOU NEED A HELPING HAND.
HUH?!?
WH-WHAT WAS THAT?
MUTTER
"HUMBLE LOOKS"?
MUTTER
MUTTER
THAT'S TORA-SAN'S SPEECH...
!
YOU MEAN...
YOU LIKE...
...TORA-SAN?

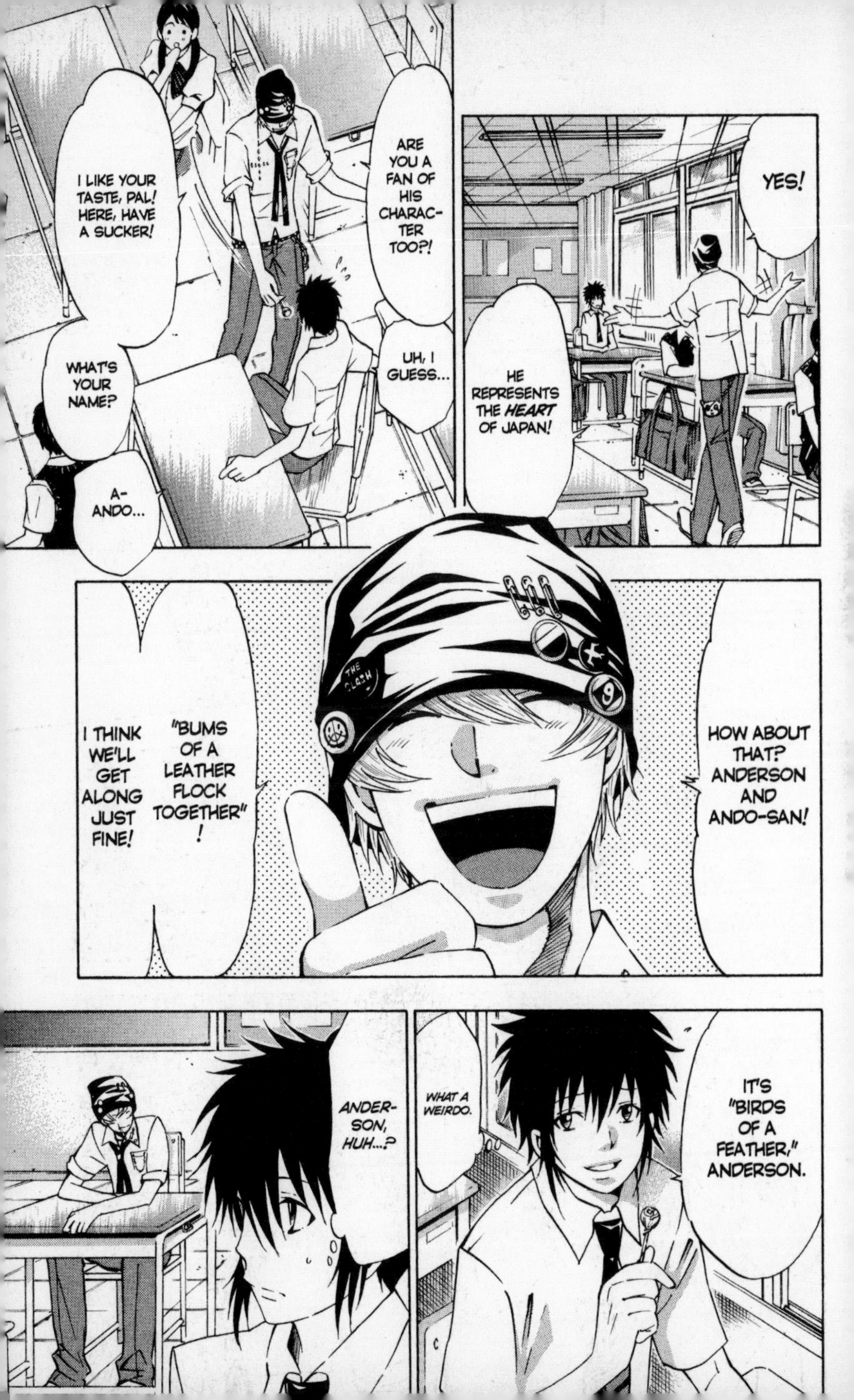
YES!
HE REPRESENTS THE *HEART* OF JAPAN!
ARE YOU A FAN OF HIS CHARAC-TER TOO?!
UH, I GUESS...
I LIKE YOUR TASTE, PAL! HERE, HAVE A SUCKER!
WHAT'S YOUR NAME?
A- ANDO...
HOW ABOUT THAT? ANDERSON AND ANDO-SAN!
"BUMS OF A LEATHER FLOCK TOGETHER"!
I THINK WE'LL GET ALONG JUST FINE!
IT'S "BIRDS OF A FEATHER," ANDERSON.
WHAT A WEIRDO.
ANDER-SON, HUH...?

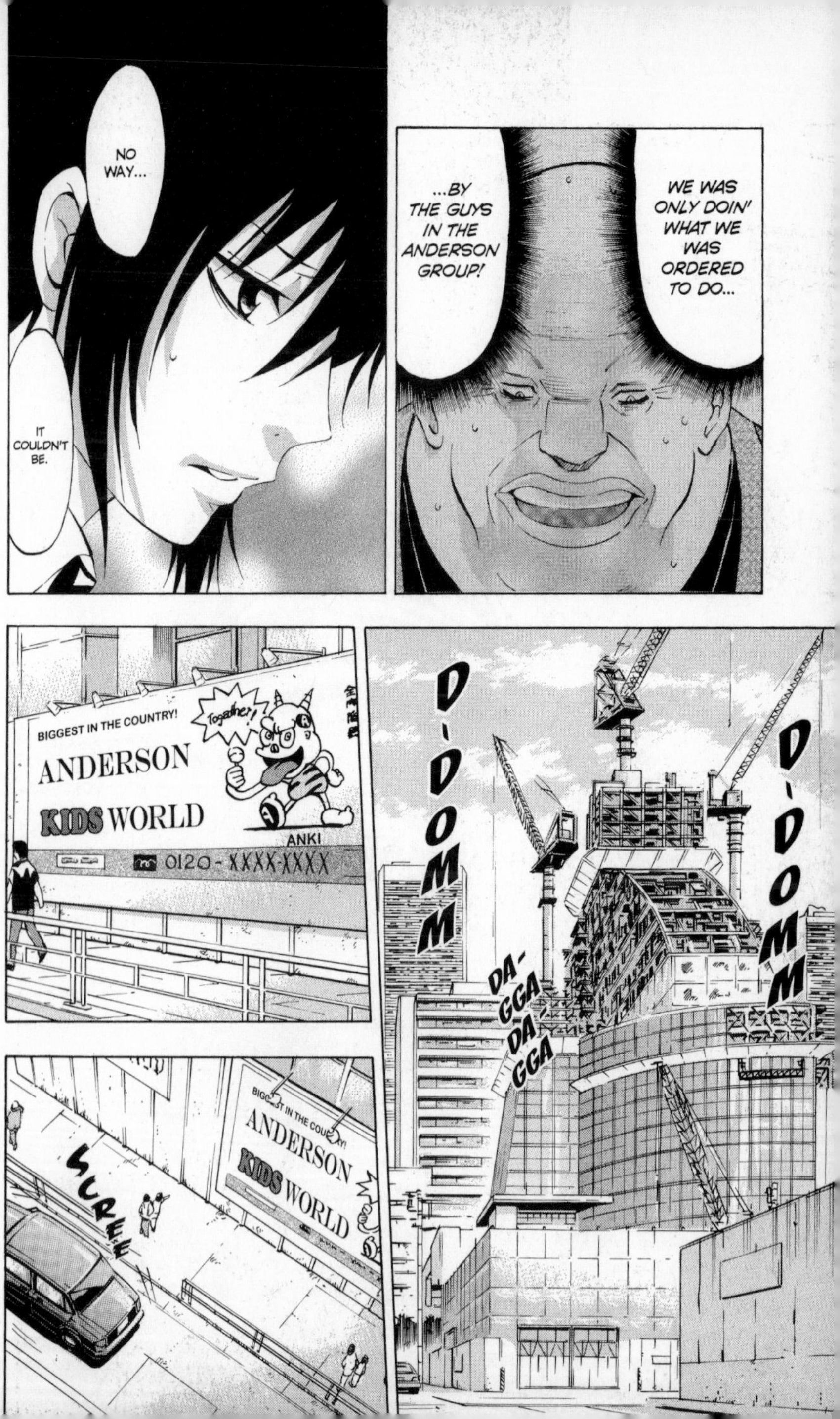
WE WAS ONLY DOIN' WHAT WE WAS ORDERED TO DO...
...BY THE GUYS IN THE ANDERSON GROUP!
NO WAY...
IT COULDN'T BE.
D-DOMM
D-DOMM
DA-GGA DA-GGA
BIGGEST IN THE COUNTRY!
ANDERSON
KIDS WORLD
Together!
ANKI
0120-XXXX-XXXX
SCREE
BIGGEST IN THE COUNTRY!
ANDERSON
KIDS WORLD

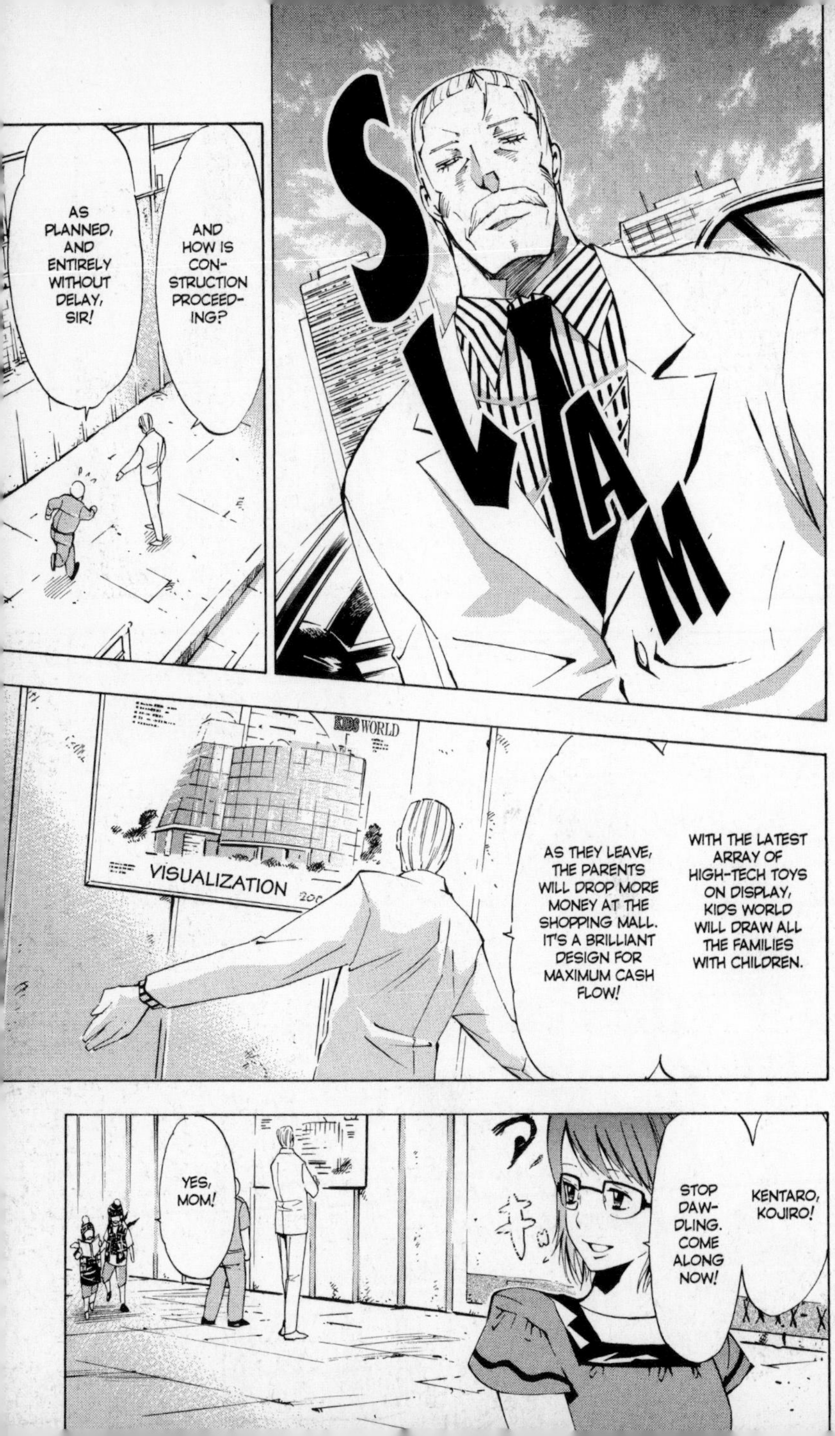
SLAM
AND HOW IS CONSTRUCTION PROCEEDING?
AS PLANNED, AND ENTIRELY WITHOUT DELAY, SIR!
KIDS WORLD
VISUALIZATION
WITH THE LATEST ARRAY OF HIGH-TECH TOYS ON DISPLAY, KIDS WORLD WILL DRAW ALL THE FAMILIES WITH CHILDREN.
AS THEY LEAVE, THE PARENTS WILL DROP MORE MONEY AT THE SHOPPING MALL. IT'S A BRILLIANT DESIGN FOR MAXIMUM CASH FLOW!
KENTARO, KOJIRO!
STOP DAWDLING. COME ALONG NOW!
YES, MOM!

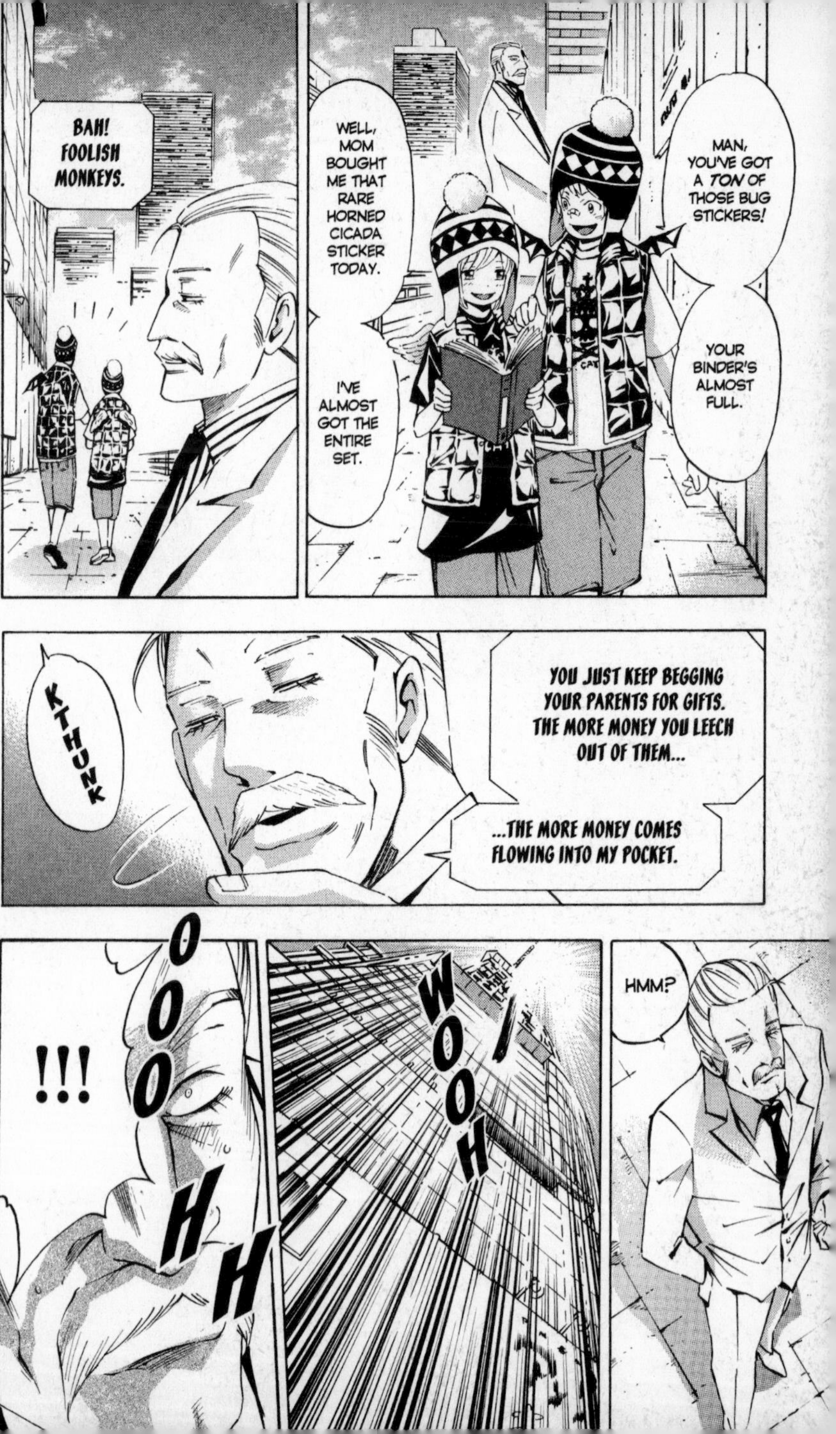
MAN, YOU'VE GOT A *TON* OF THOSE BUG STICKERS!
YOUR BINDER'S ALMOST FULL.
WELL, MOM BOUGHT ME THAT RARE HORNED CICADA STICKER TODAY.
I'VE ALMOST GOT THE ENTIRE SET.
BAH! FOOLISH MONKEYS.
YOU JUST KEEP BEGGING YOUR PARENTS FOR GIFTS. THE MORE MONEY YOU LEECH OUT OF THEM...
...THE MORE MONEY COMES FLOWING INTO MY POCKET.
KTHUNK
HMM?
WOOOH
OOOHHH
!!!

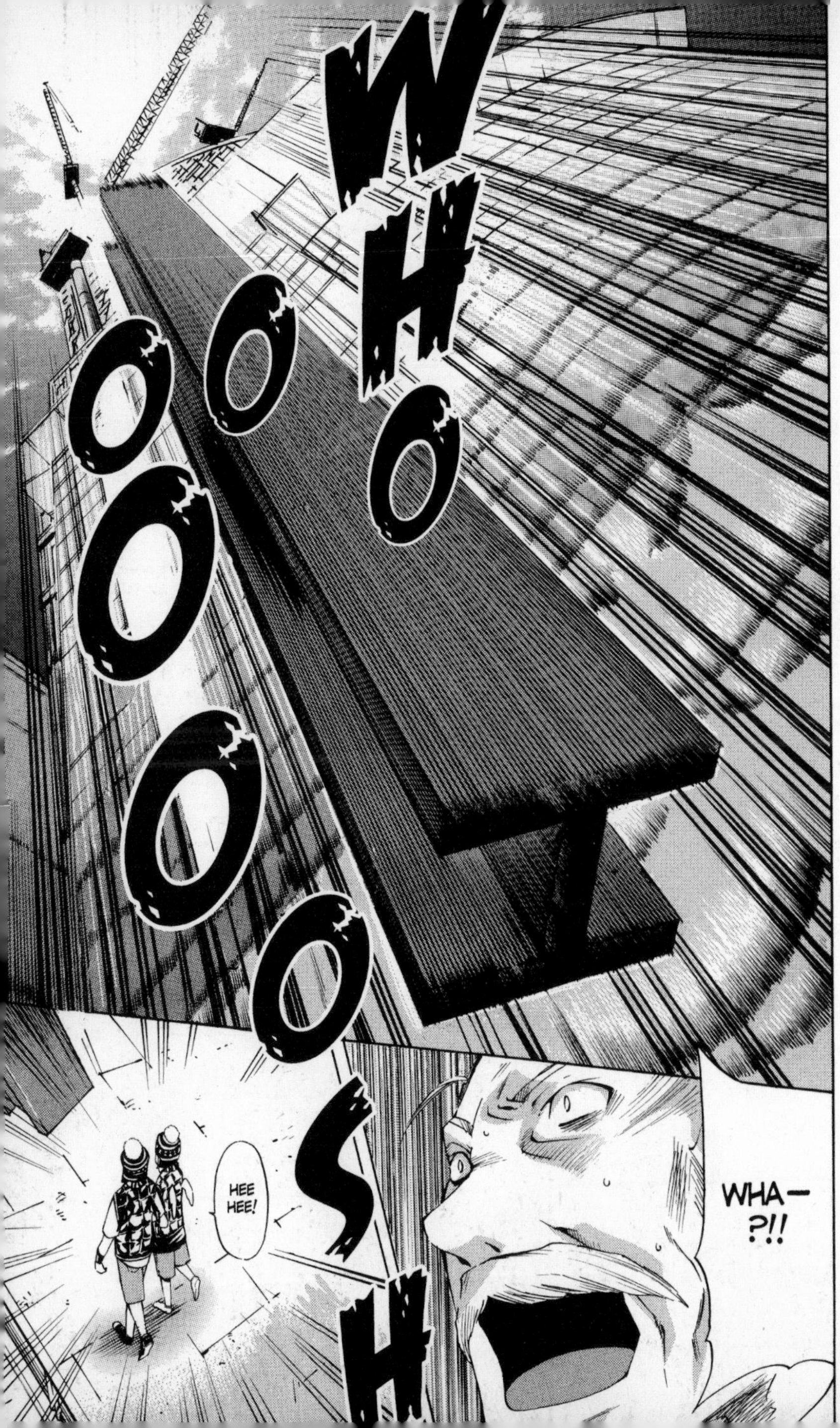
WHOOOOOOSH
WHA— ?!!
HEE HEE!

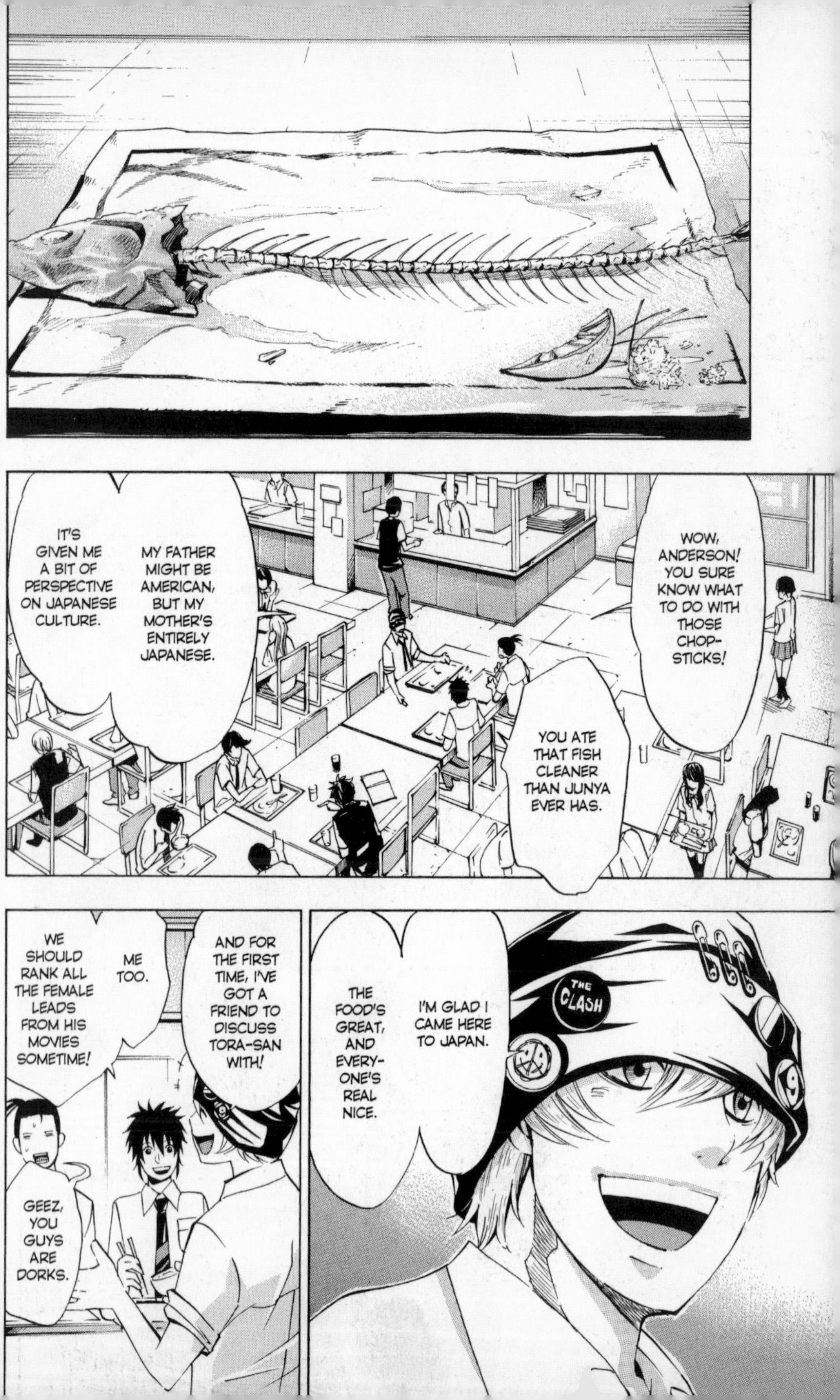
WOW, ANDERSON! YOU SURE KNOW WHAT TO DO WITH THOSE CHOP-STICKS!
YOU ATE THAT FISH CLEANER THAN JUNYA EVER HAS.
MY FATHER MIGHT BE AMERICAN, BUT MY MOTHER'S ENTIRELY JAPANESE.
IT'S GIVEN ME A BIT OF PERSPECTIVE ON JAPANESE CULTURE.
THE CLASH
I'M GLAD I CAME HERE TO JAPAN.
THE FOOD'S GREAT, AND EVERY-ONE'S REAL NICE.
AND FOR THE FIRST TIME, I'VE GOT A FRIEND TO DISCUSS TORA-SAN WITH!
ME TOO.
WE SHOULD RANK ALL THE FEMALE LEADS FROM HIS MOVIES SOMETIME!
GEEZ, YOU GUYS ARE DORKS.

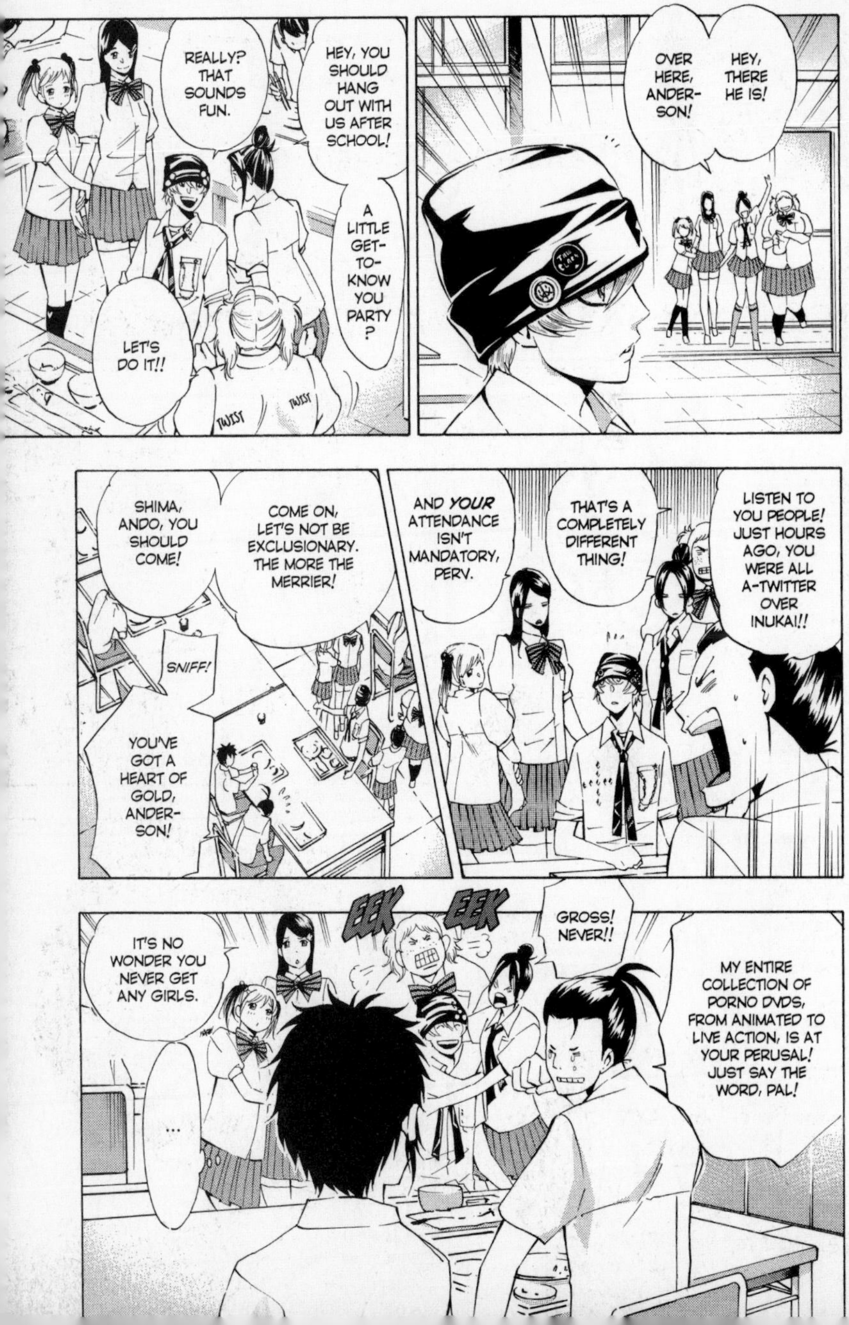
HEY, THERE HE IS!
OVER HERE, ANDER-SON!
HEY, YOU SHOULD HANG OUT WITH US AFTER SCHOOL!
A LITTLE GET-TO-KNOW YOU PARTY?
REALLY? THAT SOUNDS FUN.
LET'S DO IT!!
TWIST
TWIST
LISTEN TO YOU PEOPLE! JUST HOURS AGO, YOU WERE ALL A-TWITTER OVER INUKAI!!
THAT'S A COMPLETELY DIFFERENT THING!
AND YOUR ATTENDANCE ISN'T MANDATORY, PERV.
COME ON, LET'S NOT BE EXCLUSIONARY. THE MORE THE MERRIER!
SHIMA, ANDO, YOU SHOULD COME!
SNIFF!
YOU'VE GOT A HEART OF GOLD, ANDER-SON!
MY ENTIRE COLLECTION OF PORNO DVDS, FROM ANIMATED TO LIVE ACTION, IS AT YOUR PERUSAL! JUST SAY THE WORD, PAL!
GROSS! NEVER!!
EEK
EEK
IT'S NO WONDER YOU NEVER GET ANY GIRLS.
...

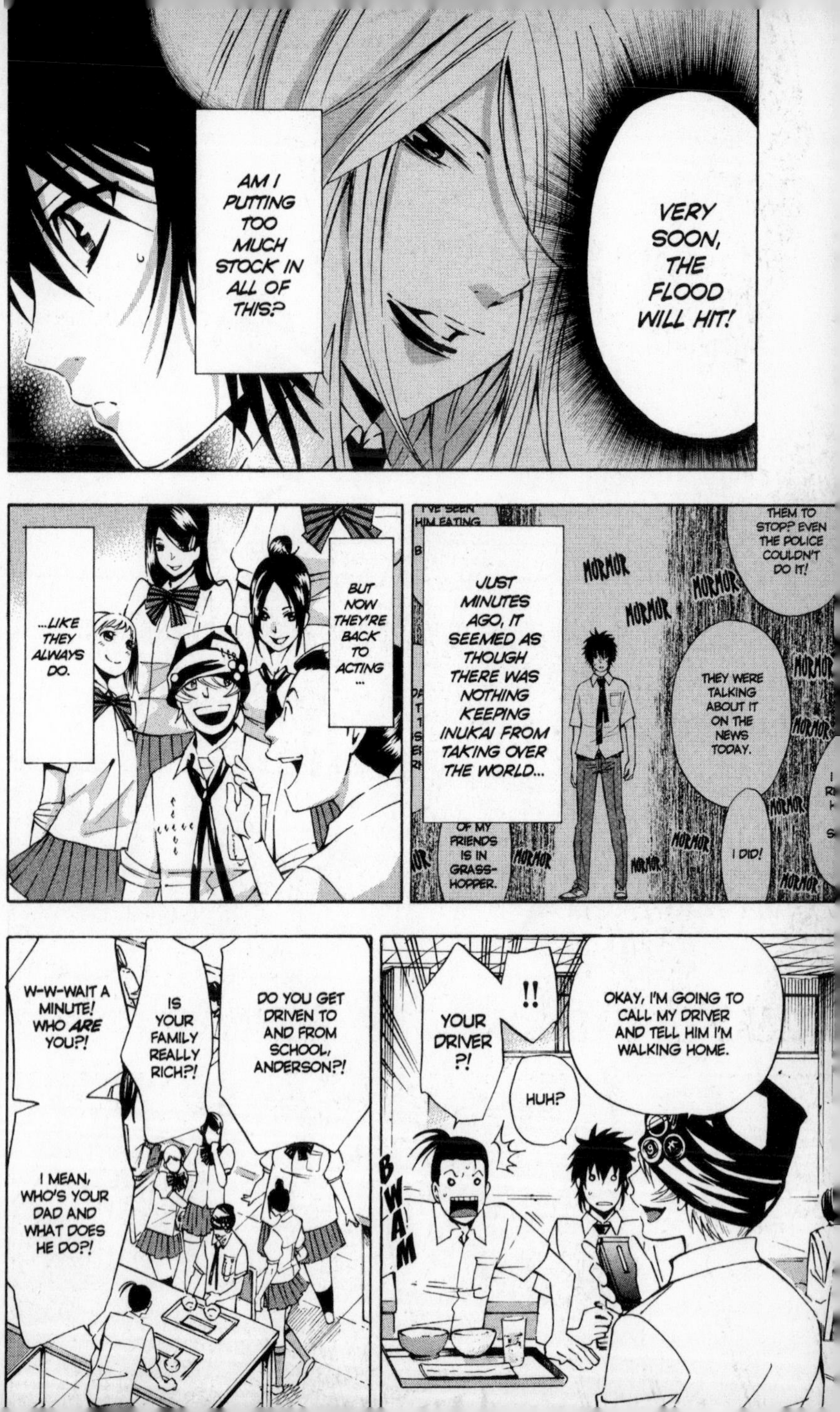
VERY SOON, THE FLOOD WILL HIT!
AM I PUTTING TOO MUCH STOCK IN ALL OF THIS?
THEM TO STOP? EVEN THE POLICE COULDN'T DO IT!
MORMOR
MORMOR
MORMOR
THEY WERE TALKING ABOUT IT ON THE NEWS TODAY.
JUST MINUTES AGO, IT SEEMED AS THOUGH THERE WAS NOTHING KEEPING INUKAI FROM TAKING OVER THE WORLD...
I DID!
MORMOR
OF MY FRIENDS IS IN GRASS-HOPPER.
BUT NOW THEY'RE BACK TO ACTING ...
...LIKE THEY ALWAYS DO.
OKAY, I'M GOING TO CALL MY DRIVER AND TELL HIM I'M WALKING HOME.
!!
YOUR DRIVER?!
HUH?
BWAM
DO YOU GET DRIVEN TO AND FROM SCHOOL, ANDERSON?!
IS YOUR FAMILY REALLY RICH?!
W-W-WAIT A MINUTE! WHO *ARE* YOU?!
I MEAN, WHO'S YOUR DAD AND WHAT DOES HE DO?!

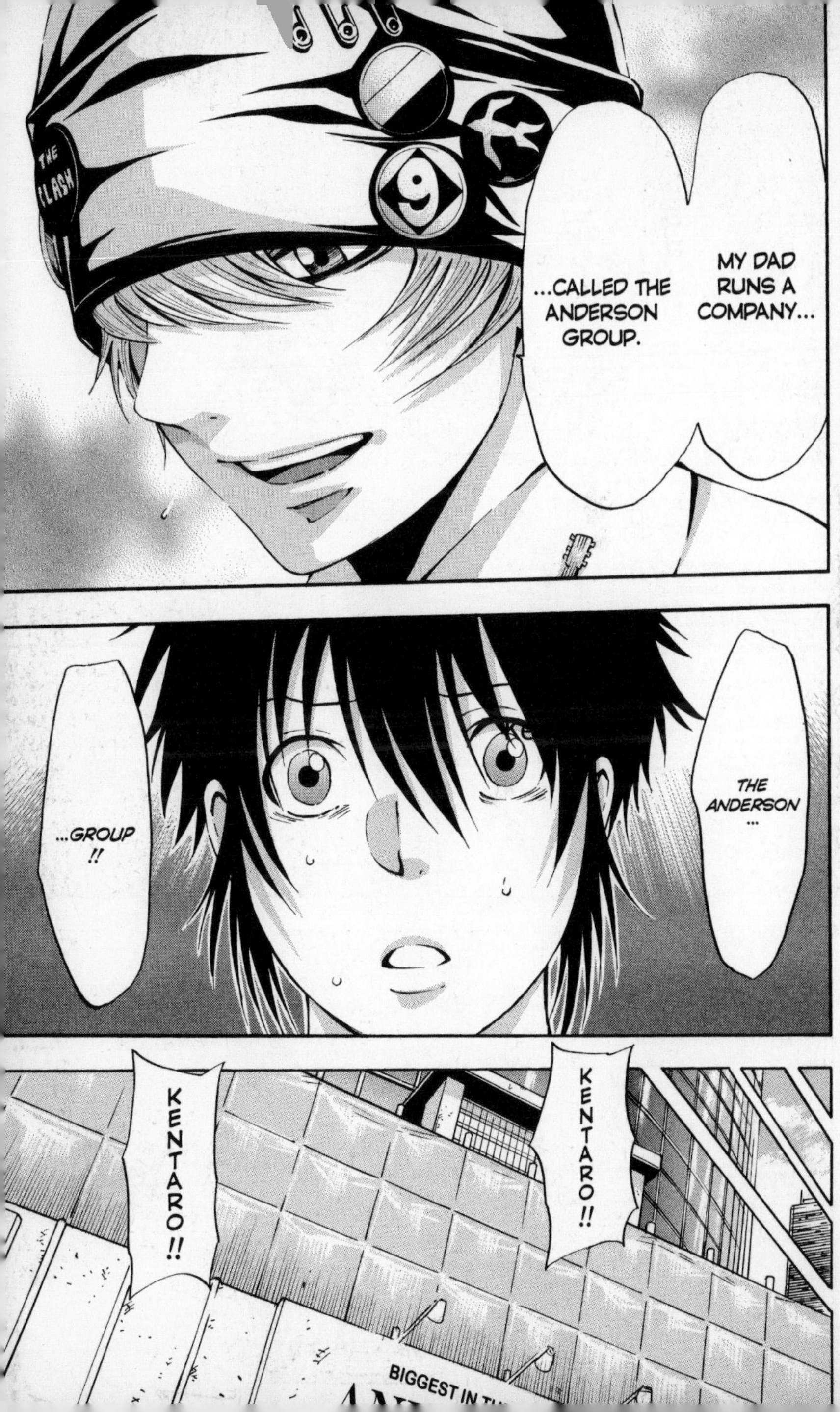
MY DAD RUNS A COMPANY...
...CALLED THE ANDERSON GROUP.
THE ANDERSON ...
...GROUP !!
KENTARO!!
KENTARO!!
BIGGEST IN

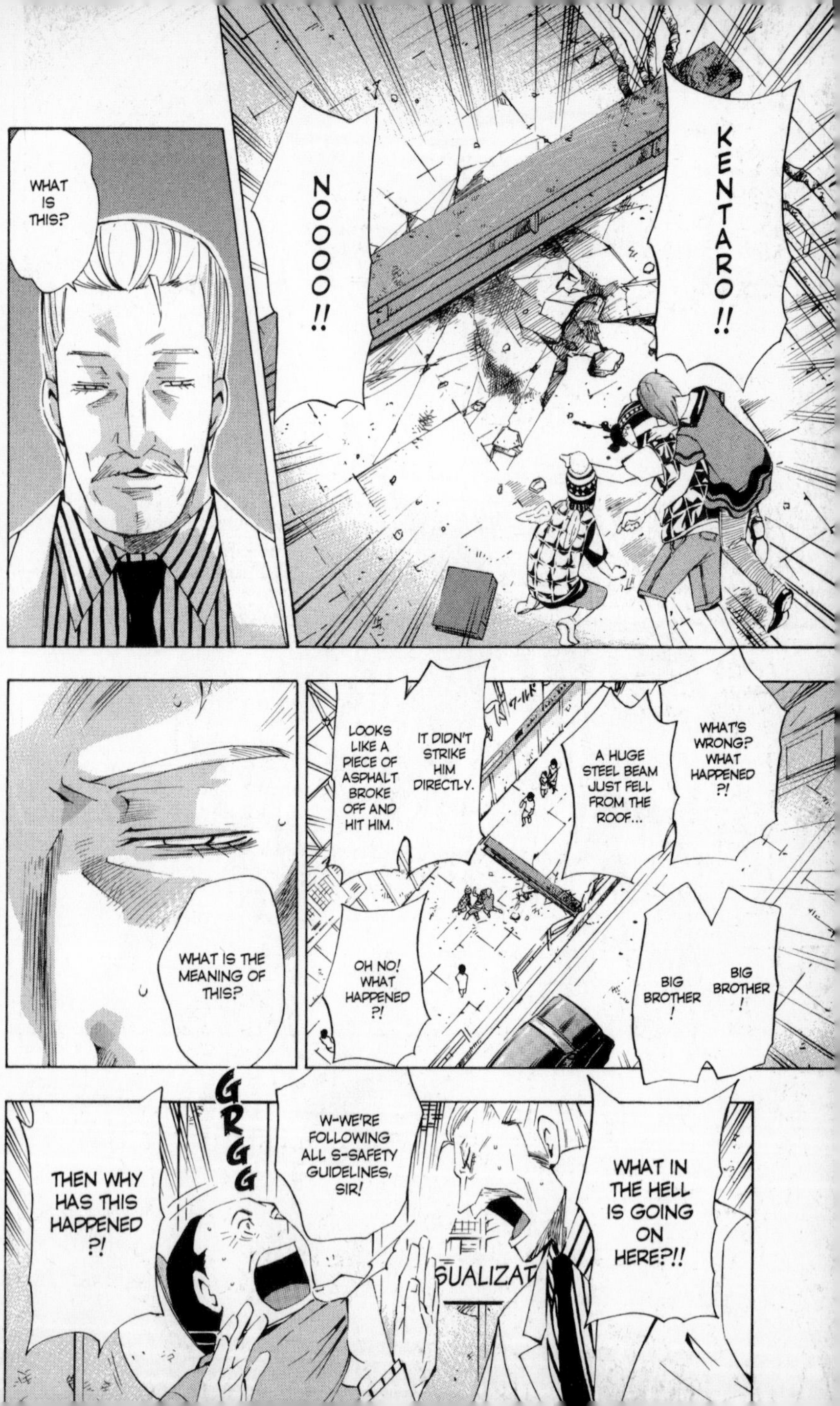
KENTARO!!
NOOOO!!
WHAT IS THIS?
WHAT'S WRONG? WHAT HAPPENED?!
A HUGE STEEL BEAM JUST FELL FROM THE ROOF...
IT DIDN'T STRIKE HIM DIRECTLY.
LOOKS LIKE A PIECE OF ASPHALT BROKE OFF AND HIT HIM.
BIG BROTHER!
BIG BROTHER!
OH NO! WHAT HAPPENED?!
WHAT IS THE MEANING OF THIS?
WHAT IN THE HELL IS GOING ON HERE?!!
W-WE'RE FOLLOWING ALL S-SAFETY GUIDELINES, SIR!
GRGG
THEN WHY HAS THIS HAPPENED?!
SUALIZAT

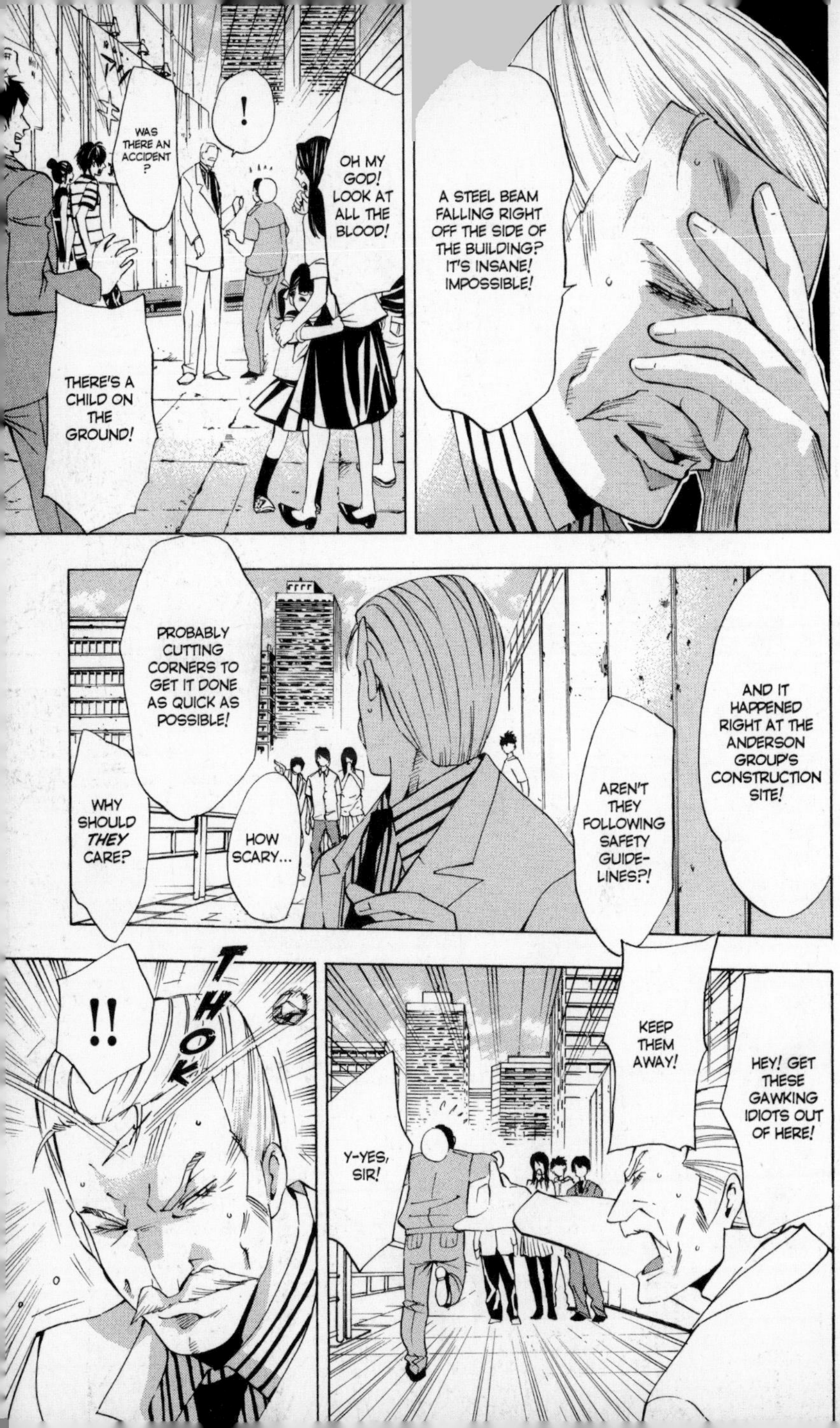
A STEEL BEAM FALLING RIGHT OFF THE SIDE OF THE BUILDING? IT'S INSANE! IMPOSSIBLE!
OH MY GOD! LOOK AT ALL THE BLOOD!
!
WAS THERE AN ACCIDENT?
THERE'S A CHILD ON THE GROUND!
AND IT HAPPENED RIGHT AT THE ANDERSON GROUP'S CONSTRUCTION SITE!
AREN'T THEY FOLLOWING SAFETY GUIDE-LINES?!
PROBABLY CUTTING CORNERS TO GET IT DONE AS QUICK AS POSSIBLE!
HOW SCARY...
WHY SHOULD *THEY* CARE?
HEY! GET THESE GAWKING IDIOTS OUT OF HERE!
KEEP THEM AWAY!
Y-YES, SIR!
THOK
!!

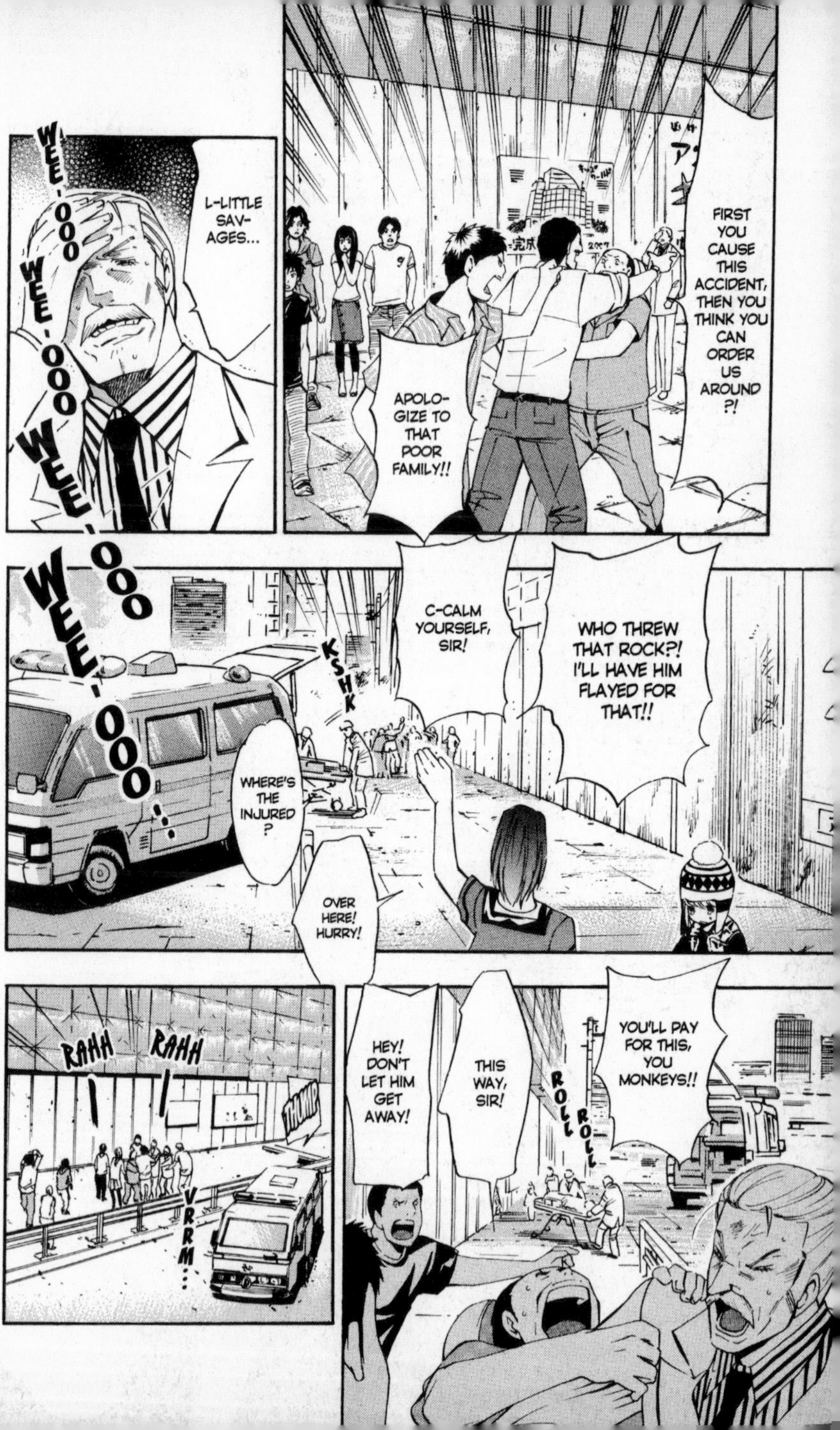
FIRST YOU CAUSE THIS ACCIDENT, THEN YOU THINK YOU CAN ORDER US AROUND?!
APOLOGIZE TO THAT POOR FAMILY!!
L-LITTLE SAV-AGES...
WEE-OOO WEE-OOO WEE-OOO WEE-OOO WEE-OOO...
WHO THREW THAT ROCK?! I'LL HAVE HIM FLAYED FOR THAT!!
C-CALM YOURSELF, SIR!
KSHK
WHERE'S THE INJURED?
OVER HERE! HURRY!
YOU'LL PAY FOR THIS, YOU MONKEYS!!
THIS WAY, SIR!
HEY! DON'T LET HIM GET AWAY!
ROLL ROLL
RAHH RAHH
THOMP
VRRM...

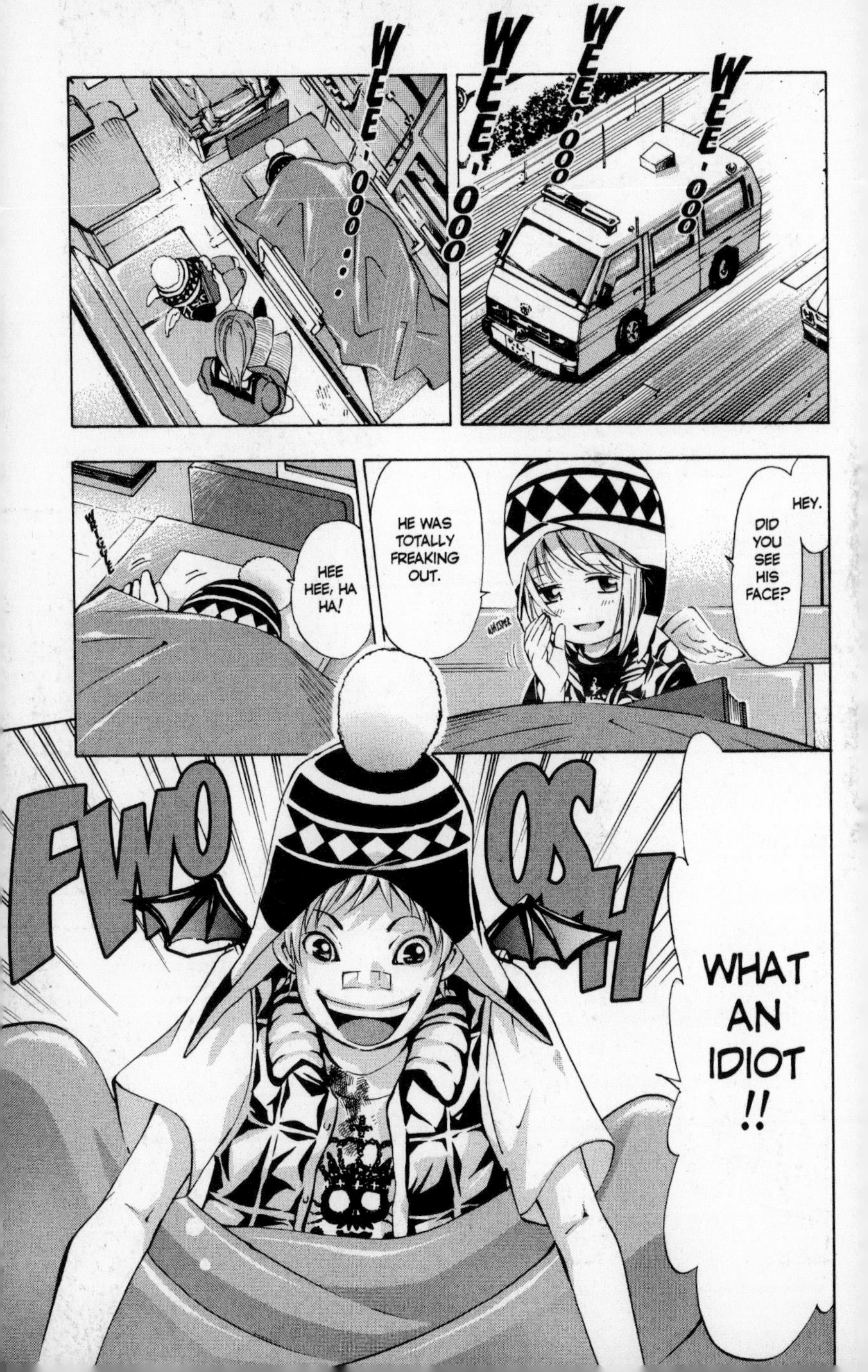
WEE-OOO
WEE-OOO
WEE-OOO
WEE-OOO...
HEY. DID YOU SEE HIS FACE?
WHISPER
HE WAS TOTALLY FREAKING OUT.
HEE HEE, HA HA!
WRIGGLE
FWOOSH
WHAT AN IDIOT!!

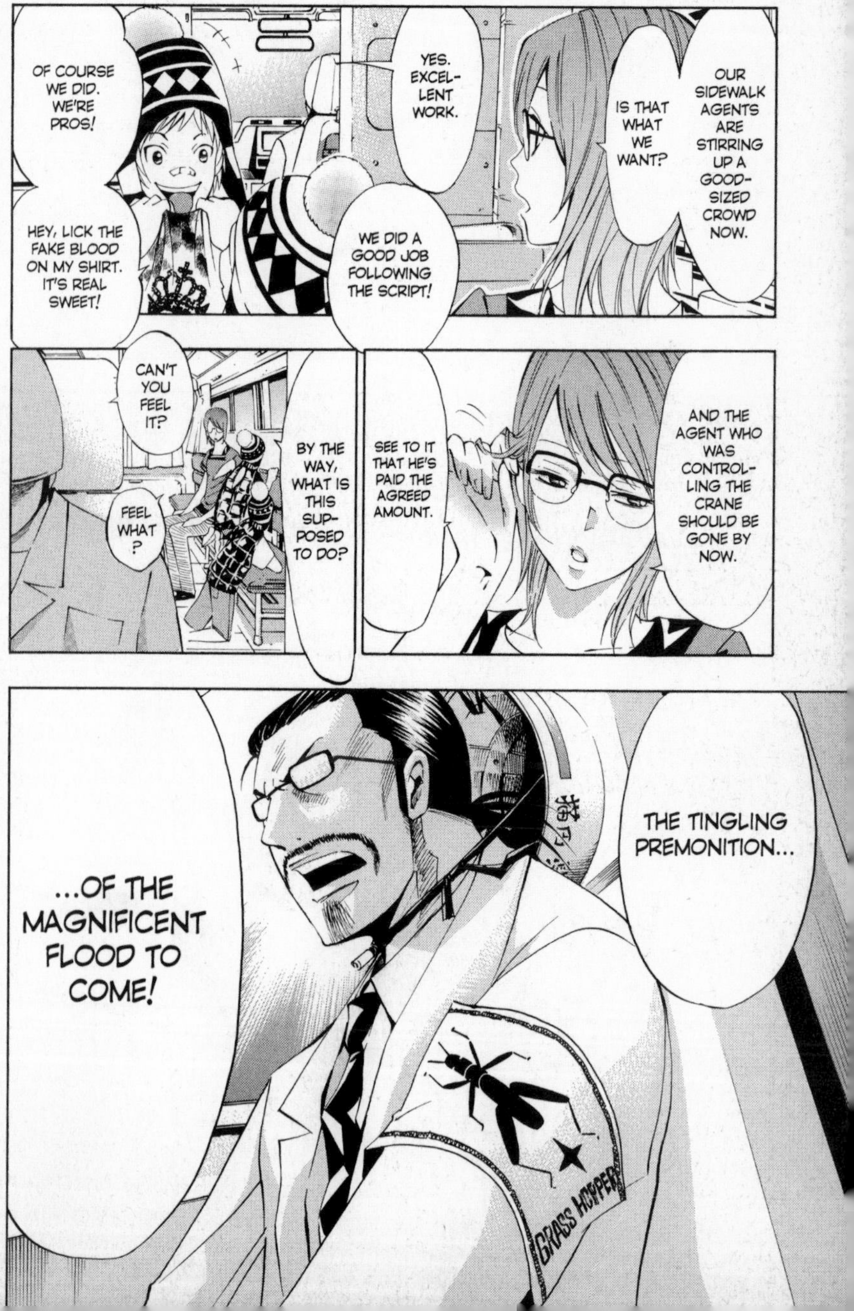
OUR SIDEWALK AGENTS ARE STIRRING UP A GOOD-SIZED CROWD NOW.
IS THAT WHAT WE WANT?
YES. EXCELLENT WORK.
WE DID A GOOD JOB FOLLOWING THE SCRIPT!
OF COURSE WE DID. WE'RE PROS!
HEY, LICK THE FAKE BLOOD ON MY SHIRT. IT'S REAL SWEET!
AND THE AGENT WHO WAS CONTROLLING THE CRANE SHOULD BE GONE BY NOW.
SEE TO IT THAT HE'S PAID THE AGREED AMOUNT.
BY THE WAY, WHAT IS THIS SUPPOSED TO DO?
CAN'T YOU FEEL IT?
FEEL WHAT?
THE TINGLING PREMONITION...
...OF THE MAGNIFICENT FLOOD TO COME!
GRASS HOPPER

Chapter 24 The Meaning of Life

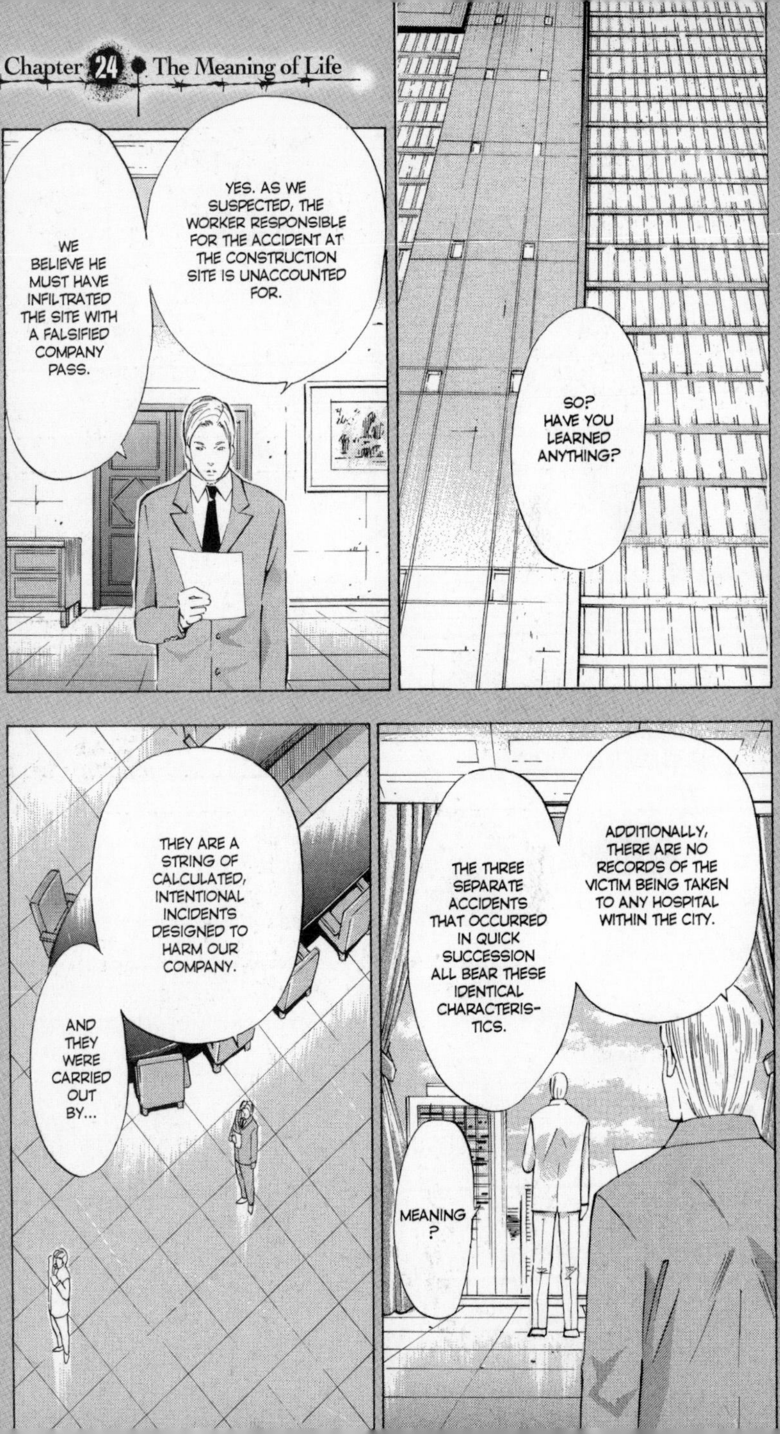
SO? HAVE YOU LEARNED ANYTHING?
YES. AS WE SUSPECTED, THE WORKER RESPONSIBLE FOR THE ACCIDENT AT THE CONSTRUCTION SITE IS UNACCOUNTED FOR.
WE BELIEVE HE MUST HAVE INFILTRATED THE SITE WITH A FALSIFIED COMPANY PASS.
ADDITIONALLY, THERE ARE NO RECORDS OF THE VICTIM BEING TAKEN TO ANY HOSPITAL WITHIN THE CITY.
THE THREE SEPARATE ACCIDENTS THAT OCCURRED IN QUICK SUCCESSION ALL BEAR THESE IDENTICAL CHARACTERIS-TICS.
MEANING?
THEY ARE A STRING OF CALCULATED, INTENTIONAL INCIDENTS DESIGNED TO HARM OUR COMPANY.
AND THEY WERE CARRIED OUT BY...

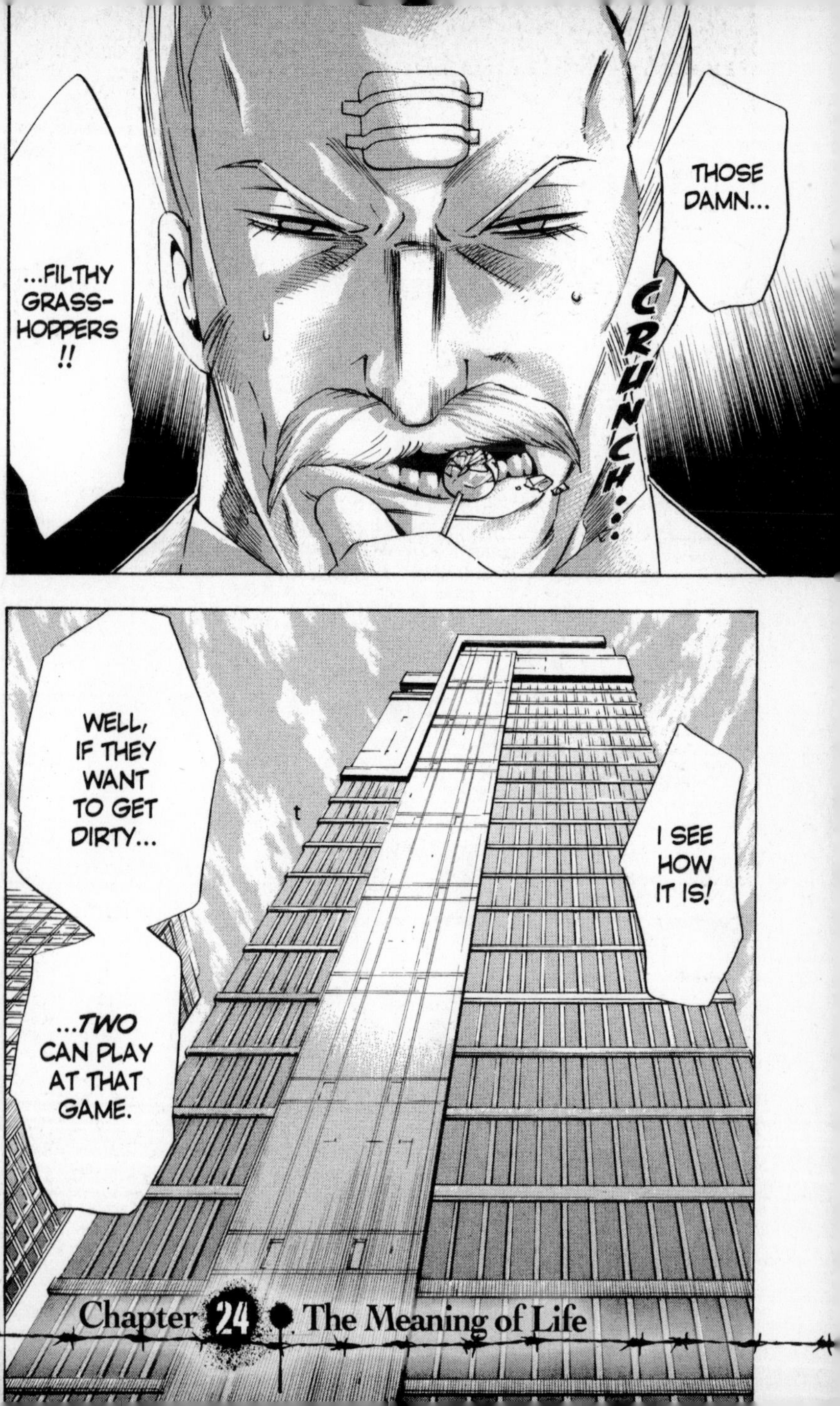
THOSE DAMN...
CRUNCH...
...FILTHY GRASSHOPPERS!!
I SEE HOW IT IS!
WELL, IF THEY WANT TO GET DIRTY...
...TWO CAN PLAY AT THAT GAME.

Chapter 24 The Meaning of Life

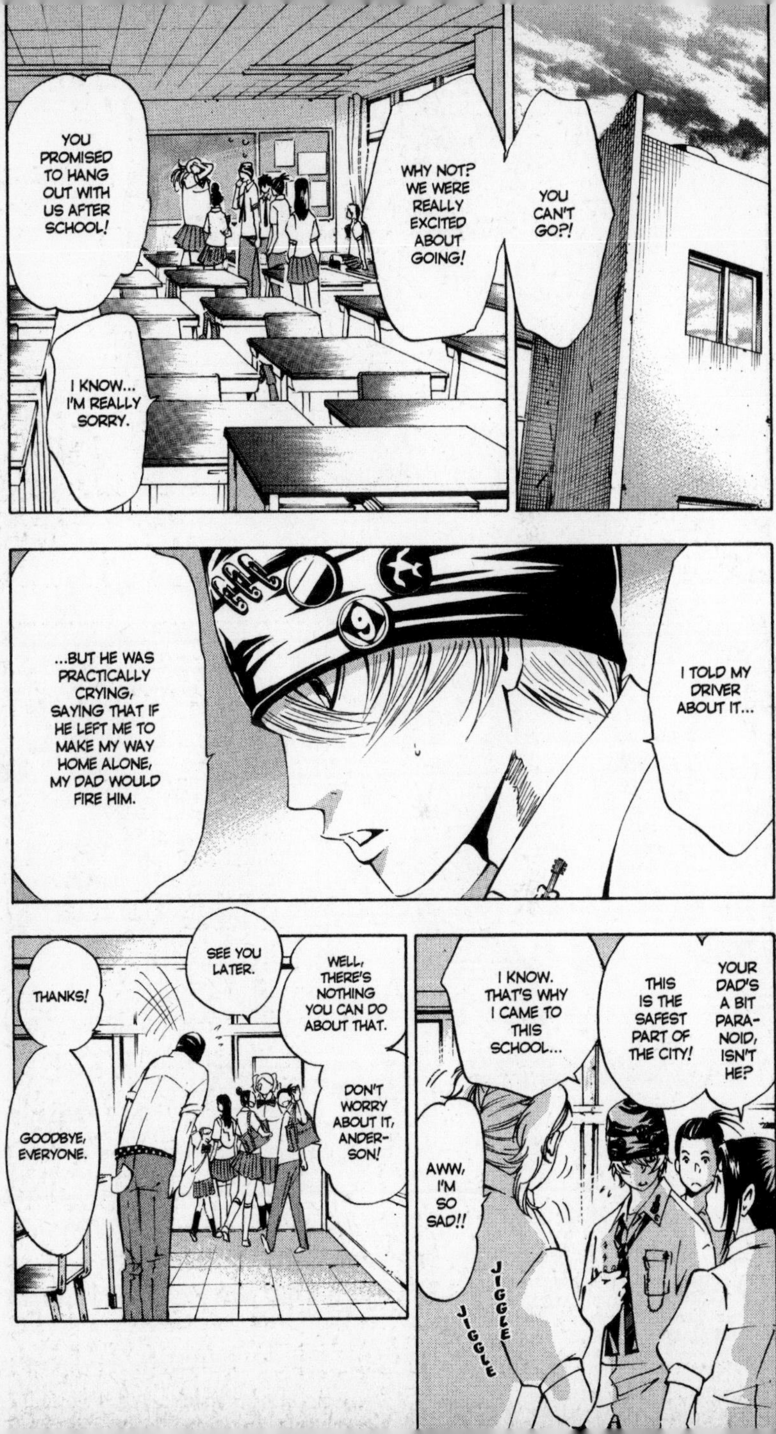
YOU CAN'T GO?!
WHY NOT? WE WERE REALLY EXCITED ABOUT GOING!
YOU PROMISED TO HANG OUT WITH US AFTER SCHOOL!
I KNOW... I'M REALLY SORRY.
I TOLD MY DRIVER ABOUT IT...
...BUT HE WAS PRACTICALLY CRYING, SAYING THAT IF HE LEFT ME TO MAKE MY WAY HOME ALONE, MY DAD WOULD FIRE HIM.
YOUR DAD'S A BIT PARA-NOID, ISN'T HE?
THIS IS THE SAFEST PART OF THE CITY!
I KNOW. THAT'S WHY I CAME TO THIS SCHOOL...
AWW, I'M SO SAD!!
JIGGLE
JIGGLE
WELL, THERE'S NOTHING YOU CAN DO ABOUT THAT.
DON'T WORRY ABOUT IT, ANDER-SON!
SEE YOU LATER.
THANKS!
GOODBYE, EVERYONE.

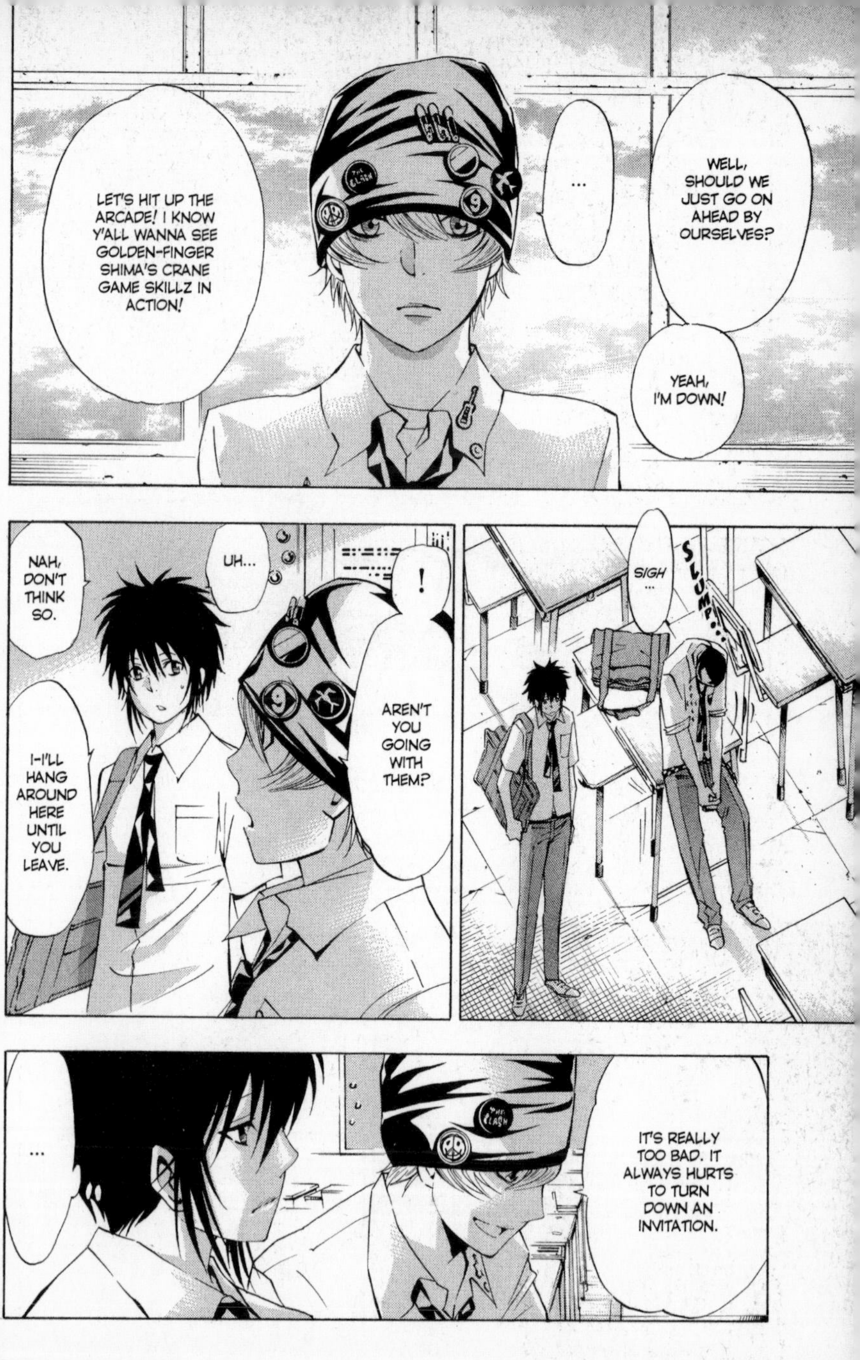
WELL, SHOULD WE JUST GO ON AHEAD BY OURSELVES?
YEAH, I'M DOWN!
...
LET'S HIT UP THE ARCADE! I KNOW Y'ALL WANNA SEE GOLDEN-FINGER SHIMA'S CRANE GAME SKILLZ IN ACTION!
SIGH ...
SLUMP...
!
AREN'T YOU GOING WITH THEM?
UH...
NAH, DON'T THINK SO.
I-I'LL HANG AROUND HERE UNTIL YOU LEAVE.
IT'S REALLY TOO BAD. IT ALWAYS HURTS TO TURN DOWN AN INVITATION.
...

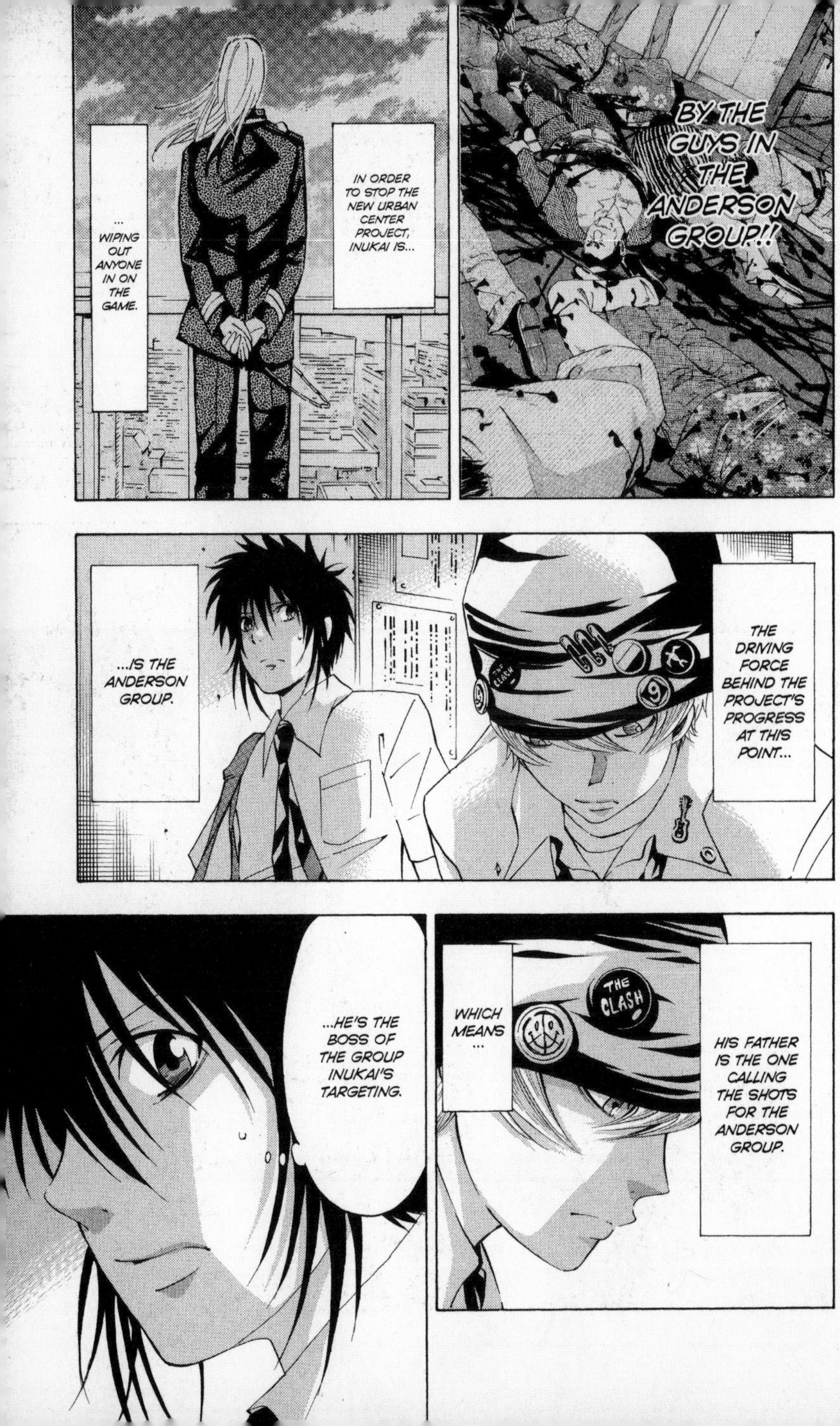

BY THE GUYS IN THE ANDERSON GROUP!!
IN ORDER TO STOP THE NEW URBAN CENTER PROJECT, INUKAI IS...
... WIPING OUT ANYONE IN ON THE GAME.
THE DRIVING FORCE BEHIND THE PROJECT'S PROGRESS AT THIS POINT...
...IS THE ANDERSON GROUP.
HIS FATHER IS THE ONE CALLING THE SHOTS FOR THE ANDERSON GROUP.
WHICH MEANS ...
...HE'S THE BOSS OF THE GROUP INUKAI'S TARGETING.

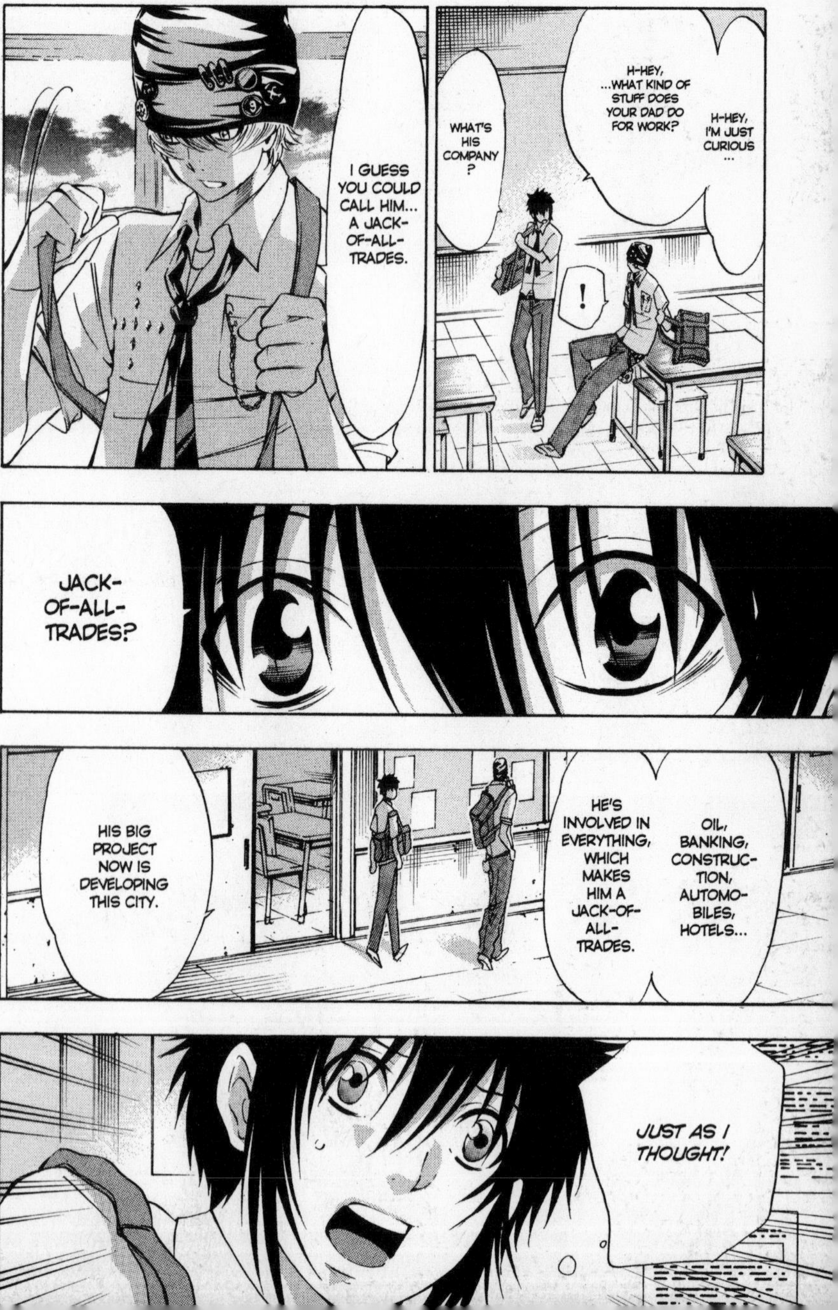
H-HEY, I'M JUST CURIOUS...
H-HEY, ...WHAT KIND OF STUFF DOES YOUR DAD DO FOR WORK?
WHAT'S HIS COMPANY?
!
I GUESS YOU COULD CALL HIM... A JACK-OF-ALL-TRADES.
JACK-OF-ALL-TRADES?
OIL, BANKING, CONSTRUCTION, AUTOMOBILES, HOTELS...
HE'S INVOLVED IN EVERYTHING, WHICH MAKES HIM A JACK-OF-ALL-TRADES.
HIS BIG PROJECT NOW IS DEVELOPING THIS CITY.
JUST AS I THOUGHT!

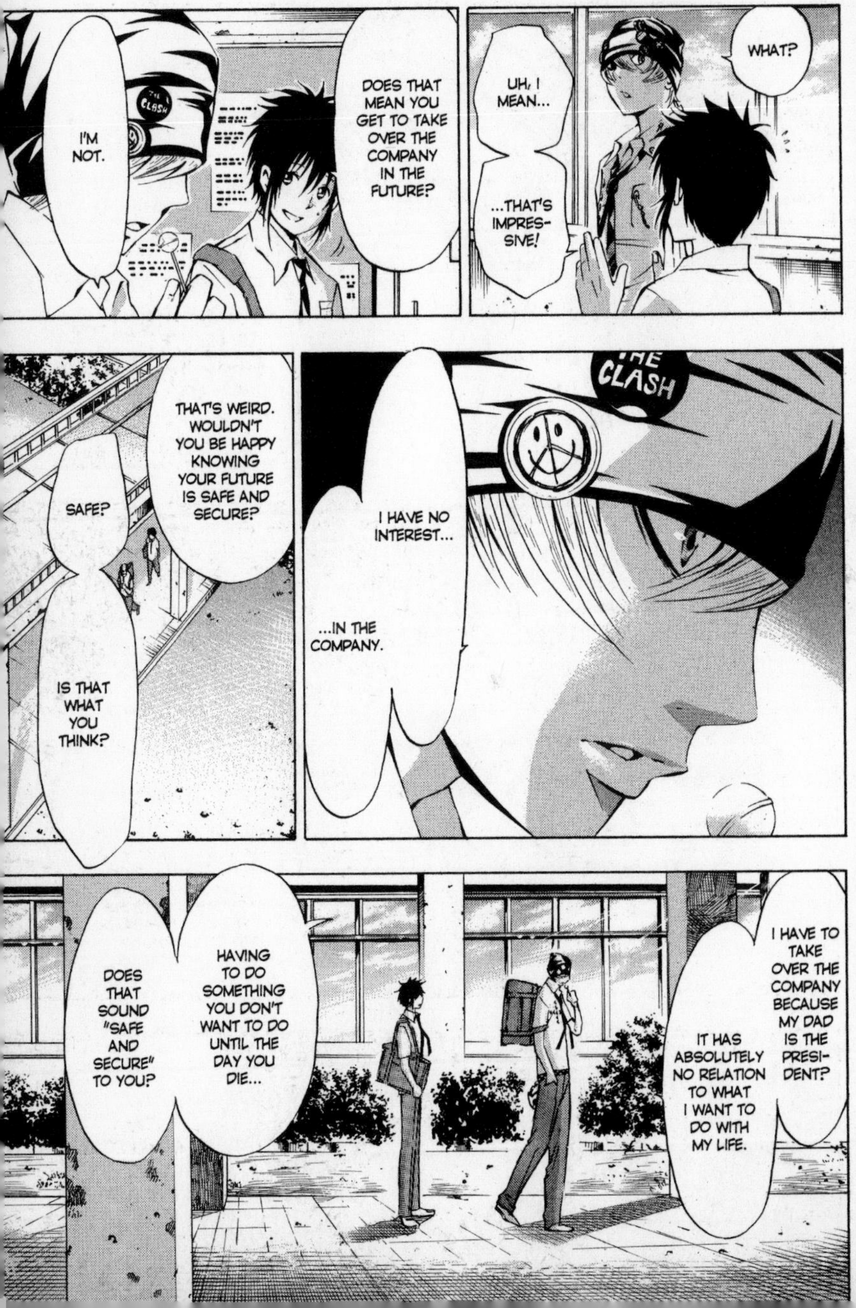
WHAT?
UH, I MEAN...
...THAT'S IMPRESSIVE!
DOES THAT MEAN YOU GET TO TAKE OVER THE COMPANY IN THE FUTURE?
I'M NOT.
I HAVE NO INTEREST...
...IN THE COMPANY.
THAT'S WEIRD. WOULDN'T YOU BE HAPPY KNOWING YOUR FUTURE IS SAFE AND SECURE?
SAFE?
IS THAT WHAT YOU THINK?
I HAVE TO TAKE OVER THE COMPANY BECAUSE MY DAD IS THE PRESIDENT?
IT HAS ABSOLUTELY NO RELATION TO WHAT I WANT TO DO WITH MY LIFE.
HAVING TO DO SOMETHING YOU DON'T WANT TO DO UNTIL THE DAY YOU DIE...
DOES THAT SOUND "SAFE AND SECURE" TO YOU?

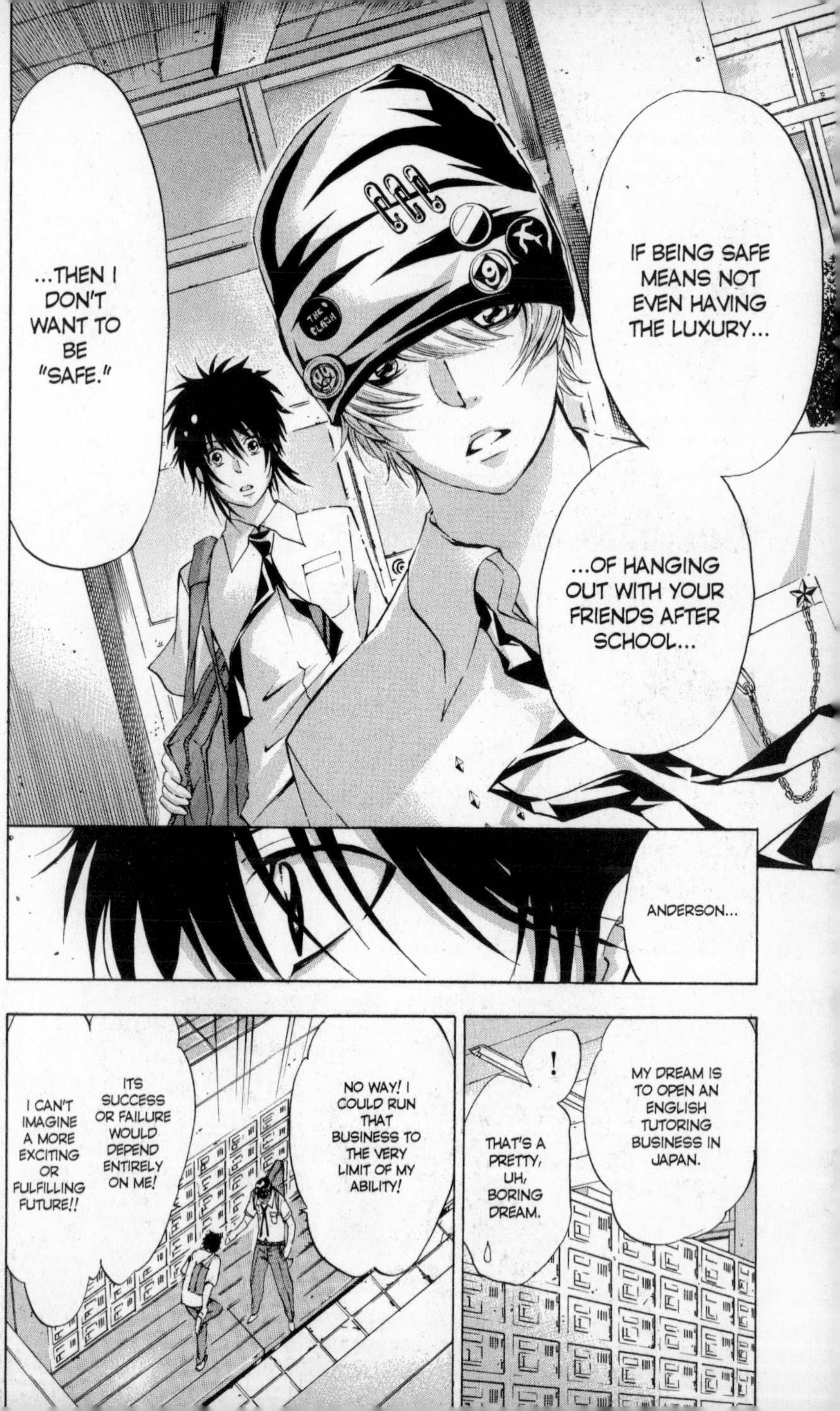
IF BEING SAFE MEANS NOT EVEN HAVING THE LUXURY...
...OF HANGING OUT WITH YOUR FRIENDS AFTER SCHOOL...
...THEN I DON'T WANT TO BE "SAFE."
ANDERSON...
MY DREAM IS TO OPEN AN ENGLISH TUTORING BUSINESS IN JAPAN.
!
THAT'S A PRETTY, UH, BORING DREAM.
NO WAY! I COULD RUN THAT BUSINESS TO THE VERY LIMIT OF MY ABILITY!
ITS SUCCESS OR FAILURE WOULD DEPEND ENTIRELY ON ME!
I CAN'T IMAGINE A MORE EXCITING OR FULFILLING FUTURE!!

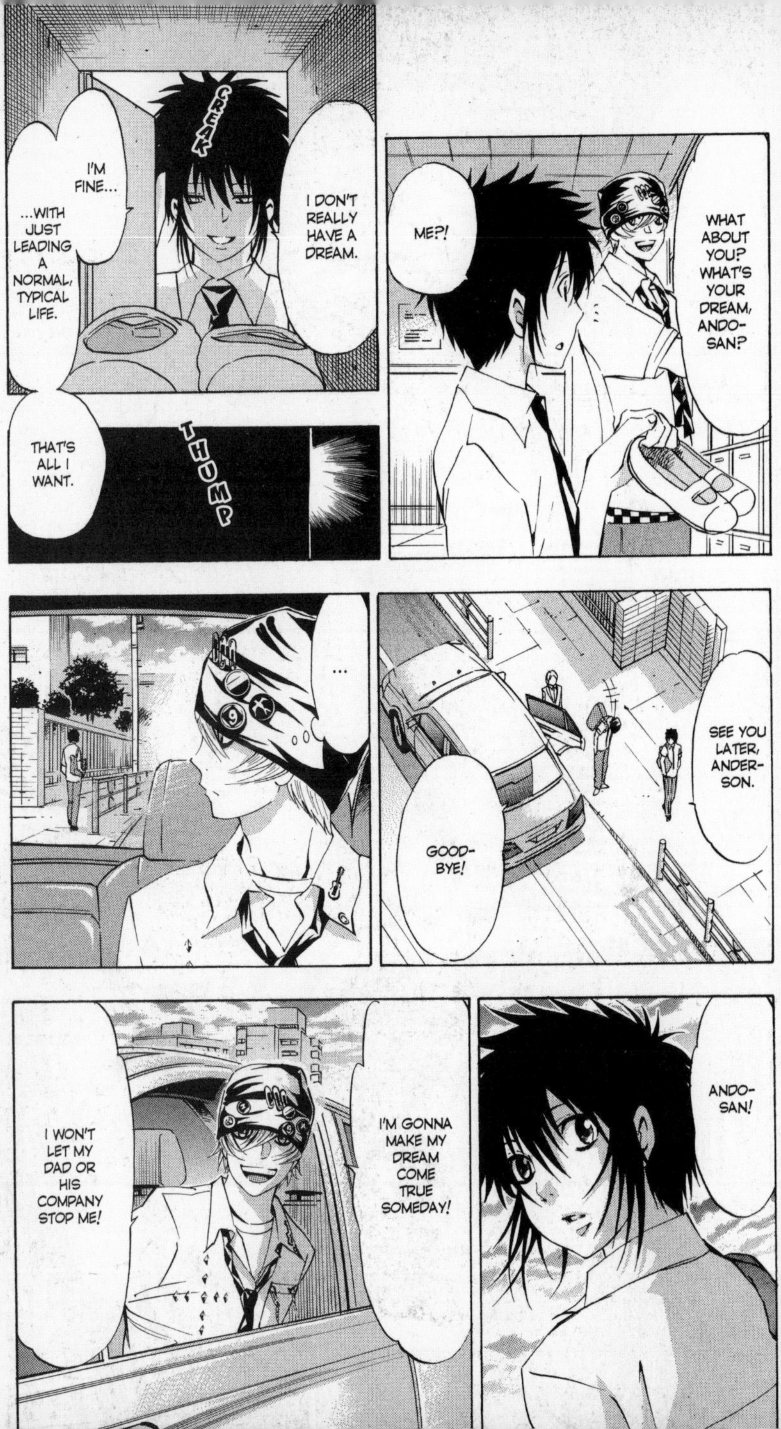
WHAT ABOUT YOU? WHAT'S YOUR DREAM, ANDO-SAN?
ME?!
CREAK
I DON'T REALLY HAVE A DREAM.
I'M FINE...
...WITH JUST LEADING A NORMAL, TYPICAL LIFE.
THUMP
THAT'S ALL I WANT.
SEE YOU LATER, ANDERSON.
GOOD-BYE!
...
ANDO-SAN!
I'M GONNA MAKE MY DREAM COME TRUE SOMEDAY!
I WON'T LET MY DAD OR HIS COMPANY STOP ME!

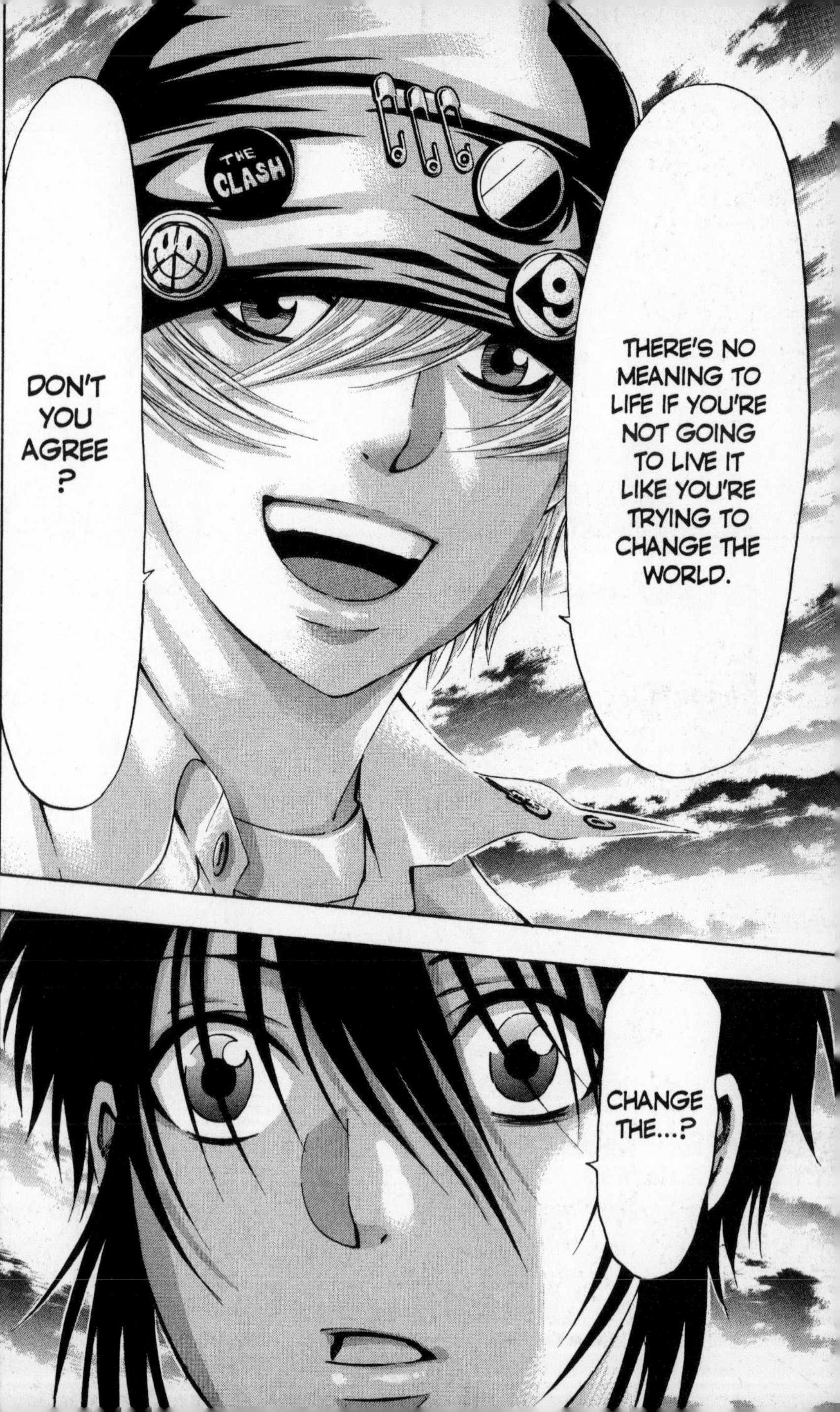
THE CLASH
THERE'S NO MEANING TO LIFE IF YOU'RE NOT GOING TO LIVE IT LIKE YOU'RE TRYING TO CHANGE THE WORLD.
DON'T YOU AGREE ?
CHANGE THE...?

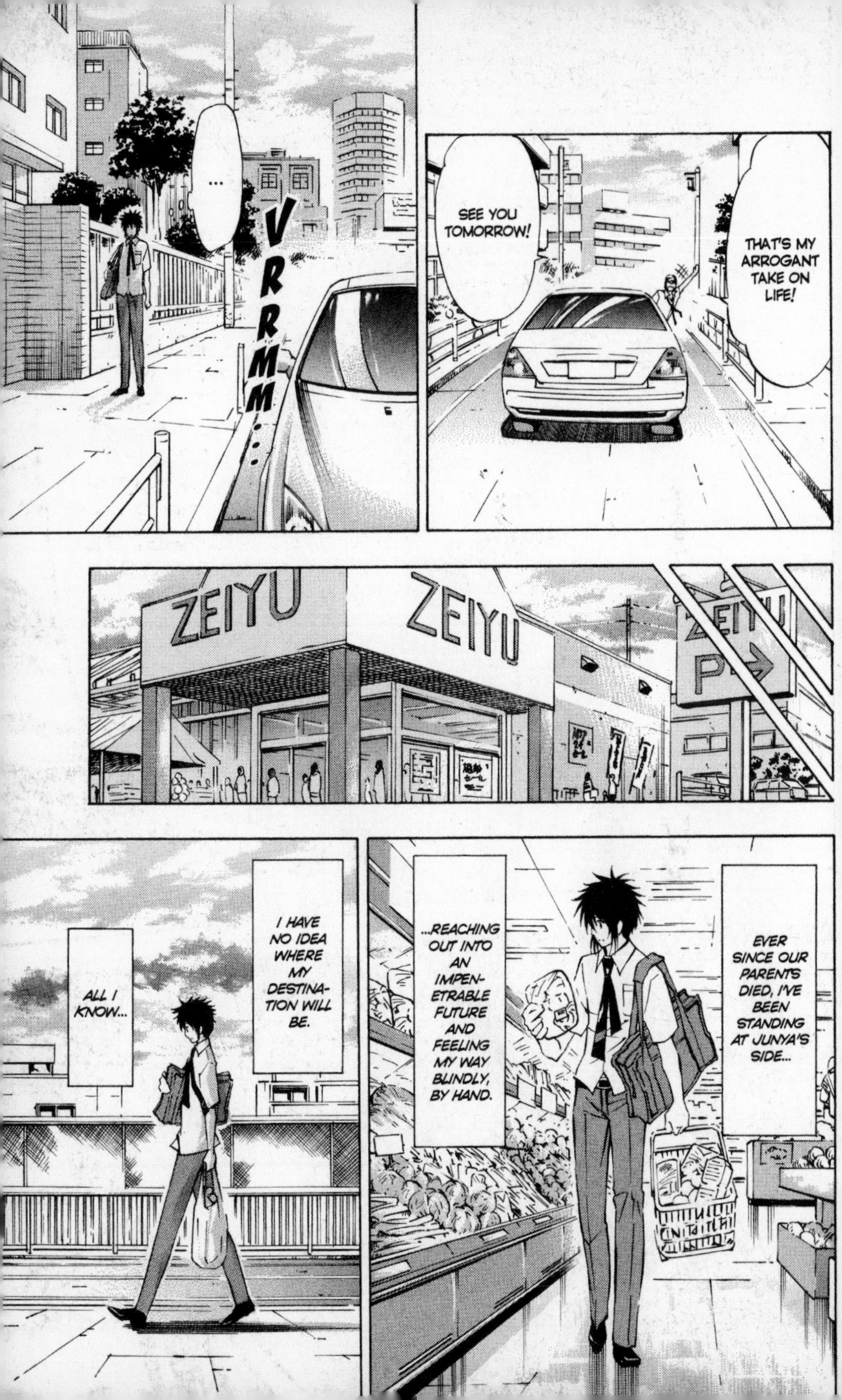
THAT'S MY ARROGANT TAKE ON LIFE!
SEE YOU TOMORROW!
...
VRRMM...
ZEIYU
ZEIYU
ZEIYU P
EVER SINCE OUR PARENTS DIED, I'VE BEEN STANDING AT JUNYA'S SIDE...
...REACHING OUT INTO AN IMPENETRABLE FUTURE AND FEELING MY WAY BLINDLY, BY HAND.
I HAVE NO IDEA WHERE MY DESTINATION WILL BE.
ALL I KNOW...

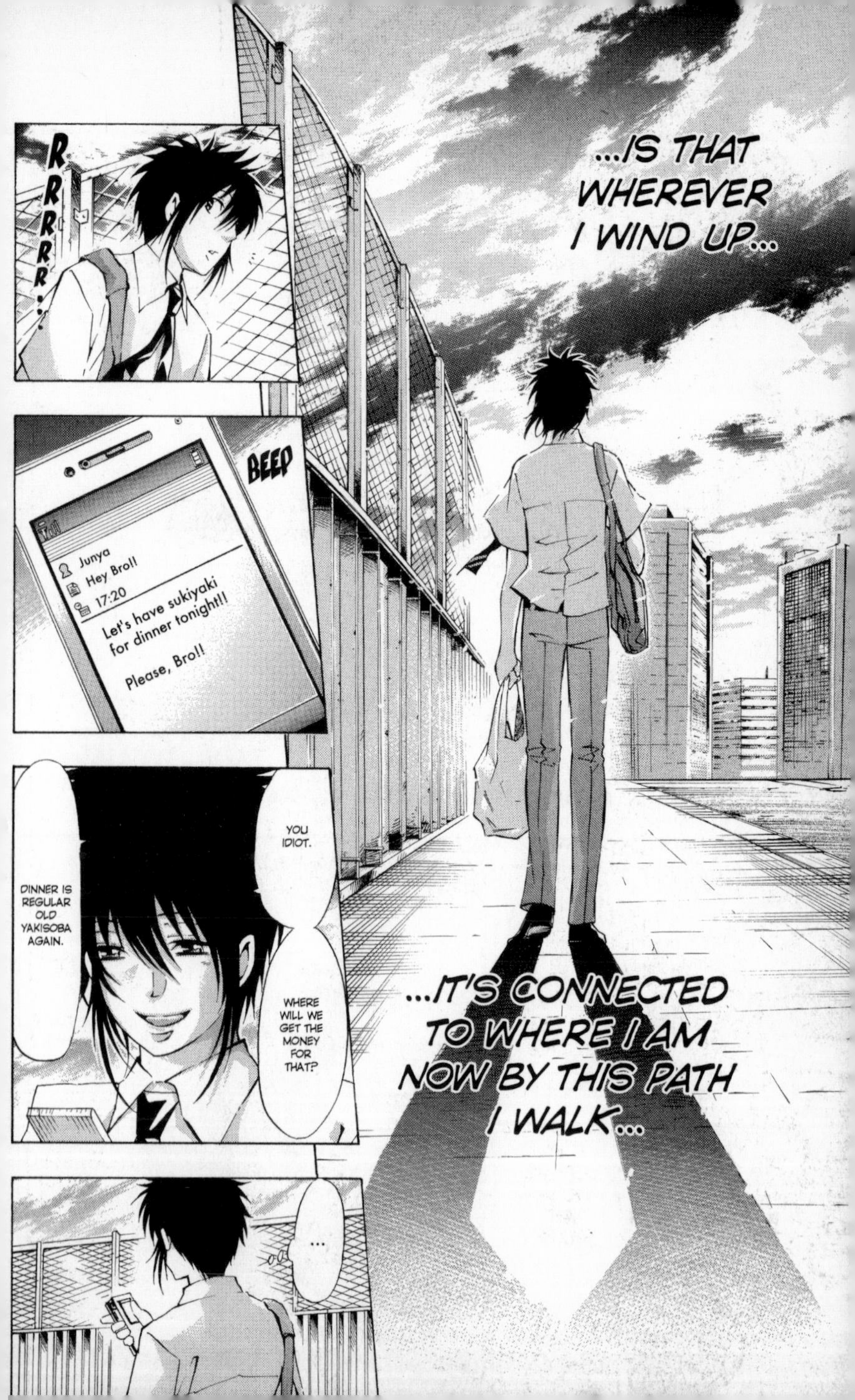
...IS THAT WHEREVER I WIND UP...
...IT'S CONNECTED TO WHERE I AM NOW BY THIS PATH I WALK...
RRRRR...
BEEP
Junya
Hey Bro!!
17:20
Let's have sukiyaki for dinner tonight!!
Please, Bro!!
YOU IDIOT.
DINNER IS REGULAR OLD YAKISOBA AGAIN.
WHERE WILL WE GET THE MONEY FOR THAT?
...

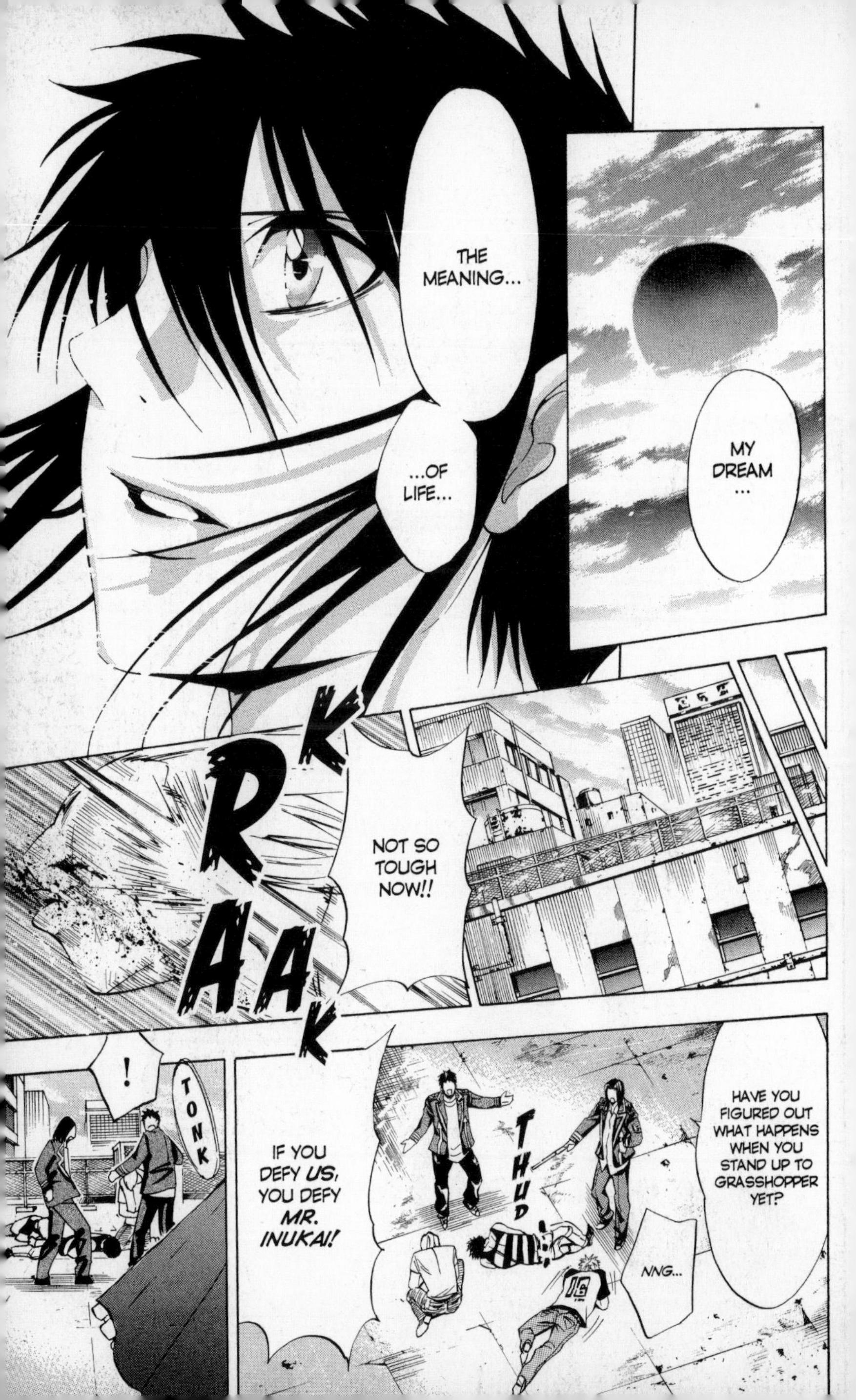
MY DREAM ...
THE MEANING...
...OF LIFE...
NOT SO TOUGH NOW!!
KRAAAK
HAVE YOU FIGURED OUT WHAT HAPPENS WHEN YOU STAND UP TO GRASSHOPPER YET?
THUD
IF YOU DEFY *US*, YOU DEFY *MR. INUKAI!*
NNG...
!
TONK

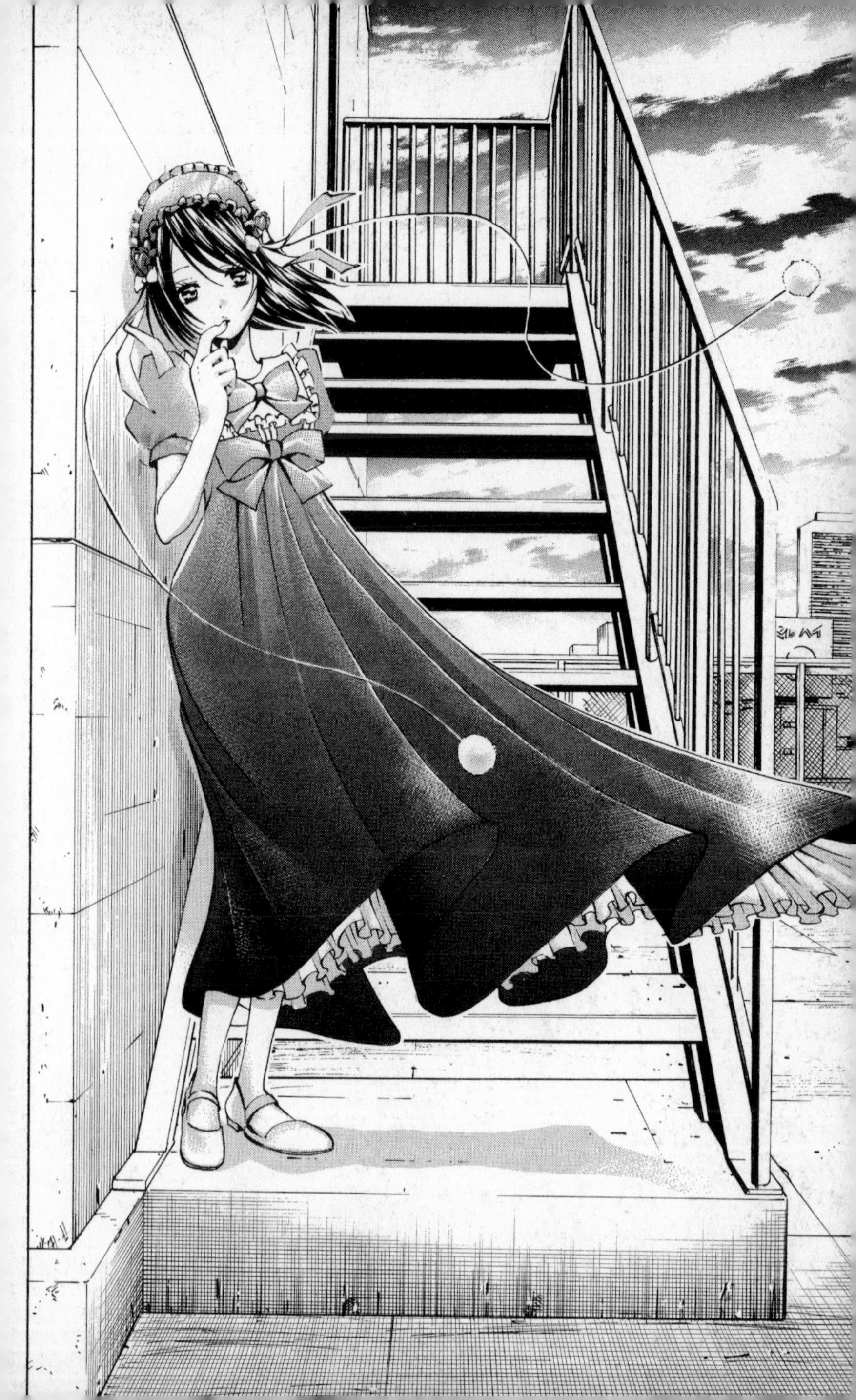
ミルハイ

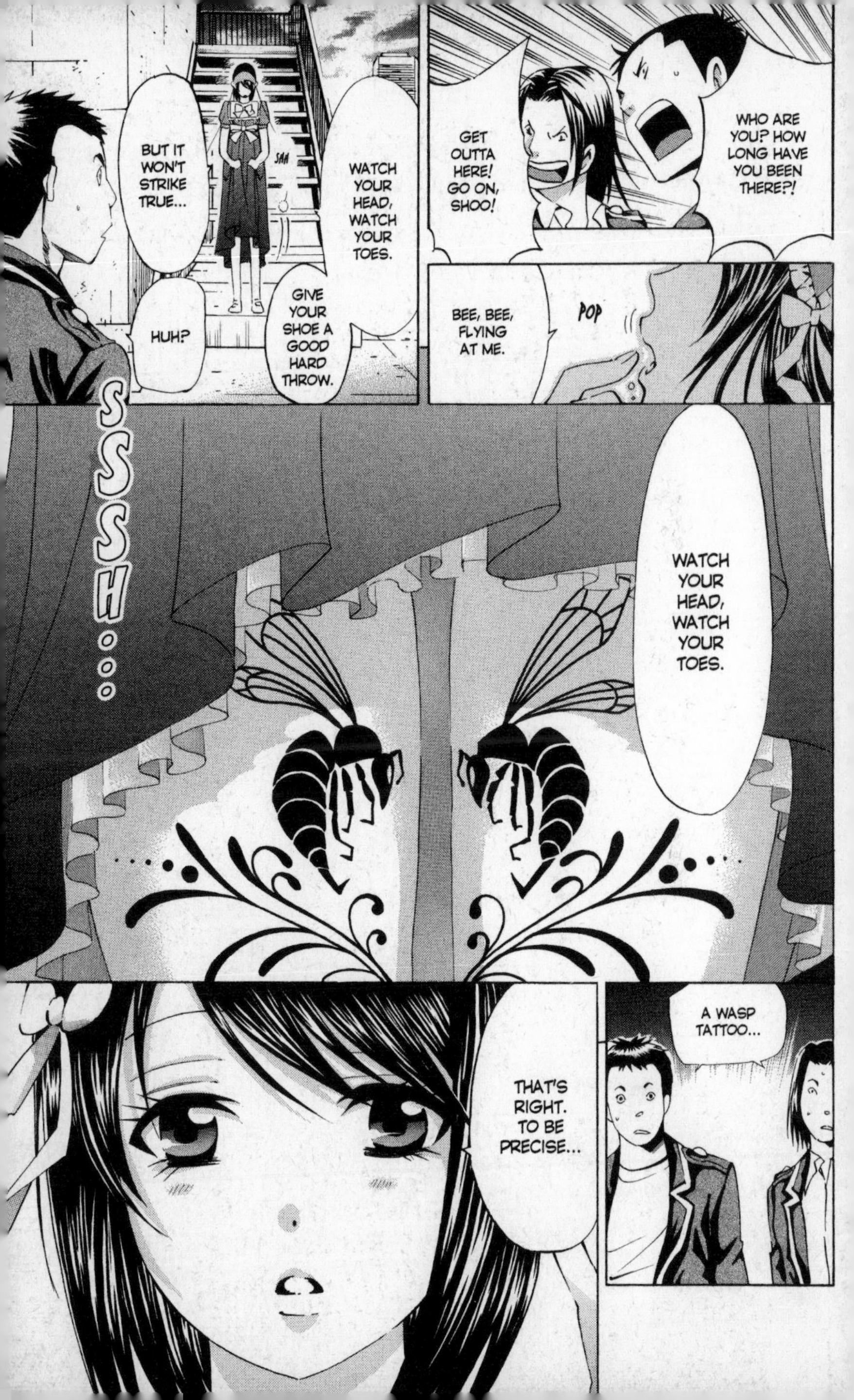
WHO ARE YOU? HOW LONG HAVE YOU BEEN THERE?!
GET OUTTA HERE! GO ON, SHOO!
POP
BEE, BEE, FLYING AT ME.
WATCH YOUR HEAD, WATCH YOUR TOES.
GIVE YOUR SHOE A GOOD HARD THROW.
SAH
BUT IT WON'T STRIKE TRUE...
HUH?
WATCH YOUR HEAD, WATCH YOUR TOES.
SSSH...
A WASP TATTOO...
THAT'S RIGHT. TO BE PRECISE...

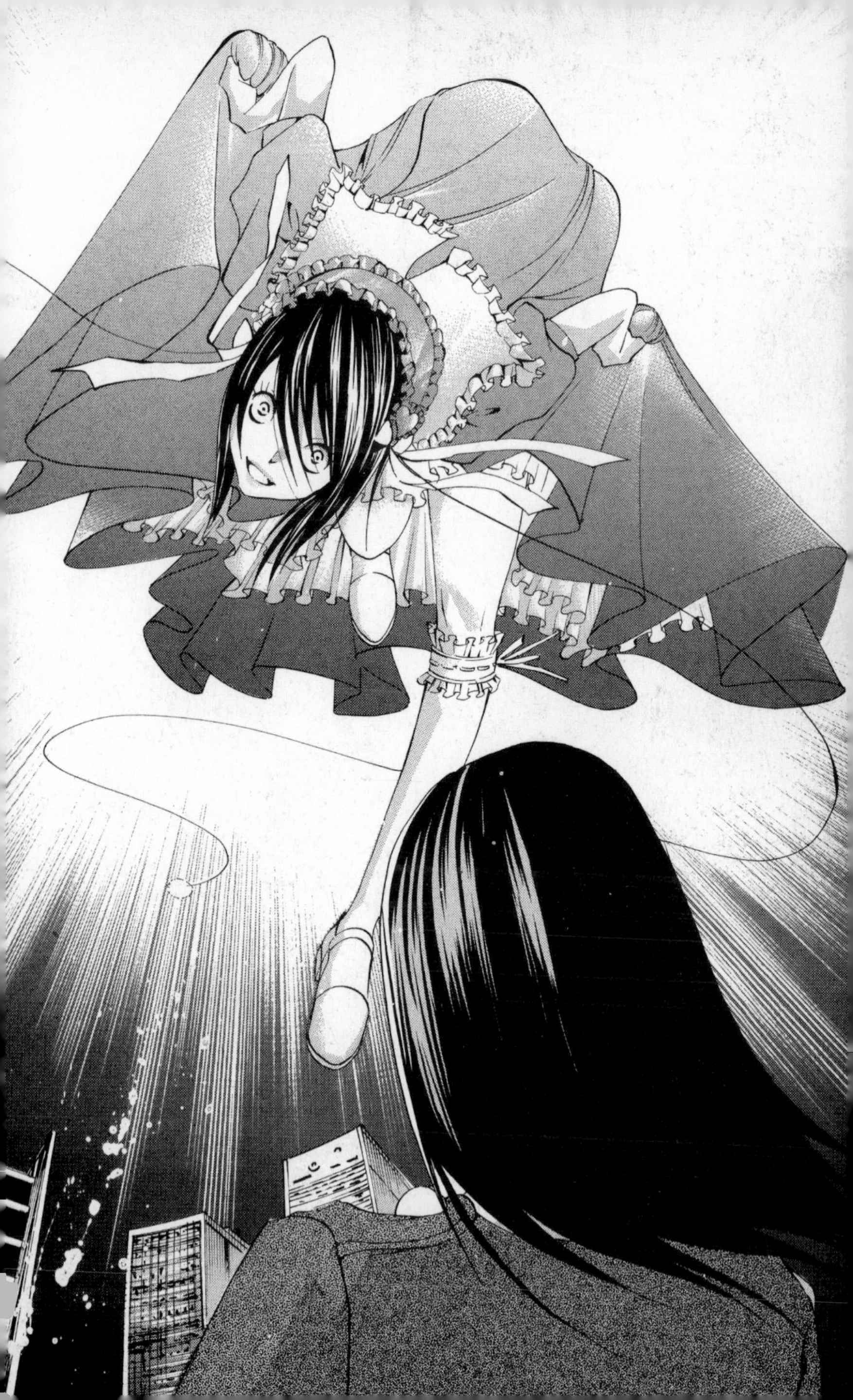

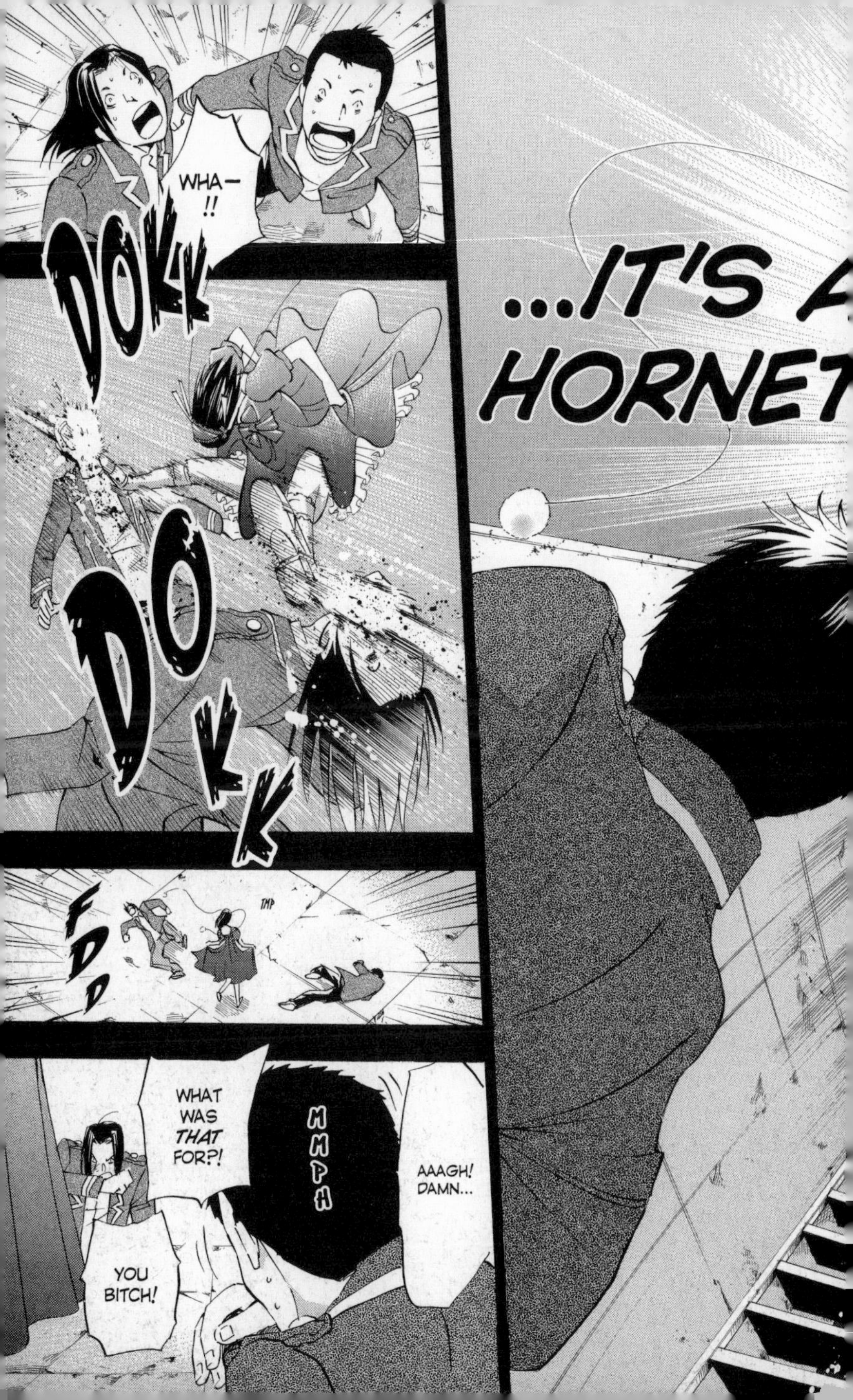

...IT'S A
HORNET
WHA— !!
DOKK
DOKK
TMP
FDD
AAAGH! DAMN...
MMPH
WHAT WAS THAT FOR?!
YOU BITCH!

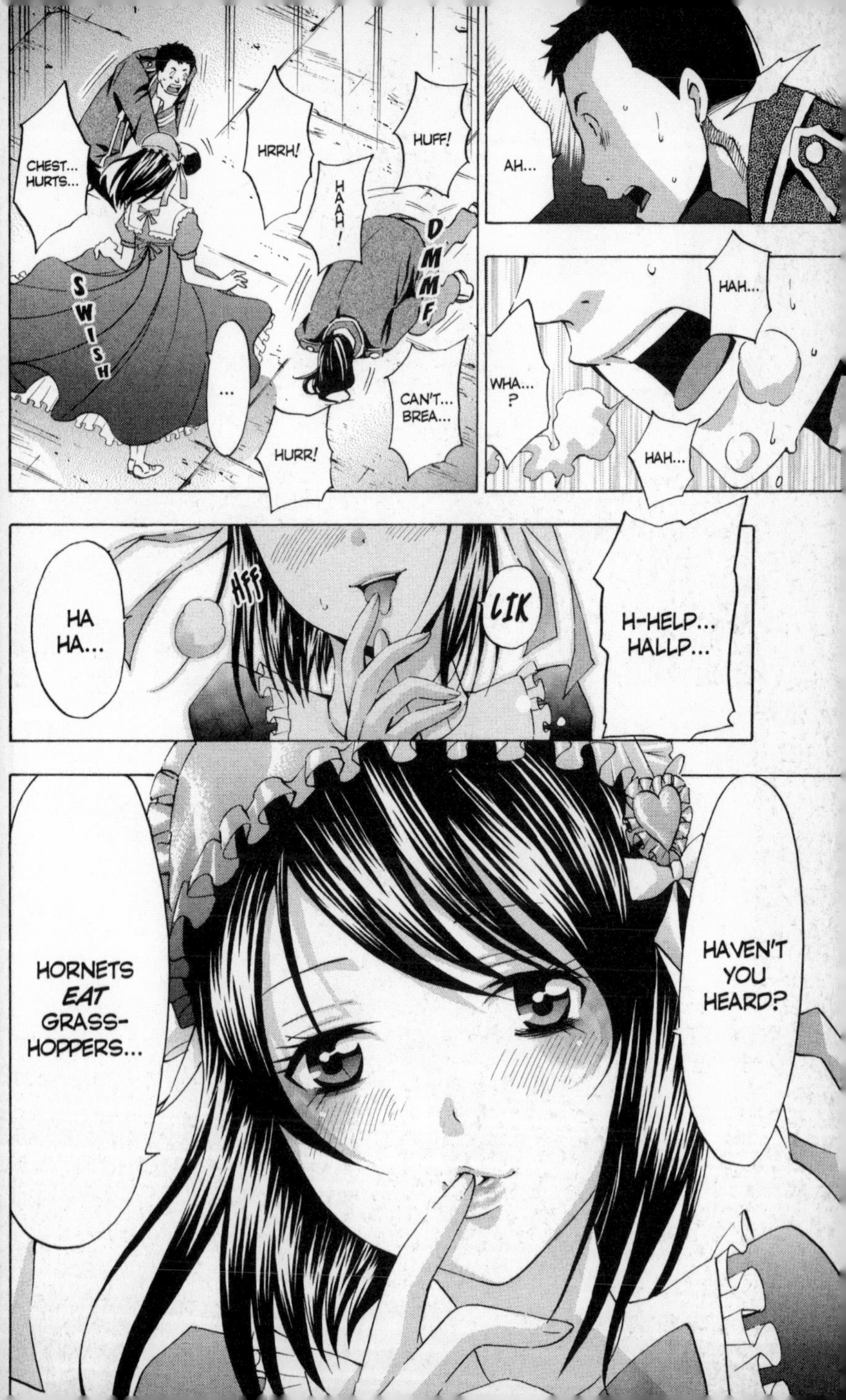
AH...
HAH...
WHA... ?
HAH...
HUFF!
HRRH!
HAAH!
CHEST... HURTS...
DMMF
CAN'T... BREA...
SWISH
...
HURR!
H-HELP... HALLP...
LIK
HFF
HA HA...
HAVEN'T YOU HEARD?
HORNETS *EAT* GRASS-HOPPERS...

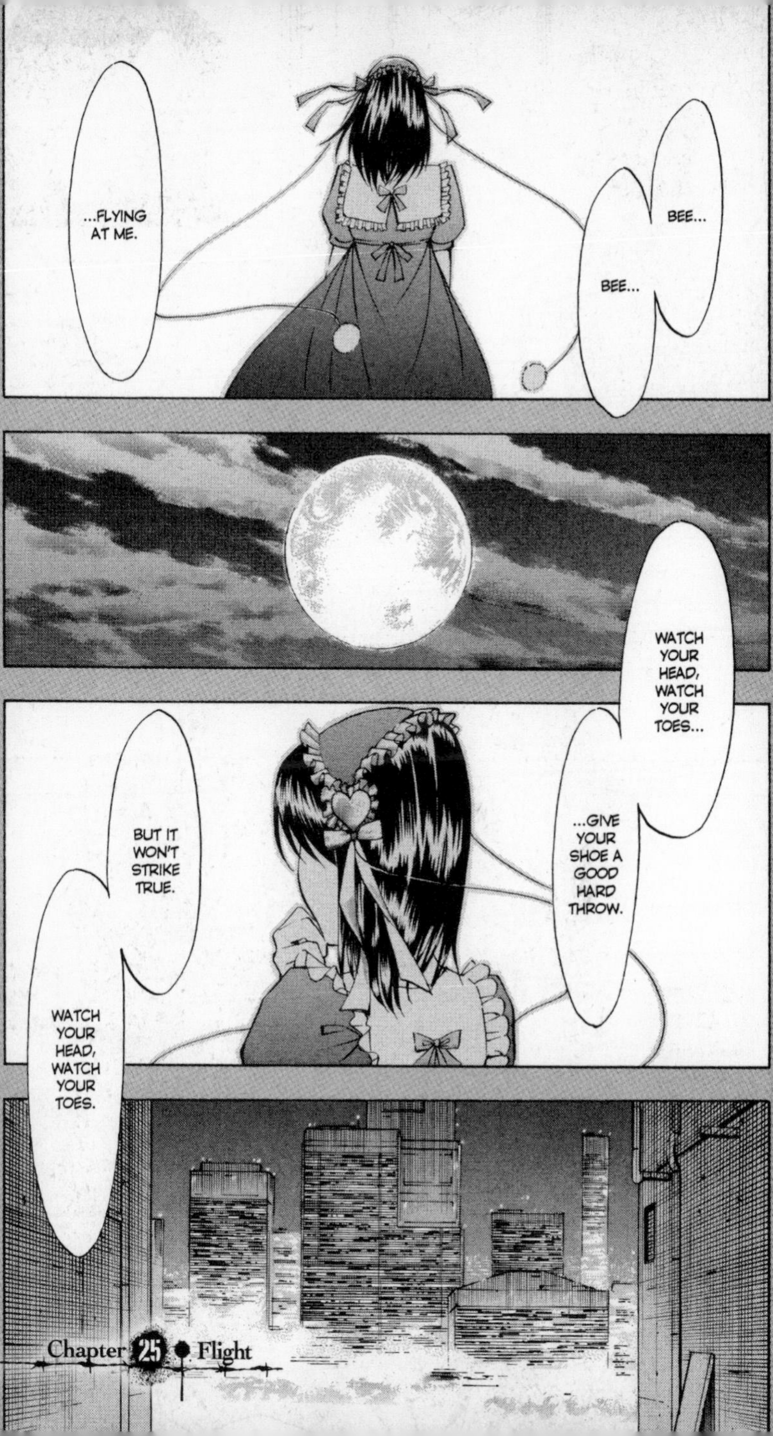
BEE... BEE...
...FLYING AT ME.
WATCH YOUR HEAD, WATCH YOUR TOES...
...GIVE YOUR SHOE A GOOD HARD THROW.
BUT IT WON'T STRIKE TRUE.
WATCH YOUR HEAD, WATCH YOUR TOES.
Chapter 25 Flight

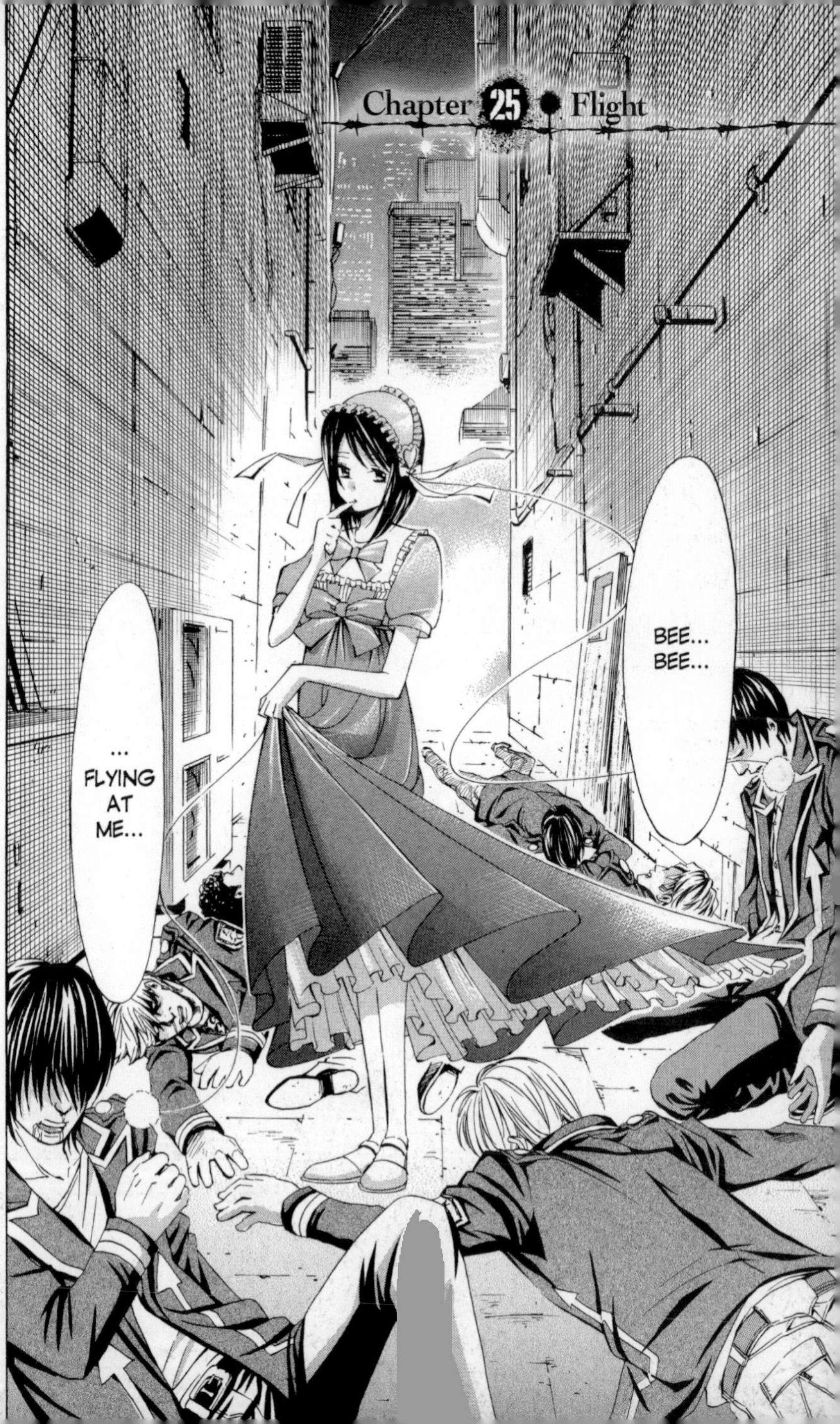
Chapter 25 Flight
BEE... BEE...
... FLYING AT ME...

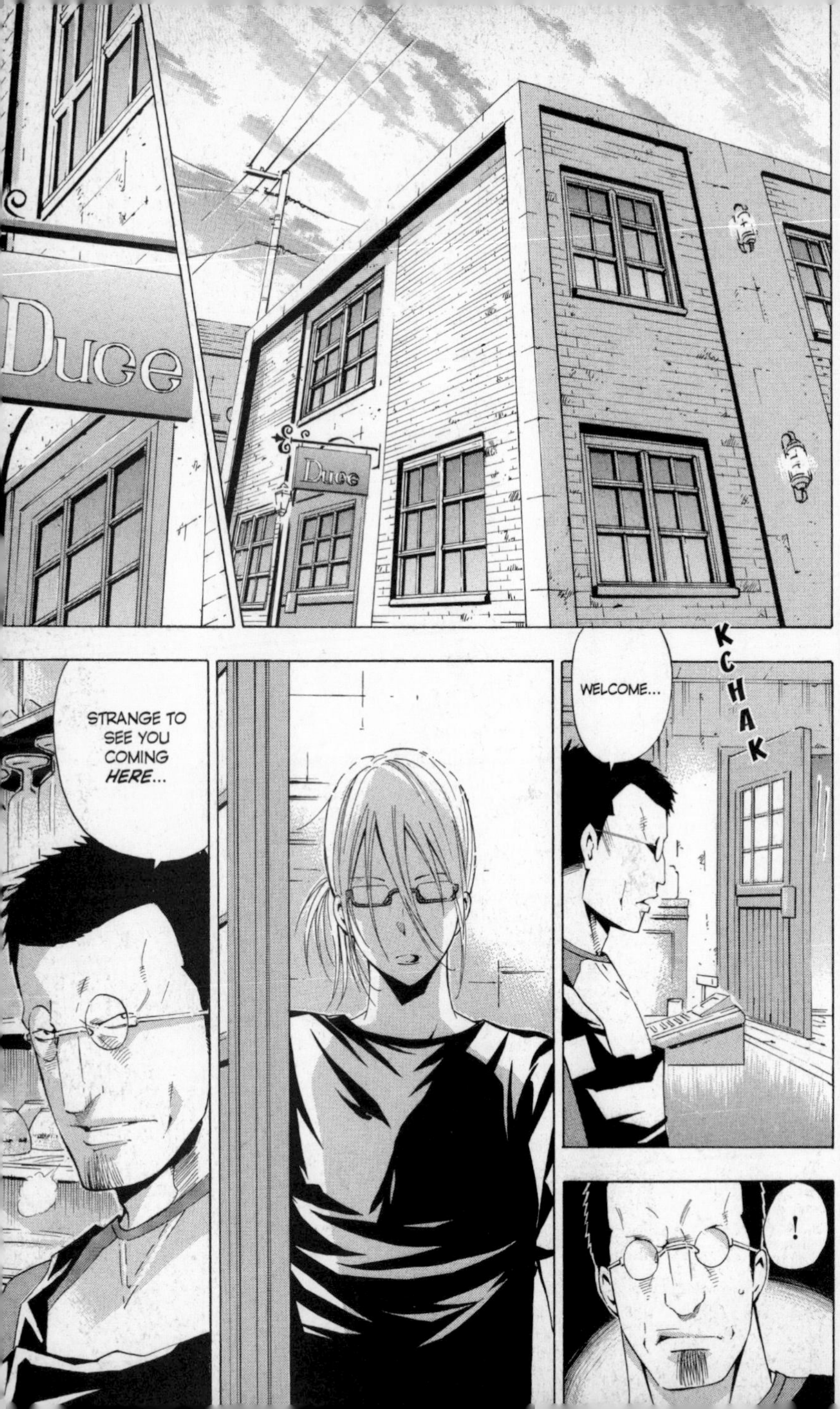
Duce
Duce
KCHAK
WELCOME...
!
STRANGE TO SEE YOU COMING *HERE*...

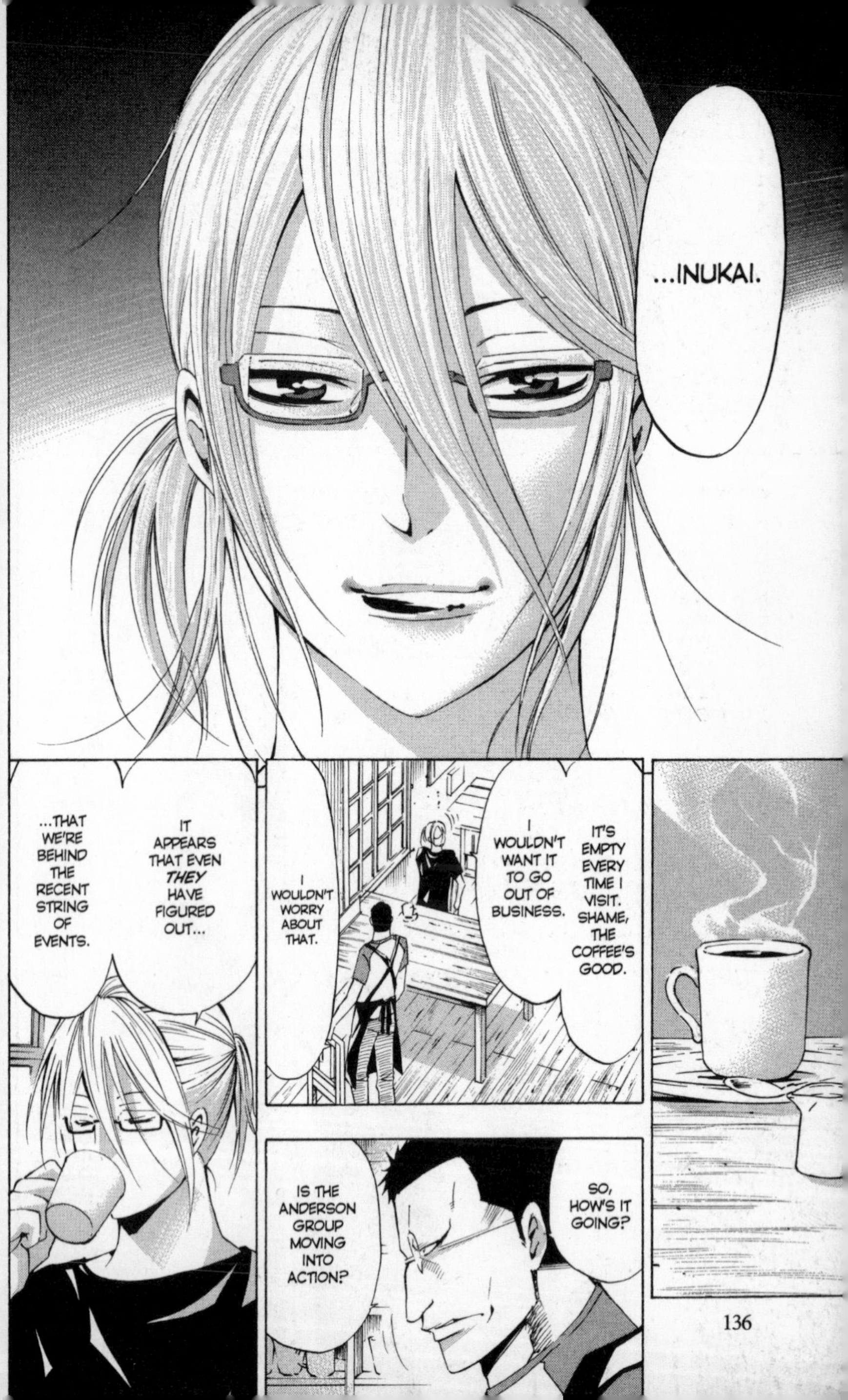
...INUKAI.
IT'S EMPTY EVERY TIME I VISIT. SHAME, THE COFFEE'S GOOD.
I WOULDN'T WANT IT TO GO OUT OF BUSINESS.
I WOULDN'T WORRY ABOUT THAT.
SO, HOW'S IT GOING?
IS THE ANDERSON GROUP MOVING INTO ACTION?
IT APPEARS THAT EVEN *THEY* HAVE FIGURED OUT...
...THAT WE'RE BEHIND THE RECENT STRING OF EVENTS.

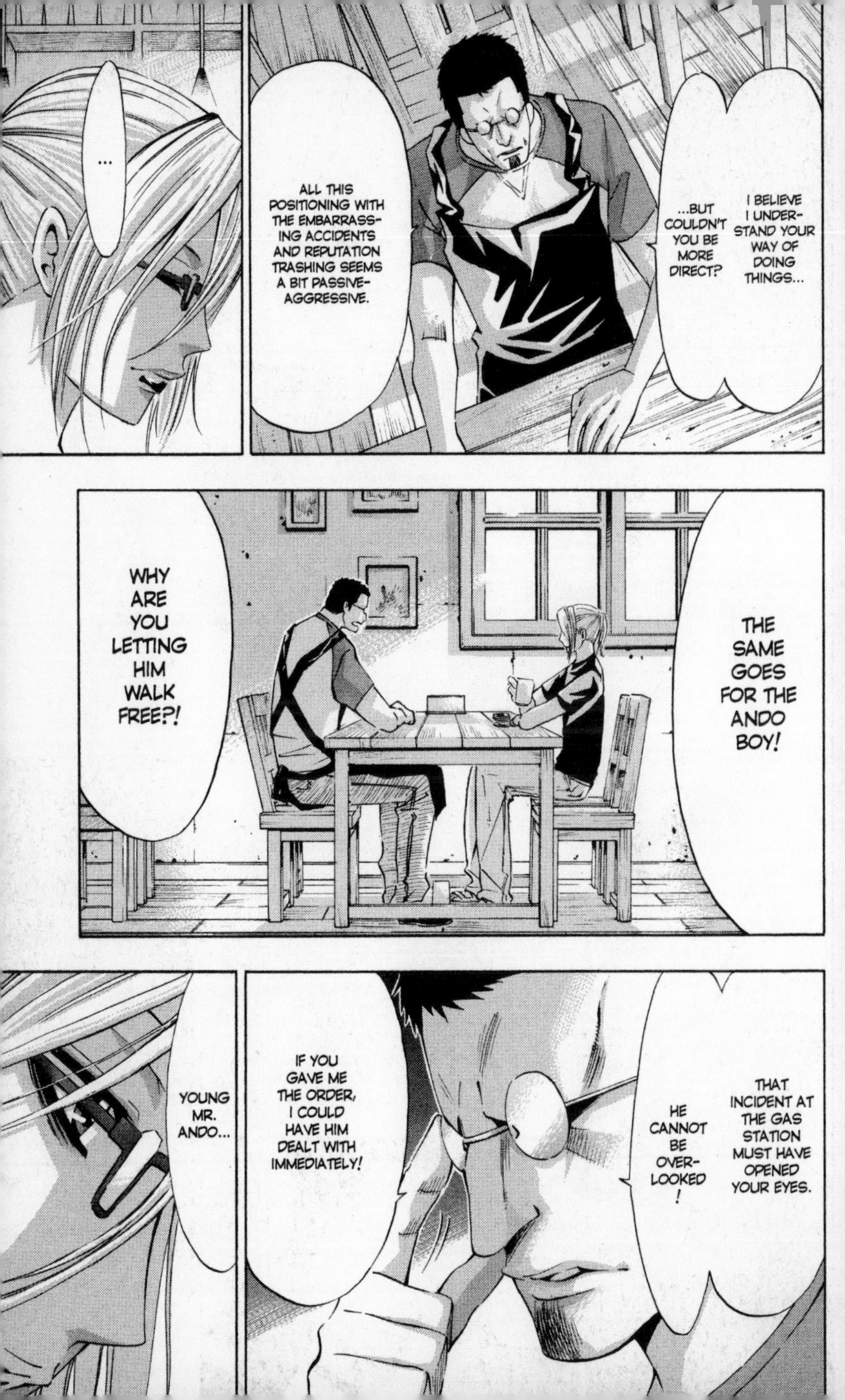
I BELIEVE I UNDERSTAND YOUR WAY OF DOING THINGS...
...BUT COULDN'T YOU BE MORE DIRECT?
ALL THIS POSITIONING WITH THE EMBARRASSING ACCIDENTS AND REPUTATION TRASHING SEEMS A BIT PASSIVE-AGGRESSIVE.
...
THE SAME GOES FOR THE ANDO BOY!
WHY ARE YOU LETTING HIM WALK FREE?!
THAT INCIDENT AT THE GAS STATION MUST HAVE OPENED YOUR EYES.
HE CANNOT BE OVERLOOKED!
IF YOU GAVE ME THE ORDER, I COULD HAVE HIM DEALT WITH IMMEDIATELY!
YOUNG MR. ANDO...

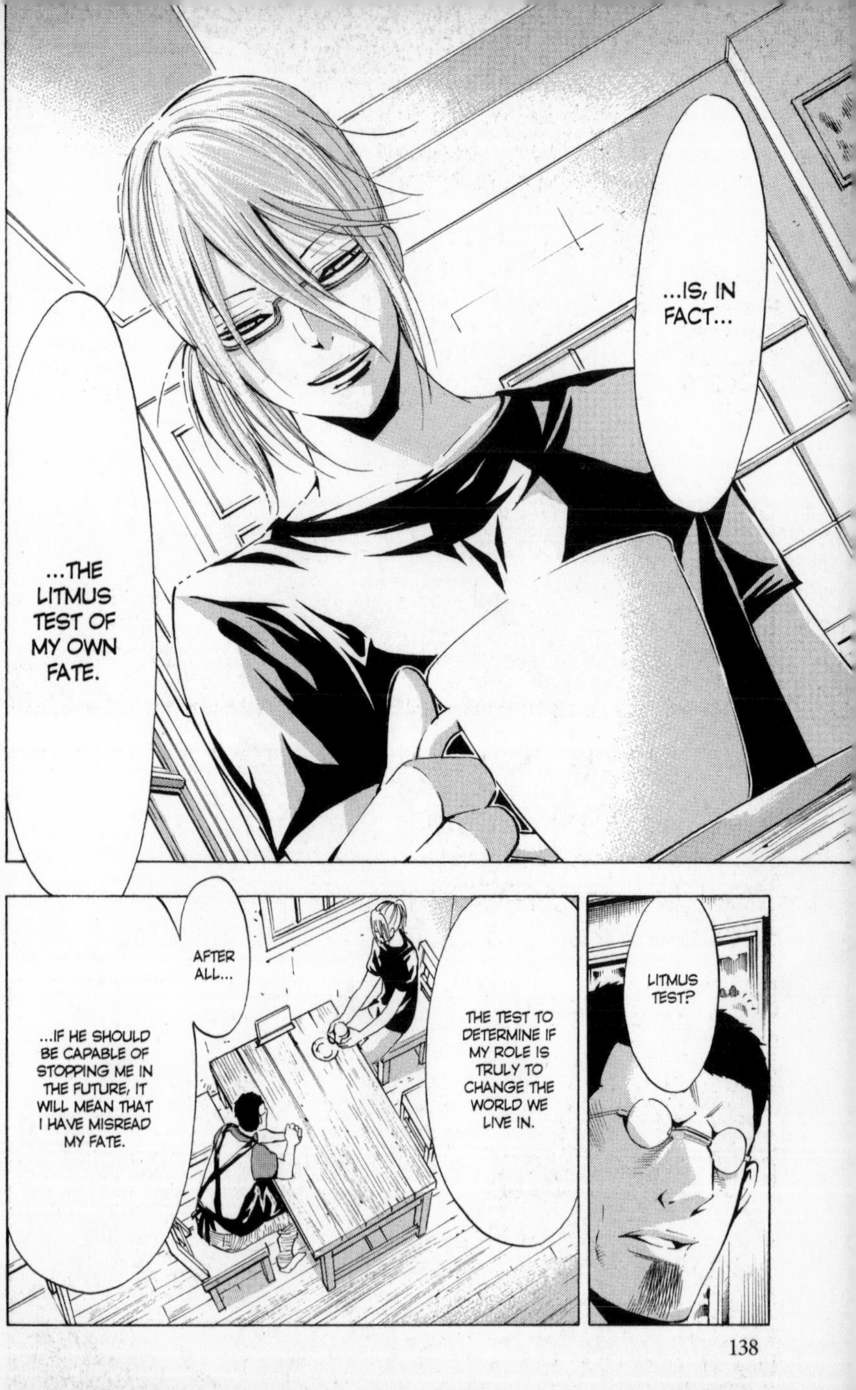
...IS, IN FACT...
...THE LITMUS TEST OF MY OWN FATE.
LITMUS TEST?
THE TEST TO DETERMINE IF MY ROLE IS TRULY TO CHANGE THE WORLD WE LIVE IN.
AFTER ALL...
...IF HE SHOULD BE CAPABLE OF STOPPING ME IN THE FUTURE, IT WILL MEAN THAT I HAVE MISREAD MY FATE.

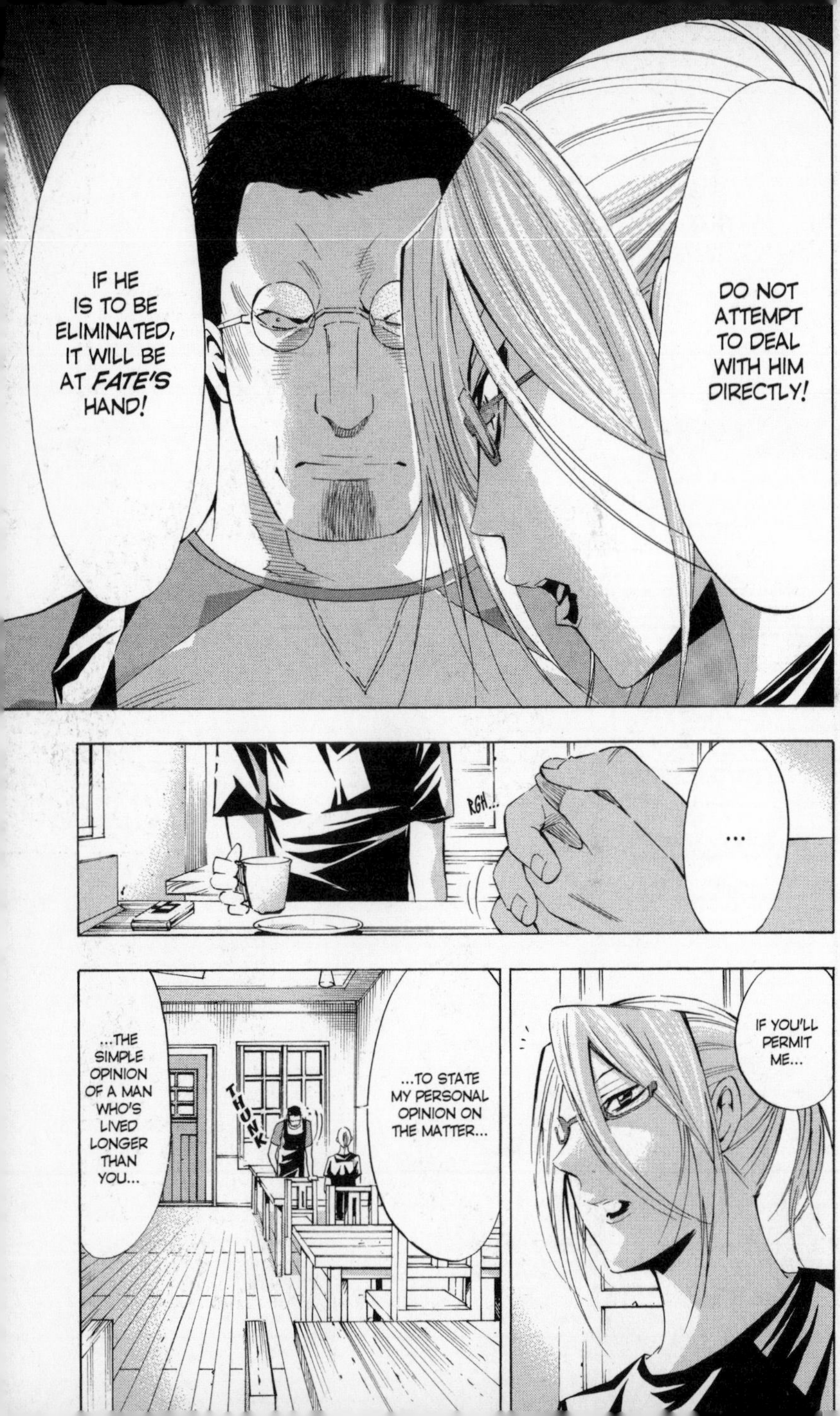
DO NOT ATTEMPT TO DEAL WITH HIM DIRECTLY!
IF HE IS TO BE ELIMINATED, IT WILL BE AT *FATE'S* HAND!
RGH...
...
IF YOU'LL PERMIT ME...
...TO STATE MY PERSONAL OPINION ON THE MATTER...
THUNK
...THE SIMPLE OPINION OF A MAN WHO'S LIVED LONGER THAN YOU...

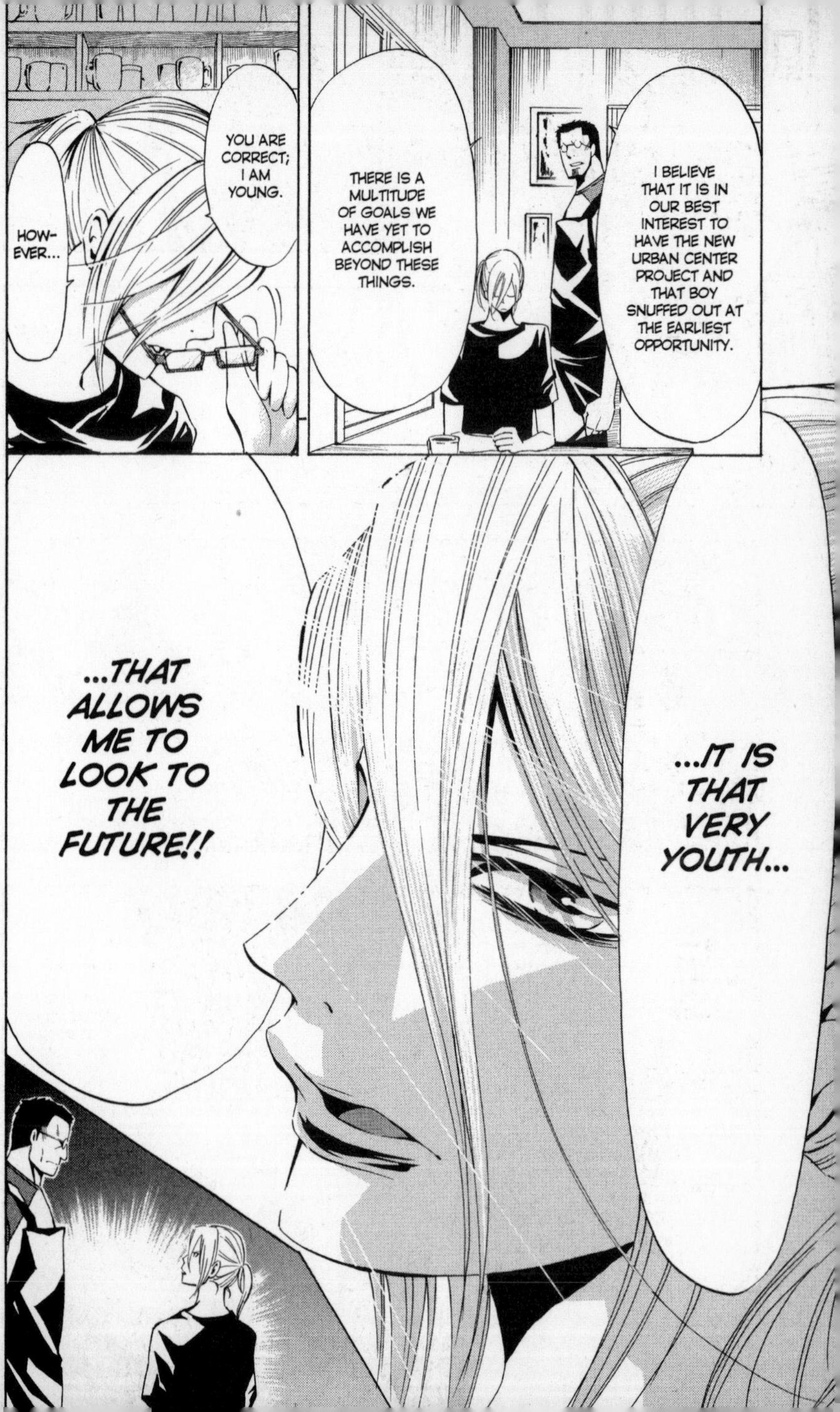
I BELIEVE THAT IT IS IN OUR BEST INTEREST TO HAVE THE NEW URBAN CENTER PROJECT AND THAT BOY SNUFFED OUT AT THE EARLIEST OPPORTUNITY.
THERE IS A MULTITUDE OF GOALS WE HAVE YET TO ACCOMPLISH BEYOND THESE THINGS.
YOU ARE CORRECT; I AM YOUNG.
HOW-EVER...
...IT IS THAT VERY YOUTH...
...THAT ALLOWS ME TO LOOK TO THE FUTURE!!

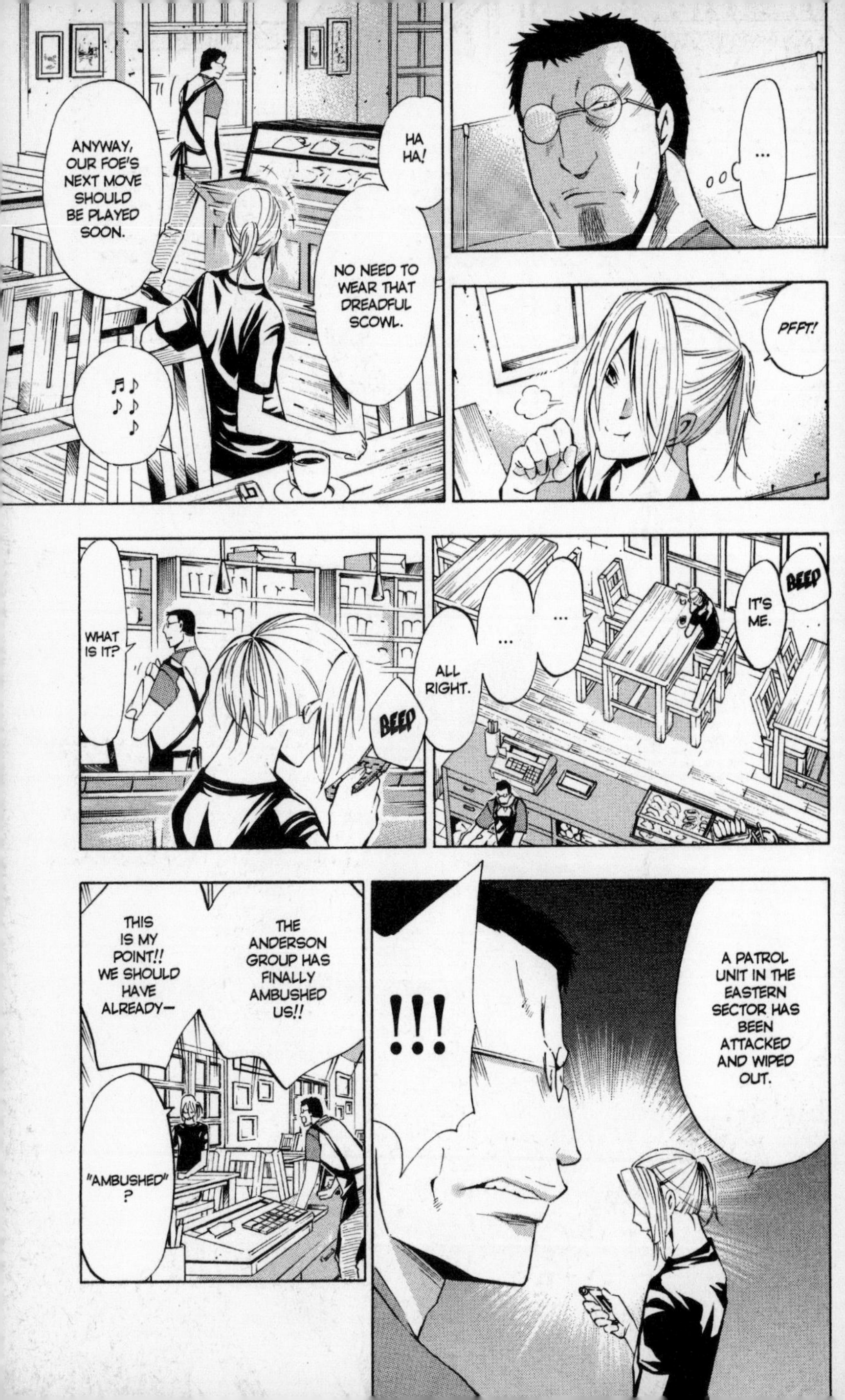
...
PFFT!
HA HA!
NO NEED TO WEAR THAT DREADFUL SCOWL.
ANYWAY, OUR FOE'S NEXT MOVE SHOULD BE PLAYED SOON.
♬♪ ♪♪ ♪
BEEP
IT'S ME.
...
...
ALL RIGHT.
BEEP
WHAT IS IT?
A PATROL UNIT IN THE EASTERN SECTOR HAS BEEN ATTACKED AND WIPED OUT.
!!!
THE ANDERSON GROUP HAS FINALLY AMBUSHED US!!
THIS IS MY POINT!! WE SHOULD HAVE ALREADY—
"AMBUSHED"?

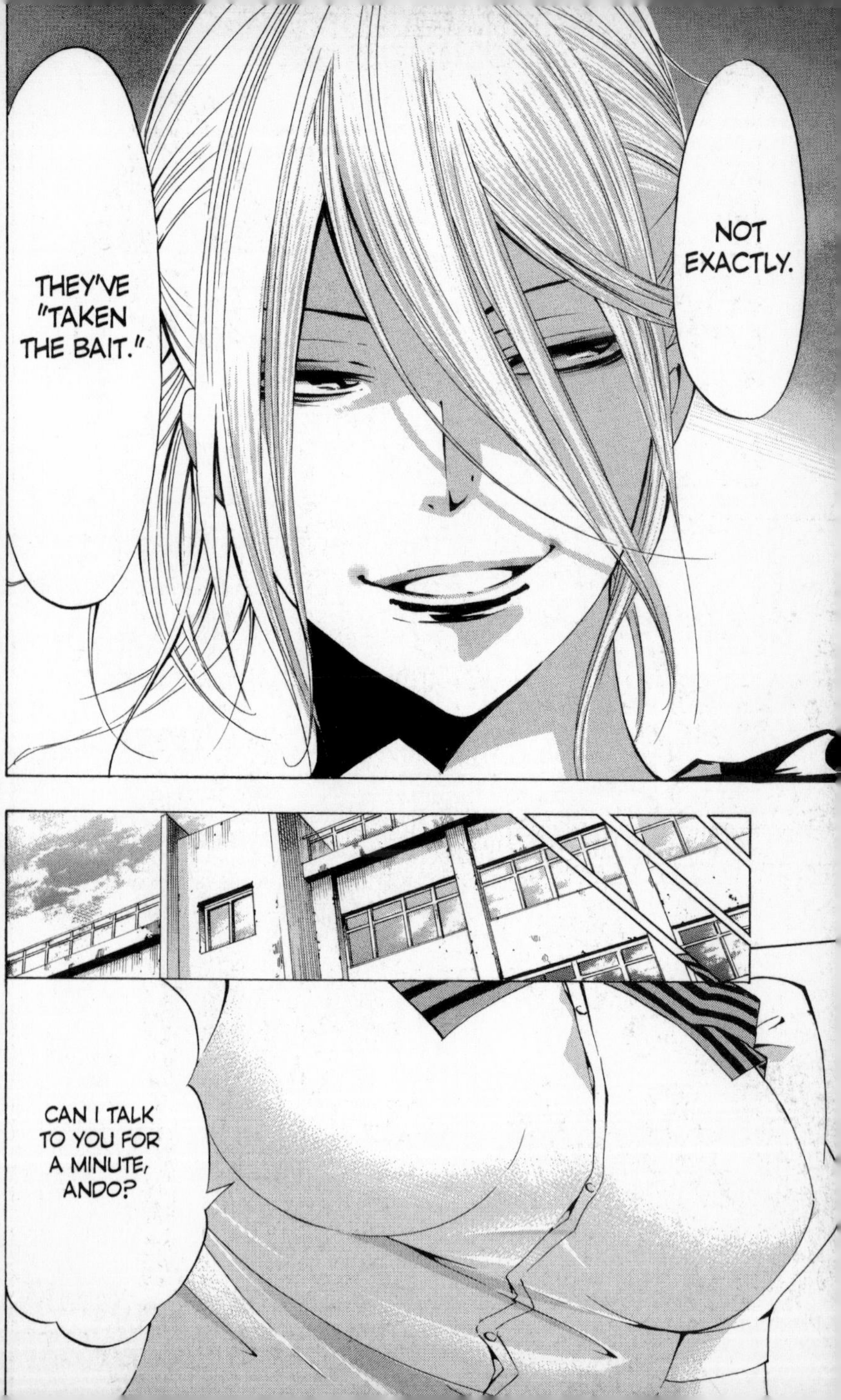
NOT EXACTLY.
THEY'VE "TAKEN THE BAIT."
CAN I TALK TO YOU FOR A MINUTE, ANDO?

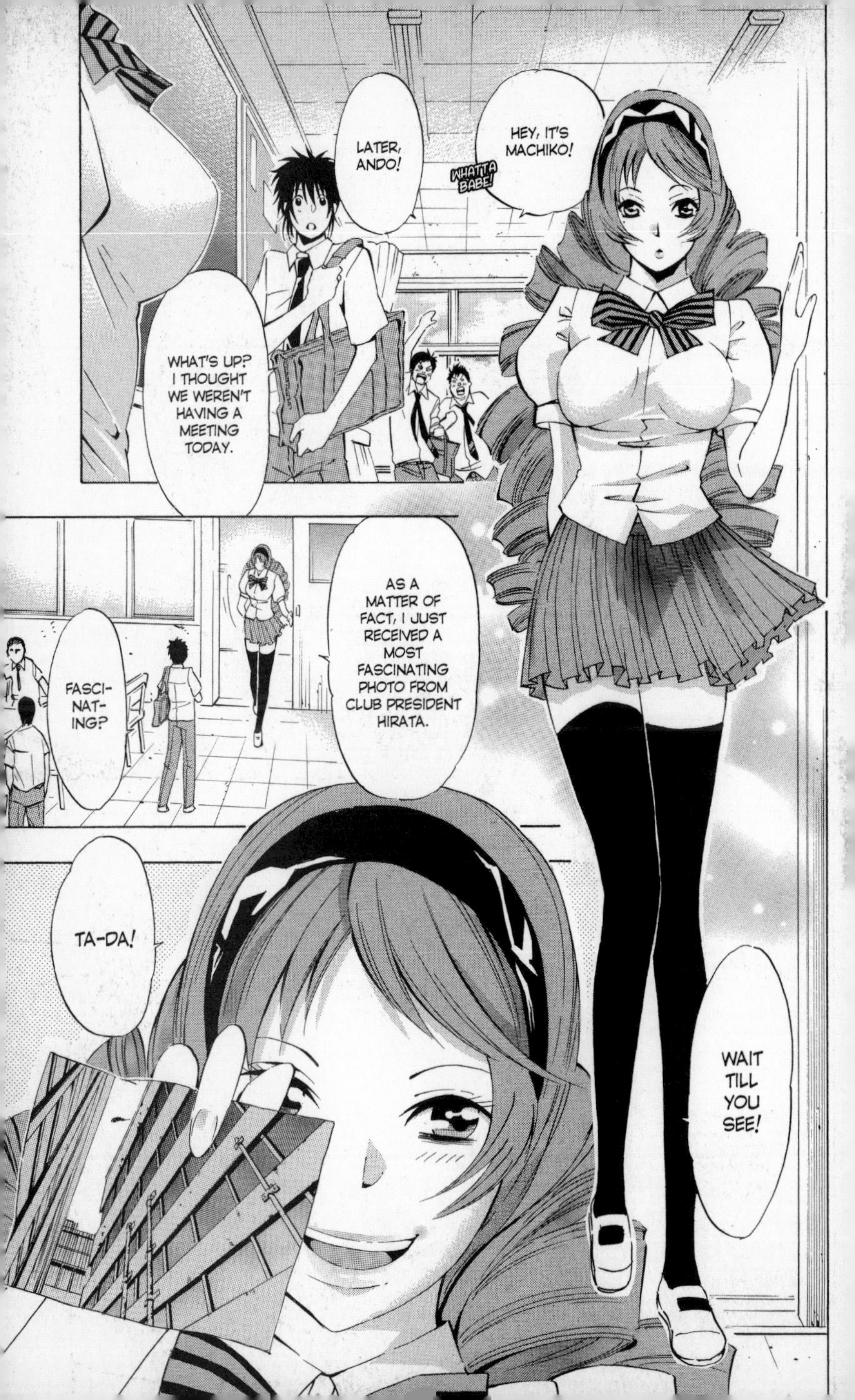
HEY, IT'S MACHIKO!
WHATTA BABE!
WAIT TILL YOU SEE!
LATER, ANDO!
WHAT'S UP? I THOUGHT WE WEREN'T HAVING A MEETING TODAY.
AS A MATTER OF FACT, I JUST RECEIVED A MOST FASCINATING PHOTO FROM CLUB PRESIDENT HIRATA.
FASCI-NAT-ING?
TA-DA!

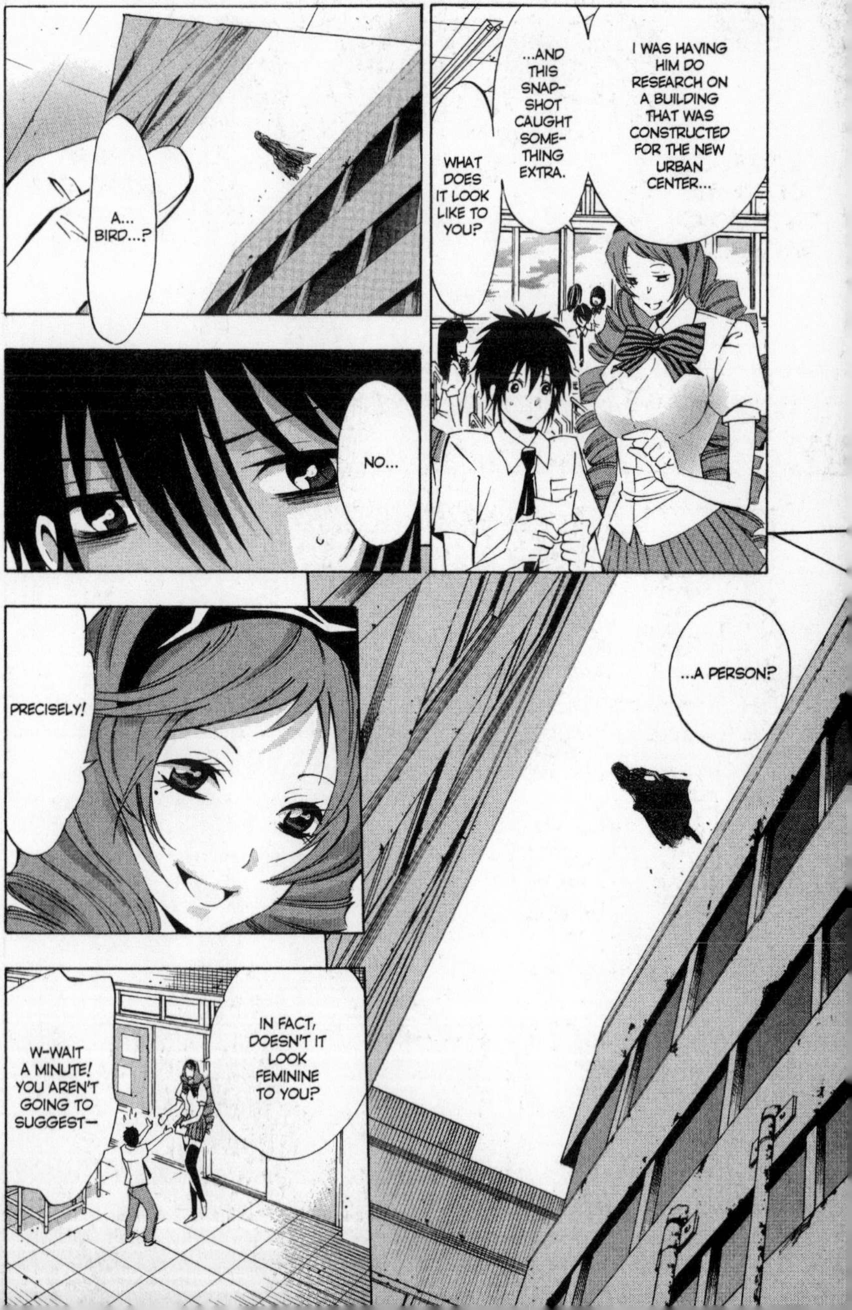
I WAS HAVING HIM DO RESEARCH ON A BUILDING THAT WAS CONSTRUCTED FOR THE NEW URBAN CENTER...
...AND THIS SNAPSHOT CAUGHT SOMETHING EXTRA.
WHAT DOES IT LOOK LIKE TO YOU?
A... BIRD...?
NO...
...A PERSON?
PRECISELY!
IN FACT, DOESN'T IT LOOK FEMININE TO YOU?
W-WAIT A MINUTE! YOU AREN'T GOING TO SUGGEST—

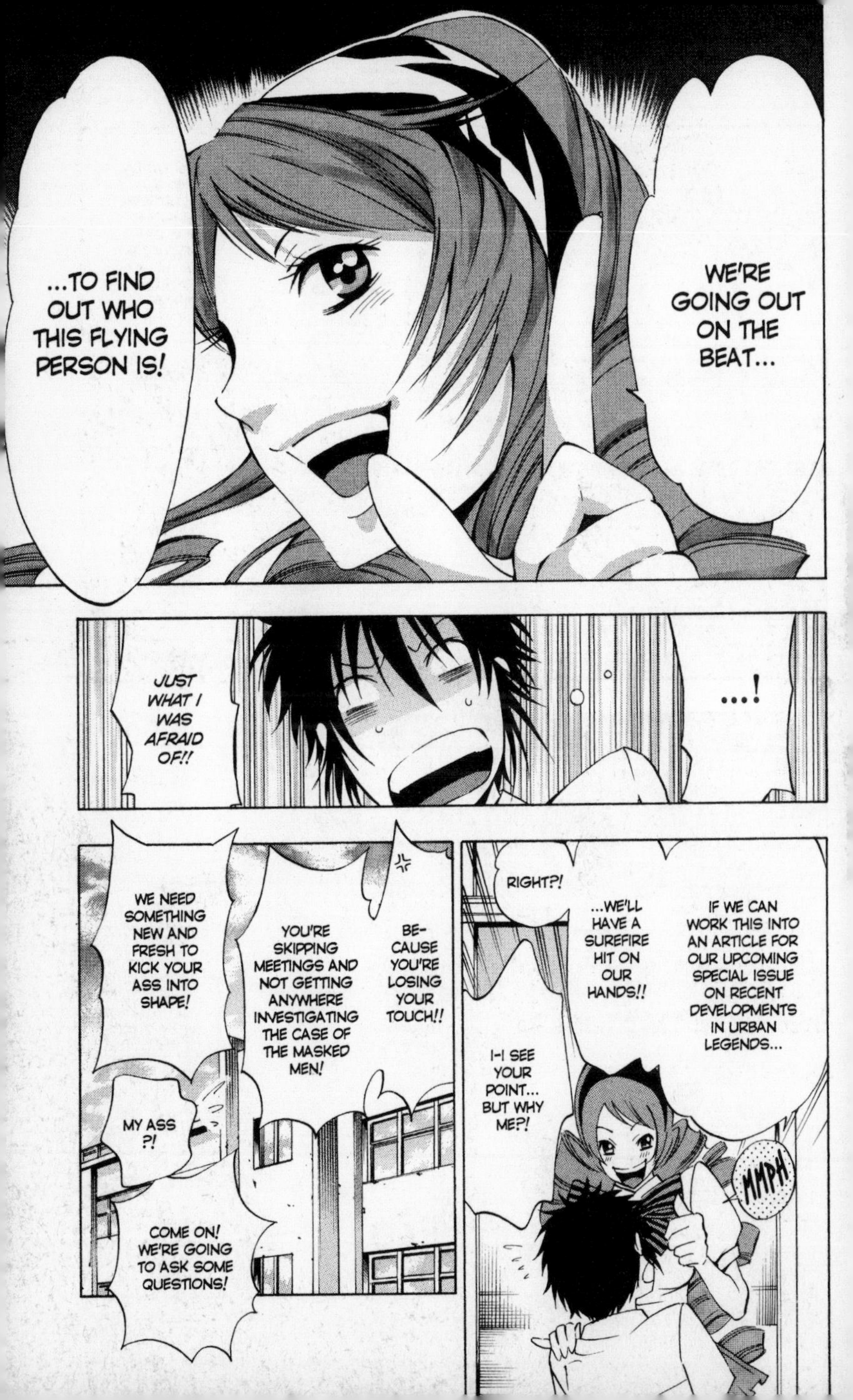
WE'RE GOING OUT ON THE BEAT...
...TO FIND OUT WHO THIS FLYING PERSON IS!
...!
JUST WHAT I WAS AFRAID OF!!
IF WE CAN WORK THIS INTO AN ARTICLE FOR OUR UPCOMING SPECIAL ISSUE ON RECENT DEVELOPMENTS IN URBAN LEGENDS...
...WE'LL HAVE A SUREFIRE HIT ON OUR HANDS!!
RIGHT?!
I-I SEE YOUR POINT... BUT WHY ME?!
MMPH
BE-CAUSE YOU'RE LOSING YOUR TOUCH!!
YOU'RE SKIPPING MEETINGS AND NOT GETTING ANYWHERE INVESTIGATING THE CASE OF THE MASKED MEN!
WE NEED SOMETHING NEW AND FRESH TO KICK YOUR ASS INTO SHAPE!
MY ASS ?!
COME ON! WE'RE GOING TO ASK SOME QUESTIONS!

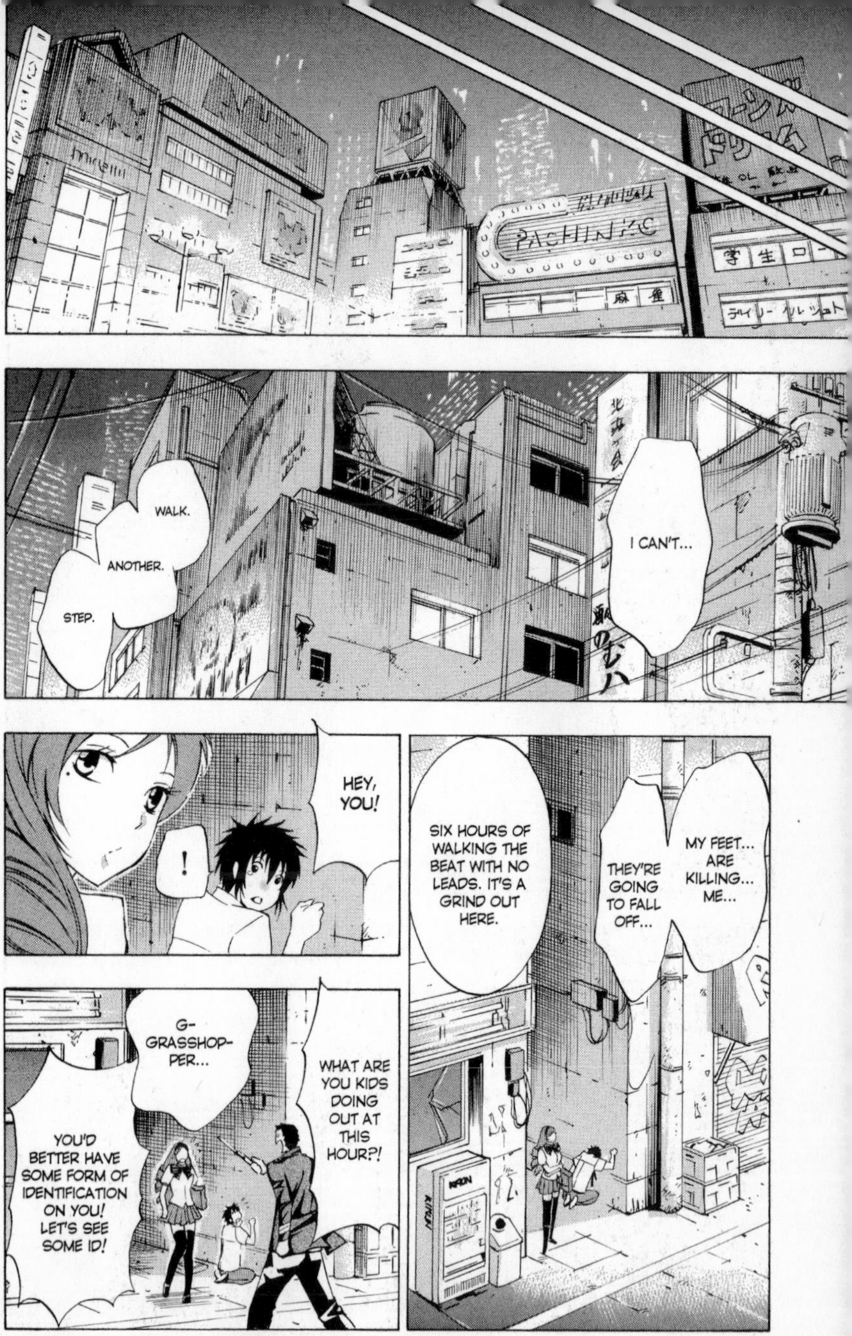
PACHINKO
麻雀
I CAN'T...
WALK.
ANOTHER.
STEP.
MY FEET... ARE KILLING... ME...
THEY'RE GOING TO FALL OFF...
SIX HOURS OF WALKING THE BEAT WITH NO LEADS. IT'S A GRIND OUT HERE.
HEY, YOU!
!
WHAT ARE YOU KIDS DOING OUT AT THIS HOUR?!
G-GRASSHOPPER...
YOU'D BETTER HAVE SOME FORM OF IDENTIFICATION ON YOU! LET'S SEE SOME ID!

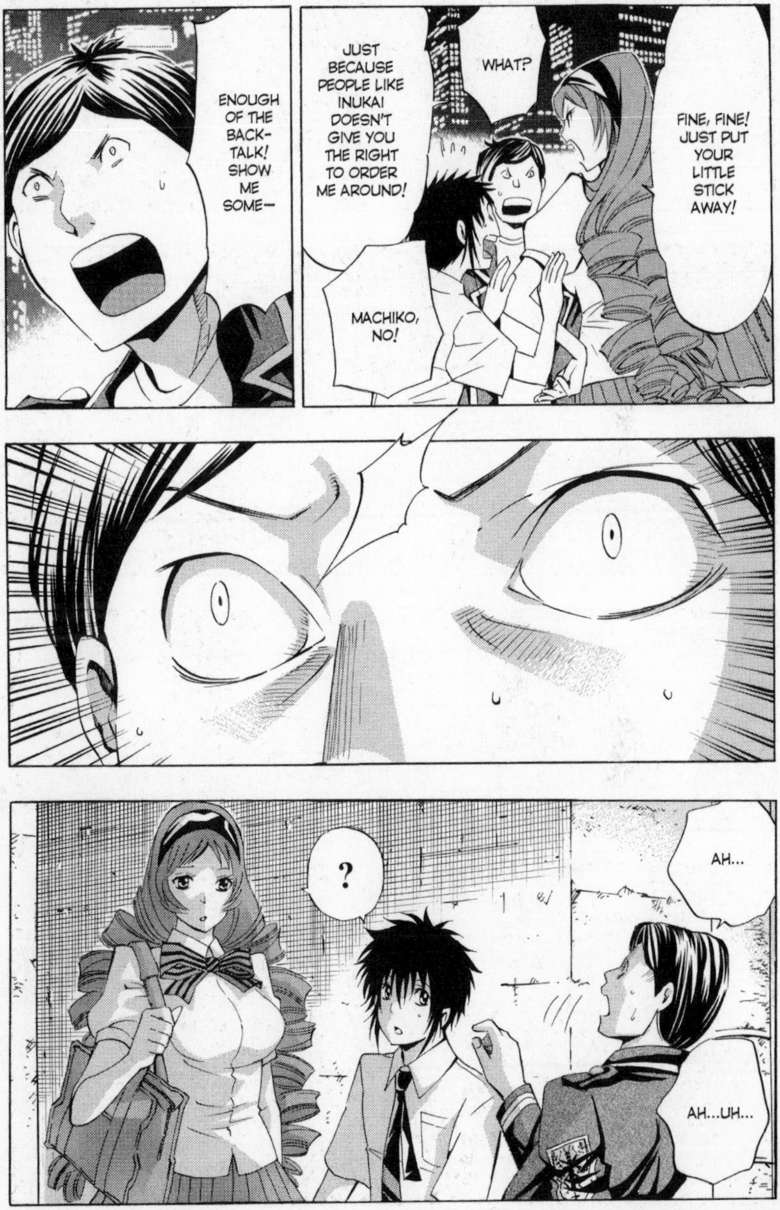
FINE, FINE! JUST PUT YOUR LITTLE STICK AWAY!
WHAT?
JUST BECAUSE PEOPLE LIKE INUKAI DOESN'T GIVE YOU THE RIGHT TO ORDER ME AROUND!
MACHIKO, NO!
ENOUGH OF THE BACK-TALK! SHOW ME SOME—
AH...
AH...UH...
?

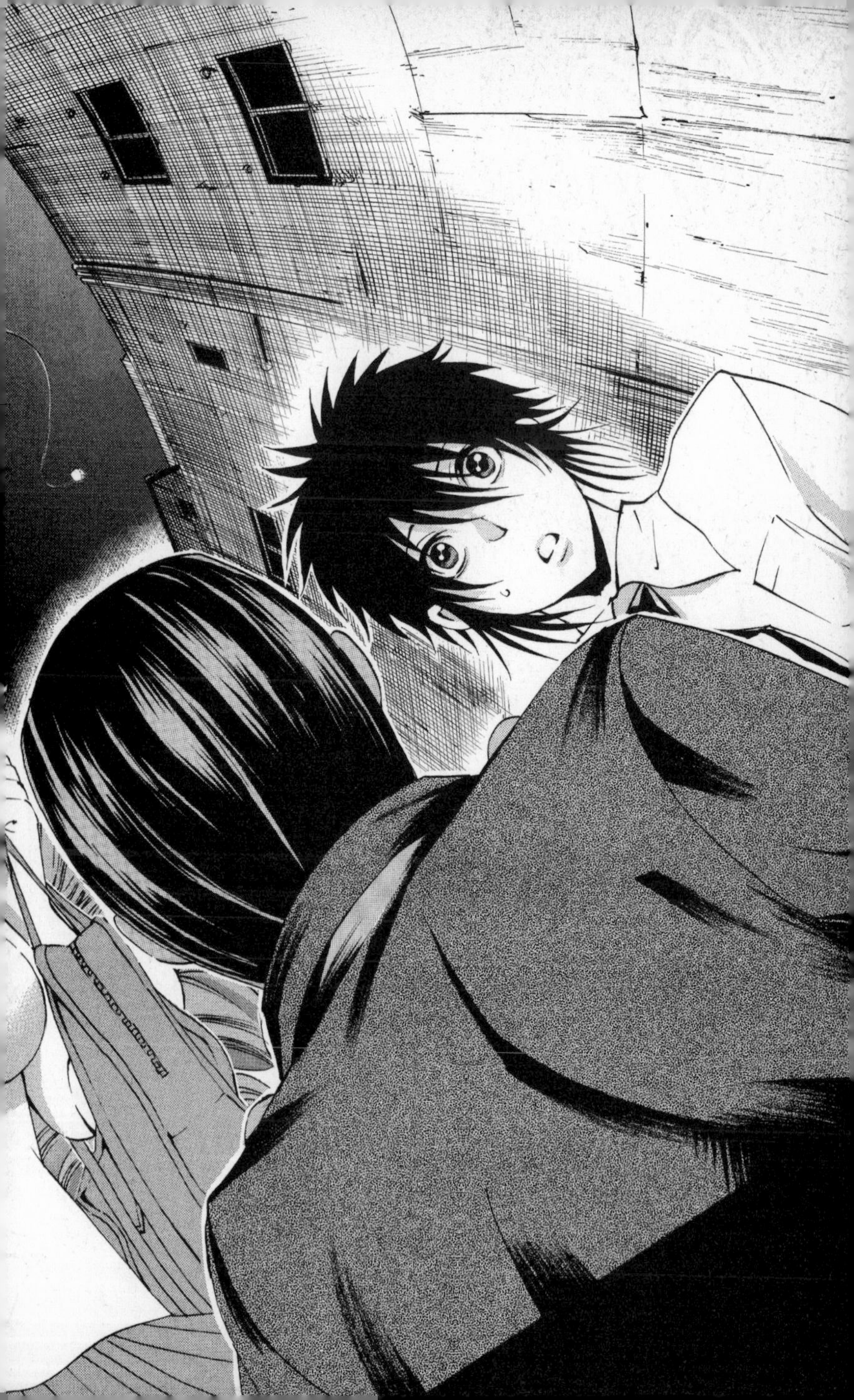

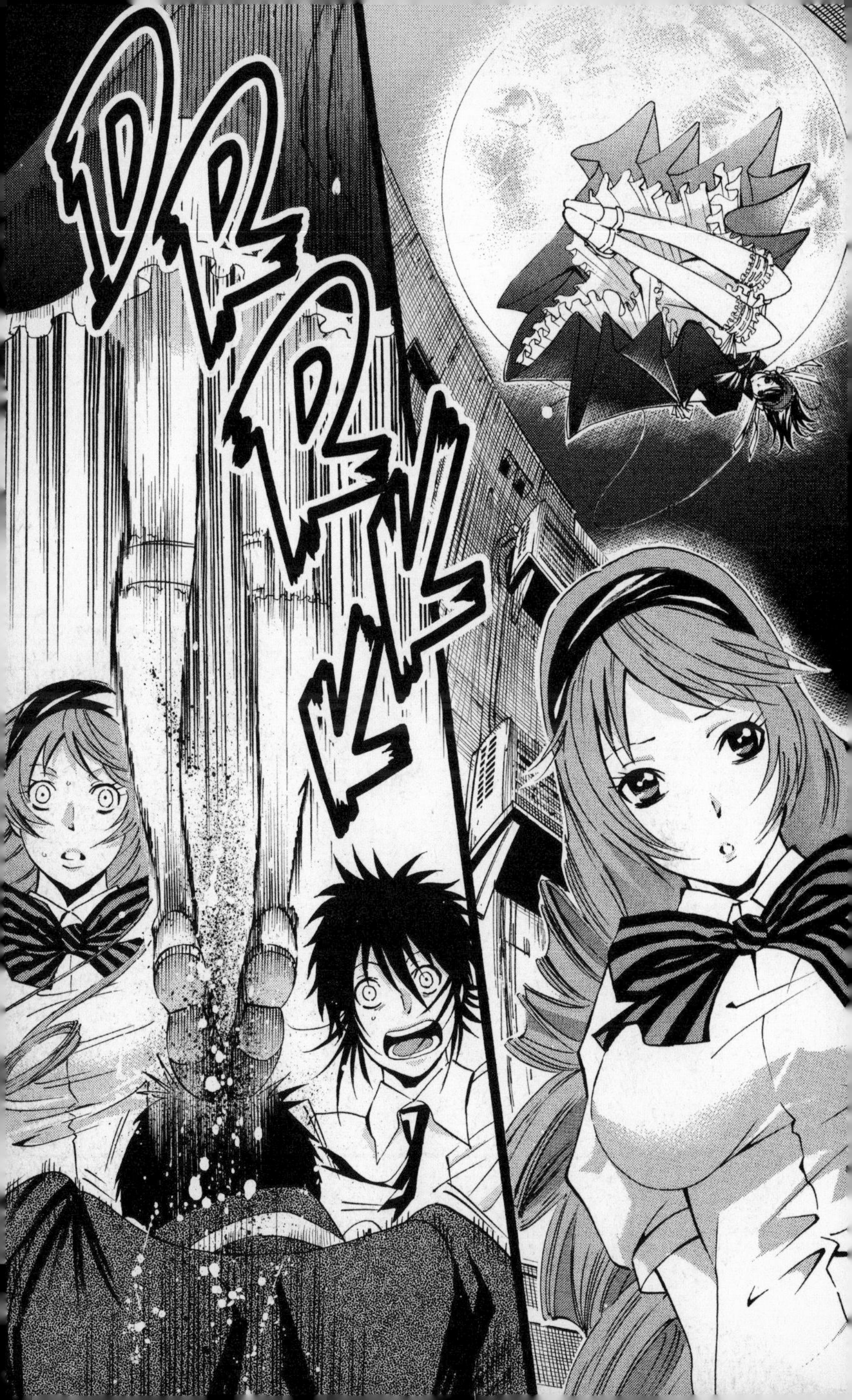
DRRNK

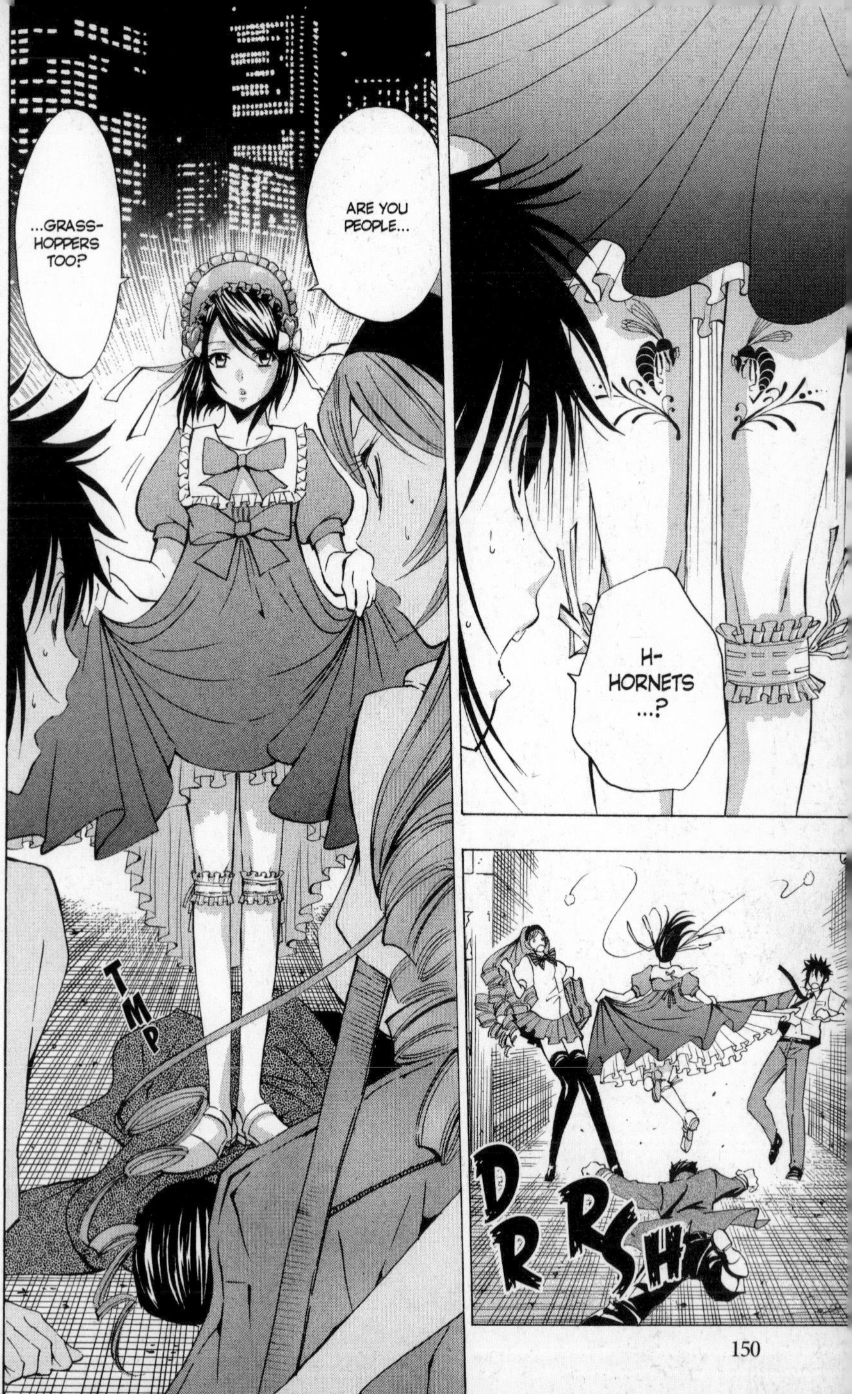
H-HORNETS...?
DRRSH
ARE YOU PEOPLE...
...GRASS-HOPPERS TOO?
TMP

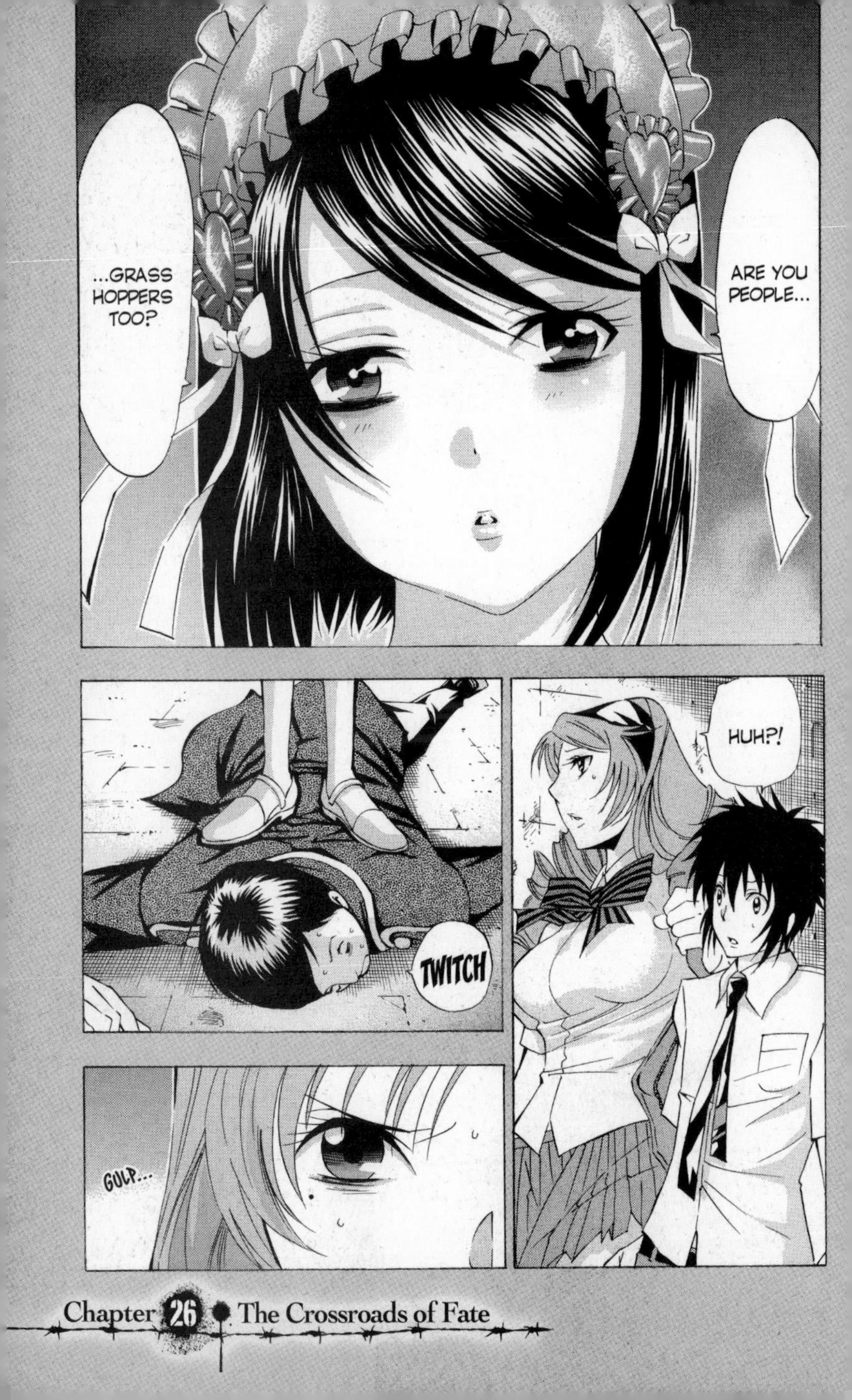
ARE YOU PEOPLE...
...GRASS HOPPERS TOO?
HUH?!
TWITCH
GULP...

Chapter 26 The Crossroads of Fate

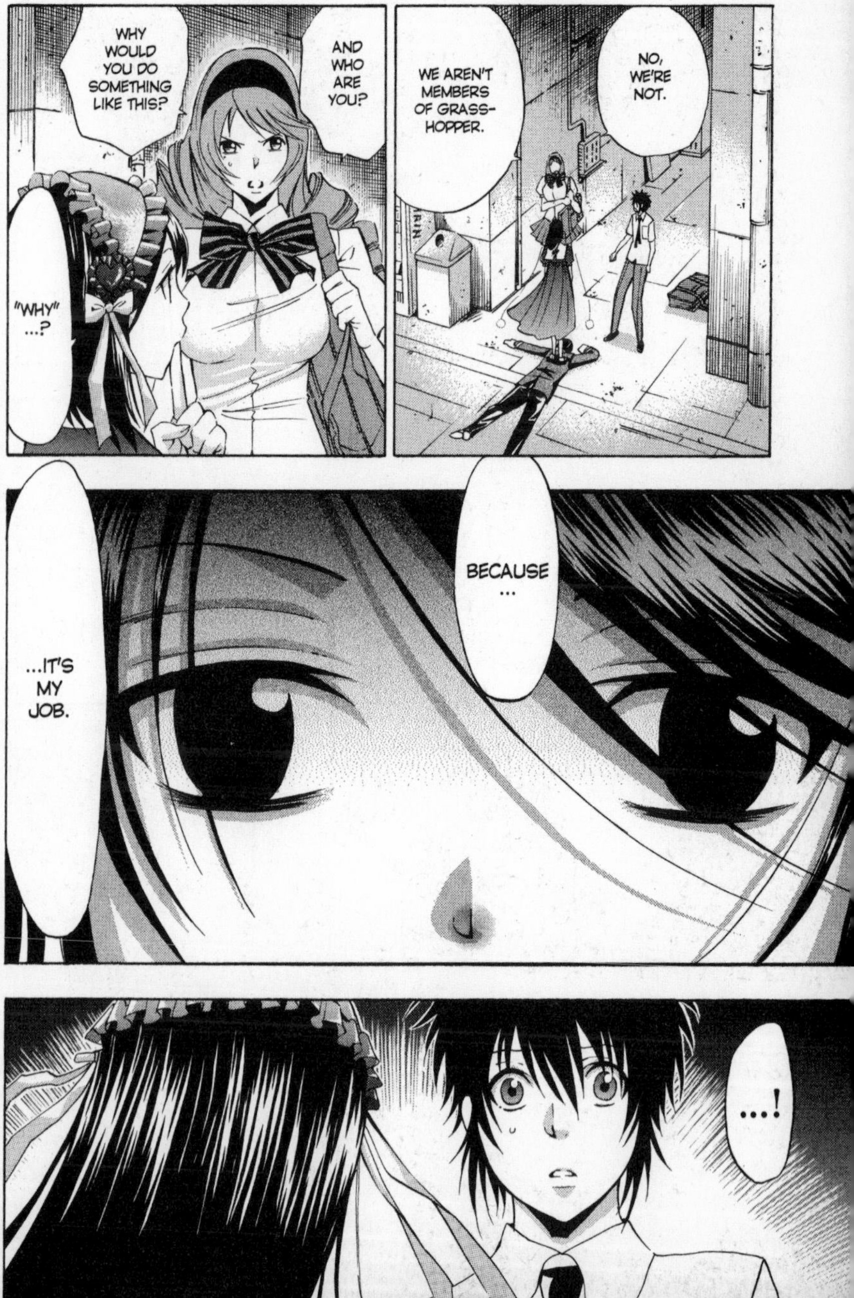
NO, WE'RE NOT.
WE AREN'T MEMBERS OF GRASS-HOPPER.
WHY WOULD YOU DO SOMETHING LIKE THIS?
AND WHO ARE YOU?
"WHY" ...?
BECAUSE ...
...IT'S MY JOB.
...!

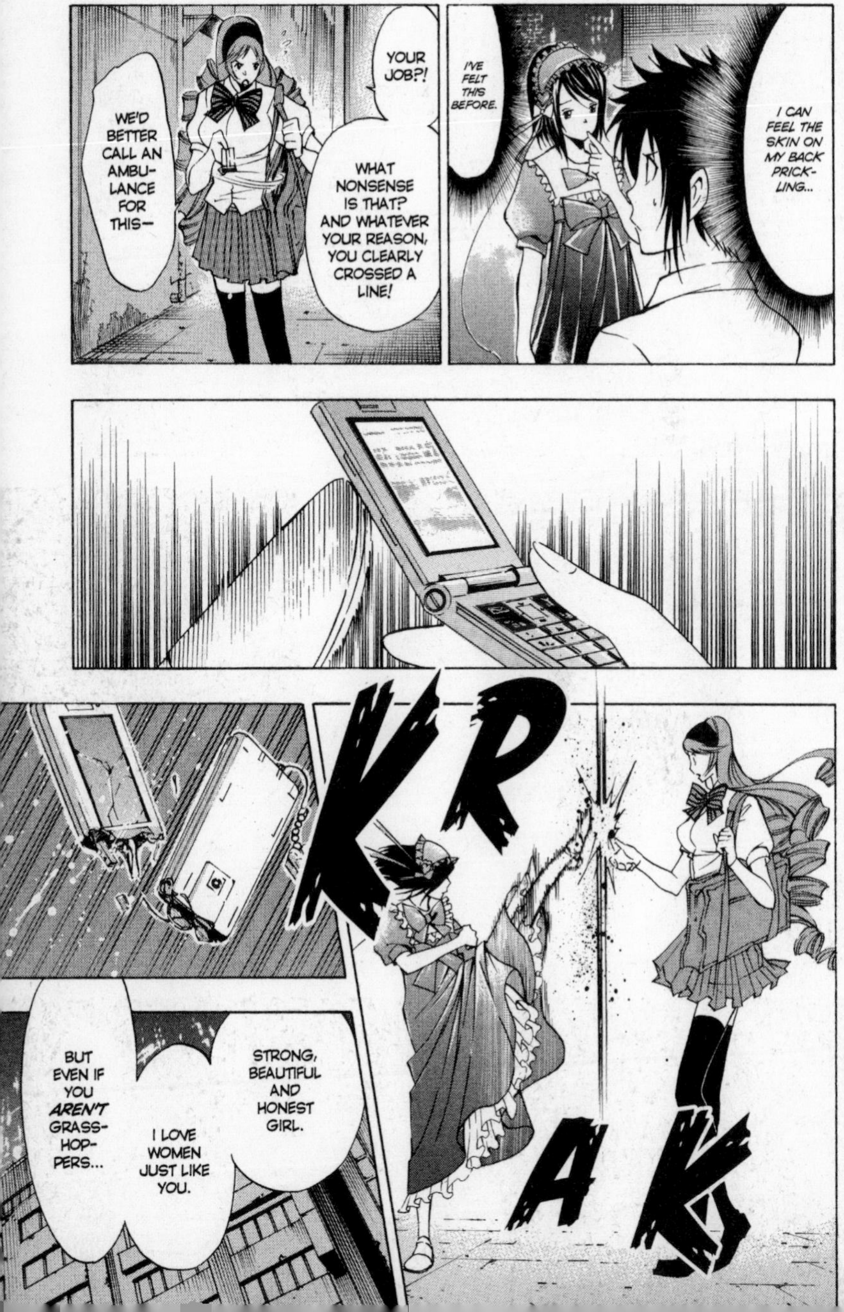
I CAN FEEL THE SKIN ON MY BACK PRICKLING...
I'VE FELT THIS BEFORE.
YOUR JOB?!
WHAT NONSENSE IS THAT? AND WHATEVER YOUR REASON, YOU CLEARLY CROSSED A LINE!
WE'D BETTER CALL AN AMBULANCE FOR THIS—
KRAK
STRONG, BEAUTIFUL AND HONEST GIRL.
I LOVE WOMEN JUST LIKE YOU.
BUT EVEN IF YOU *AREN'T* GRASSHOPPERS...

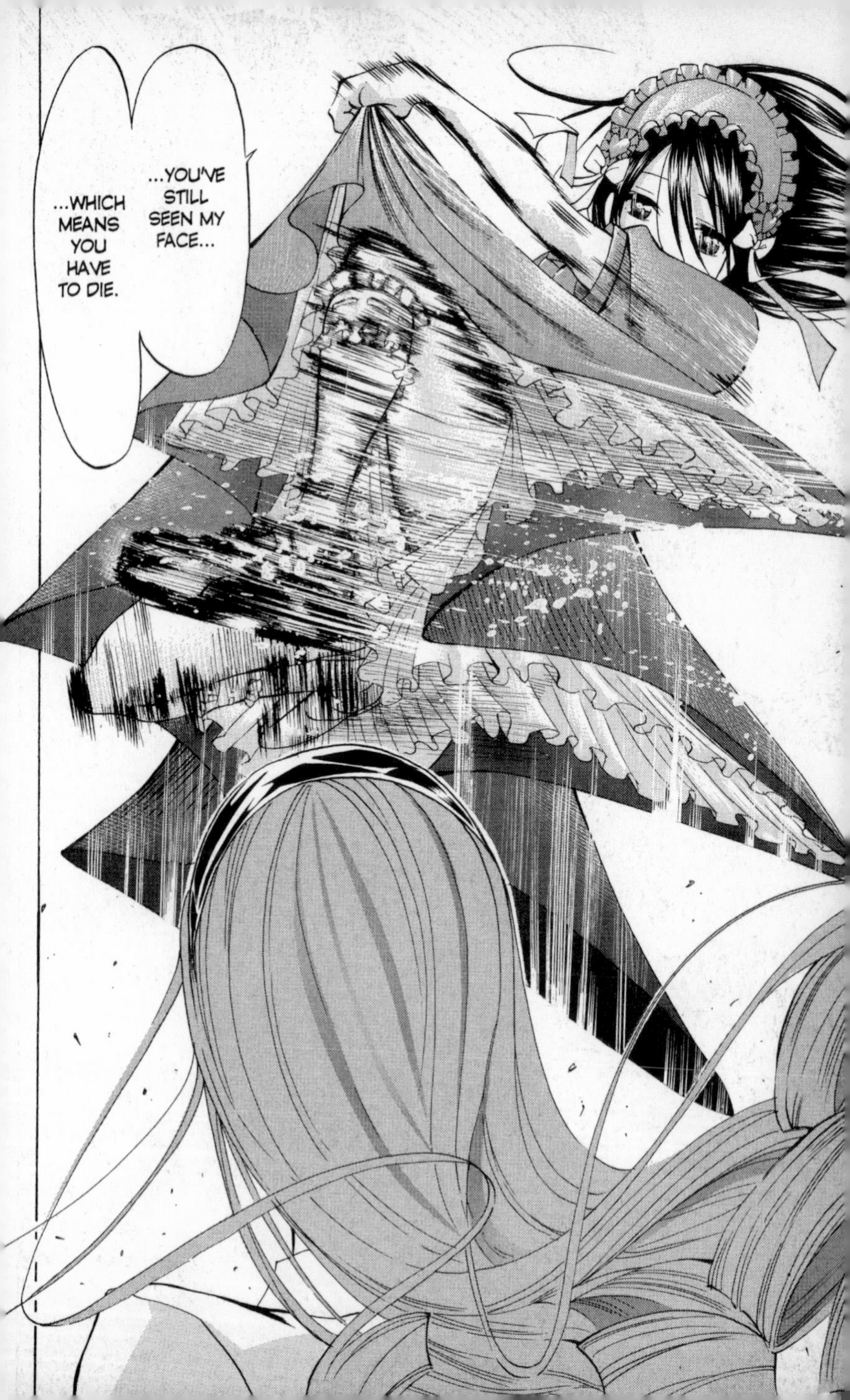
...YOU'VE STILL SEEN MY FACE...
...WHICH MEANS YOU HAVE TO DIE.

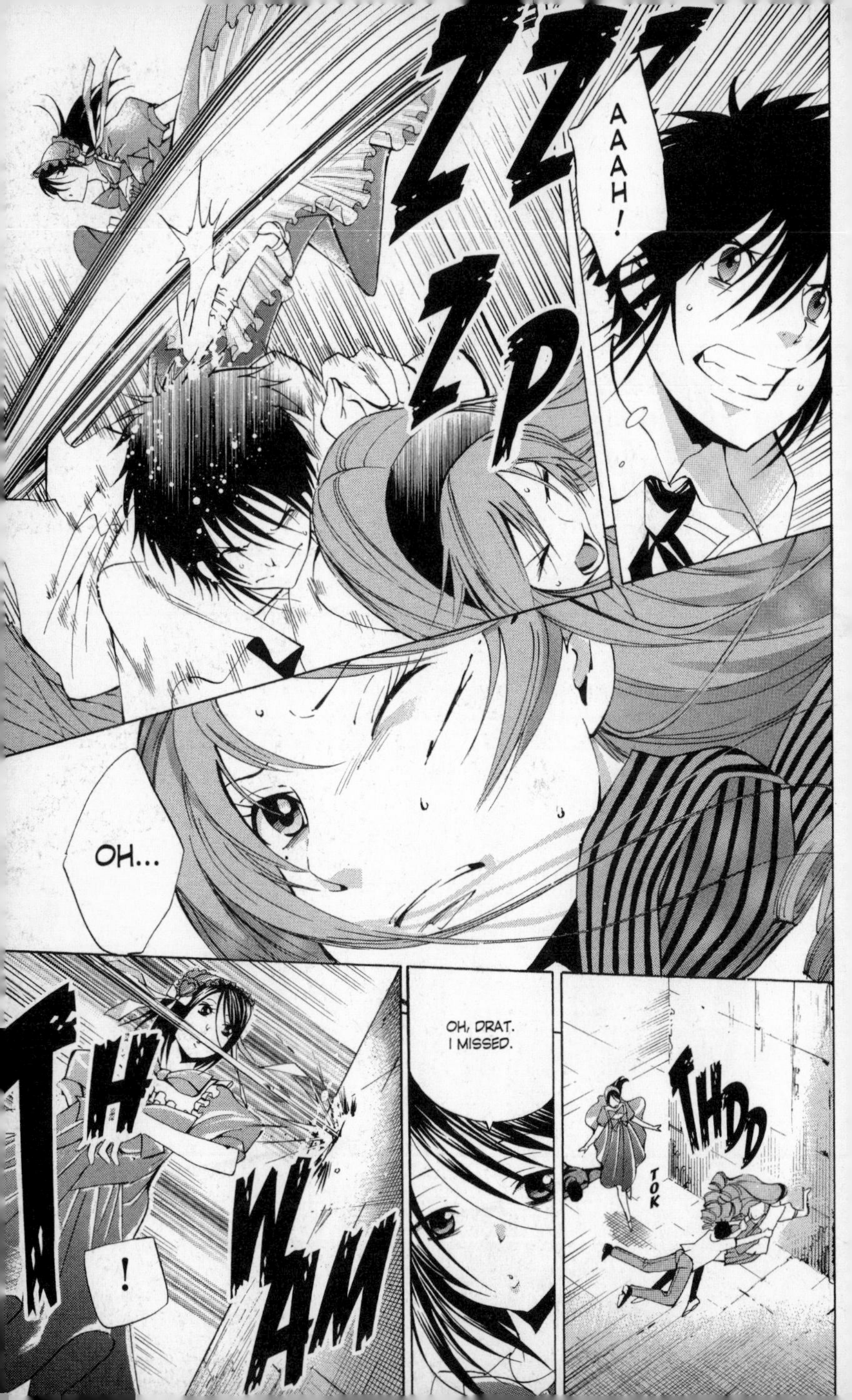
AAAH!
ZZZIP
OH...
THDD
TOK
OH, DRAT. I MISSED.
THWAM
!

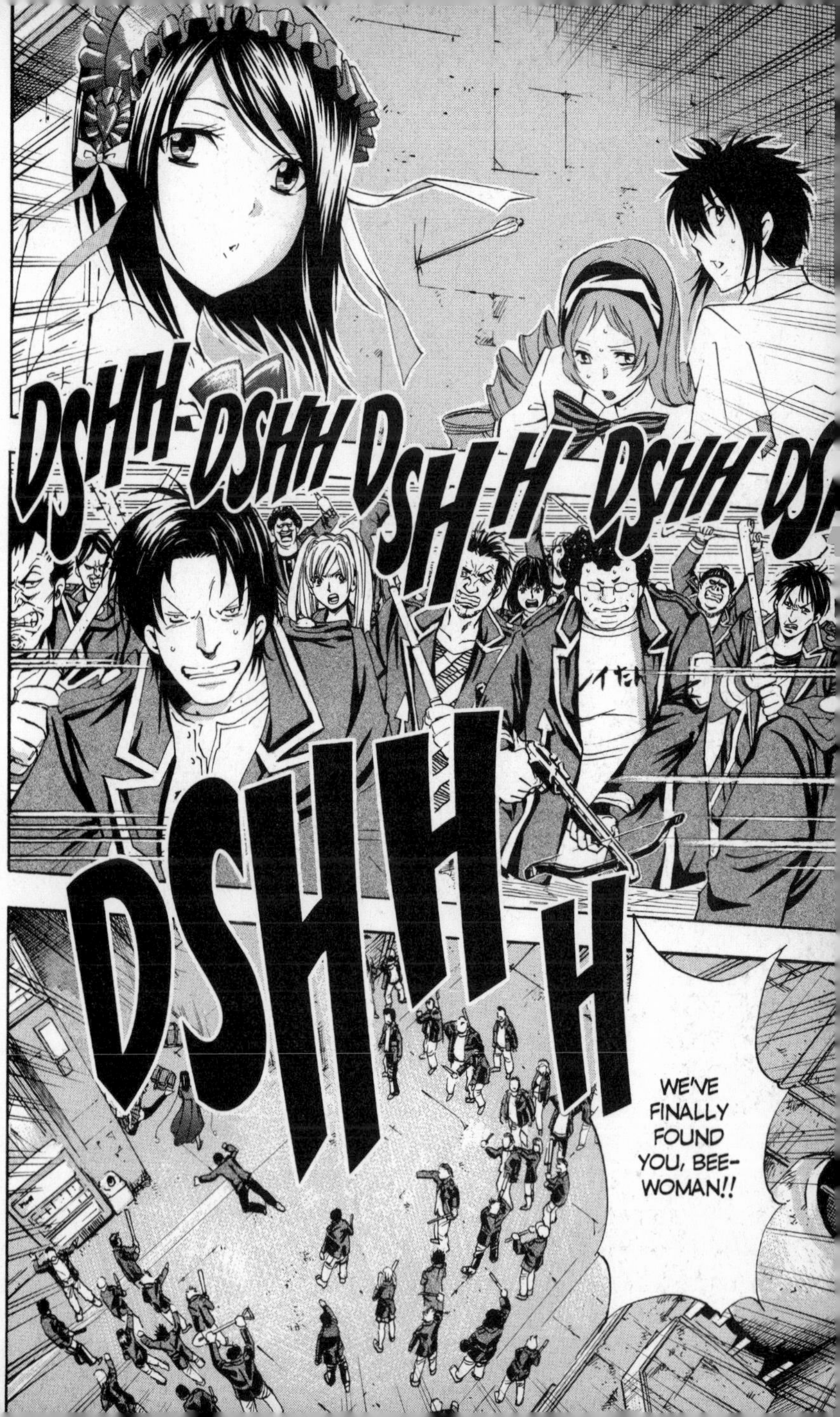
DSHH DSHH DSHH DSHH DS
DSHHH
WE'VE FINALLY FOUND YOU, BEE-WOMAN!!

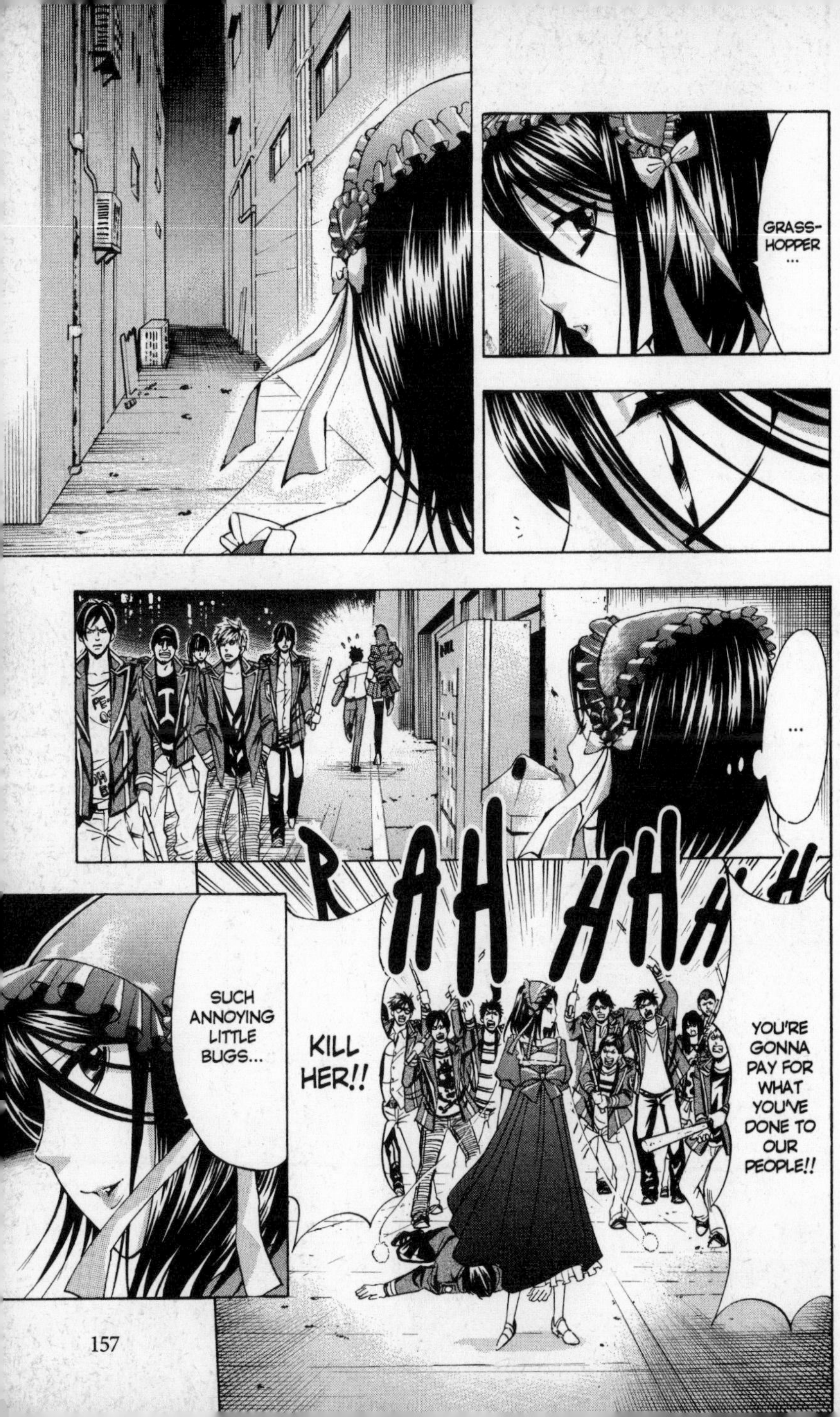
GRASS-HOPPER ...
...
RAAHHHAH
YOU'RE GONNA PAY FOR WHAT YOU'VE DONE TO OUR PEOPLE!!
KILL HER!!
SUCH ANNOYING LITTLE BUGS...

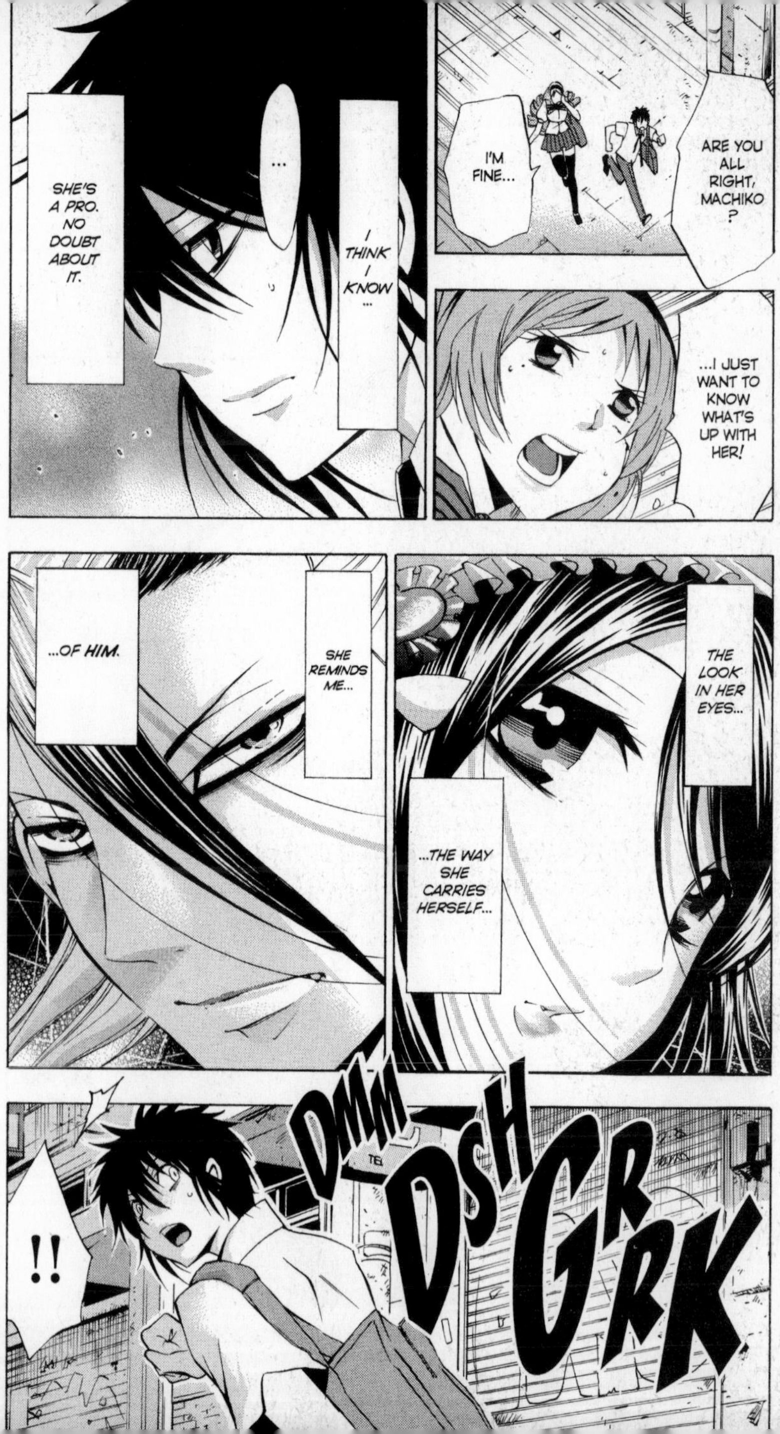
ARE YOU ALL RIGHT, MACHIKO?
I'M FINE...
...I JUST WANT TO KNOW WHAT'S UP WITH HER!
I THINK I KNOW...
...
SHE'S A PRO. NO DOUBT ABOUT IT.
THE LOOK IN HER EYES...
...THE WAY SHE CARRIES HERSELF...
SHE REMINDS ME...
...OF HIM.
GRGRK
DSH
DMM
!!

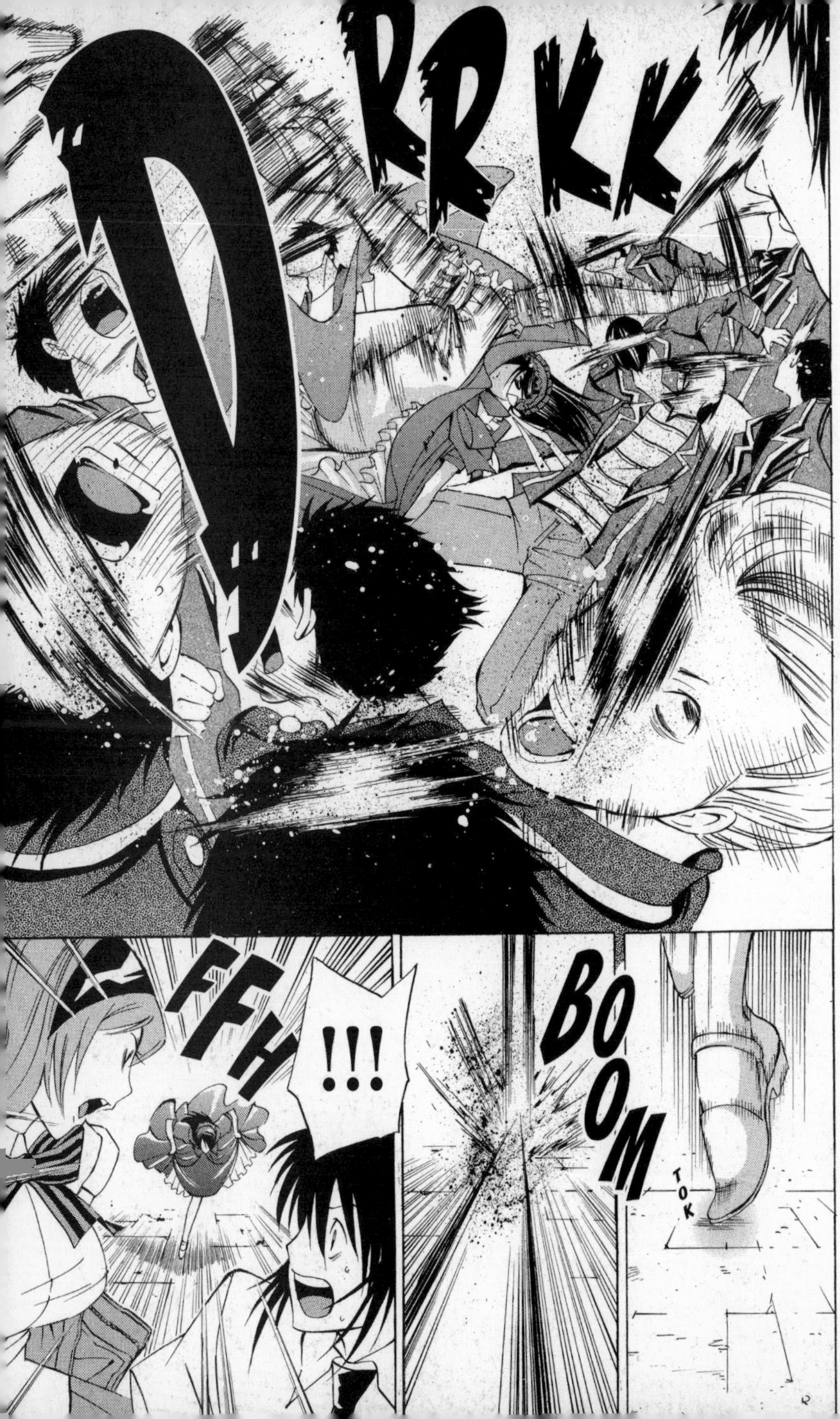
DRRKK
TOK
BOOM
FFH
!!!

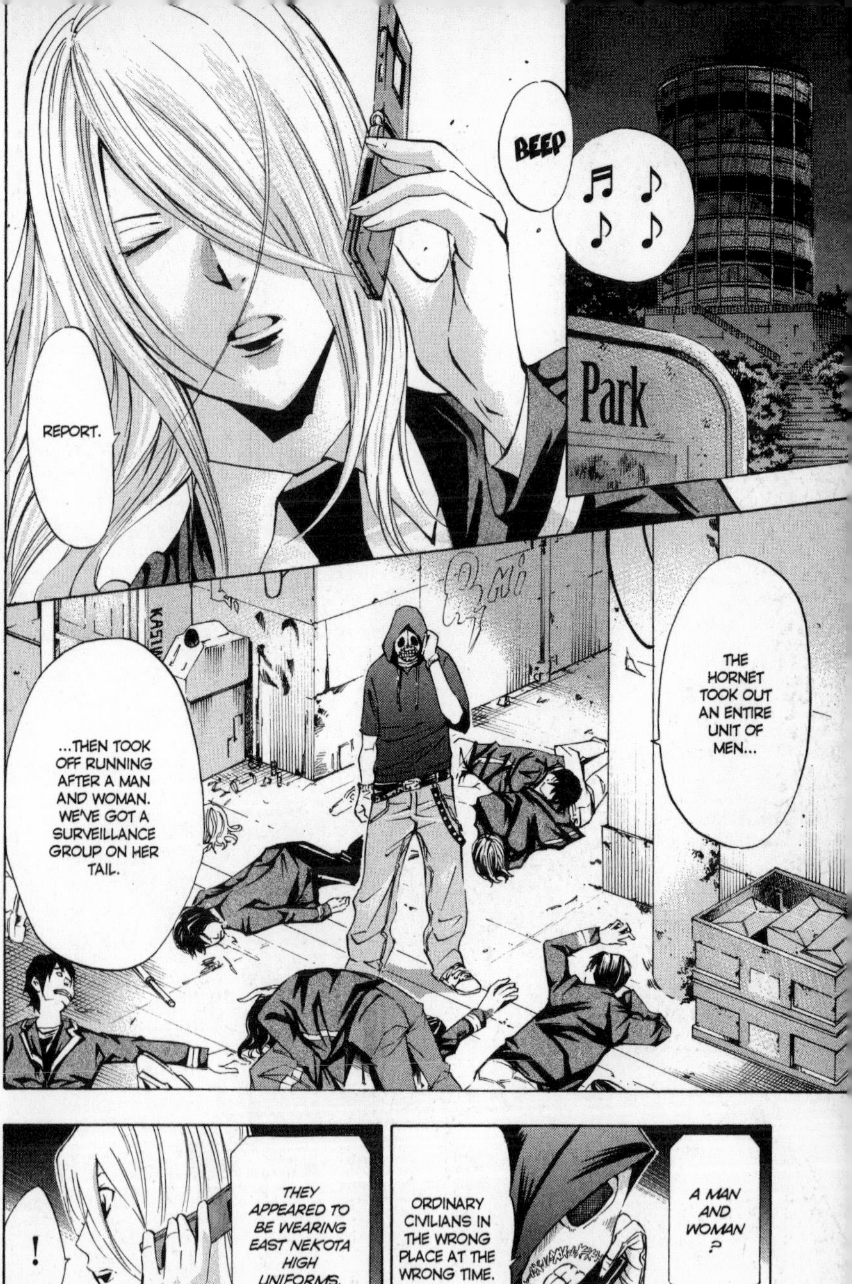
BEEP
♬ ♪
♪ ♪
Park
REPORT.
THE HORNET TOOK OUT AN ENTIRE UNIT OF MEN...
...THEN TOOK OFF RUNNING AFTER A MAN AND WOMAN. WE'VE GOT A SURVEILLANCE GROUP ON HER TAIL.
A MAN AND WOMAN?
ORDINARY CIVILIANS IN THE WRONG PLACE AT THE WRONG TIME.
THEY APPEARED TO BE WEARING EAST NEKOTA HIGH UNIFORMS.
!

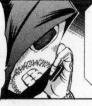

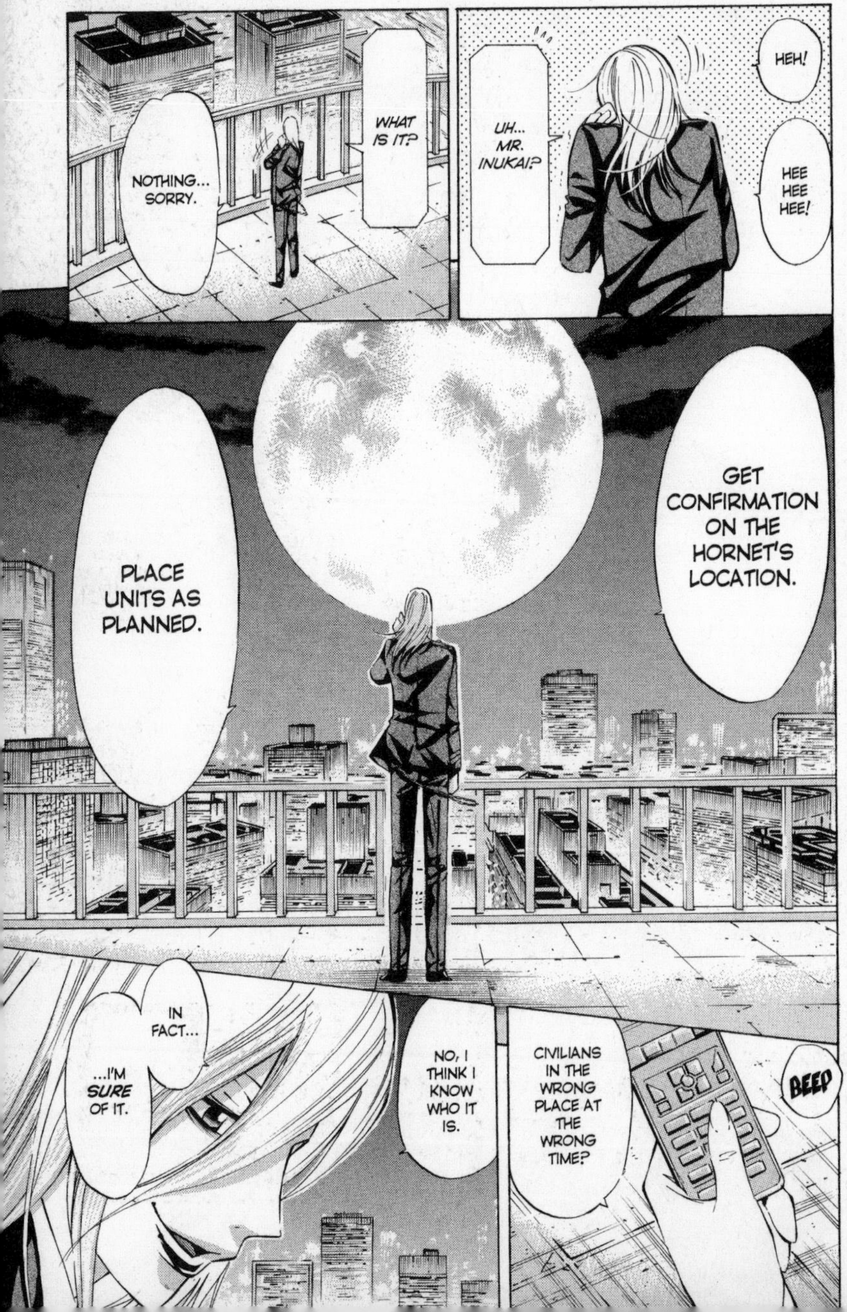
HEH!
HEE HEE HEE!
UH... MR. INUKAI?
WHAT IS IT?
NOTHING... SORRY.
GET CONFIRMATION ON THE HORNET'S LOCATION.
PLACE UNITS AS PLANNED.
BEEP
CIVILIANS IN THE WRONG PLACE AT THE WRONG TIME?
NO, I THINK I KNOW WHO IT IS.
IN FACT...
...I'M *SURE* OF IT.

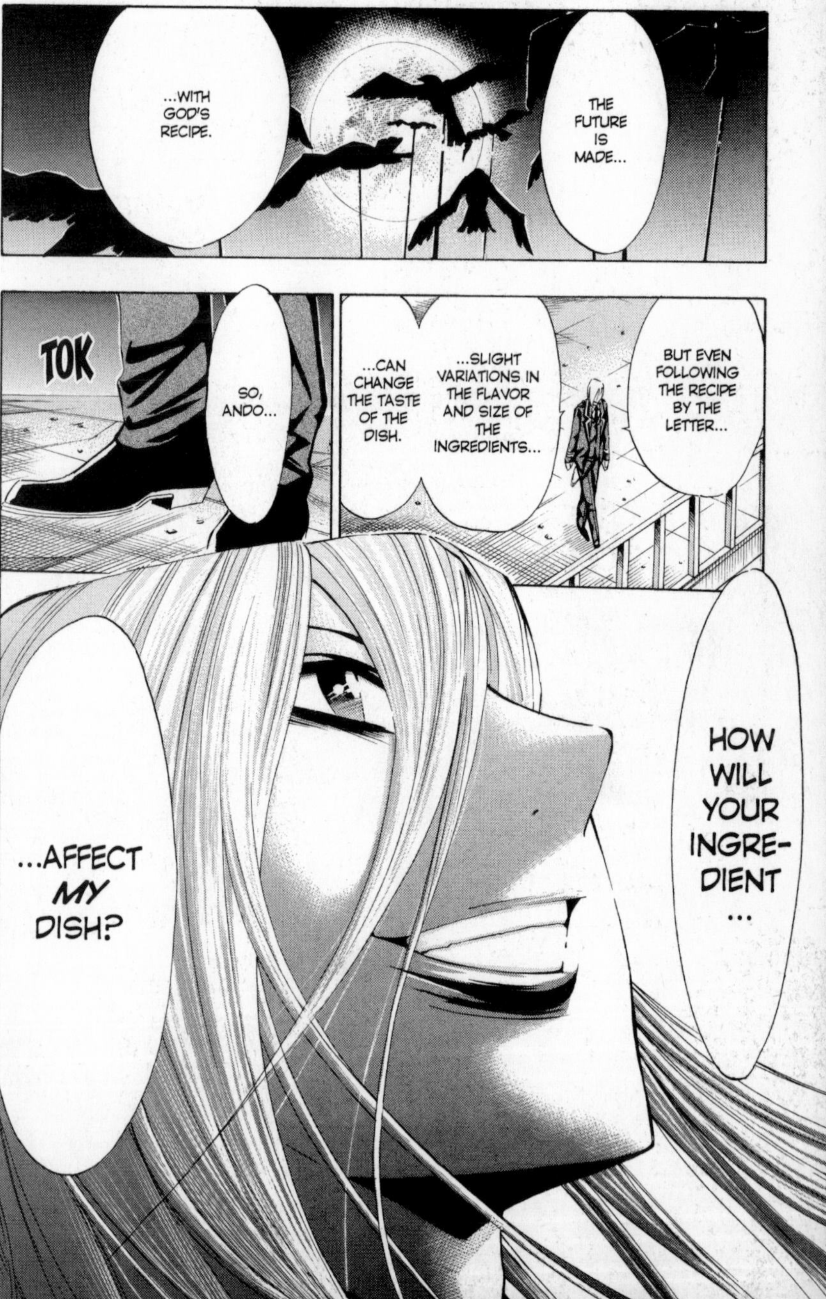

THE FUTURE IS MADE...
...WITH GOD'S RECIPE.
BUT EVEN FOLLOWING THE RECIPE BY THE LETTER...
...SLIGHT VARIATIONS IN THE FLAVOR AND SIZE OF THE INGREDIENTS...
...CAN CHANGE THE TASTE OF THE DISH.
SO, ANDO...
TOK
HOW WILL YOUR INGRE-DIENT ...
...AFFECT *MY* DISH?

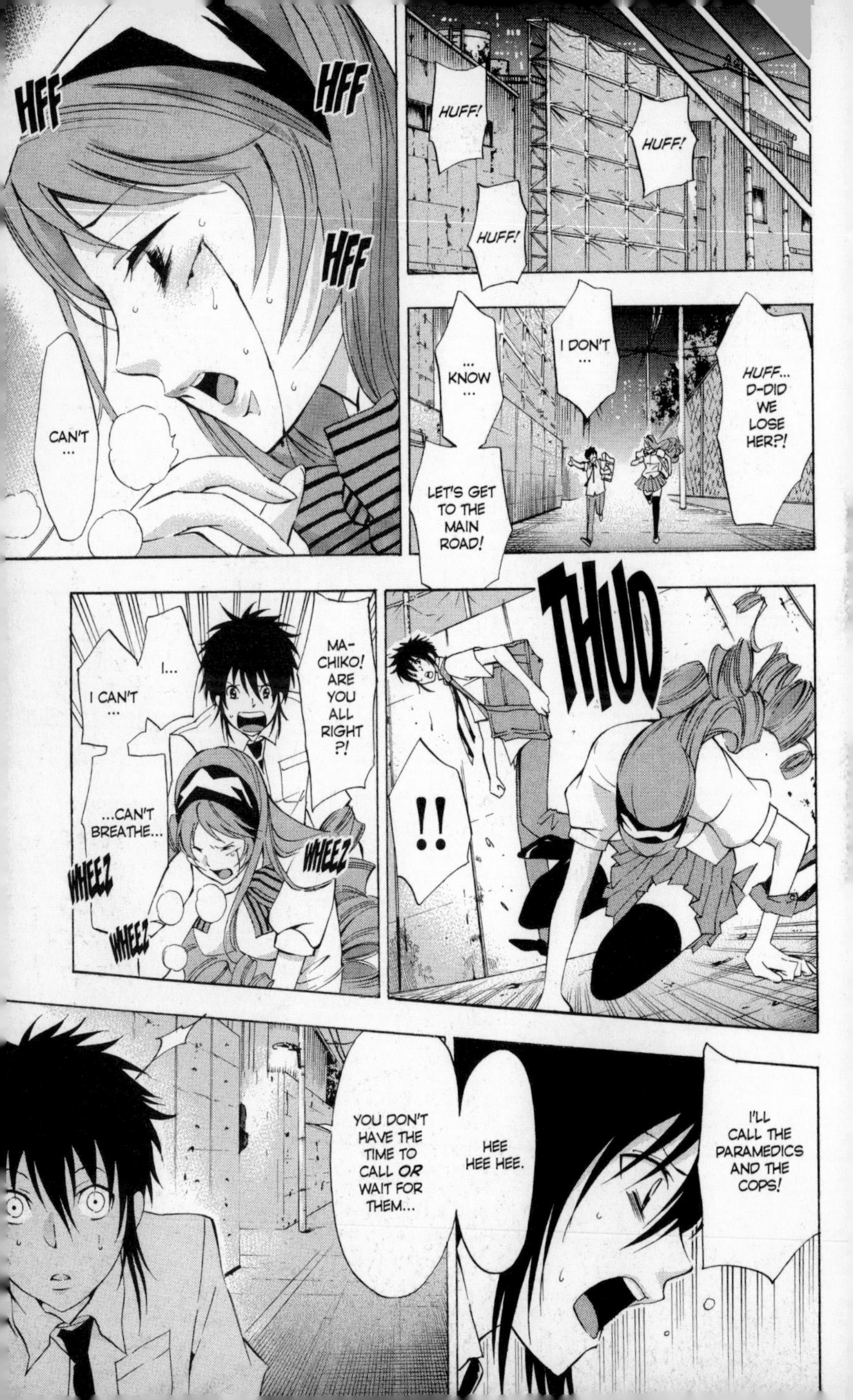
HUFF!
HUFF!
HUFF!
HUFF... D-DID WE LOSE HER?!
I DON'T ...
... KNOW ...
LET'S GET TO THE MAIN ROAD!
HFF
HFF
HFF
CAN'T ...
THUD
!!
MA-CHIKO! ARE YOU ALL RIGHT?!
I...
I CAN'T ...
...CAN'T BREATHE...
WHEEZ
WHEEZ
WHEEZ
I'LL CALL THE PARAMEDICS AND THE COPS!
HEE HEE HEE.
YOU DON'T HAVE THE TIME TO CALL *OR* WAIT FOR THEM...

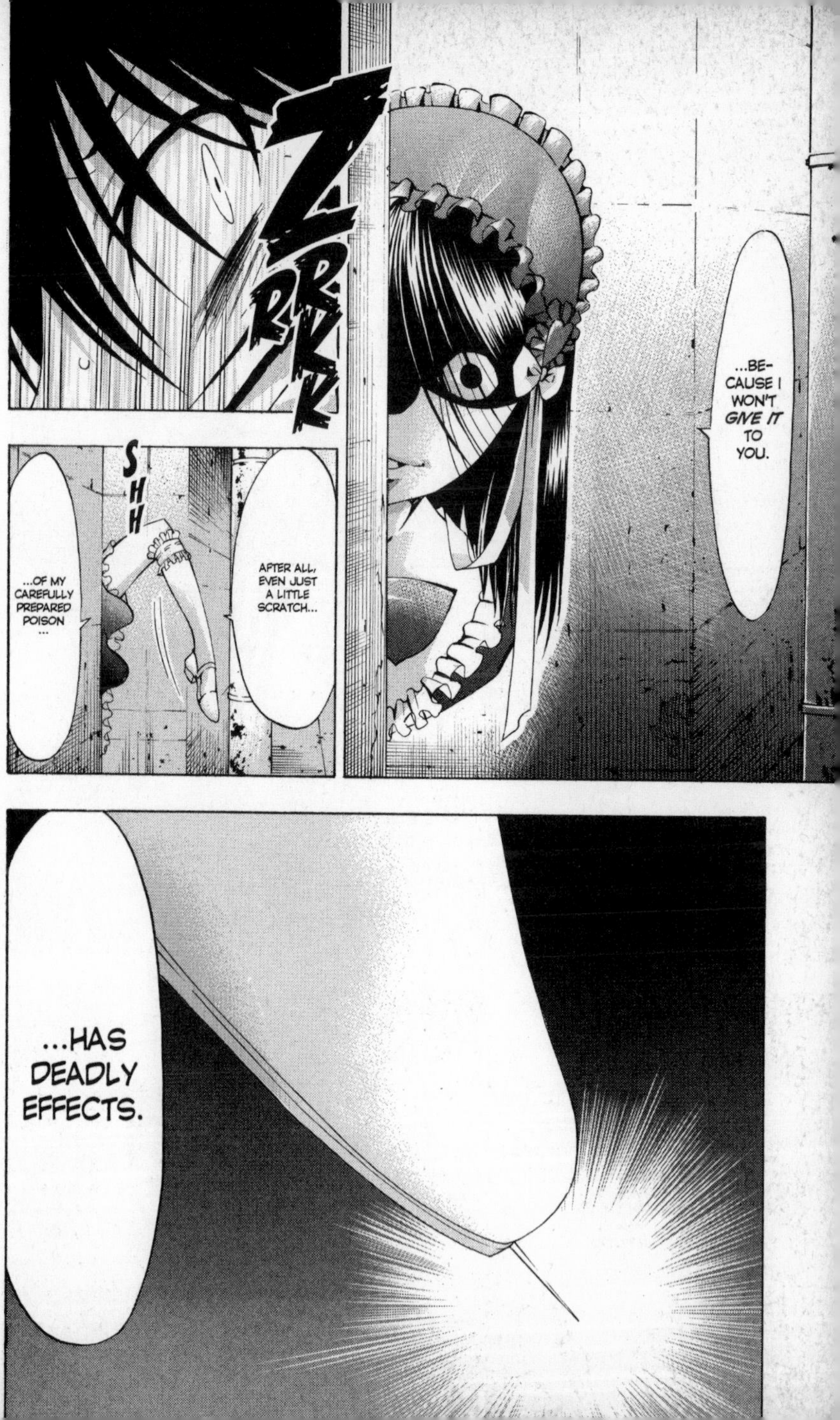
...BE-CAUSE I WON'T *GIVE IT* TO YOU.
ZRRK
SHH
AFTER ALL, EVEN JUST A LITTLE SCRATCH...
...OF MY CAREFULLY PREPARED POISON ...
...HAS DEADLY EFFECTS.

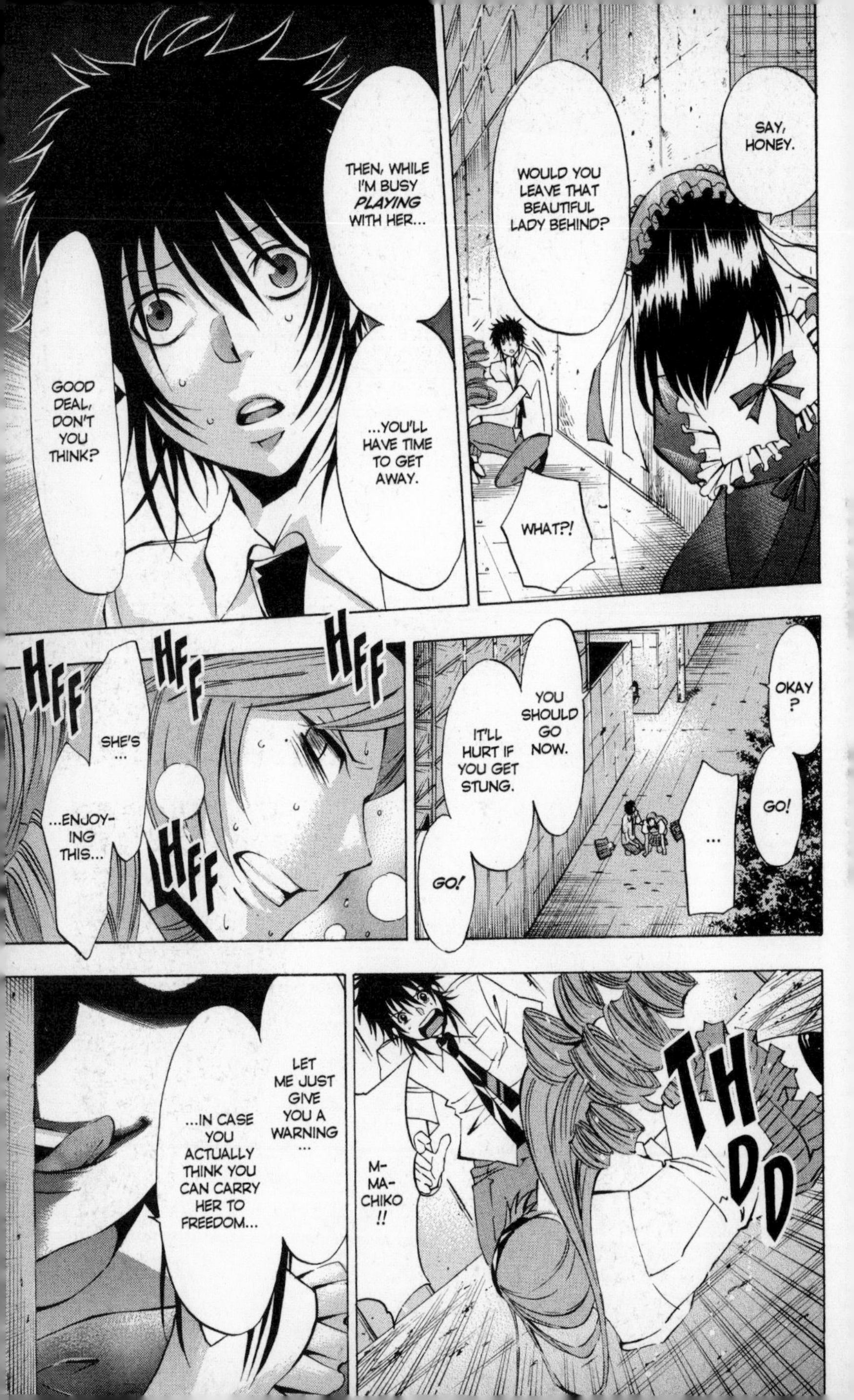
SAY, HONEY.
WOULD YOU LEAVE THAT BEAUTIFUL LADY BEHIND?
WHAT?!
THEN, WHILE I'M BUSY *PLAYING* WITH HER...
...YOU'LL HAVE TIME TO GET AWAY.
GOOD DEAL, DON'T YOU THINK?
OKAY?
GO!
...
YOU SHOULD GO NOW.
IT'LL HURT IF YOU GET STUNG.
GO!
HFF
HFF
HFF
HFF
SHE'S...
...ENJOYING THIS...
THDD
M-MACHIKO!!
LET ME JUST GIVE YOU A WARNING...
...IN CASE YOU ACTUALLY THINK YOU CAN CARRY HER TO FREEDOM...

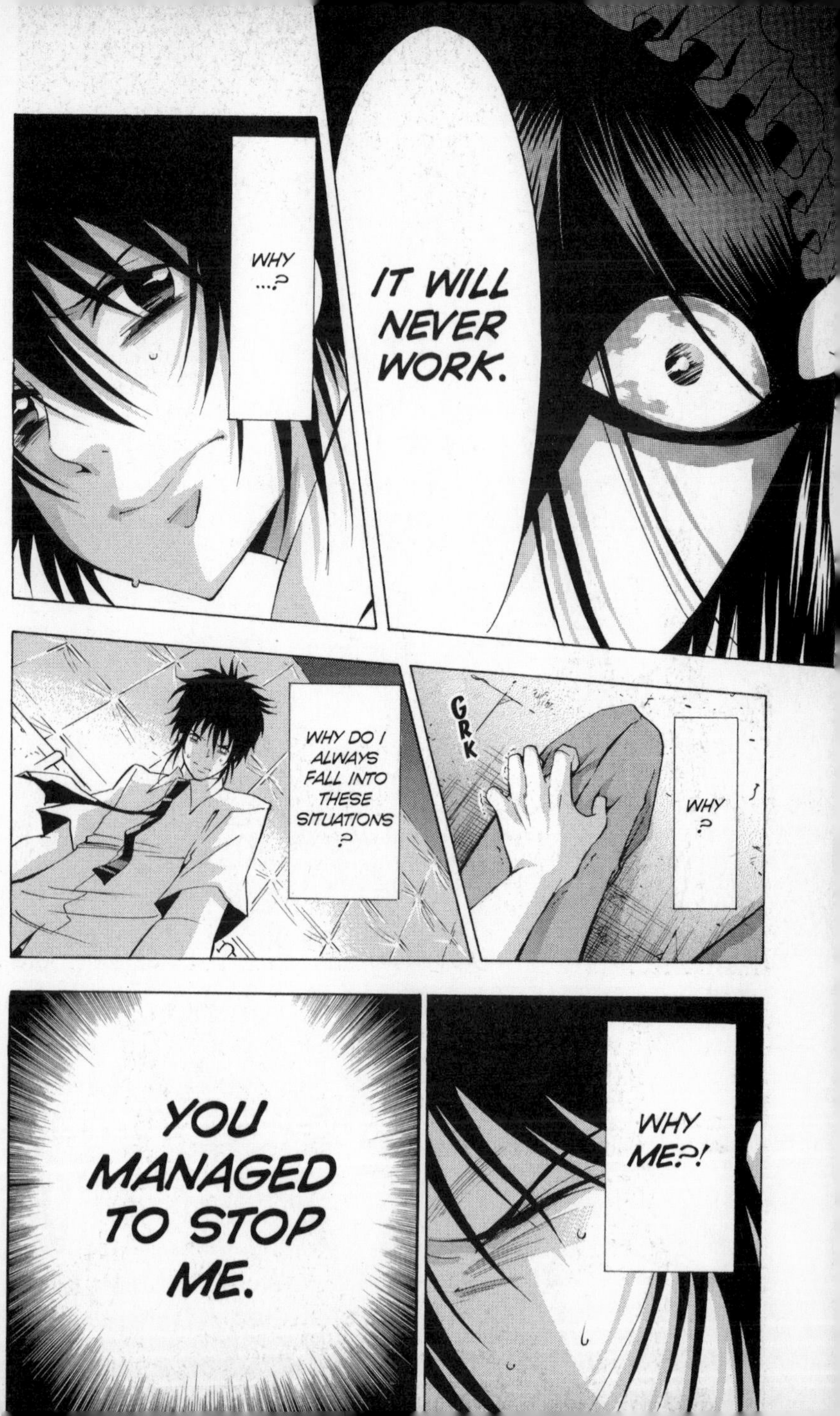
IT WILL NEVER WORK.
WHY ...?
WHY?
GRK
WHY DO I ALWAYS FALL INTO THESE SITUATIONS?
WHY ME?!
YOU MANAGED TO STOP ME.

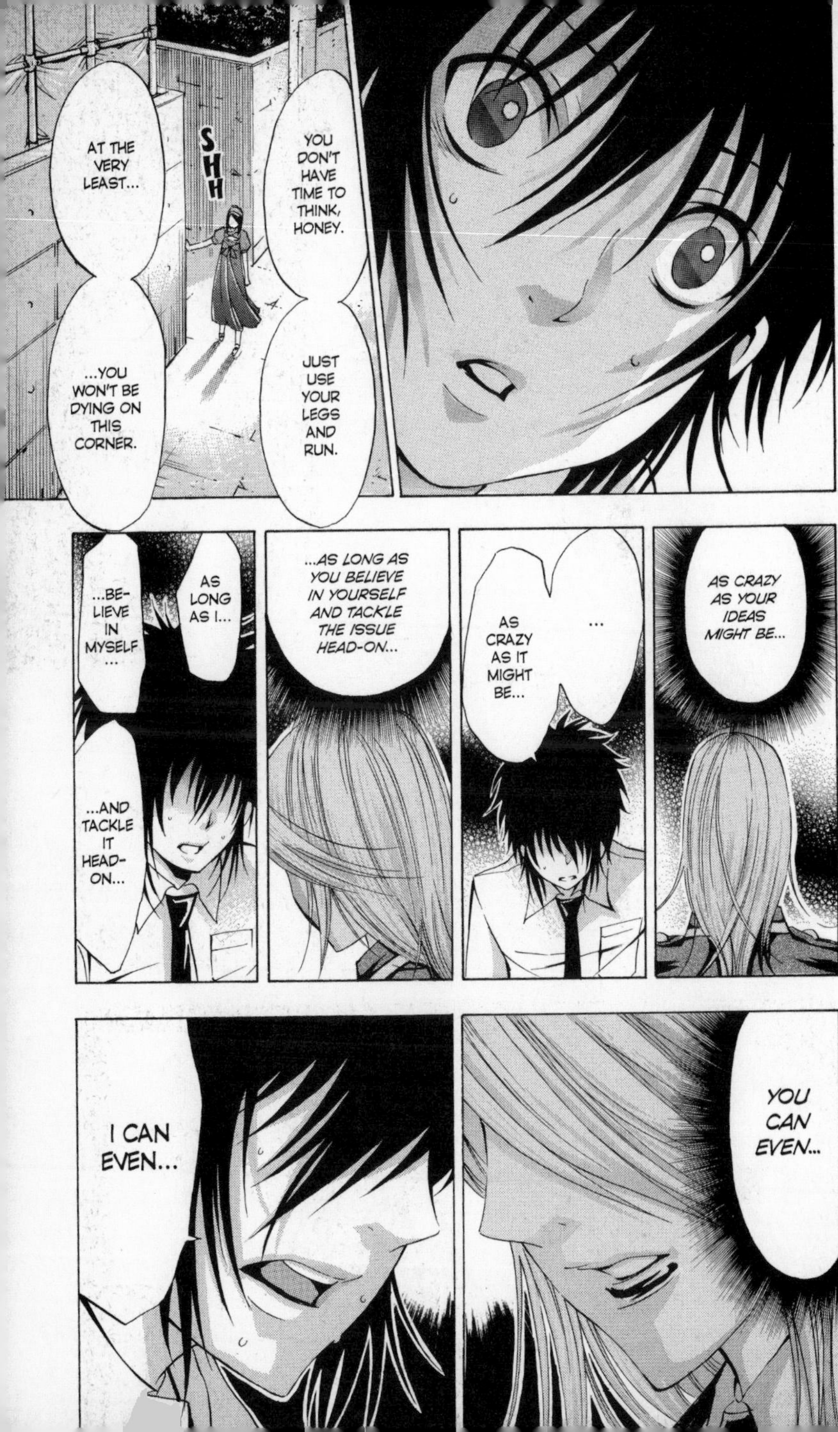
YOU DON'T HAVE TIME TO THINK, HONEY.
JUST USE YOUR LEGS AND RUN.
SHH
AT THE VERY LEAST...
...YOU WON'T BE DYING ON THIS CORNER.
AS CRAZY AS YOUR IDEAS MIGHT BE...
...
AS CRAZY AS IT MIGHT BE...
...AS LONG AS YOU BELIEVE IN YOURSELF AND TACKLE THE ISSUE HEAD-ON...
AS LONG AS I...
...BE-LIEVE IN MYSELF...
...AND TACKLE IT HEAD-ON...
YOU CAN EVEN...
I CAN EVEN...

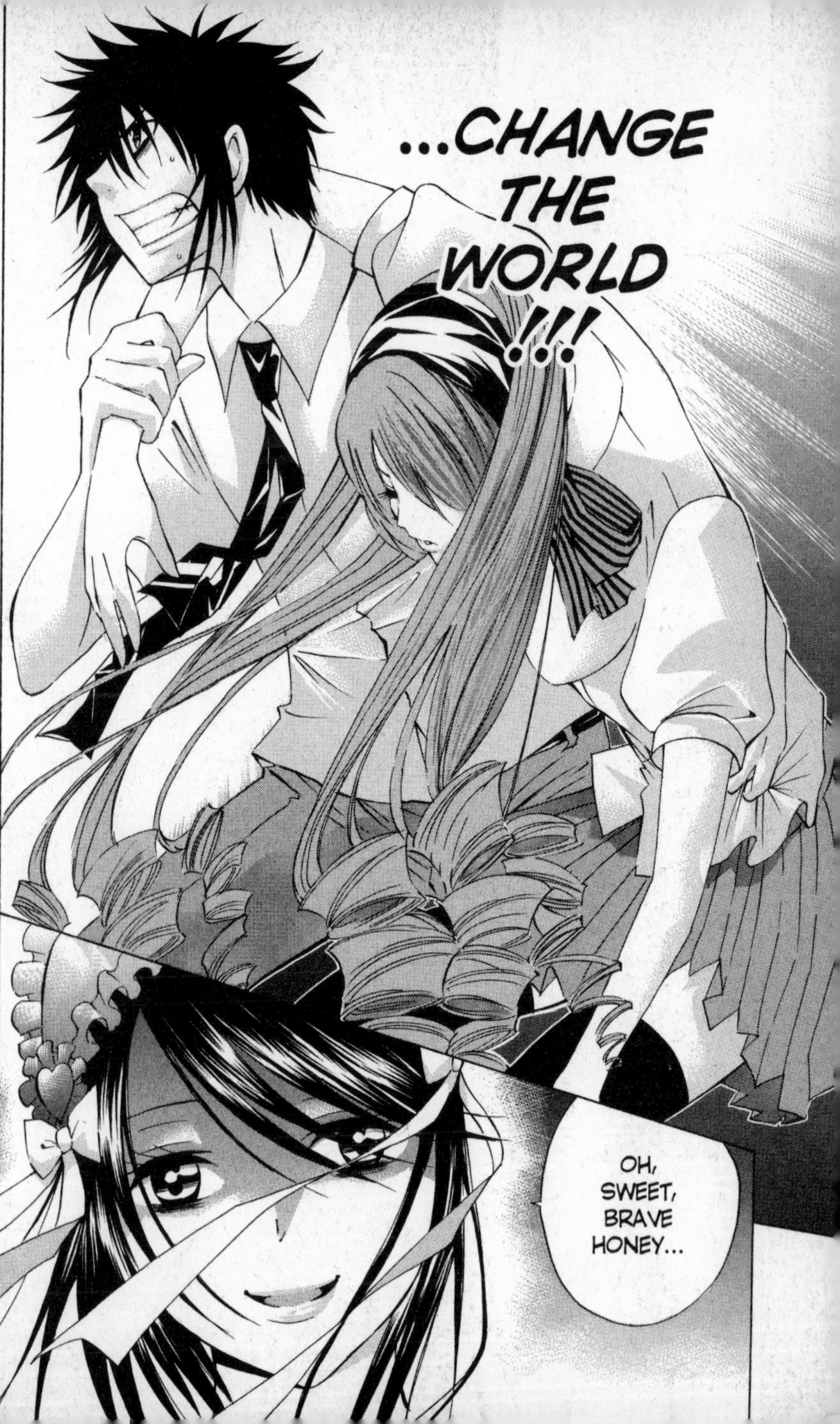
...CHANGE THE WORLD !!!
OH, SWEET, BRAVE HONEY...

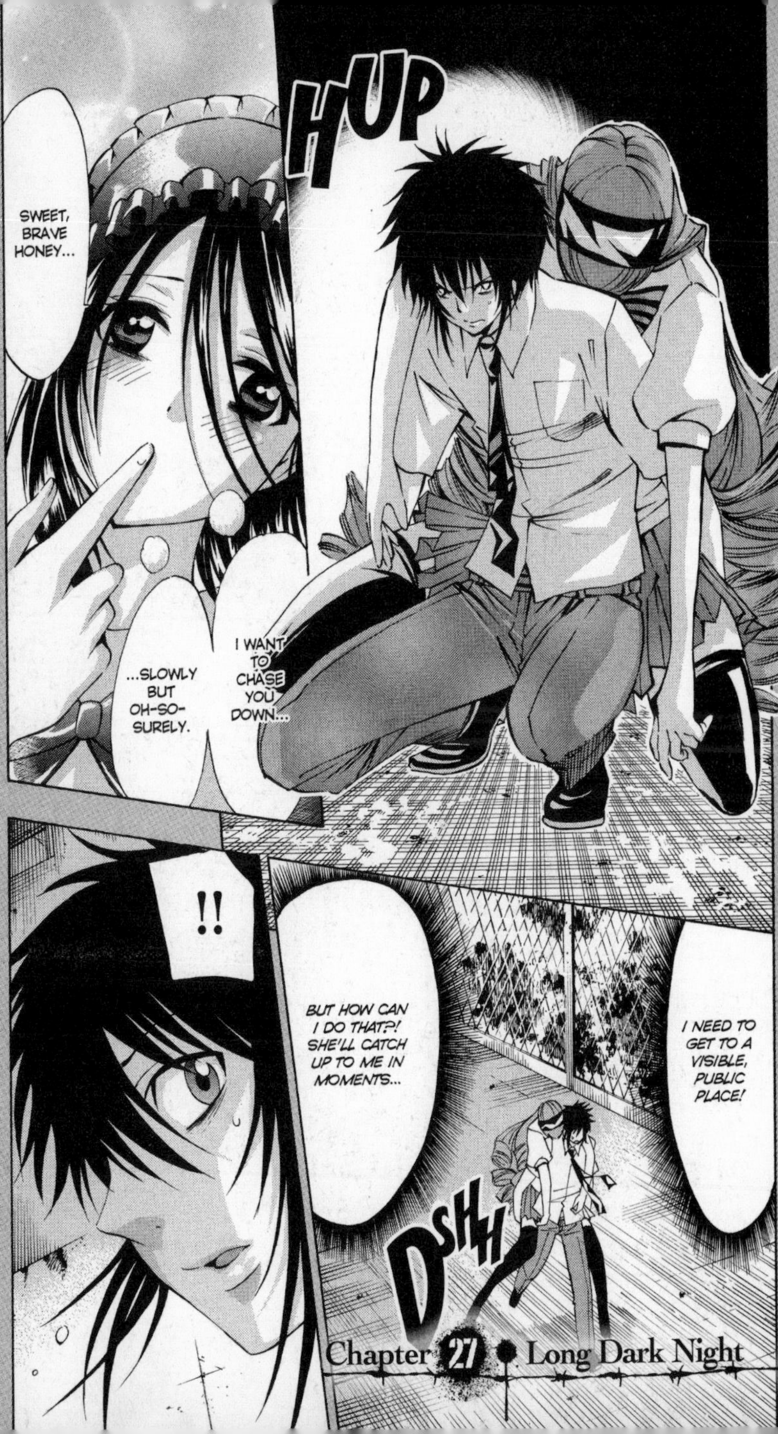
HUP
SWEET, BRAVE HONEY...
I WANT TO CHASE YOU DOWN...
...SLOWLY BUT OH-SO-SURELY.
I NEED TO GET TO A VISIBLE, PUBLIC PLACE!
BUT HOW CAN I DO THAT?! SHE'LL CATCH UP TO ME IN MOMENTS...
DSHH
Chapter 27 Long Dark Night
!!

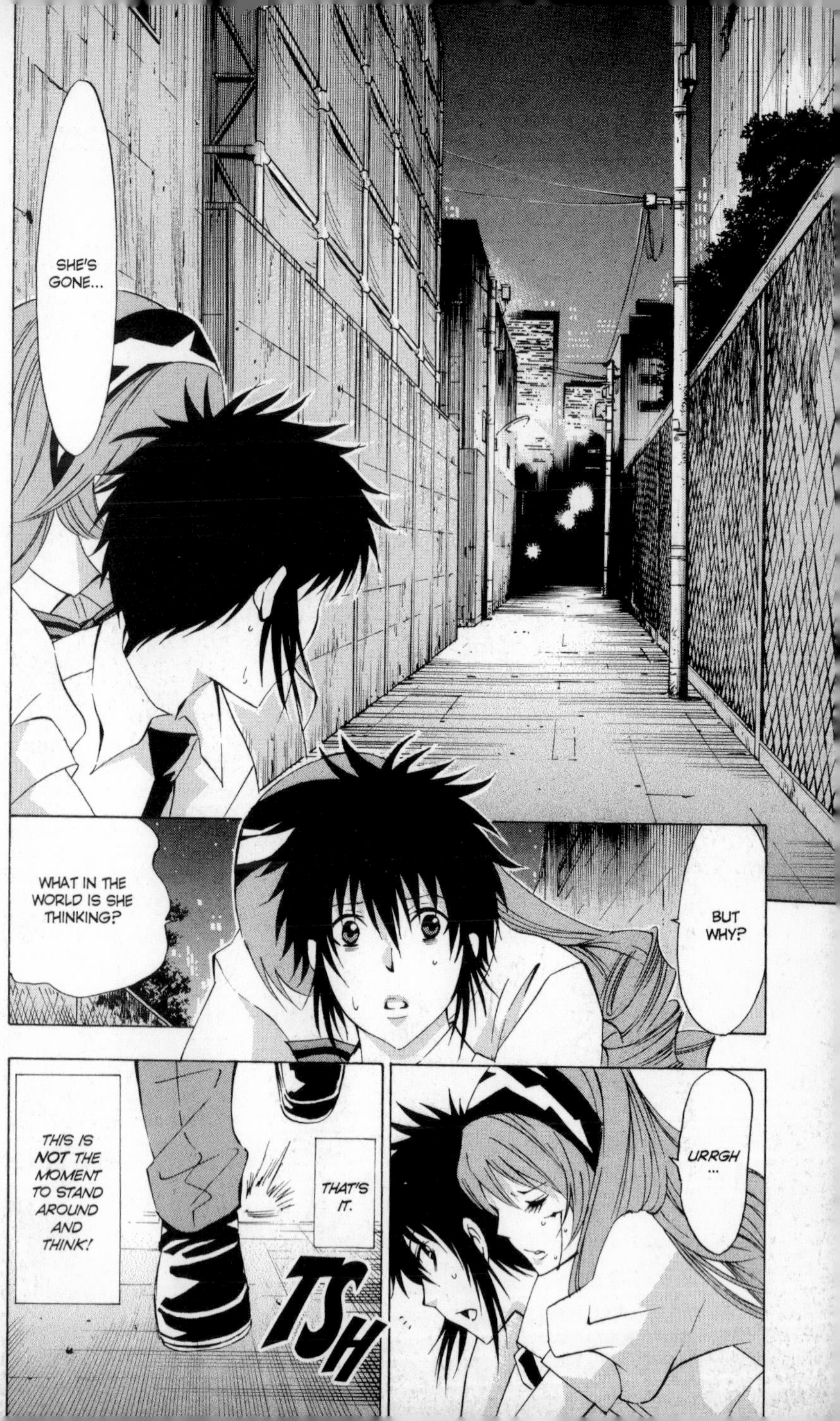
SHE'S GONE...
BUT WHY?
WHAT IN THE WORLD IS SHE THINKING?
URRGH ...
THAT'S IT.
THIS IS NOT THE MOMENT TO STAND AROUND AND THINK!
TSH

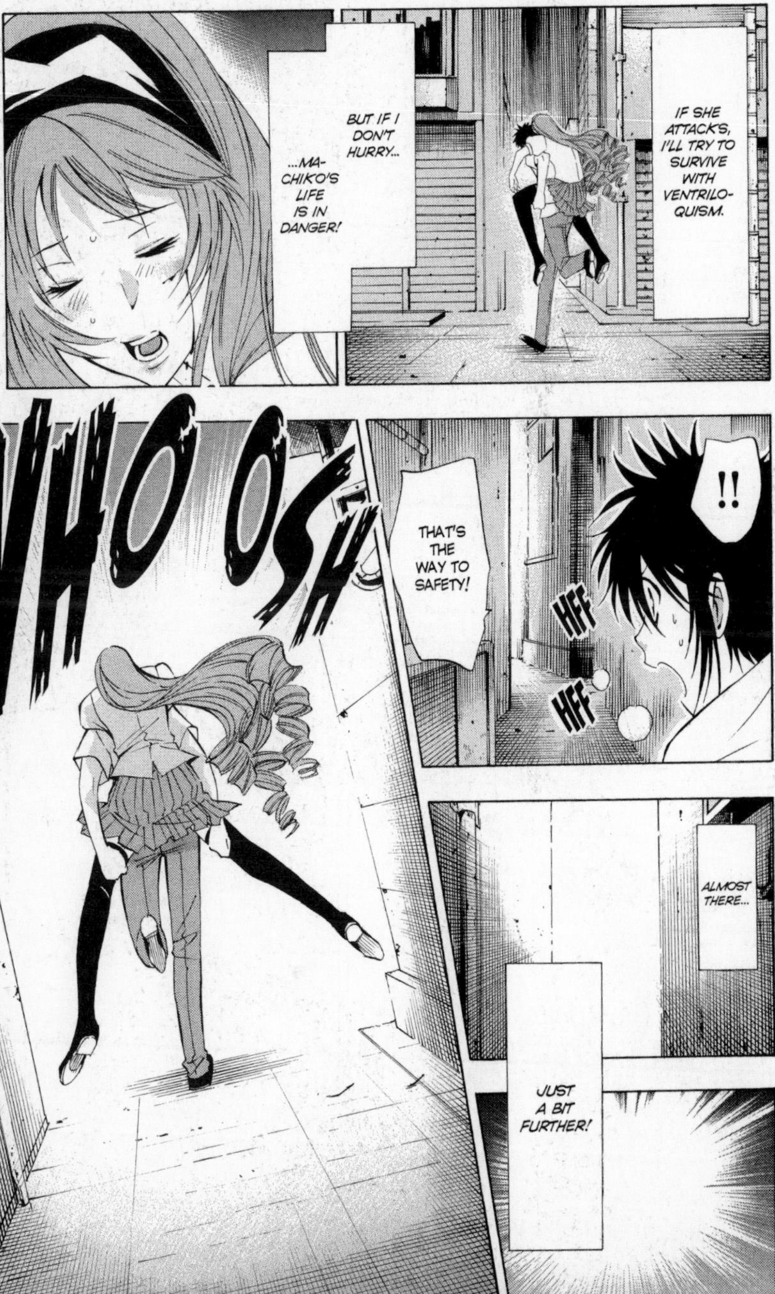
IF SHE ATTACKS, I'LL TRY TO SURVIVE WITH VENTRILO-QUISM.
BUT IF I DON'T HURRY...
...MA-CHIKO'S LIFE IS IN DANGER!
!!
THAT'S THE WAY TO SAFETY!
HFF
HFF
ALMOST THERE...
JUST A BIT FURTHER!
WHOOSH

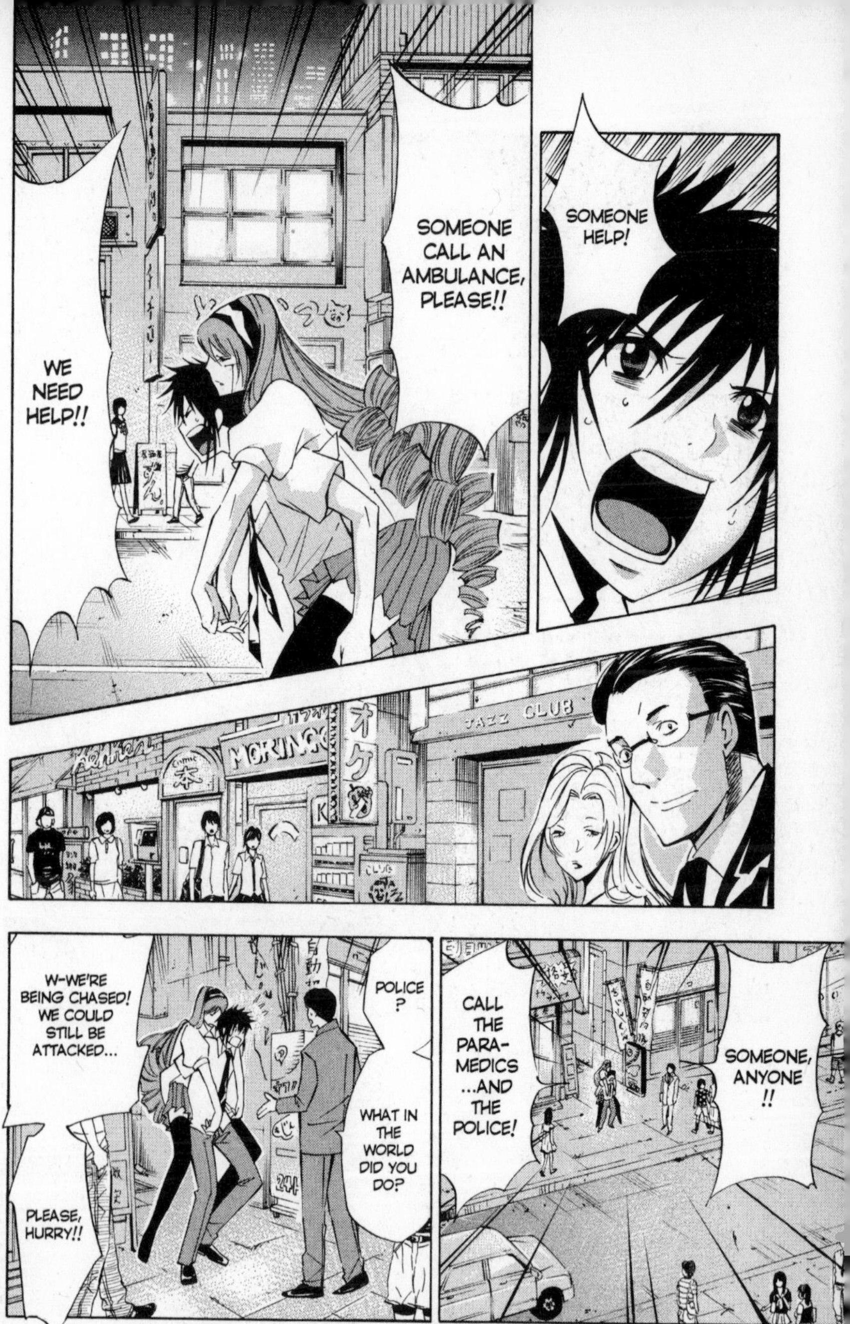
SOMEONE HELP!
SOMEONE CALL AN AMBULANCE, PLEASE!!
WE NEED HELP!!
JAZZ CLUB
SOMEONE, ANYONE!!
CALL THE PARA-MEDICS ...AND THE POLICE!
POLICE?
WHAT IN THE WORLD DID YOU DO?
W-WE'RE BEING CHASED! WE COULD STILL BE ATTACKED...
PLEASE, HURRY!!

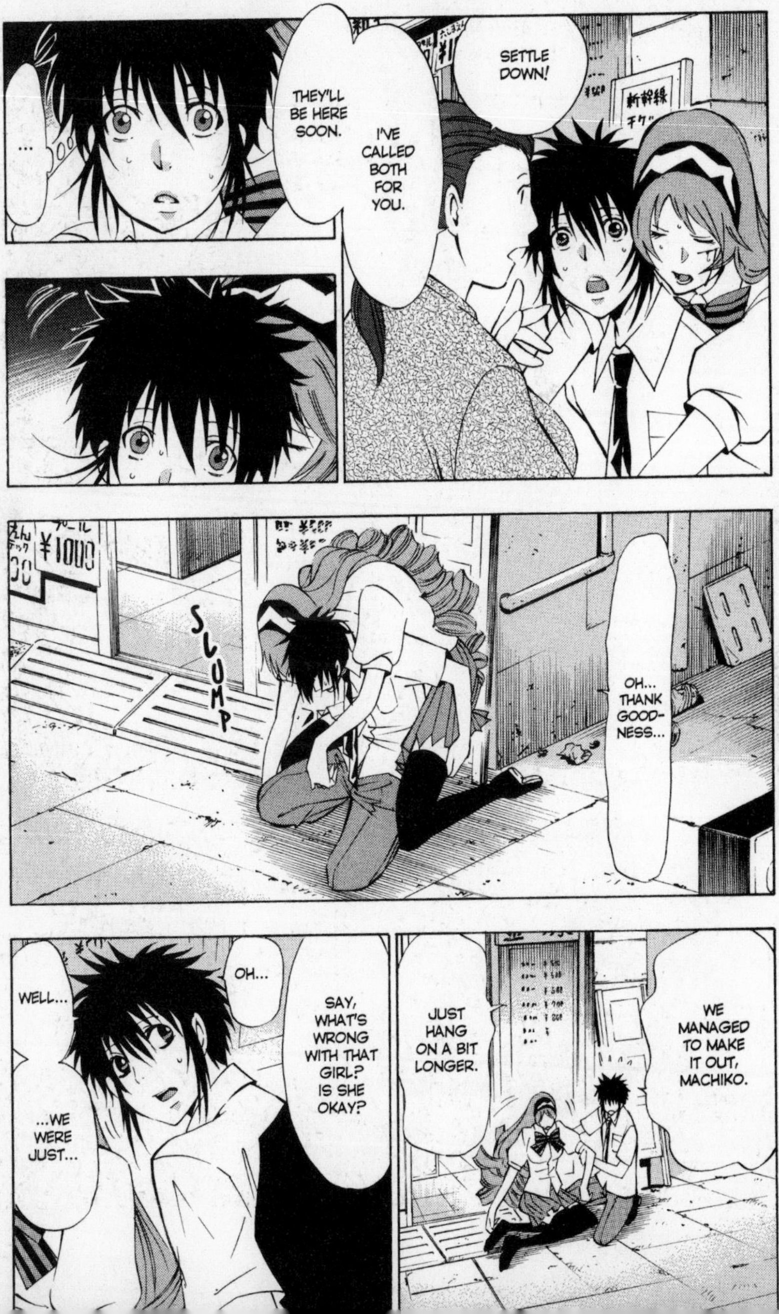
SETTLE DOWN!
I'VE CALLED BOTH FOR YOU.
THEY'LL BE HERE SOON.
...
OH... THANK GOODNESS...
SLUMP
WE MANAGED TO MAKE IT OUT, MACHIKO.
JUST HANG ON A BIT LONGER.
SAY, WHAT'S WRONG WITH THAT GIRL? IS SHE OKAY?
OH...
WELL...
...WE WERE JUST...

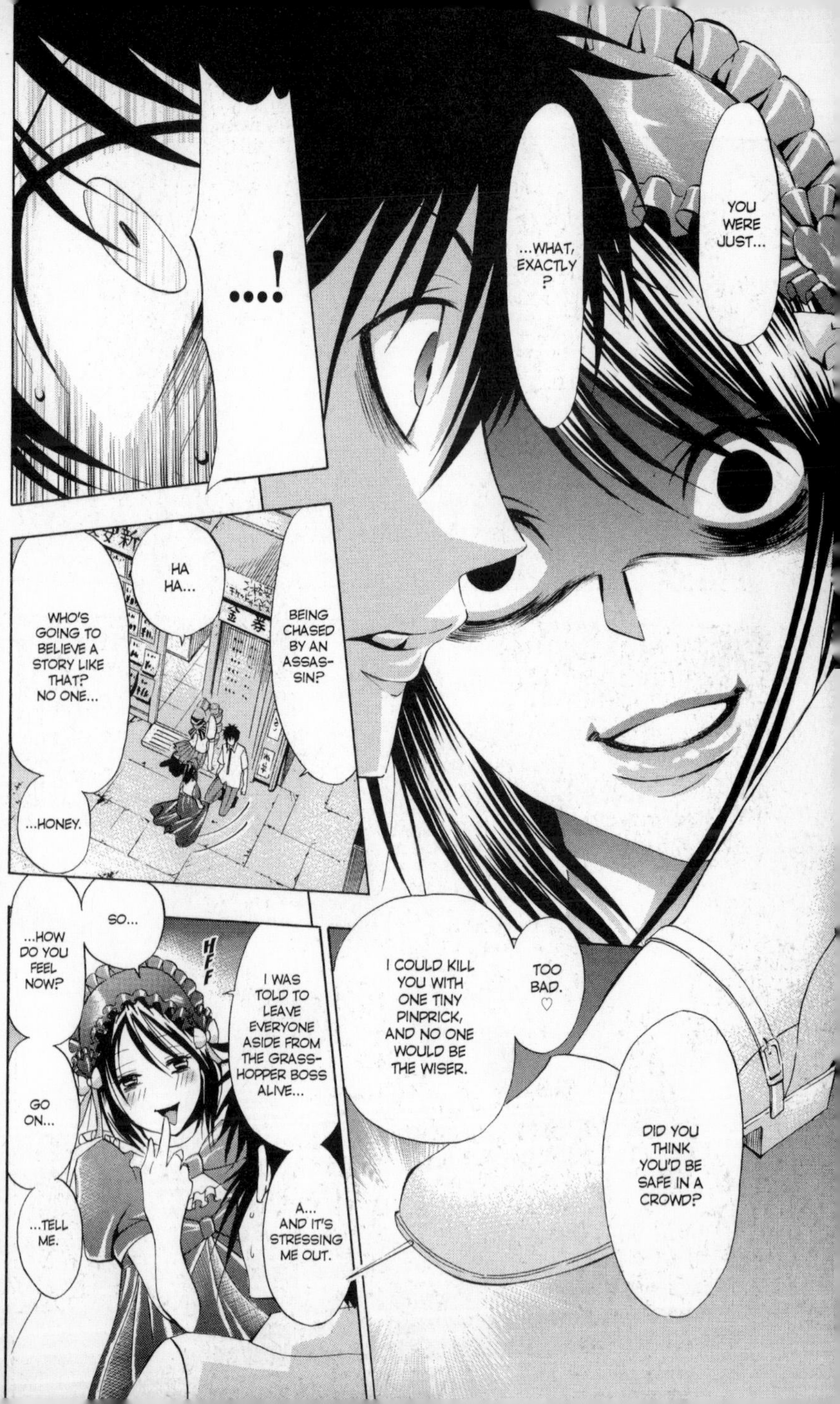
YOU WERE JUST...
...WHAT, EXACTLY?
...!
BEING CHASED BY AN ASSAS-SIN?
HA HA...
WHO'S GOING TO BELIEVE A STORY LIKE THAT? NO ONE...
...HONEY.
TOO BAD. ♡
I COULD KILL YOU WITH ONE TINY PINPRICK, AND NO ONE WOULD BE THE WISER.
DID YOU THINK YOU'D BE SAFE IN A CROWD?
HFF
I WAS TOLD TO LEAVE EVERYONE ASIDE FROM THE GRASS-HOPPER BOSS ALIVE...
SO...
...HOW DO YOU FEEL NOW?
GO ON...
A... AND IT'S STRESSING ME OUT.
...TELL ME.

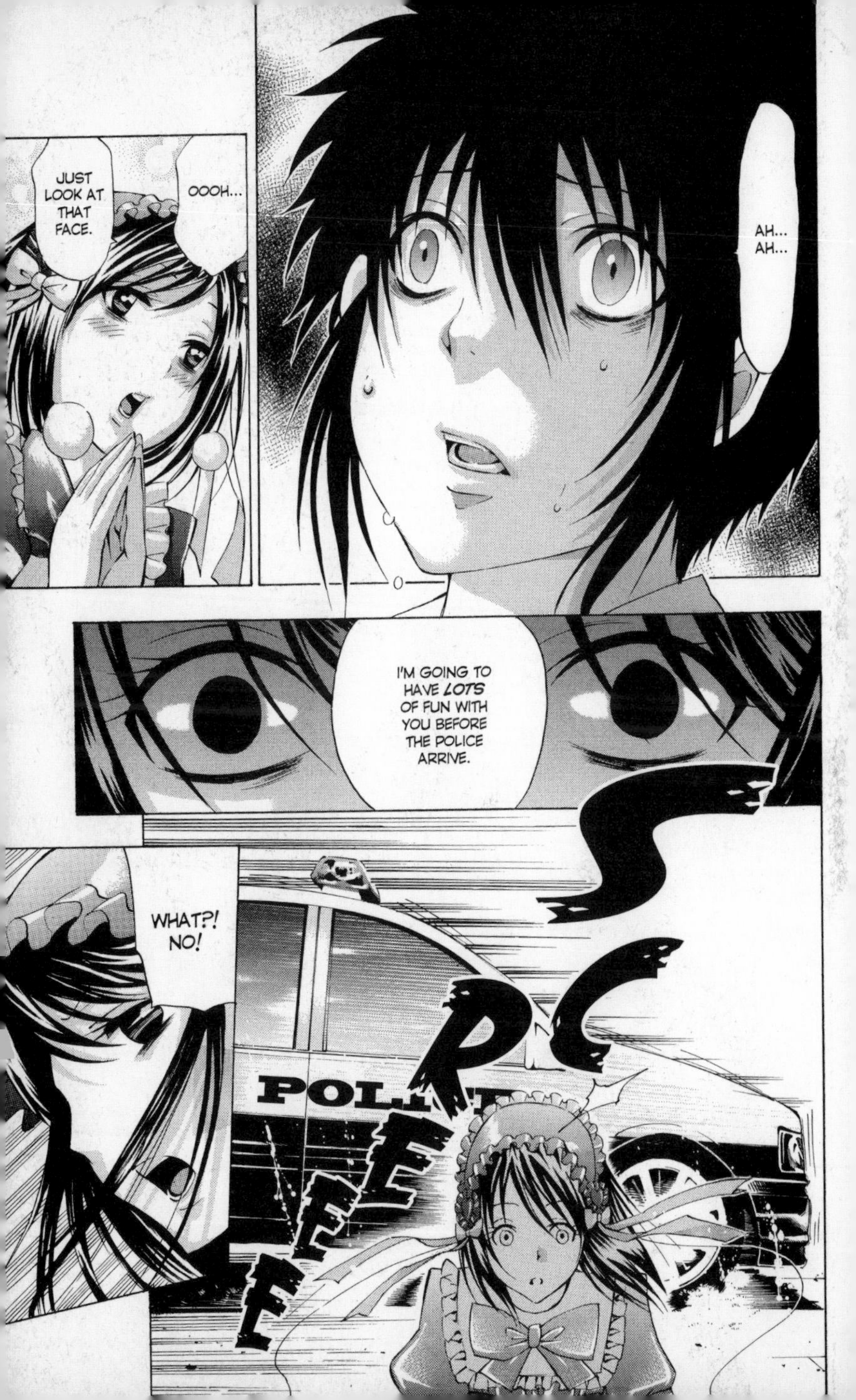
AH... AH...
OOOH...
JUST LOOK AT THAT FACE.
I'M GOING TO HAVE *LOTS* OF FUN WITH YOU BEFORE THE POLICE ARRIVE.
SCREEEE
WHAT?! NO!

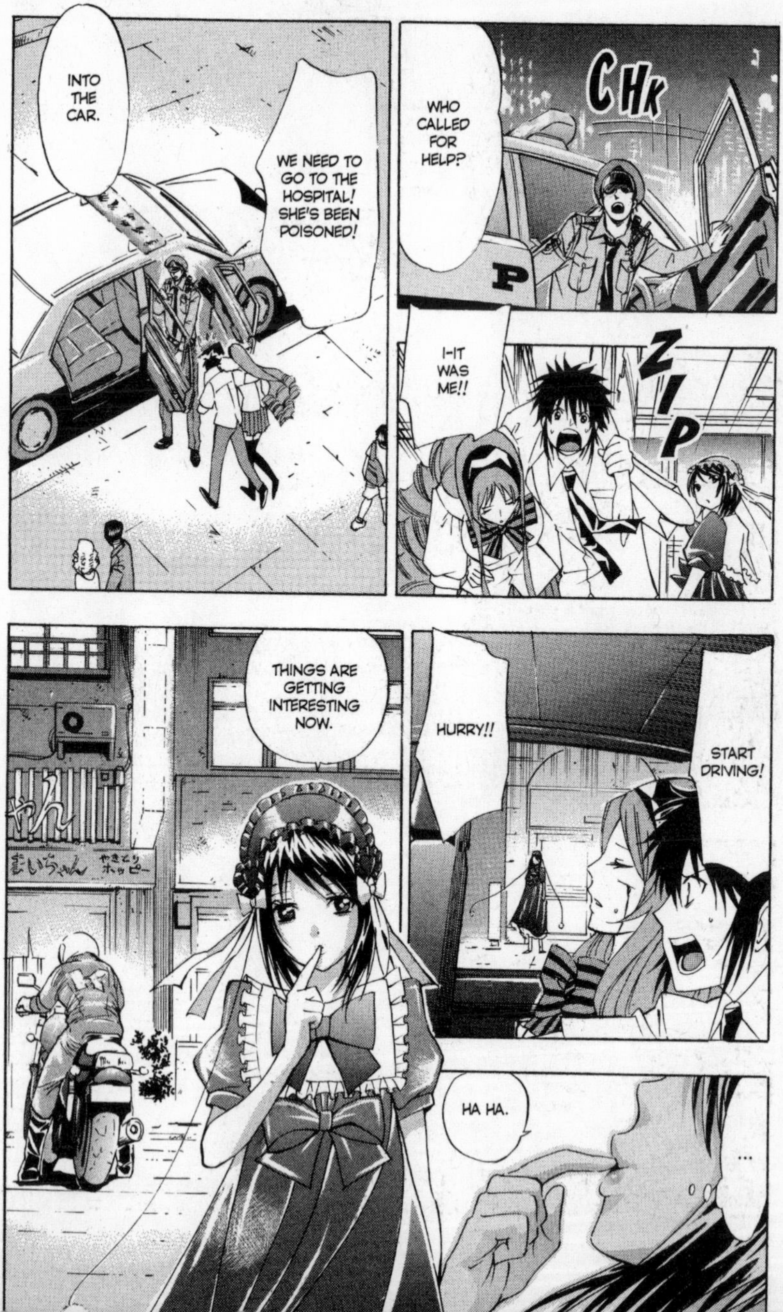
CHK
WHO CALLED FOR HELP?
I-IT WAS ME!!
ZIP
WE NEED TO GO TO THE HOSPITAL! SHE'S BEEN POISONED!
INTO THE CAR.
START DRIVING!
HURRY!!
HA HA.
...
THINGS ARE GETTING INTERESTING NOW.
まいちゃん
やきとり ホッピー

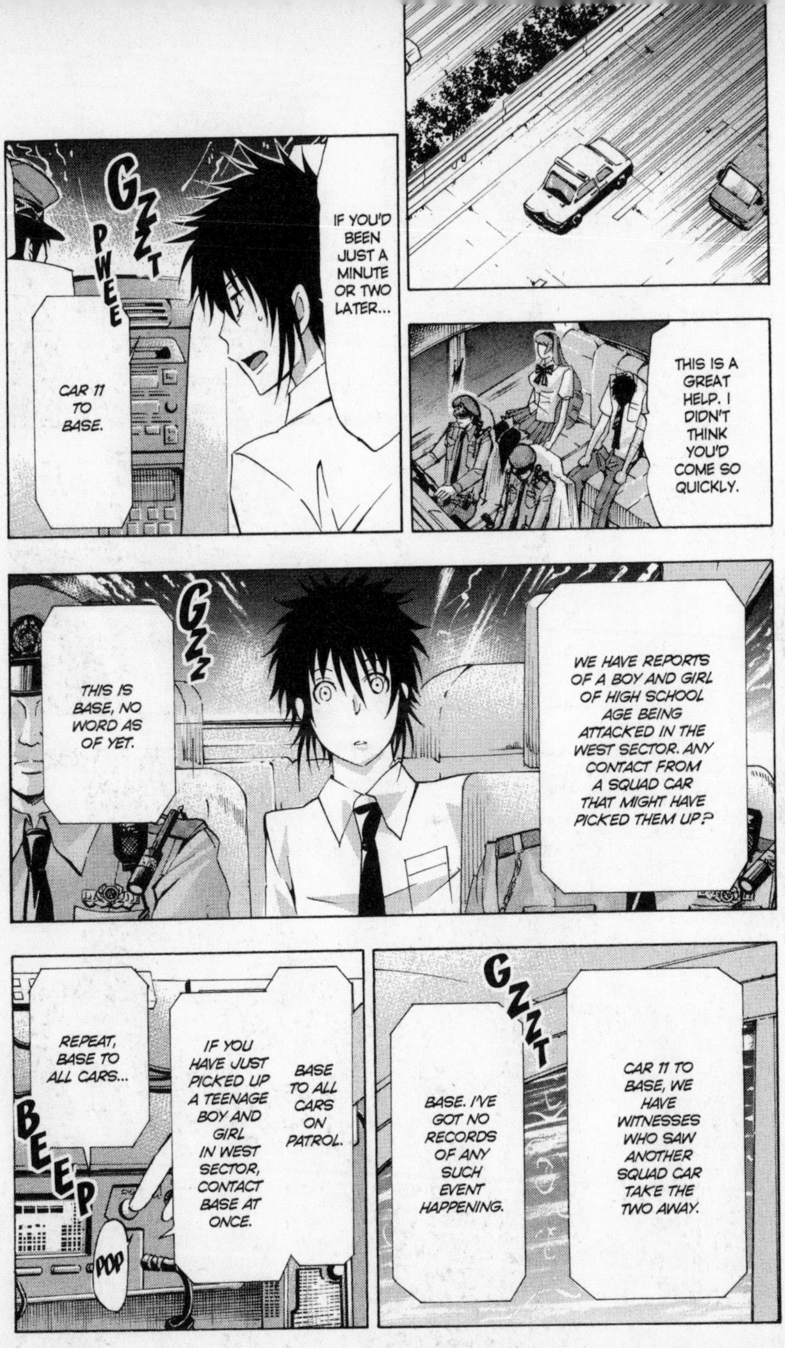
THIS IS A GREAT HELP. I DIDN'T THINK YOU'D COME SO QUICKLY.
IF YOU'D BEEN JUST A MINUTE OR TWO LATER...
GZZT
PWEE
CAR 11 TO BASE.
WE HAVE REPORTS OF A BOY AND GIRL OF HIGH SCHOOL AGE BEING ATTACKED IN THE WEST SECTOR. ANY CONTACT FROM A SQUAD CAR THAT MIGHT HAVE PICKED THEM UP?
GZZ
THIS IS BASE, NO WORD AS OF YET.
CAR 11 TO BASE, WE HAVE WITNESSES WHO SAW ANOTHER SQUAD CAR TAKE THE TWO AWAY.
GZZT
BASE. I'VE GOT NO RECORDS OF ANY SUCH EVENT HAPPENING.
BASE TO ALL CARS ON PATROL.
IF YOU HAVE JUST PICKED UP A TEENAGE BOY AND GIRL IN WEST SECTOR, CONTACT BASE AT ONCE.
REPEAT, BASE TO ALL CARS...
BEEP
POP

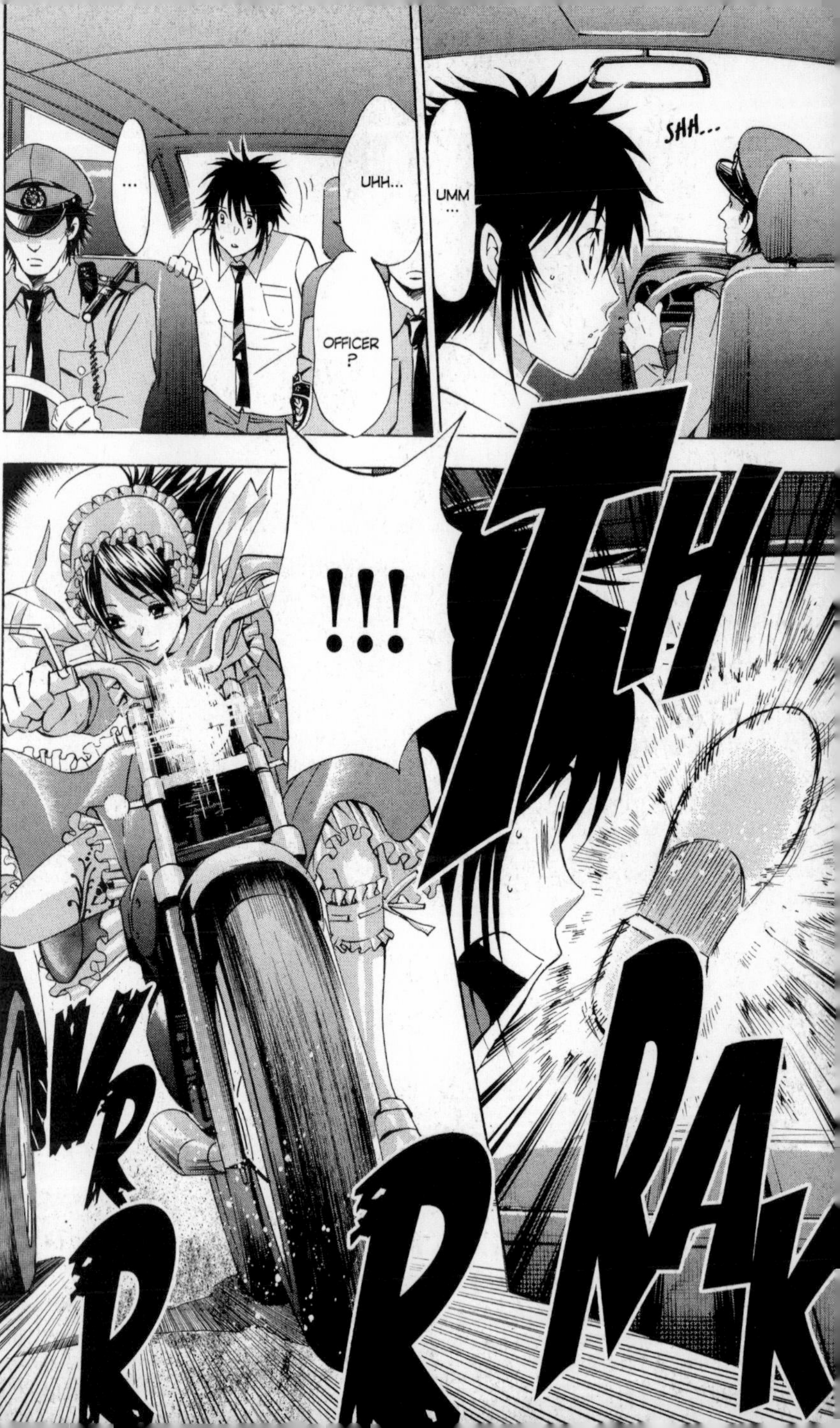
SHH...
UMM...
UHH...
...
OFFICER?
!!!

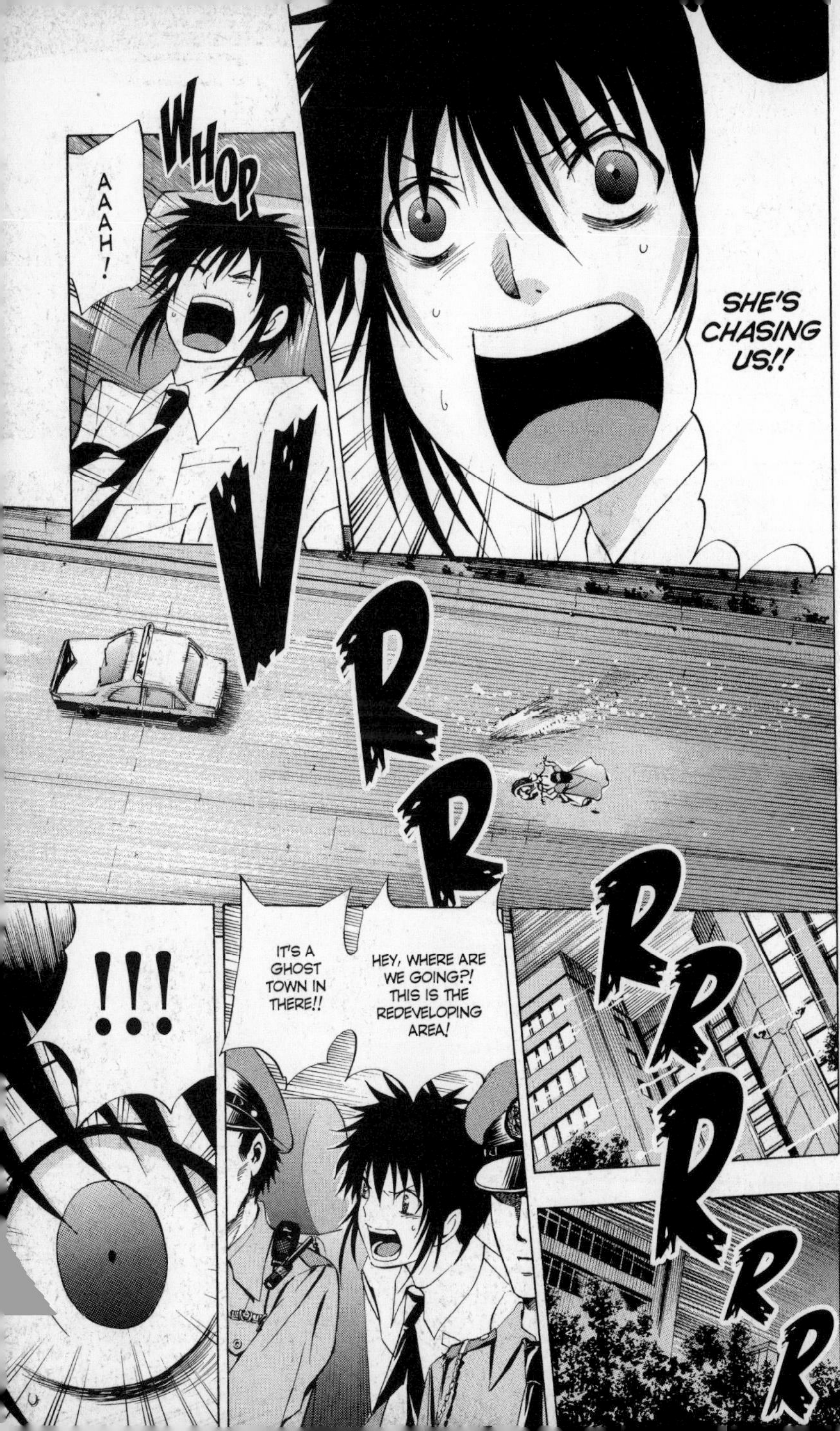

SHE'S CHASING US!!
WHOP
AAAH!
VRRRRRRR
HEY, WHERE ARE WE GOING?! THIS IS THE REDEVELOPING AREA!
IT'S A GHOST TOWN IN THERE!!
!!!

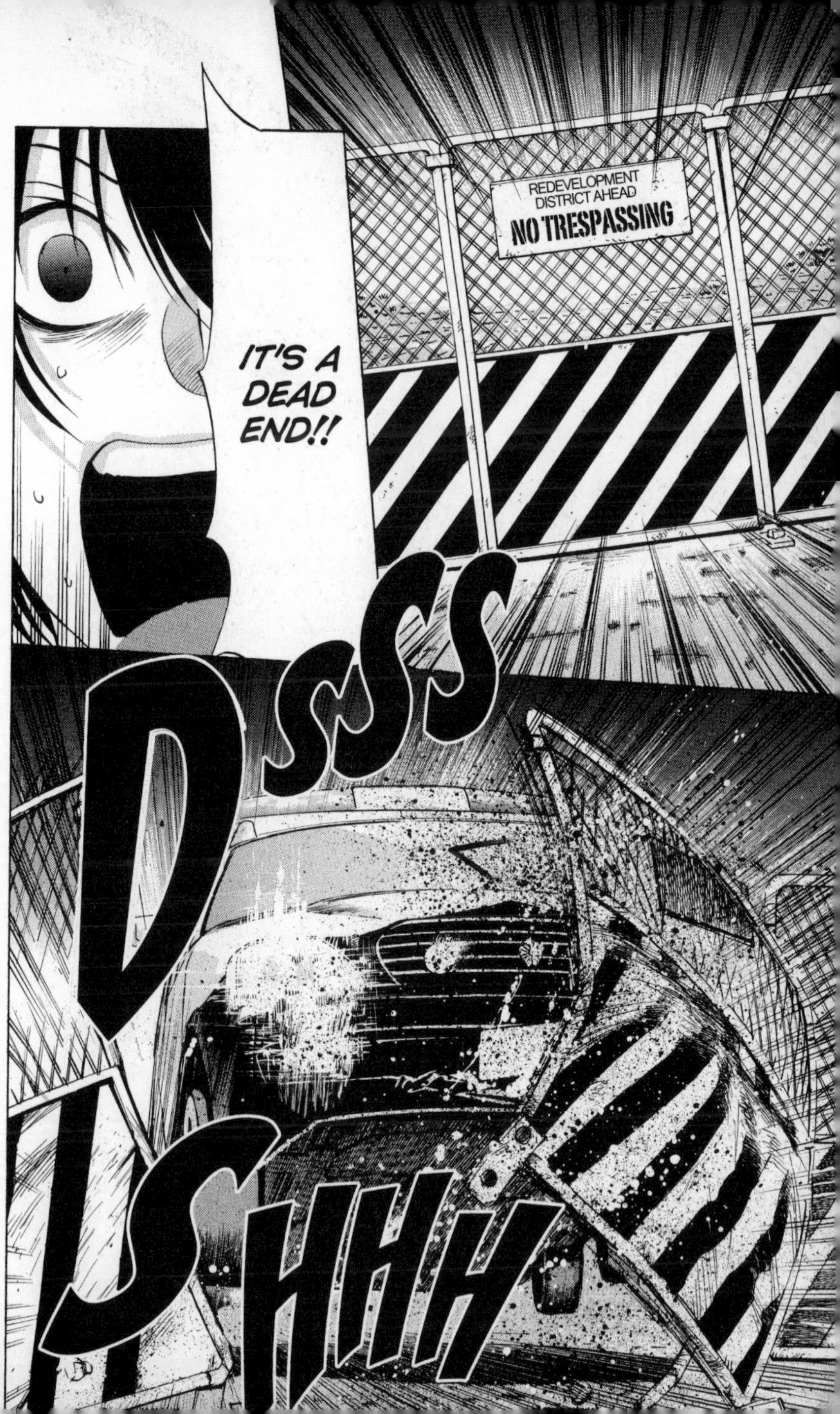
REDEVELOPMENT DISTRICT AHEAD
NO TRESPASSING
IT'S A DEAD END!!
DSSSS
SHHH

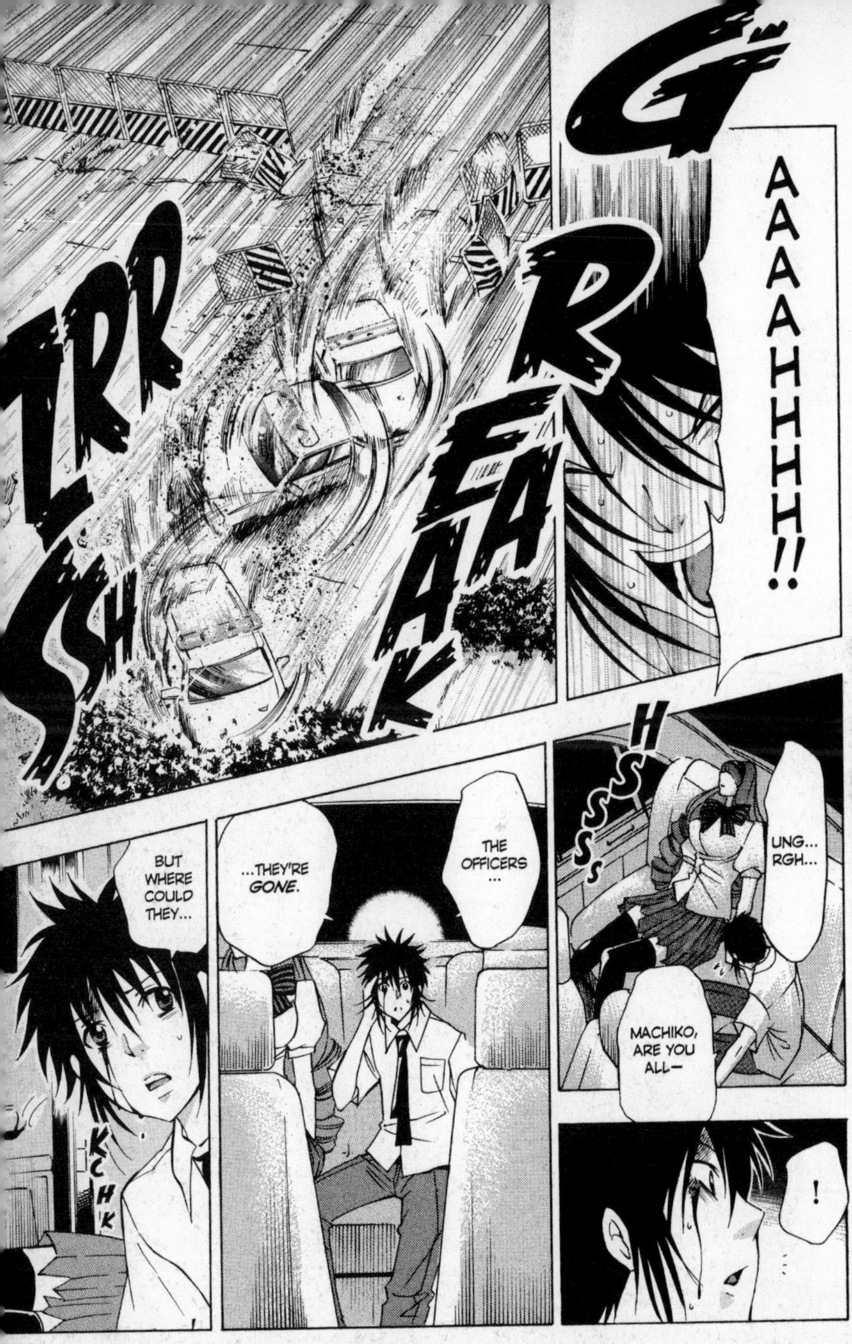
AAAAHHHH!!
GREAAK
ZRRSH
HSSSSS
UNG... RGH...
MACHIKO, ARE YOU ALL—
!
THE OFFICERS...
...THEY'RE *GONE*.
BUT WHERE COULD THEY...
KCHK

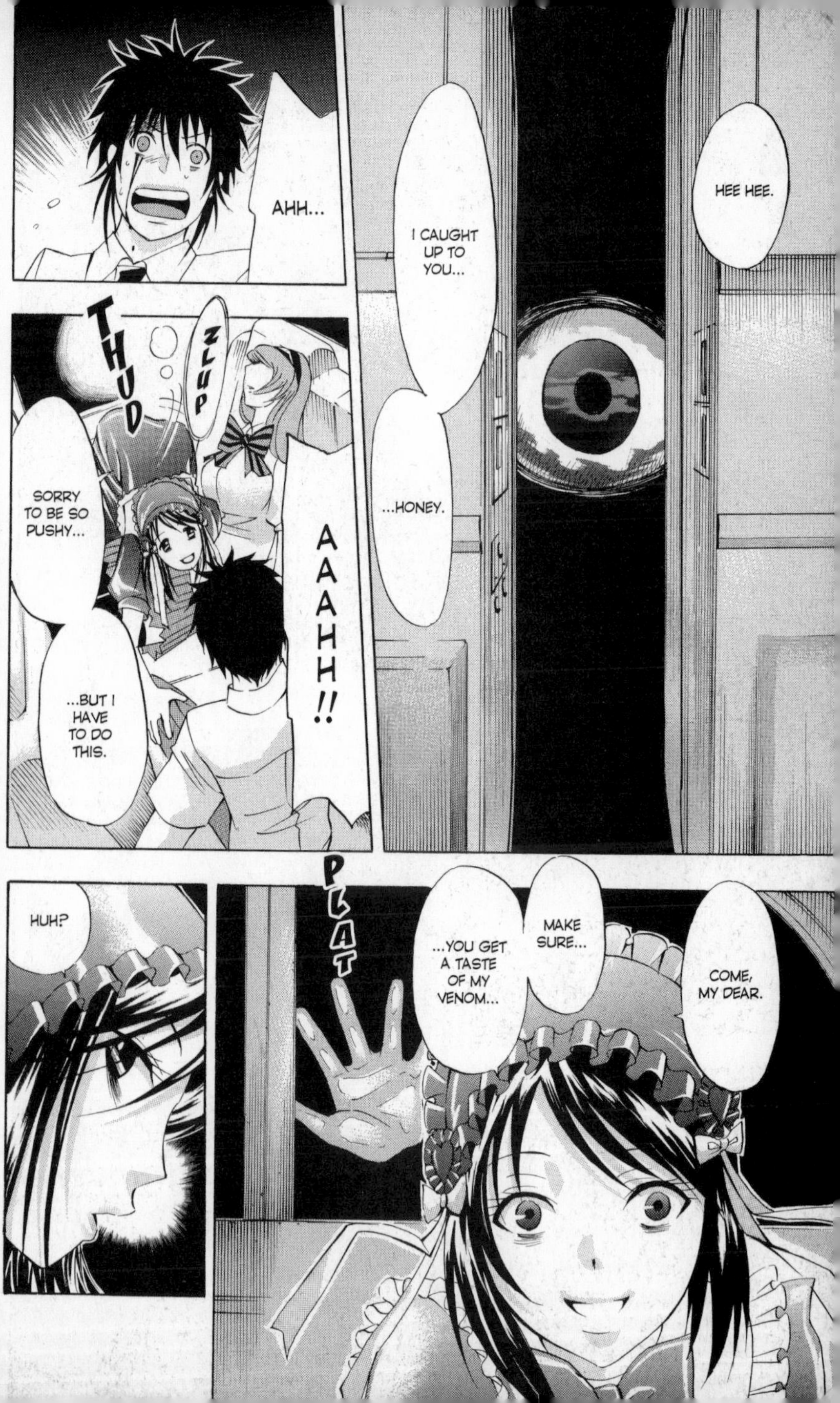
HEE HEE.
I CAUGHT UP TO YOU...
...HONEY.
AHH...
ZLUP
THUD
AAAAHH!!
SORRY TO BE SO PUSHY...
...BUT I HAVE TO DO THIS.
PLAT
COME, MY DEAR.
MAKE SURE...
...YOU GET A TASTE OF MY VENOM...
HUH?

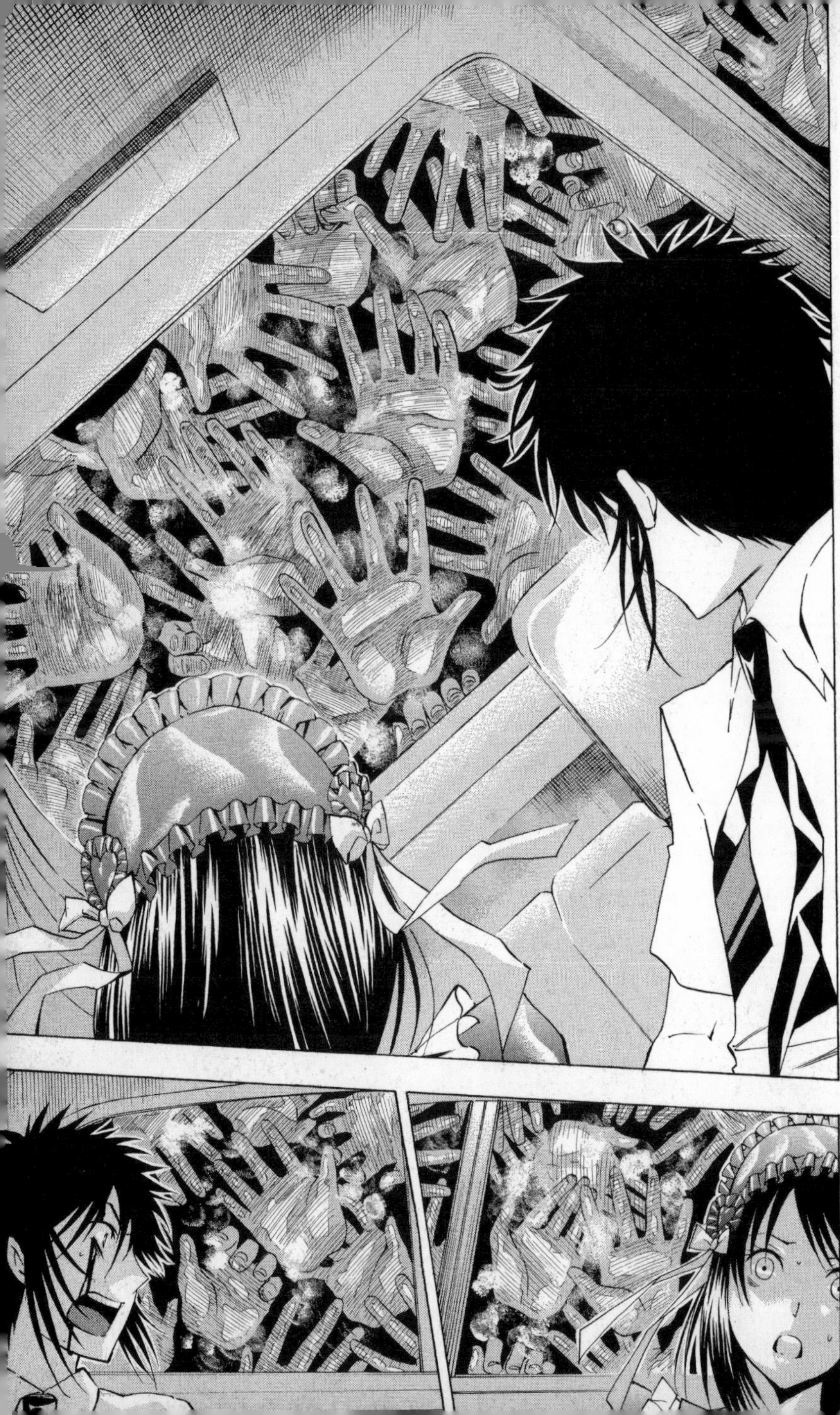

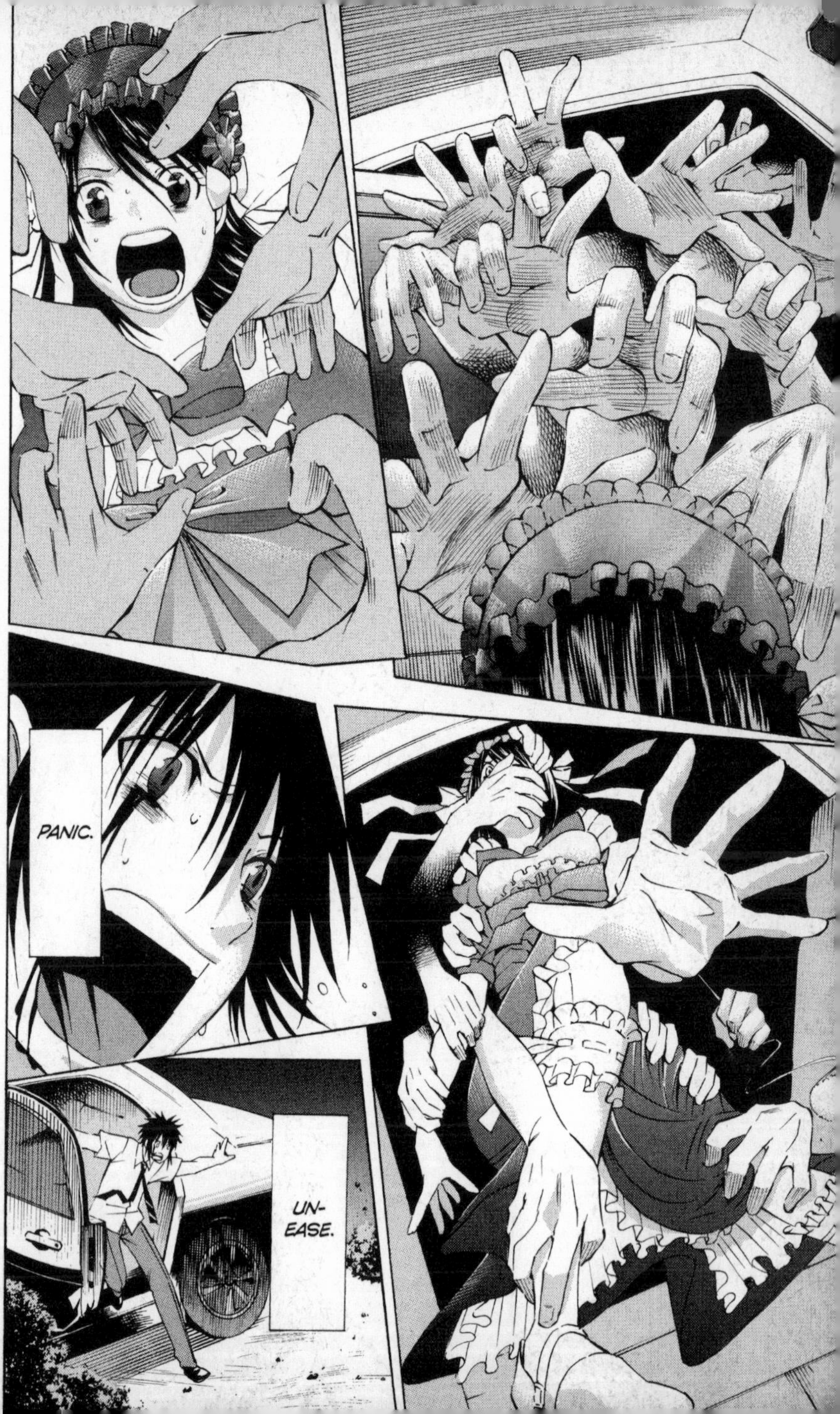
PANIC.
UN-EASE.

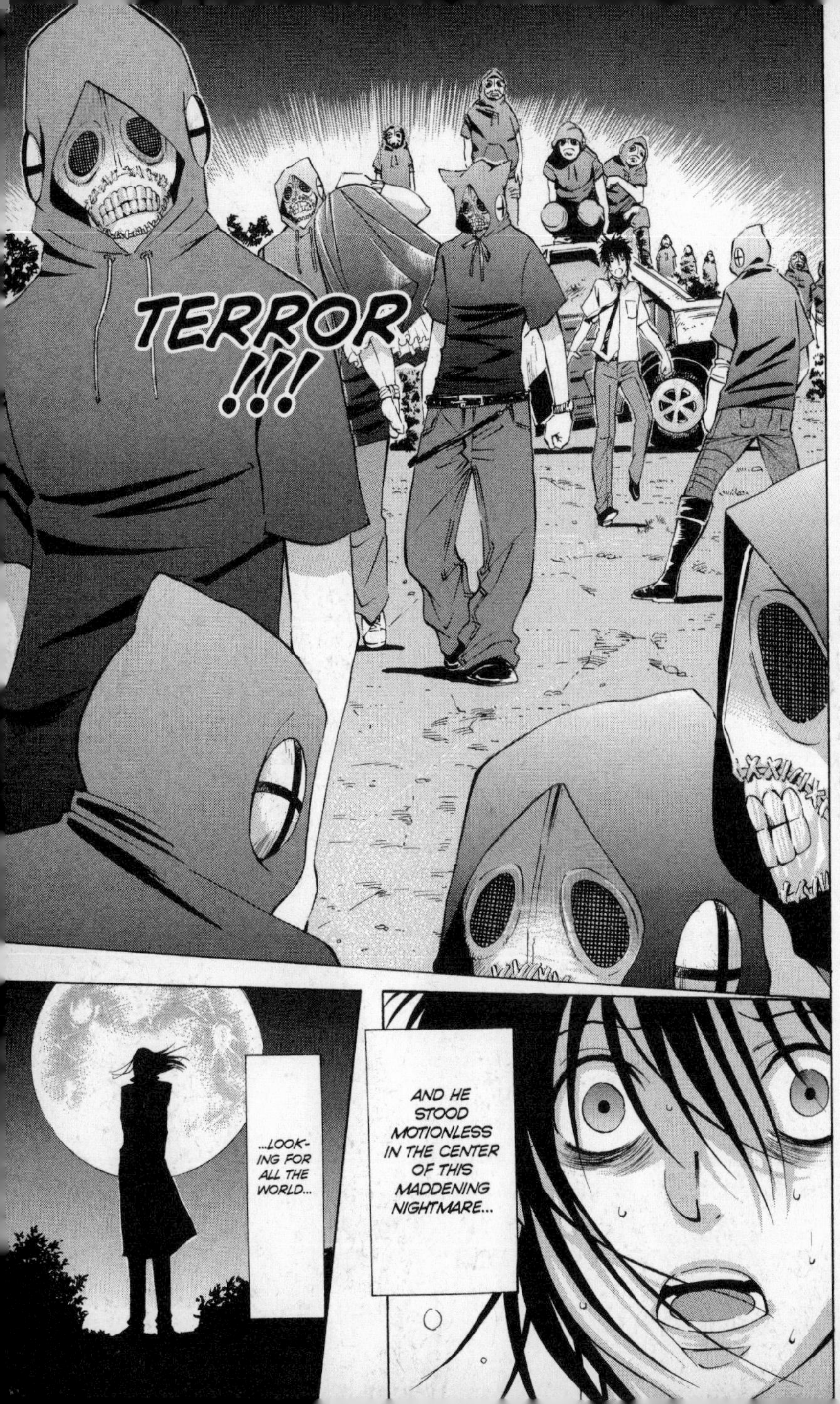
TERROR!!!
AND HE STOOD MOTIONLESS IN THE CENTER OF THIS MADDENING NIGHTMARE...
...LOOKING FOR ALL THE WORLD...

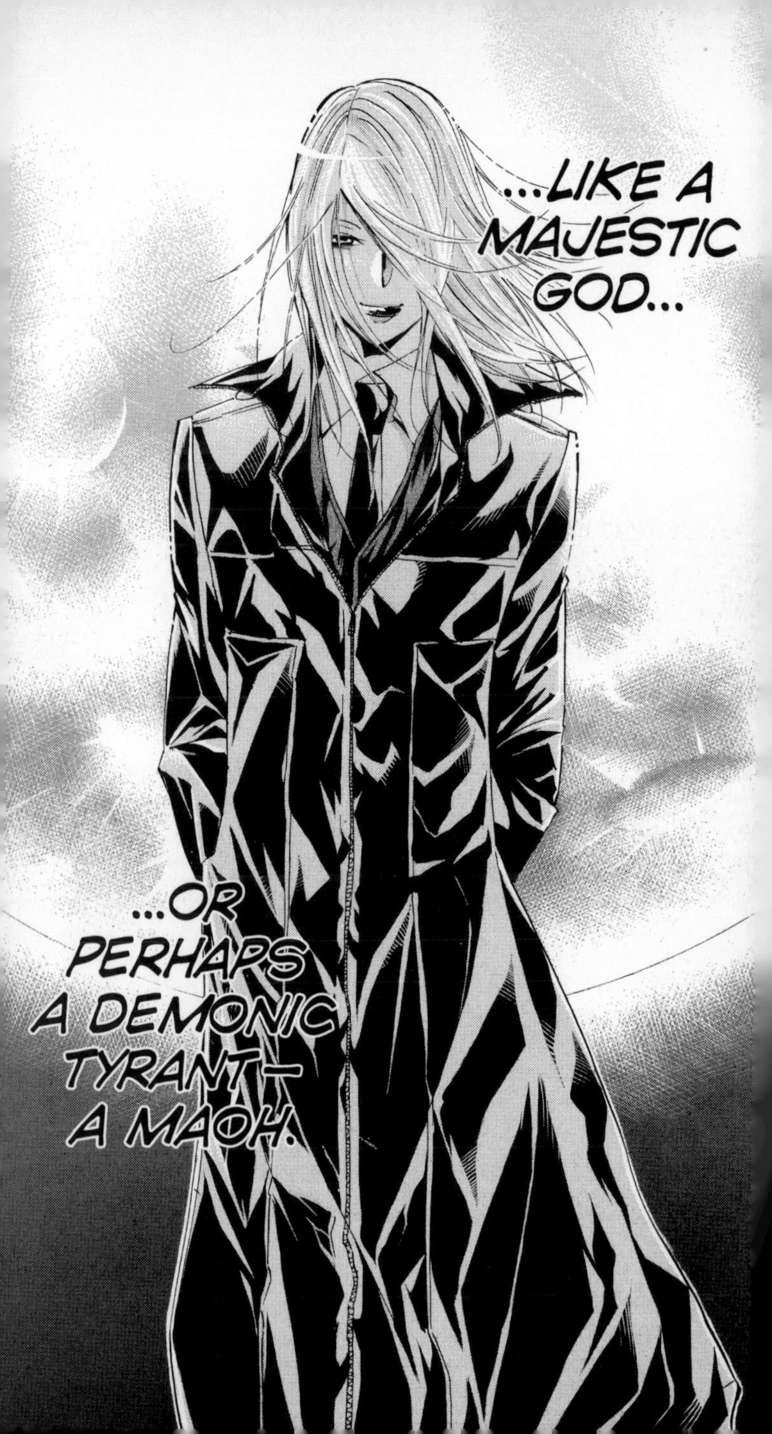
...LIKE A MAJESTIC GOD...
...OR PERHAPS A DEMONIC TYRANT— A MAOH.

IT CONTINUES IN Vol.04

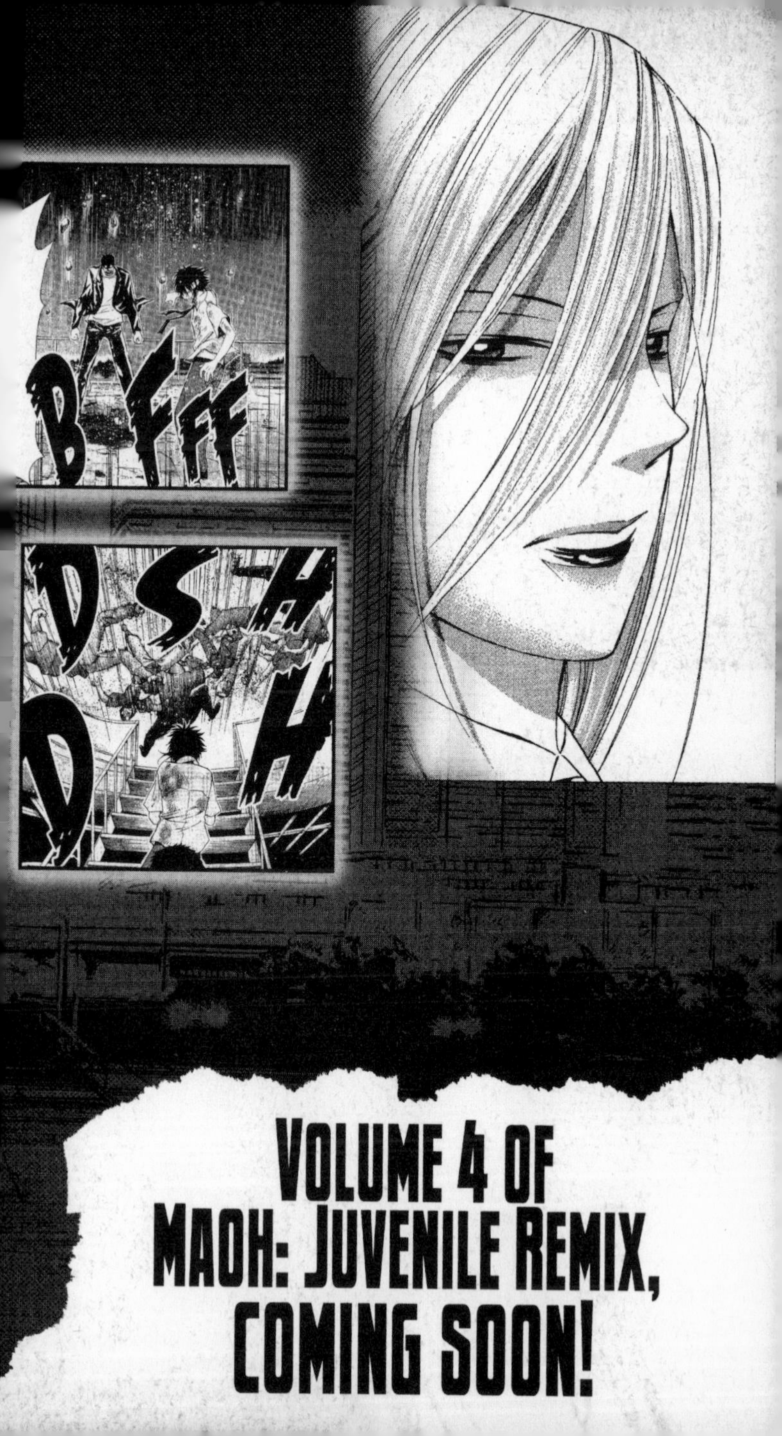
BFFF
DSHH
VOLUME 4 OF
MAOH: JUVENILE REMIX,
COMING SOON!

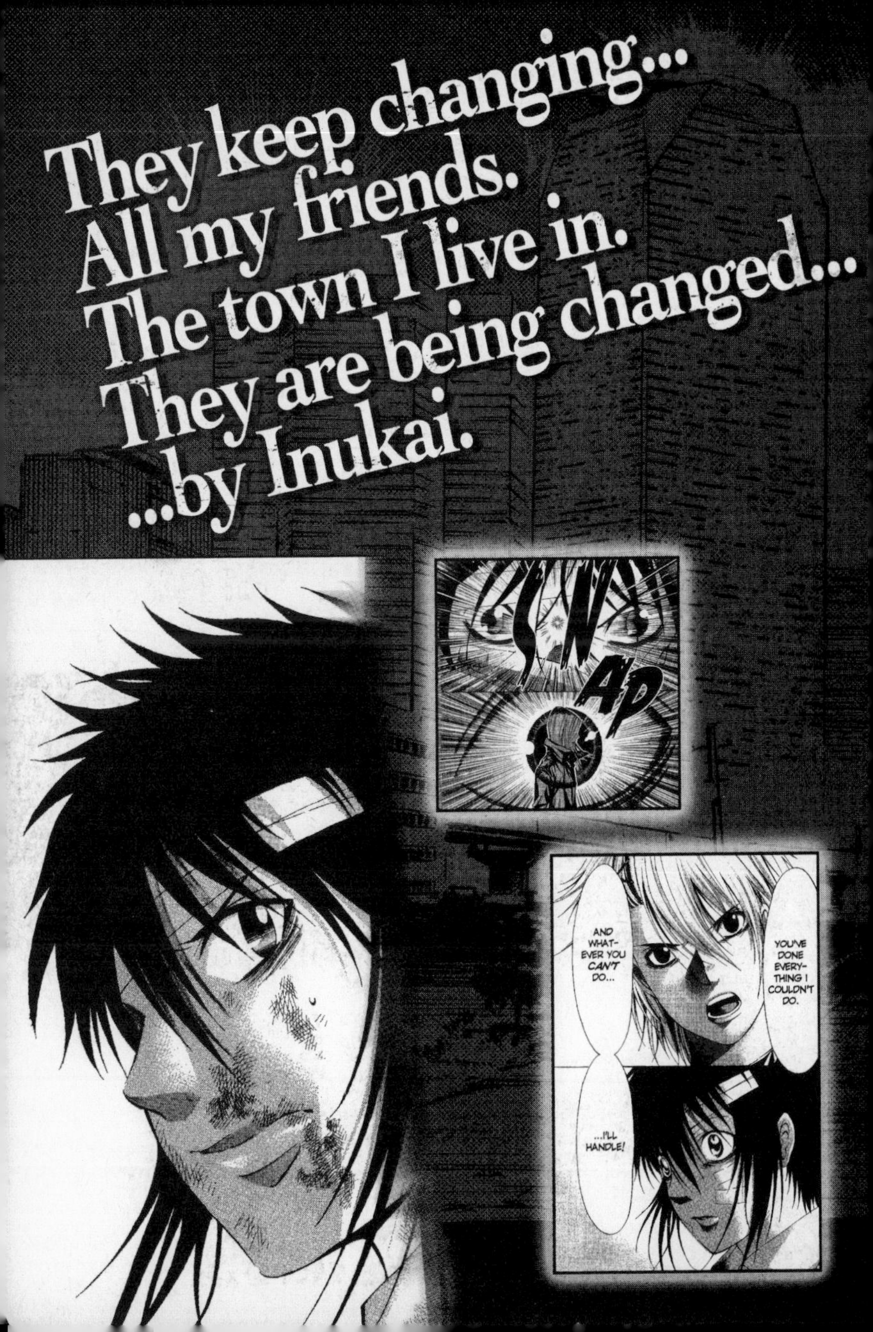
They keep changing...
All my friends.
The town I live in.
They are being changed...
...by Inukai.
YOU'VE DONE EVERYTHING I COULDN'T DO.
AND WHATEVER YOU CAN'T DO...
...I'LL HANDLE!